PHILOSOPHY AND ROMANTIC NATIONALISM

PHILOSOPHY AND ROMANTIC NATIONALISM: THE CASE OF POLAND

BY

ANDRZEJ WALICKI

CLARENDON PRESS · OXFORD
1982

Oxford University Press, Walton Street, Oxford OX2 6DP
London Glasgow New York Toronto
Delhi Bombay Calcutta Madras Karachi
Kuala Lumpur Singapore Hong Kong Tokyo
Nairobi Dar es Salaam Cape Town
Melbourne Auckland
and associates in
Beirut Berlin Ibadan Mexico City Nicosia

Published in the United States by
Oxford University Press, New York

British Library Cataloguing in Publication Data

Walicki, Andrzej
  Philosophy and romantic nationalism: the
  case of Poland.
  1. Nationalism—Poland—History
  I. Title
  320.5'4'09438   DK437

  ISBN 0–19–827250–2

Library of Congress Cataloging in Publication Data

Walicki, Andrzej.
  Philosophy and romantic nationalism.

  Bibliography: p.
  Includes index.
  1. Poland—Intellectual life—1795–1918.
  2. Nationalism—Poland.   3. Philosophy, Polish—
  19th century.   4. Messianism, Polish.
  5. Romanticism—Poland.   I. Title.
  DK4358.W34   320.5'4'09438   81–18120
  ISBN 0–19–827250–2   AACR2

Typeset by Oxprint Ltd., Oxford
Printed in Great Britain
at the University Press, Oxford
by Eric Buckley
Printer to the University

TO MARIA

Acknowledgements

This book owes much to a number of people and institutions. In the first place I should acknowledge my gratitude to Professor Wiktor Weintraub whose works on Adam Mickiewicz inspired some of my interpretations and whose interest in my studies of the Polish romantic ideologies strongly encouraged me to make an effort to present them to English-speaking readers. I should also mention my friends and colleagues—B. Baczko, L. Kolakowski, J. Szacki and others—who in the 1960s, because of a certain community of life experience and of philosophical, social, and methodological interests, were often called 'the Warsaw school in the history of ideas'. Although my peculiar interest in the philosophical heritage of Polish romantic nationalism has not been fully shared by them, the present book is, partially at least, a product of the vivid exchange of ideas which was taking place in this informal group of scholars.

The book is a result of many years of my research work in the Institute of Philosophy and Sociology, Polish Academy of Sciences, in Warsaw. Its first version, in English, was written during my visiting fellowship in the Woodrow Wilson International Center For Scholars in Washington DC (1977–8). It took final shape in summer 1980, during my three months' fellowship in the Humanities Research Centre of the Australian National University in Canberra. Its publication was facilitated by a subsidy from the Alfred Jurzykowski Foundation, Inc., New York. To all these institutions I owe a real debt of gratitude.

Andrzej Walicki
Warsaw, October 1980

Contents

Contents

Introduction

The present book, based on the results of about 25 years of study in nineteenth-century Polish, Russian, and West-European intellectual history, was written specially for Western readers. There were many reasons why I decided to embark on this difficult task.

It would be no exaggeration to say that—in spite of the valuable contributions of a few European and American scholars—Polish intellectual history is almost entirely unknown in the West and interest in it is almost non-existent. During my visits to Great Britain and to the United States I was told by many people that 'polonica non leguntur' because the knowledge of Polish history is limited to a small number of specialists and the general public is reluctant to buy and read books on unknown subjects. What is true of Polish history in general is even more true of Polish *intellectual* history. As a rule it is unknown in the West even in the milieu of specialists in European intellectual history. Should the unknown remain unknown? Some people, with whom I have talked about it in the West, expressed their personal regrets but did not hesitate to give an unambiguous answer to this question: yes, it should. It should remain unknown because Western universities, at the present moment at least, cannot afford to develop new fields of historical studies, because specialists in Polish intellectual history would hardly find jobs for themselves in a situation where there are not enough jobs on the academic market, even for scholars with more important specializations.

I assume that this is really so, but I have always felt that there is a certain *non sequitur* in the above argument. It may be true that Western Universities cannot expand their Polish studies by paying more attention to Polish intellectual history, but it does not follow from this that efforts should not be made to increase knowledge of it among historians, Slavists, and historians of ideas. One cannot understand European history while remaining ignorant of the history of East-Central Europe. Poland was for centuries the most important country of this area and her intellectual history provides many keys to a better understanding not only of her own history, but of European history as a whole. One cannot understand the rise of modern, post-revolutionary nationalism in Europe without a good knowledge of Polish nationalism and Polish national-liberation movements. This should be self-evident, but, unfortunately, there are many books on nationalism whose authors are fully ignorant of the Polish case.[1] A specialist in European Romanticism cannot excuse himself for being ignorant of Polish Romanticism; he should attempt to understand why Jean Fabre called it 'le plus expressif, le plus vivant et le plus complet des "romantismes"' (B. 36, p. x). The same is true for the historian of Hegelianism in Europe: he *should* know that the controversy about Hegel was especially intense in partitioned Poland and that it gave birth to a number of quite interesting philosophical systems.

To sum up: there are, I think, at least two important reasons why Polish intellectual history should be of some interest even to those scholars who do not intend to specialize in Polish studies. First, some Polish thinkers and some Polish ideas were of an all-European significance. Secondly, the knowledge of them enables us to see the intellectual history of other European countries in a broader comparative perspective. As a specialist in Russian intellectual history I wish to add that the ignorance of Polish history, including intellectual history, is, perhaps, especially detrimental to Russian studies, and that a true Slavist, even if he specializes in Russian history, should be able to see his subject in an all-Slavonic perspective. In writing this book I wanted, among other things, to give Western Slavists a necessary comparative background for such problems as: the ancient Slavonic commune in the ideologies of gentry revolutionism, different kinds of broadly conceived 'Slavophilism', Polish precursors of Russian populism, parallels between Polish and Russian post-Hegelian 'philosophies of action', national Messianism in both countries, and even (in spite of the general hostility towards Panslavism among the Poles) the Polish contributions to the ideology of pro-Russian Panslavism. Needless to say, I have analysed also the direct interrelations between

Polish and Russian thought, such as Cieszkowski's influence on Herzen, Bakunin's influence on Dembowski, Mickiewicz's Lectures on Slavonic literature and Russian Slavophilism, and so on.

The title of the book was suggested by the study of Alexandre Koyré, *La Philosophie et le problème national en Russie au début du XIXe siècle* (Paris 1939). As I shall try to show, the relations between German-inspired philosophy and the 'national problem' were even closer and more significant in the case of Poland than in that of Russia. Polish philosophers of the 1840s were more speculative and systematic than their Russian counterparts and, at the same time (with the exception of Bakunin), more directly involved in political activities. They represented a quite unique phenomenon: a philosophical move-ment consciously motivated by patriotic feelings, aiming at patriotic ends, trying to create a deliberately 'national' philo-sophy—a philosophy, however, which would be able to com-bine 'nationalism' with a genuine universalism.

The book deals primarily ·with the period between the November uprising of 1830 and the revolutionary events of 1848–9. In the intellectual history of Poland this period was characterized by an unprecedented richness of philosophical and social ideas, borrowed mainly from France and Germany, but always reinterpreted in an original way to suit the specific exigencies of the ideological situation in Poland. The 'Polish question' was then of international significance. The Polish progressive national movement became a model for the national and social movements in other countries and was highly appre-ciated by the European Left (among others by Marx and Engels). Polish ideas (especially those of Mickiewicz and Cieszkowski) had influenced such thinkers as Mazzini, Michelet, Quinet, Lamennais, Herzen, and others. It seems justified to treat the Poland of this time as a classic country of romantic nationalism and to claim that the Polish national-liberation movement, together with its intellectual counter-parts, played an important role in nineteenth-century European history.

The four parts of the book are relatively autonomous. Each of them differs from a conventional, chronological account of his-torical facts. Instead, each of them concentrates on a compara-tive and structural analysis of ideas. The political and social

history of Poland is, of course, always present in them, because
ideas are analysed in their relations to political situations and
social structures. Nevertheless, one should not expect to find in
this book a more-or-less detailed separate account of Polish
political and social history during this epoch. It presents
enough facts to be read and fully understood without previous
studies in Polish history, but it deals with ideas, patterns of
thought, and does not pretend to give a full picture of Polish
political and social development during the years 1831–49.

The first part ('The Main Patterns of Political and Social
Thought of the Polish National-Liberation Movement of the
Epoch') analyses the most important currents of Polish political
and social thought—both in the homeland and in the emigration. Consequently, it deals with different variants of broadly
conceived Polish 'nationalism' and with the different solutions
to social questions in their relation to the 'national cause'.
Among other things it tries to show that some peculiar features
of the Polish political thought of the epoch were closely bound
up with the traditions of the Polish 'democracy of the gentry'.
To prove this I had to go beyond the chronological framework
of this book and to present a brief synthetic view of the legacy
and historical vicissitudes of this original and extremely interesting form of political structure. In particular, I set forth the
thesis that the idea of the 'sovereignty of the nation of the
gentry' in its relation to the king paved the way for the modern
ideas of national sovereignty and the right to national self-
determination—ideas which appeared in Poland earlier than in
any other European country. Another contribution of the
legacy of the old Polish commonwealth to nineteenth-century
Polish nationalism was the idea of a multilingual and multiethnic political nation. Thus, contrary to widespread opinions
about the differences between West-European and East-
European nationalism, Polish nationalism was born as a
political nationalism and only later began to place more emphasis on linguistic and cultural/ethnic criteria. The first step in
this direction was made under the impact of (1) the French
Revolution, which stressed the linguistic homogeneity of the
state, and (2) German Romanticism. A peculiarly Polish
admixture to this—the belief in the brotherhood of nations and
in the necessity of putting an end to the divorce between morality
and politics in international relations—was a product of the

situation in which the Polish struggle for independence was directed against the reactionary Holy Alliance and, by the same token, had natural allies in the revolutionary movements, undermining the foundations of the 'old world'. As a result of all these circumstances Poland brought a peculiarly rich contribution to European nationalist thought, creating her own model of progressive romantic nationalism and showing the possibility of combining its different aspects with different types of social radicalism. In the last chapters of the first part of this book I have tried to confront this Polish contribution with some influential theories and typologies of nationalism. The results of this confrontation provide, I think, concrete proofs of the importance of a deeper knowledge of Polish nationalism for the improvement, or correction, of some existing theories, typologies, and comparative histories of nationalism.

One important reservation is necessary in this context. It is well known that the term 'nationalism' is used in a variety of meanings. In the West-European, especially Anglo-Saxon, usage the word 'nationalism' comprises, as a rule, *every* concern with winning national independence, awakening national consciousness, or preserving the national identity. 'In simplest terms', wrote C. J. H. Hayes, 'nationalism may be defined as a fusion of patriotism with a consciousness of nationality' (B. 50, p. 2). Considered in this way, Polish romantic nationalism *is*, of course, an example of the most ardent and highly developed nationalism. In Poland, however, as well as in other socialist countries, the term 'nationalism' is used in a different, much narrower sense: it is a pejorative term, meaning, approximately, the same as chauvinism, narrow national egoism, state expansionism, intolerant attitudes towards national minorities, and so forth. Already in nineteenth-century Poland the word 'nationalism' was used as a synonym for national egoism, and was sharply distinguished from 'patriotism', i.e. from the legitimate and humanitarian manifestations of the love of one's own nation. It is obvious that from this point of view the Polish nationalists of the Romantic Epoch were not 'nationalists' but 'patriots': the average educated Pole would be surprised and indignant if he were told that Adam Mickiewicz was not only the greatest Polish poet but also one of the greatest Polish 'nationalists'.

I think that the contemporary English usage of the term

'nationalism' has many obvious advantages; it is perhaps preferable to have a common term for all the different—both positive and negative—manifestations of national feeling and national consciousness at different stages of their historical evolution. Moreover, this book was written for English-speaking readers and I will not try to change their linguistic habits.[2] Nevertheless, in order to avoid any misunderstanding, I would like to stress that although the word 'nationalism' is used in this book in its *broadest* meaning, one of my main aims was to contribute towards a clearer understanding of important *differences* between the various types of nationalist thinking. I strongly feel that the word 'nationalism' should be used with more discrimination (i.e. with adjectives added), if we intend to eliminate unjustified associations and to avoid reducing qualitatively different ideas to an allegedly common denominator.

The second part of the book is devoted to philosophical problems. The so-called Polish 'national philosophy' of the 1840s should be of interest to historians of nationalist ideas as a peculiarly ambitious attempt to give nationalism a solid philosophical basis. Its significance, however, cannot be reduced to this. First of all, an acquaintance with this philosophy completes and enriches the picture of heterogeneous tendencies in which the crisis of Hegelian absolute idealism found expression. This was a quite important addendum because the influence of German idealism in Poland at that time—despite the very different character of historical and cultural conditions—was considerably broader and deeper than in the countries of Western Europe. Secondly, Polish philosophy of the 1840s was an original implementation of two postulates which were very popular among the German Left-Hegelians and which gave birth to the philosophy of Marx: the postulate of a 'philosophy of action' (or 'philosophy of praxis'), as well as the postulate of the so-called 'German-French intellectual alliance', i.e. of creating a synthesis of German philosophy with French political and social thought. The first of these postulates strongly appealed to Polish thinkers because the peculiar situation of their subjugated and partitioned country made them peculiarly aware of the necessity of creating bridges between theory and practice. It is not by chance, therefore, that the Polish Hegelian, August Cieszkowski, was the first thinker who set forth the idea of the 'Philosophie der Tat'. The realization of the second postulate was greatly facilitated by the fact that Poland was more open to German influences than France and, at the same time, more open to French influences than Germany. It should be added that the Polish philosophy of the epoch was also a product of the intellectual culture of Polish Romanticism. Especially interesting from this point of view is the philosophy of the young revolutionary, the leader of the Cracow uprising of 1846, Edward Dembowski: it was a very original synthesis of German philosophy with French socialism and Polish romantic populism.

The next part of this book deals with the national and religious Messianism of the prophetic poets: Mickiewicz, Słowacki, and Krasiński. Their ideas presented the most extreme and the best-articulated variant of the messianic-millenarian tendencies of European romantic thought. Therefore, they should be of interest to many categories of scholars: to the Slavists, because of the mere fact that they were proclaimed by some of the greatest Slavonic poets of the epoch; to historians of literature and historians of ideas who are interested in the comparative study of European romanticisms; to historians and theoreticians of nationalism, as perfect material for a case study of a national Messianism; finally, to those scholars, quite numerous in our times, who are studying millenarianism and Messianism (from sociological, anthropological, historical, or philosophical points of view) as the archetypal, always recurring, patterns of thought underlying so many religious and secular social movements, and throwing light on the phenomenon of irrational hope, whose value, as history shows, should not be easily rejected.

The last chapter of this part of the book presents the ideas of yet another great Polish poet—Cyprian Norwid. He was a profound critic of both religious and national Messianism. His views deserve to be known not only as an interesting page in Polish intellectual history but also because of their own autonomous values, as one of the most penetrating warnings against the dangers inherent in millenarian structures of thought.

The fourth and last part of the book ('Changing Perspectives') is composed of two autonomous chapters each of which deals with the question: what happened to the legacy of Polish romantic nationalism in the second half of the nineteenth century. The first, entitled 'The Legacy of Political Romanticism and the Emergence of Integral Nationalism', provides a short historical outline of Polish nationalism after the breakdown of its romantic illusions. The next chapter presents an analysis of Marx's and Engels's views on the 'Polish Question'. I felt that their pro-Polish attitude deserves to be better known and that it should not be dismissed as merely a question of political tactics, stemming from their hatred of the despotic tsarist Empire. Therefore, I have tried to show the inner connections between their profound sympathy for Polish romantic nationalism and their general approach to national questions. Such an analysis, in turn, has enabled me to explain the emergence of a Marxist-inspired 'nationalism' within the Polish socialist movement.

Thus, Polish nationalism during 1831–49—its political, social, religious, and philosophical ideas—is presented and analysed in this book in a similar way to that in which Russian Slavophilism has been analysed in my earlier book *The Slavophile Controversy* (B. 180). It is shown in its relations with contemporary Western and Russian ideas, as well as against the background of the views of its predecessors, opponents and later critics, defenders and partial followers in Poland.

PART ONE

The Main Patterns of Political and Social Thought of the Polish National-Liberation Movement of the Epoch

I. The Legacy and Historical Vicissitudes of the Democracy of the Gentry

According to a Western historian, 'the Polish revolution of November 1830 and the war which followed it were the last challenge of the old Poland to the Russian hegemony in Eastern Europe' (B. 98, p. vii). There is a grain of truth in this statement, although its one-sidedness is also evident: it obscures the fact that the small Congress Kingdom fighting for ten months against the powerful Russian Empire had undergone a process of modernization which made it very different from the ancient Polish Commonwealth. Nevertheless, it is certainly true that the political thinking of the Polish insurgents of 1830–1 was connected in many ways with the ancient traditions of the Polish 'democracy of the gentry'.

Among other things, a proof of this was the fact that they perceived their revolution as a perfectly legal act, resulting from the violations of the Polish Constitution and the non-observance of the relevant clauses of the Vienna settlement of 1815 by Nicholas I—the autocrat of all the Russias and simultaneously the constitutional king of Poland. The roots of this conviction can and, indeed, should be traced back to the contractual conception of the state which emerged in Poland in the sixteenth century and which made the king answerable to society for observing the limitations of his power. If he did not respect the agreed conditions, society had a legal right of resistance, formulated in the Polish Constitution as the 'ius de non praestanda obedientia' (B. 148, pp. 51–4).

The inadequacy of knowledge of Eastern Europe or, rather, of East-Central Europe among educated Westerners manifests itself perhaps most clearly in the widespread belief that such notions as 'limited government', 'government by consent', 'civil rights' and so forth are products of a peculiarly 'Western' or, even, a peculiarly Anglo-Saxon historical development. Western students, even students of history, are, as a rule, not aware, or not fully aware, of the fact that the Polish-Lithuanian Commonwealth, which was, after all, the largest European state after Muscovy, could rightly claim to represent the fullest development of the principle of 'government by consent' in contemporary Europe (cf. B. 98, p. 10). Equally widespread is the lack of knowledge of, and the lack of interest in, the history of representative institutions in Hungary.

One of the reasons for this is to be found, I think, in a mechanistic understanding of historical determinism and of the so-called theory of modernization. Eighteenth-century Poland was, to be sure, a non-modernized country, characterized by the decline of its cities and by the unchallenged rule of the nobility. If so, the reasoning goes, what could be the relevance of her institutions to modern, 'bourgeois' constitutionalism? At first sight it can indeed appear that the Golden Freedom of the Polish gentry was only a historical anomaly or a strange ana-chronism—a relic of the pre-absolutist feudal anarchy, quite unrelated to the principles of the modern representative government. It is questionable whether real history was as simple as this would seem to indicate. If the social conscious-ness of people can be treated as a kind of historical testimony, it is important to point out that the eighteenth-century Polish 'republicans', representing, as a rule, the conservative part of the nobility, were guilty of a quite different kind of over-simplification. For them the most important question was the criterion of 'freedom versus despotism', quite irrespective of the *social* content of a given theory or the *social* structure of a given country. Therefore, they enjoyed reading John Locke and found in his writings many arguments supporting their own political views (B. 108). For the same reason, in spite of their conservatism in social questions, they wholeheartedly sym-pathized with the American revolution (B. 56). It is worth while to remember that Kazimierz Pułaski, who became an American national hero, was also one of the leaders of the Confederation of Bar—a movement of the traditional Polish nobility, devoted to freedom, but socially and religiously conservative, fighting the Russians in the name of 'Freedom and the [Catholic] Church'.

The tendency to ignore the libertarian traditions of Poland and to stress, instead, her economic and social backwardness, seems to be related to the results of World War II. Because of the political division of Europe the notion of the 'West' became unduly politicized and narrowed. As a result of this, Poland, which for centuries had been seen as a 'bulwark of the West', ceased to be perceived as a 'Western' country and, as might be expected, attempts were made to justify this by historical studies. In the first half of the nineteenth century the situation was different. Not only in Europe, but also in the distant United States, the Polish insurrection of 1830–1 was greeted as a heroic defence of the West and public meetings were organized to support the Polish cause (B. 97, p. 19). In the Appeal to the American People on Behalf of the American-Polish Committee in Paris (issued on 5 September 1831), James Fenimore Cooper wrote:

The crime of Poland was too much liberty; her independent existence, in the vicinity of those who had reared their thrones on arbitrary will, was not to be endured. Fellow-citizens, neither the ancient institutions nor the ancient practices in Poland have been understood. The former had, in common with all Europe, the inherited defects of feudal practices, but still were they among the freest of this hemisphere. (B. 97, p. 168)

European historians of the Romantic Epoch held quite similar views (see B. 140, pp. 177–244). In the later period, especially after the abortive uprising of 1863–4, the general climate of opinion changed and the dominant views on Polish history (not uninfluenced by official Prussian and Russian historiography) became much more severe. Nevertheless, the 'other side of the coin' was also seen, and some historians paid due attention to it. Let us quote, for example, the opinion of the distinguished American specialist in Polish history, R. H. Lord:

The old Polish Commonwealth was an experiment of a highly original and interesting character. It was a republic both in name and in fact, although nominally it had a king as its first magistrate. It was the largest and the most ambitious experiment with a republican form of government that the world had seen since the day of the Romans. Moreover, it was the first experiment on a large scale with a federal republic down to the appearance of the United States. In the sixteenth and the seventeenth centuries this republic was the freest state in Europe, the state in which the greatest degree of constitutional, civic and intellectual liberty prevailed. . . . Like the United States today, Poland was at that time the melting-pot of Europe, the haven for the poor and the oppressed of all the neighbouring countries—Germans, Jews, Greeks, Magyars, Armenians, Tartars, Russians . . . Finally, the oldest republic represented an effort to organize the vast open plain between the Baltic and the Black Sea—a region containing so many weak and underdeveloped races and a region so much exposed to Germanic ambitions on the one side and to

Turco-Tartar onslaughts on the other side—into a compact and powerful realm, which was directed indeed by the strongest and most advanced voice within its borders . . . but which in its better period allowed a genuine equality to the other voices and extensive self-government to some of them. (B. 48, pp. 22–3.)

Similar opinions are voiced today by the eminent Belgian Slavist, Claude Backvis. In one of his works he put forward the thesis that Polish society in the Renaissance period combined the best features of organic 'Gemeinschaft' with those of rational 'Gesellschaft' (B. 4). He expressed his admiration for the fact that the ancient Poles treated their state as a genuine *res publica*—the 'commonwealth', or 'matter of common concern', and rightly pointed out that the popularity of the Polish word for *res publica* (*Rzeczpospolita*) had prevented, or, rather, retarded for centuries, the emergence of the Polish word for 'state' (*państwo*) (B. 5). He tried even to defend the notorious *liberum veto*, seeing it, quite rightly, as a logical consequence of the assumption that the only source of legitimacy of legislative and executive power is the unanimous consent of the entire body of citizens (B. 6).

Perhaps this is a somewhat over-idealized picture. It cannot be denied, however, that the quoted opinions are based on facts which should be known not only to students of sixteenth- and seventeenth-century Europe, but to students of nineteenth-century Polish thought as well. The heated controversy over the legacy of the Polish past was extremely characteristic of the Romantic Epoch, and the tendency to rehabilitate 'ancient Polish freedom' was very common in the nineteenth century both in Poland and in the West. It seems proper, therefore, to present here a brief account of the main facts concerning the Polish 'democracy of the gentry'.

First, a series of facts should show the development of the political structure and the juridical system of this unique phenomenon in European history.

In 1422, by the so-called Czerwińsk privilege, the Polish gentry was granted the inviolability of their private property. A few years later—in 1430, that is, two and a half centuries before the English Habeas Corpus Act of 1679—they obtained from the king the firm assurance of personal immunity: 'Neminen captivabimus nisi iure victum.' In 1558 legislation was passed concerning the inviolability of private households—king's servitors could not enter a nobleman's house even if an outlaw were sheltered in it. Parallel to the increase of 'negative freedom' of the gentry went the process of increasing their strictly political rights and their share in ruling the state. In 1454, King Kazimierz IV of the Jagellonian dynasty had to pledge himself never to declare war without the agreement of the local gentry councils (dietines). The year 1493 was the date of the formal establishment of the parliamentary system in Poland with the Great Diet as a legislative power. It was composed of two Chambers and of three 'executive Estates'—King, Senate, and the Chamber of Deputies—whose agreement was necessary to enact a law. The members of the Chamber of Deputies were dependent on the 'instructions' they had received from their local dietines. The towns had the right to send their representatives to the lower Chamber and to participate in debates concerning urban legislation. In practice, however, with the important exception of Cracow, they neglected the exercise of this privilege. Besides proclaiming the laws, the Great Diet fixed taxation, controlled the administration and the finances of the state, received the reports of foreign ambassadors and envoys, and, above all, decided on all important questions of foreign politics, especially on peace and war. The king was forbidden to declare war for personal or dynastic reasons. In 1505 the Great Diet in Radom strengthened this constitutional development by promulgating the famous law of 'Nihil Novi'—the law which obliged the king to refrain from introducing any changes in the established system, except with the agreement of the Diet.

Further constitutional development took place after the extinction of the Jagellonian dynasty. In theory Poland had been an elective monarchy since 1382, that is, since the extinction of the Piast dynasty; in practice, however, until the death of the last of the Jagellons (1572)—mainly because of the fact that the Jagellons had hereditary rights to the Lithuanian throne—the dynastic principle was observed. Afterwards, from the time of the election of Henry de Valois in 1573, every newly elected King of Poland had to swear to protect the existing laws and liberties of the country and never to violate them (the so-called 'Henrician articles' which Henry de Valois had to accept and which henceforth were made obligatory for all elected kings of Poland). Each Polish noble felt proud not only of being the 'elector' of the king but also of the right to become king himself.

This was by no means a purely theoretical right. In fact four kings were elected in Poland not from among royal families but from the ranks of the Polish nobility. One of these was Jan Sobieski, who in 1683 defended the Habsburg Empire against the Turkish invasion.

In such a manner the peculiar political system known as 'the democracy of the gentry' came into being. It was a 'democracy' because it was based upon the principle of the sovereignty of the people. It was a 'democracy of the gentry' because the sovereign 'people' were composed of, and limited to, the members *of the gentry*. Moreover, the development of this system ran parallel with the growing enserfment of the Polish peasantry. This was not felt to be incompatible with democratic principles: on the contrary, some prominent ideologists of the 'gentry democracy' were convinced that a democratic form of government was impossible without the enslavement of part of the population, and to support this thesis they pointed to the example of ancient Greece.[1]

To do justice to the Polish 'democracy of the gentry', one should realize that the Polish nobility, in contrast to the nobility of England or France, was a very numerous social estate. In the sixteenth century, 11–13 per cent of the total population of the Commonwealth consisted of noblemen. This meant that 11–13 per cent of the population were represented in the parliament, while in sixteenth-century England—another country with a parliamentary form of government—the respective figure was only 5 per cent. At the end of the eighteenth century at least 9–10 per cent of the inhabitants of the Polish Republic belonged to the nobility,[2] whereas the respective figure for contemporary France was less than 1.5 per cent. Because of property qualifications, even in the bourgeois France of Louis Philippe only 1.5 per cent of the population had the right to vote; in Britain—after the Reform Bill of 1832—the number of voters was 3.2 per cent (or 7.1 per cent of population aged 20 and over. See British Enc. Parliament).

From the socio-economic point of view the Polish (or polonized) nobility was an extremely differentiated group. At the top of it were great magnates, at the bottom the noble proletariat, the *nobiles pauperes* who had to work for their living and who were often as poor as the peasantry. In spite of these differences all the members of the nobility embraced the doctrine of the juridical and political equality of all the nobles. The ideal to which they aspired was expressed in their favourite saying: 'the nobleman on his little plot of land is the equal of the Palatine' (*Szlachcic na zagrodzie równy wojewodzie*). Of course, in reality it was not so. It is a rather general rule that societies cannot live up to their values. Nevertheless, it was true that many efforts were made to equalize the nobility, or at least, to uphold the image of their theoretical equality. The Polish king had no right to bestow aristocratic titles on the nobility of his country; only some ancient Lithuanian and Ruthenian families were allowed to use their inherited ducal titles. The difference between the most powerful magnate and the poorest nobleman was accepted as a difference in wealth, but not as a difference in political or social status. The accepted form of addressing every member of the noble estate by another noble was 'Sir brother'.

The 'Golden Age of gentry democracy'—the sixteenth century—was indeed a 'Golden Age' in Polish history. The gentry could by then combine their freedom with civic virtues and an acute sense of responsibility for their 'common wealth'. Their state was one of the most powerful states in Europe. Its Western, ethnically Polish part cannot be classified as 'backward'. The question of its economic development is somewhat controversial: some historians emphasize its relatively high level, others pay more attention to the fact that already in the sixteenth century the unlimited domination of the nobility had begun to hamper the development of cities. There is no doubt, however, that from the point of view of cultural development— the number of schools, books, and the general diffusion of knowledge—it was on the level of the advanced West European countries (cf. B. 194). Its political culture was well developed, its Diet was one of the best-functioning parliaments in Europe (cf. B. 109). The University of Cracow, founded in 1364, flourished. Polish literature (and literature written in Latin as well) reached brilliant heights: its greatest poet, the 'Polish Ronsard', Jan Kochanowski (1530–84), ranks certainly among the greatest poets of the European Renaissance. Polish political thought had its best representative in Andrzej Frycz Modrzewski (1503–72), whose book *De Republica Emendanda* (1554; translated into German, French and—in manuscript—Spanish and Russian) is considered to be 'the first treatise in Europe to discuss problems of State as a whole' (B. 119, p. 40). Among other things he proclaimed that laws should be the same for all estates, that everybody should work, that burghers and peasants should be treated as free citizens, and that the peasants should be granted security of tenure and should pay rent to their lords in amounts strictly defined by law. It shows that the democratic tendency inherent in the contractual theory of the state could be levelled against the class interests of the gentry.

The following century is usually seen as an epoch of cultural decline. However, this decline can only be seen as relative. Poland was still the most powerful and culturally developed country in Eastern Europe. It was during this period that the Polish language became a language of high culture in the vast territories of the East: from Moscow, where it was spoken at the tsarist court, to Moldavia, whose leading historiographer and a distinguished poet, Miron Costîn (1663–91), wrote his works in beautiful Polish.

One of the most attractive features of the Polish 'Golden Age' was a religious tolerance, conceived as a corollary of political freedom. In sharp contrast to other European countries, six-teenth-century Poland was a 'country without stakes', pro-viding asylum for the heretics persecuted in other countries (cf. B. 161). Protestantism spread freely in Poland, especially among the upper stratum of the nobility, so that Protestants became a majority in the Senate. Even the so-called 'radical Reformation', banned in most Protestant countries, found shelter in Poland and produced the unique phenomenon of Polish Socinianism (known also as Polish Arianism or Uni-tarianism)—the most radical form of religious rationalism, paving the way for the secular rationalism of the Enlightenment (cf. B. 126 and B. 190). The doctrine 'cuius regio, eius religio' was alien to the Polish kings, who consciously avoided any interference in matters of conscience. Shortly after the famous massacre of Huguenots in Paris (Saint Bartholomew's Day, 24 August 1572), the Polish law 'de pace inter dissidentes' (en-acted on 28 January 1573) secured equal rights for all con-fessions and declared that nobody could be persecuted for religious reasons.

In a mood of self-flagellation some nineteenth-century critics of the Polish past threw doubt on the inner value of the Polish tradition of tolerance by claiming that it had stemmed from religious indifference prevailing allegedly among the Catholic gentry. This severe judgement does not seem just. It can be proved by much evidence that the Polish tolerance stemmed from respect for the dignity of the human person. This attitude found beautiful expression in the words of the Crown Chancellor, Jan Zamoyski (1542–1605): 'If it would lead you back to Catholicism I would gladly give up half of my life and with the other half I would live rejoicing in this union. But if anyone should try to compel you, then I would give up all my life, rather than be obliged to witness this compulsion' (see B. 26, p. 37).

The religious tolerance was extended also to the Jews, who were given the right to full autonomy and self-government, not merely in religious matters. This fact is widely acknowledged by Jewish scholars, quite irrespective of their friendly or unfriendly feelings towards contemporary Poland. The local Jewish communities (*kehilla* or *kahal*) were united into provincial councils under the rule of the Council of Four Lands. (The 'four lands' were: Great Poland, Little Poland, the Lvov Land, and Volhynia. The Grand Duchy of Lithuania had its own, separate council.) This Council (to quote a Jewish-American scholar) 'was the supreme legal, judicial, and executive body of Polish Jewry. It manifested the greatest degree of Jewish autonomy ever attained by Jews in Europe' (B. 53, p. 24).[3]

Another characteristic feature of the 'republic of the gentry' was its capacity for peaceful expansion by voluntary 'unions'. The first and most important of these unions was the union with Lithuania, based upon the simple principle: 'Uniting the free with the free and equals with equals.' In 1454 the Prussian estates, i.e. the German burghers and German or Germanized nobility, rebelled against the arbitrary rule of the Teutonic Knights and asked Poland for protection. Soon afterwards, in 1466, West Prussia and the city of Gdańsk (Danzig) became an integral, although autonomous, part of the Commonwealth. Almost a hundred years later similar developments took place in Livonia. In 1561 it was voluntarily united with Poland, preserving its native institutions and internal autonomy.[4] Unfortunately for Poland, the fate of the Ukraine was different. In 1569 it ceased to be part of the Grand Duchy of Lithuania and instead became part of the Polish Crown. In September 1658, at Hadiach, an attempt was made to give the Ukraine the status of Lithuania, i.e. to unite her with Poland through the person of king as a separate, autonomous body politic. It was, however, too late: after the long, bloody war (1648–54) in which the Ukrainian Cossacks and peasants under Hetman Khmelnytsky (Chmielnicki) had fought against the Poles and the polonized Ukrainian nobility, the anti-Polish feelings in the Ukraine were too strong and the 'union of Hadiach' did not materialize. One of the reasons for this failure was the fact that in 1569 the Ukrainian nobility was satisfied with obtaining the same privileges as the Polish gentry, and did not care to demand territorial autonomy for their land (cf. B. 131).

The Polish–Lithuanian union had passed through three stages (personal union through the accession of the Lithuanian Grand Duke Jagello to the Polish throne in 1386; the union of Horodlo in 1413; and the union of Lublin in 1569), and it lasted until the final partition of the Commonwealth. The estimation of its final results is a very controversial matter. Many Polish historians have tried to show that it benefited Lithuania and weakened Poland, whose material resources and intellectual potential were quite sufficient for ensuring for herself the Western level of development, but not enough for 'civilizing work' on the enormous territories of the Grand Duchy. On the other hand, Lithuanian historians are convinced, as a rule, that the union was very detrimental to Lithuanian interests, since it resulted in the polonization of the Lithuanian nobility and retarded for centuries the emergence of a distinctively Lithuanian national consciousness and culture. It is not simple to decide who has been right in this controversy, and, in fact, an analysis of this complicated question does not fall within the scope of the present book. However, if we want to understand the social psychology and the type of patriotism represented by the Polish (or polonized) gentry, two points, at least, must be made clear. First, the polonization of the Lithuanian nobility was the result of the attractiveness of the Polish culture and not of any conscious effort on the part of the Poles; among other things, this is shown by the fact that the official language of the Grand Duchy was Belorussian (or proto-Belorussian), and that this language continued to be obligatory in official documents long after it had ceased to be spoken by Lithuanian and Belorussian nobles. Secondly, the questions for ethnic and linguistic nationality were not important for the citizens of the Commonwealth. Their patriotism consisted in loyalty to *res publica*, in proud attachment to its traditions and institutions. Nicolaus Copernicus was a great Polish patriot, although his native language was probably German.

The best-known (although, as a rule, very superficially understood) peculiarity of the political system of the Polish–Lithuanian Commonwealth was the famous *liberum veto*. It is easy to see it as a nonsensical privilege, making impossible the normal functioning of the parliament. The real problem, however, is to explain how it was possible that in fact the Polish parliament functioned so well for such a long time, and what was the reason for the rejection of the majority principle in the Diet.

If a 'free protest' was voiced by a deputy in the Diet, the Diet was automatically dissolved and *all* laws voted during the session were annulled. Every member of the Diet knew that making use of the right of veto would result in preventing not only the legislation which his constituency did not desire, but desired legislation as well. Therefore, as Claude Backvis has rightly pointed out (B. 6), it was in the interests of all deputies to come to agreement based on compromise. Thus the threat of veto functioned against the polarization of opinions in the Diet and strengthened the will for mutual understanding and co-operation. The right of veto was the other side of the striving for unanimity, and the ideal of unanimity was based upon the assumption that the *essential* values and interests of all citizens were the same and that everybody was ready to give up insistence on his particular interests if required for the common good. No wonder that for more than one hundred years it remained a right acknowledged in theory but not used in practice. It was exercised for the first time in 1652, and the man who dared to make use of it was most severely condemned by public opinion.

One of the reasons for this stubborn clinging to the right of the veto was the pluralist character of the Commonwealth. It was a federation of nobles of different ethnic and cultural backgrounds and, at the same time, a federation of different, self-governing provinces. Legislation in accordance with the simple majority principle would have created a danger of uniformity, of imposing the will of a mechanical majority against the wishes and interests of different minorities. The right of veto was seen as a safeguard that no legislation would be passed without taking into account the will and separate interests of every province of the state (cf. B. 127). With such a safeguard the Commonwealth could be held together avoiding the danger of separatist movements. The most important and extremely dangerous exception to this rule was the separatist movements in the Ukraine—movements growing in strength from the social grievances of the peasant masses, and led by Cossacks who were denied nobilitation and, therefore, were not represented in the Diet. It should be stressed, however, that even in the Ukraine the separatist tendencies appeared surprisingly late. Khmelnytsky's rebellion was not started under a separatist banner. It was a struggle against Polish (or polonized) magnates and Jesuits, but not against the king; a struggle for an autonomous, Cossack-controlled Ukraine within the boundaries of the Commonwealth, and not a 'war for independence'.

The Cossack wars of the middle of the seventeenth century, followed by war with Muscovy and by the Swedish invasion, were a real watershed in Polish history. The first half of the century was in many respects a continuation of Poland's 'Golden Age'. True, it witnessed the growing oppression of the peasants and the decisive victory of the Jesuit counter-reformation which, among other things, wasted the possibility of Poland's union with Muscovy through the accession of the Polish Crown Prince, the future Polish king, Władysław IV, to the Russian throne (if such a union had materialized, it might have changed the future pattern of Russian history). Nevertheless, in the first half of the seventeenth century Poland was still a powerful, culturally developed, and religiously tolerant country. Later, however, the years of bloody and exhausting wars with Cossacks, Russians, and Swedes brought about a series of disastrous consequences and marked the beginning of the process which, in the final analysis, resulted in the downfall of the Polish state. The economic ruin and depopulation of the country, in conjunction with the monopolization of the export of grain by the nobility (leading, as it did, to the decline of the cities), made Poland an incurably backward state; a state whose economic backwardness was bound to increase because of its petrified social structure. The so-called 'betrayal' of the Polish Protestants, many of whom were in fact guilty of supporting the Swedes, resulted in growing intolerance, which found expression in the expulsion of the Arians in 1658 and in a series of legal acts restricting the political rights of religious dissidents; anti-Protestant feelings were apparently so rampant in the Diet that no deputy dared to oppose this legislation by using his right of veto. In consequence, in the next century Poland came to be seen as an example of intolerant religious fanaticism, and the cause of Polish dissidents became a handy pretext for the multiple Russian and Prussian interferences in the internal affairs of the Commonwealth. Last but not least, the Right-Bank Ukraine (which after the partition of the Ukraine in 1667 remained part of Poland) was in the eighteenth century a scene of bloody peasant revolts (1734, 1750, and 1768), led by so-called Haidamaks and incited by Orthodox priests who wanted to liquidate the Uniate Church and to unite with their Orthodox brethren in Muscovy.[5] Needless to say, these violent proto-nationalistic rebellions greatly contributed to the further weakening and disorganization of the multiethnic republic of the gentry.

However, the most dangerous tendency manifested itself in the inner degeneration of the democracy of the gentry. As the result of a long process, the beginnings of which could be traced back to the first half of the seventeenth century, the knightly estate (as the gentry used to call themselves) came to see the great magnates, 'the elder brothers', as their natural leaders and the best protectors of 'Golden liberty', finding in this an excuse for gradually withdrawing from public affairs. Another excuse was found in the famous saying that 'Poland stands not by government' (*Polska nierządem stoi*),[6] which meant that Poland stands because of the strength of her unpolitical social ties (religion, traditional customs, family) and, therefore, that she could afford not to care about strong government. Added to this was the common illusion that the existence of Poland was completely safe because of the demands of the international balance of power and, moreover, that her safety depended precisely on her political passivity and weakness, because a weak state creates no danger for its neighbours. The development of such an attitude accompanied the process of transforming the democracy of the gentry into an oligarchy of magnates. The most active supporters of the magnates were the numerous landless nobles who administered their estates, served in their private armies, and, at the same time, enjoyed theoretical equality with the oligarchs by drinking with them and calling them 'Sir brothers'. At the beginning of the eighteenth century this process of degeneration of the gentry democracy, manifesting itself in the cultural sphere as well, had been completed. The neighbouring absolutist powers were quick to take advantage of this. Foreign meddling in domestic Polish affairs, paralysing the work of Polish Diets by bribing individual deputies to make use of their *liberum veto*, became a common practice.

The 1730s and 1740s witnessed the first attempts to awaken the Commonwealth from its lethargy. The king in exile, Stanislaw Leszczyński, wrote his *Free Voice Securing Freedom* (1733–7, published 1749)[7] advocating restriction of the right of veto, abolition of serfdom, and commutation of peasants' compulsory labour into rent. A Piarist, Stanislaw Konarski, initiated the modernization of the educational system by founding in 1740 the Collegium Nobilium in Warsaw—an institution in which the future leaders of the republic were educated in the spirit of the European Enlightenment (Konarski's programme was later adopted by all Piarist schools). The powerful Czartoryski family (generally called simply 'The Family') became the rallying point for all people who saw the necessity of suppressing anarchy and strengthening the power of the state. However, no legislation had a chance to pass since all Diets were dissolved by the hirelings of conservative magnates or foreign courts.

Aware that Poland was too weak to stand alone against the three absolutist powers, the Czartoryskis chose an alliance with Russia. During the interregnum period of 1763–4 armed Russian intervention enabled the Czartoryskis' party to defeat their opponents and secure the election of a member of their family and the protégé of Catherine II, Stanislaw August Poniatowski. The Convocation Diet, assembled in the form of a General Confederation (which was a legal form of suspending the right of veto and adopting the principle of majority vote), initiated some necessary reforms. Soon, however, 'the Family' and the new king became bitterly disappointed. In 1767 the conservative magnates, encouraged by support from the Russian ambassador, Prince Nikolai Repnin, formed a confederation at Radom and asked Catherine to guarantee the 'Golden Freedom' (that is to say, the existing anarchy) of the republic. The Empress responded favourably and the Diet was ordered to give up the proposed reforms. Unexpectedly, in spite of Repnin's threats and the presence of Russian troops, the Diet showed a truly patriotic spirit and refused to comply with Catherine's demands. Her will had to be enforced by an act of most brutal violence: the arrest of the patriotic leaders of the Diet (among them two bishops) by Russian grenadiers and their deportation to Kaluga. In such a manner the so-called 'cardinal laws' of the republic (among them, of course, the *liberum veto*) were declared unalterable and placed under the guarantee of Russia. The Radom confederates, however, had no reason to rejoice since at the same time, against their will, religious dissidents in Poland received full political rights and the special protection of the Empress.

Indignation against the Russian violence and, simultaneously, against the dissidents, found expression in the Confederation of Bar (1768–72) which for four years fought Russian and Royal (Stanislaw August's) troops in all the provinces of the Commonwealth. The ideology of the Confederates was permeated by the spirit of so-called 'Sarmatism', i.e. by gentry traditionalism, praising ancient customs and combining ardent republicanism with equally ardent Catholicism and hostility towards everything foreign. The majority of the confederation were especially hostile to the French Enlightenment, seeing it as a source of demoralization and as the intellectual weapon of 'enlightened despotism'. Little wonder that many Polish historians treated the Bar Confederation as a reactionary movement. Recently, however, another interpretation has come to prevail (see B. 108, and the same author in B. 42). The Bar movement is seen as combining the features of a traditionalist Polish Confederation with those of a modern national uprising. It is rightly emphasized that, in contrast to the Confederation of Radom, it was not a movement of conservative magnates and their clients but a movement of the broad masses of the gentry who rejected, at last, the political tutelage of their 'elder brothers' and saw the magnates as traitors to the national cause. Finally, it is pointed out that the intellectual leaders of the Bar Confederation, especially Michał Wielhorski (the author of the book *On the Restoration of the Ancient Government in Accordance with Fundamental Laws of the Republic*, Paris 1775), were by no means adverse to all kinds of modernization, although, to be sure, they wanted only such reforms as would not destroy the republican character of the state. It is worth while to add that

Wielhorski was inspired by John Locke and by some thinkers of
the French Enlightenment and, in his turn, inspired Rousseau
to write his famous *Considerations On the Government of Poland*—a
book which (in sharp contrast to the opinions of Voltaire and
other ideologists of 'enlightened absolutism') praised the republican institutions of Poland and supported their defenders.

On the whole, the reign of Stanislaw August—the king who
had to witness the three partitions of Poland (1772, 1793, and
1795)—was a period of humiliating dependence on Russia and,
at the same time, an epoch of great cultural achievements, of the
full bloom of the Polish Enlightenment. In 1773 the Diet established the Commission of National Education, the first Ministry
of Education in Europe; this Commission took possession of the
network of schools belonging to the recently dissolved Jesuit
Order and thoroughly modernized the entire system of education
in the Commonwealth. In 1788 the so-called Great Diet, or
Four Years' Diet, was convened in Warsaw and, having agreed
to form a Confederation (i.e. to suspend the right of veto),
started to work out necessary reforms. First, it demanded the
withdrawal of the Russian troops and resolved to enlarge the
ridiculously small Polish army (20,000 men) to 100,000 soldiers.
(In fact the number of soldiers was increased to only 65,000.)
Then it embarked on long-range legislative work which resulted
in the promulgation—in an atmosphere of almost universal
enthusiasm—of the new fundamental law known as the Constitution of 3 May 1791. It abolished the much-abused forms of
'ancient freedom' (*liberum veto*, free elections, confederations,
and so forth) and transformed the Commonwealth into a
hereditary constitutional monarchy with modern government
(whose ministers were called 'Guardians of the Law') and
biennial parliaments. Political rights were made dependent on
the ownership of land: this meant that many burghers (owners
of houses) were raised to the status of 'active citizens', while the
landless gentry—the clients of the magnates—were deprived of
political influence. Thus not only were republican principles
replaced by monarchical ones but even the most cherished idea
of the gentry democracy—the equality of all the nobles—was
abandoned.

This was not because of any change in the basic attitude
towards 'republican freedom' as such. Stanislaw Staszic (1775–
1826), one of the most outstanding thinkers of the Polish En-

lightenment and the chief spokesman of the Polish bourgeoisie, conceded in his *Warnings for Poland* (1790) that a political system based upon republican freedom and respect for human rights was in itself the best system. He added, however, that even an orderly republic could not defend itself if its neighbours were absolute monarchies, and concluded that it was necessary to curtail some freedoms in order to face the dangers from without. The reasoning of another outstanding thinker, the main architect of the Constitution of 3 May, Hugo Kołłątaj (1750–1812), was very similar. He put even more stress on the intrinsic value of republicanism and claimed that this value would be preserved in Poland: she would not be a real monarchy since sovereignty would rest not with the king but with the entire body of citizens.

It is widely accepted today that the rise of nationalism in modern European history was closely linked with the origins of popular sovereignty and with the theory of government by the active consent of the governed (cf. B. 77 and B. 66, p. 14). If so, the case of Poland seems to be of particular importance. The principles of government by consent of the governed and of the sovereignty of the people (or, rather, the sovereignty of the political 'nation' consisting of the gentry) were known in Poland long before modern nationalism was born. For a very long time, however, the 'gentry nation' believed that its sovereignty was endangered only from within; hence, it came to oppose any strengthening of royal power and to see the *liberum veto* as the best guarantee *absolutum dominium*. The bitter eighteenth-century experiences taught it that the real danger was coming from without and that the necessary condition for national sovereignty was national independence. In such a manner the doctrine of the sovereignty of the 'nation of the gentry' became transformed in Poland, earlier, perhaps, than anywhere else, into the modern doctrine of national self-determination. Its beginnings could be traced back to Leszczyński, whose ideas, as has been shown by Jean Fabre (B. 36, pp. 131–49), had some influence on the republican current in the French Enlightenment. Its fully articulated formulation can be found in the works of Staszic and Kołłątaj. The latter expressed it in the following words:

That every nation should be free and independent, that every nation should be allowed to embrace such a form of government as it likes the best and that

no foreign nation is entitled to interfere in its constitutional development—
this is the first and most important maxim of the law of nations, so evident in
the light of our century that no proofs are needed to justify it. A nation which
has no right to rule in its own country is not a nation. A foreign guarantee
imposed on a nation means that the given nation is deprived of its sovereignty,
deprived of the right which is the basis of its independent existence. (A. 37,
p. 5.)

This is, however, only the first part of the story. The second
part began when the name of Poland was wiped from the map of
Europe. Having lost their state, the Poles had to prove that even
without statehood it was possible to remain a nation. Immediately after the last partition of 1795, Polish refugees formed
a legion in Italy which was to fight on the side of the French
army against Austria and the other partitioning powers. 'This
was something new: a national idea, deprived of statehood, in
arms; a nation in exile with nationals owing allegiance to no
king and no government, but to a vision, a myth, a hope'
(B. 159, p. 267). The song of this legion, which was to become
the Polish national anthem, expressed the continuity of the
national will to exist:

> Poland has not yet been lost
> As long as we are living.

In the new conditions created by the defeat of the Kościuszko
uprising (1794) and the complete loss of independence which
followed, the legacy of gentry democracy began to play a different role than previously. Maurycy Mochnacki, the famous
literary critic who in the November uprising emerged as an
outstanding publicist of the Left, asserted with good reason that
after the downfall of the state the republican traditions of gentry
democracy, quite irrespective of their functioning in the past,
greatly contributed to supporting the inner vitality of the nation
and the spirit of resistance against the partitioning powers (see
A. 78, p. 358). If Poland had been an absolute monarchy, he
argued, her society would have become passive, devoid of civic
spirit, unable to organize and to defend itself. In other words,
the downfall of the Polish state would have amounted in such a
case to the dissolving of the Polish nation. If 'Poland has not yet
been lost', it was due to the fact that a large percentage of her
population felt themselves to be a nation, endowed with an
inalienable right of sovereignty.

Many contemporary historians fully agree with this view. One of the great experts in the history of the Polish gentry, Janusz Tazbir, has recently pointed out that in the changed conditions even the ancient vices of the gentry showed their positive side: stubborn conservatism changed into a stubborn will to preserve national tradition and identity, the long habit of opposing royal power turned into resisting the foreign yoke, and so forth (B. 162, pp. 71–2).

In order to understand the social psychology of the Polish gentry on the eve of the November uprising one should be aware of their number and of their changed status in the Congress Kingdom. Both the Grand Duchy of Warsaw, established by Napoleon in 1807, and the Kingdom of Poland, called into being by the Vienna settlement of 1815, were constitutional monarchies occupying only a small, central part of the former Commonwealth. Although in the entire territory of the former Commonwealth the gentry constituted about 9–10 per cent, this was not so in its central, ethnically Polish and Catholic part: here, especially in Masovia and in the Podlasie region, which were parts of the Congress Kingdom, the number of the gentry was as high as 25 per cent of the total population. It should be remembered also that only a small minority of this gentry—about 4.7 per cent—could be classified as relatively wealthy landowners. The rest were petty gentry (about 35–45 per cent) and landless gentry (about 50–5 per cent), whose influence was greatly reduced or (in the case of the 'noble proletariat') completely eliminated, due to the introduction of property qualifications to vote (B. 44, pp. 60–2). It is understandable, therefore, that the broad masses of poor gentry could not be satisfied with the constitutional regime of the kingdom. In particular the landless gentry, formerly the clients of magnates and supporters of the reactionary, pro-Russian Targowica Confederation (1792), became increasingly inclined to political radicalism. After all, only a democratic and independent Polish republic could return to them their lost political rights, their political equality with the landowners, and their feeling of citizenship. Moreover, only an independent, strong, and modernized Poland could give them enough jobs in the army, in self-government, and in the bureaucratic apparatus of the state.[8]

We are told by an American scholar that Poland, along with

Hungary, provided the best example of the 'aristocratic' type of nationalism.[9] In reality, however, this was not so. Polish nationalism originated among the petty and landless gentry who constituted a large percentage of the population, were imbued with the anti-aristocratic spirit of the 'gentry democracy', and felt themselves bitterly resentful of the attempts made by the partitioning powers to establish a formal hierarchy within the gentry and to deprive the poorest part of them of their noble status. Equally untrue is the thesis that the Western ideas of popular sovereignty, natural rights of nations, and so forth, were used in Poland 'as an additional argument in favour of the established order' (B. 155, p. 26). It could be so in the eighteenth century, as was shown by the Bar Confederation,[10] but not after the Kościuszko uprising. The favourite idea of the gentry revolutionaries in Poland was to restore the sovereignty of the gentry and to transform it into a truly popular sovereignty. Their 'republicanism' was no longer a defence of outdated principles and privileges. On the contrary, their favourite idea was, as Mochnacki put it, the ennobling of the entire population of Poland, i.e. the raising of every Pole to membership in a 'political nation'.

II. Republicanism versus Monarchism

In 1807, as a result of Polish participation in the Napoleonic wars, a small central part of the former Polish state regained its independence in the form of the Grand Duchy of Warsaw. In reality it was only a semi-independent state, one of the many vassal states of imperial France. Its constitution, dictated by Napoleon, was framed on the French model and was among the most progressive constitutions of contemporary Europe. Its hereditary ruler was Frederick August, King of Saxony. It was, thus, a constitutional monarchy of the modern bourgeois type. In spite of a certain discrepancy between its backward social realities and its constitutional framework, it was the first thoroughly modern, bureaucratic, and centralized form of statehood on Polish lands. Its achievements in the economic, educational, and military fields were sometimes truly amazing (see B. 184, p. 48).

The Congress Kingdom, although created by the victorious Russian tsar, was also a French-modelled constitutional monarchy. The November uprising (1830) started as a reaction against the multiple violations of its constitution and autonomous status by the Russian authorities. Later, however, when it became clear that Nicholas I was not willing to make any concessions to the Poles, the Polish Diet decided to deprive the tsar of his Polish throne, without, however, changing the constitution. After the defeat of the insurrection the constitution was abolished and the Congress Kingdom lost its semi-independent status. Almost 10,000 political leaders and soldiers of the uprising had to leave their country and settle abroad— mainly in France but also in England, Belgium, and Switzerland. Thus, the major part of the political and intellectual élite of the nation found itself abroad, resolving not to give up the struggle for an independent Poland, seeing itself as the spokesman for the cause of all oppressed nations and as the vanguard in all-European struggle against the reactionary Holy Alliance.

I cannot embark here on writing a history of the multifarious activities of this so-called 'Great Emigration'. It is necessary, however, briefly to present the main ideological controversies which took place among these Polish exiles and in which the main currents of the Polish political thought of the epoch were shaped.

Characteristically enough, one of the most heated controversies revolved around the old issue of 'Republicanism versus Monarchism'. The leader of the constitutional monarchists was Prince Adam Jerzy Czartoryski (1770–1861), member of the famous 'Family', formerly a Russian statesman and a personal friend of Alexander I, and head of the insurrectionary national government in 1831. The main figure among the republicans was, at the beginning, the great historian Joachim Lelewel (1788–1861), chief representative of the Left in the insurrectionary government and, at the same time, the chairman of the radical Patriotic Society whose pressure on the government and the Diet brought about the dethronement of the Romanovs. Czartoryski's party, called usually Hotel Lambert (after the name of Czartoryski's residence), claimed to have inherited the progressive tradition of eighteenth-century reformers. Lelewel's estimation of the historical role of 'The Family' was bitter and one-sidedly critical; his view of the Constitution of 3 May was milder, but critical too. He was careful, however, to make a clear distinction between his republicanism and the republicanism of conservative eighteenth-century magnates. The crucial difference consisted in the violently anti-aristocratic spirit of his republican views. In Lelewel's eyes both the conservative magnates and the progressive Czartoryskis belonged to the same aristocratic oligarchy whom he held responsible for the degeneration of the gentry democracy and the downfall of the Commonwealth.

In order to see the peculiarity of Lelewel's place in the history of Polish republicanism it is useful to compare his ideas with those of Hugo Kołłątaj who also claimed to be a republican and who saw the strengthening of royal power as the only way to save republican principles. In a monarchy, Kołłątaj argued, the king is the father of small children who have no chance to come of age, whereas in Poland the king will be a father of mature, responsible citizens (A. 36, II. 47–8). Although his power will be hereditary and not elective (the elective principle being dangerous in the neighbourhood of three absolute monarchies), he will be in fact not a monarch but the head of a republic, like the president of the United States. The sovereignty will belong to the entire body of the active citizens of the state. Their number, however, should be restricted. Influenced by the French physiocrats, Kołłątaj wanted to base 'active citizenship' on ownership of the land. A landless man, he maintained, even if he should be very rich, can take his wealth with him and, therefore, can easily change his loyalty, while in the case of a landowner patriotism is indissolubly bound up with his enlightened self-interest (A. 36, I. 292–3).[11] The inevitable conclusion of this reasoning (a conclusion which became part of the Constitution of 3 May) was simple: both the noble proletariat and the wealthy but landless burghers should be given all civil rights but they should, at the same time, be deprived of political influence. An even more inferior position was to be the status of the peasants who, in Kołłątaj's view, were not entitled to the legal ownership of their land. They were to be brought under the protection of law, compulsory labour services were to be replaced by free contracts; the peasants' land, however, was to be treated not as their full property but only as a form of tenure dependent on agreements with landowners.

For Lelewel all these conclusions were entirely unacceptable. In his view the democratic principles of the ancient republic of the gentry should be made a universal law by means of which *all* the inhabitants of Poland should be given equal political rights, quite irrespective of their status, ethnic background, or property qualifications. He wrote a special historical treatise on the 'lost citizenship' of the Polish peasants and demanded that their lost rights should be fully restored (A. 48). According to his historical theory democratic–republican principles were inherent in the ancient Slavonic communalism and, as such, belonged to the common heritage of all Slavonic nations.[12] He put special emphasis on the existence of a republican tradition in Russia, exemplified by the flourishing city-republics of Novgorod and Pskov, and spoke with great sympathy of the Decembrists who had tried to restore 'ancient Russian freedom'.[13] On the whole, however, Russia was for him a sad example of a Slavonic country in which the democratic and republican traditions of ancient Slavdom had been most cruelly suppressed by absolutism, deeply alien and hostile to the Slavic nature of the Russian people. The case of Poland was entirely different: here the Slavonic principles had been weakened under the influence of Western feudalism and Catholicism, but later re-emerged and re-established themselves in the form of 'gentry democracy'. True, the ancient Slavonic freedom was confined to one estate only. Nevertheless, Lelewel argued, the natural tendency of the 'gentry democracy' was to expand freedom, and not to restrict it. If this truly Slavonic tendency did not prevail and result in the full democratization of the Commonwealth, this was due to kings, who never got rid of monarchical leanings, and to the magnates, who distorted the egalitarian principles of the gentry republic while paying lip service to it.

It is easy to see that such a conception combined a severe criticism of the Polish past with extreme, romantic idealization of it. The objects of criticism were kings and magnates; the objects of idealization were republican institutions. Contemporary Poles, Lelewel claimed, should humbly bow down before their freedom-loving ancestors (A. 47, p. 390). Rousseau—'the last defender of the Polish people' (A. 47, p. 218)—was completely right when he advised the Poles to cling to their traditions, to reform and improve their republican institutions, but never to destroy them. Unfortunately, the eighteenth-century reformers did not listen to him, preferring rather to follow the advice of Mably, who saw the old Polish institutions as inherently bad and unimprovable. The Constitution of 3 May made a long step in the wrong direction. Lelewel did not hesitate even to put forward the risky hypothesis that Poland might have been saved by liquidating the royal power altogether instead of making it hereditary (A. 47, p. 623).

Lelewel's final conclusion as to the legacy of the Polish past sounded very optimistic, even boastful. Poland had nothing to learn from the West. On the contrary, the contemporary West, decayed as it was, should learn from Poland, because what it needed for its political regeneration were precisely the same republican principles which were once adopted, although in restricted confines, by the Polish 'democracy of the gentry' (cf. B. 32, p. 167).

In the political life of the emigration Lelewel represented the most moderate Left and was often accused of being 'a man of palliatives'. Much more radical was the Polish Democratic

Society (TDP—Towarzystwo Demokratyczne Polskie)[14] whose 'Act of Foundation' was signed on 17 March 1832 by twenty-two *émigrés*, mostly former members of the Patriotic Society. Its ideological platform was formulated in the so-called Great Manifesto (or Poitiers Manifesto), written by Wiktor Heltman (1796–1878), discussed by all sections of the Society, and then voted and signed by all its members. It was published in December 1836 as the definitive ideological creed of the Society. Earlier, in June 1835, the organizational status of the TDP was elaborated, discussed, and accepted. From that time on the Society, numbering 1,135 members in 1836, functioned as the best-organized and most influential political party of the Polish democrats in exile. There is no exaggeration in Peter Brock's words that 'the *émigré* Society came to provide for the first time in the history of East European peoples a democratically run political party which was at the same time centralized, well disciplined and with definite goals' (B. 17, p. 94).

Unlike Lelewel, the ideologists of the TDP, at the beginning at least, were influenced not so much by Polish republican traditions but rather by modern French republicanism. They read the works of Robespierre, Marat, and Saint-Just, participated in the activities of the Charbonnerie Démocratique Universelle and in such neo-Jacobin French organizations as the Society of the Friends of the People and the Society For the Rights of Man and Citizen. A characteristic document of this early stage of their ideological evolution, the 'Brief Political Catechism' (1833; see A. 2, pp. 41–51), was written by one of the founders of the TDP, the son of a simple peasant Jan Nepomucen Janowski (1803–88). He violently condemned all kinds of monarchy, arguing that the monarchical principle as such is utterly incompatible with a genuine social life. Monarchy is based on compulsion, while the precondition of a truly social life is goodwill and a capacity for voluntary association. Constitutional monarchy is only a 'despotisme mis en régles'. A republic is the only form of government which would accord with the inalienable Rights of Man. A true republic, however, is inconceivable without a true democracy, that is, without the full political equality of all the inhabitants of a given state. Needless to say, neither the Polish oligarchy of magnates nor even the 'gentry republic' of the Golden Age of Polish history deserved to be called 'republics' in Janowski's sense of the term.

In fact, according to Janowski, a true democratic republic had never existed anywhere in the world as yet. The French republic of 1792–5, constantly threatened by internal and external dangers, had to suppress its own principles by transforming itself into a dictatorship. The governments of the United States and Switzerland were not democratic because the first sanctioned slavery and the second tolerated aristocracy.

A little later, under the influence of the defeat of carbonari-inspired movements which were to start an all-European revolution, the ideologists of the TDP underwent an evolution from 'the foreign faith' to 'the national faith', from the slogan 'through mankind for Poland' to its reversal, 'through Poland for mankind' (A. 27, p. 30). In accordance with this they came closer to Lelewel in putting emphasis on the native, Polish sources of their thought.' In the 'Great Manifesto' of 1836 they paid tribute to the tradition of Polish 'gentry republicanism', although they tried at the same time (in contrast to Lelewel and the moderates who followed him) to cut themselves off from any idealization of Poland's past (except the earliest epoch of ancient Slavonic democracy). They did not deny the alleged causal relation between ancient Slavonic communalism and the Polish gentry's love for freedom. They agreed also to see the 'gentry republic' as a society comparatively better than Western absolute monarchies. They wholeheartedly accepted and deepened Lelewel's criticism of the Constitution of 1791, indicating that the espousal of royalism had been contrary not only to the Polish national spirit but to the spirit of the age as well. At the same time, however, they saw the 'gentry democracy' as a deep distortion of correct principles, and refused to praise or continue any traditions specific to the gentry. The moderates treated this standpoint as a complete break with national tradition and imputed to the TDP a desire to create on the shores of the Vistula an entirely new nation, preserving only the name of the former one (see A. 54, p. 374).

It should be added that the theorists of the TDP were capable of combining the emphasis of their national roots and national tasks with profound studies of democratic ideologies and theories of democracy produced in the West. Particular attention was paid by them to two books: Tocqueville's *Democracy in America* and A. Billard's *Essai sur l'organisation démocratique en France* (Paris 1837). Both of these were discussed by the Society's sections and summarized in lengthy reviews published in the Society's theoretical journal (cf. B. 198, pp. 43–4). As might be expected, the French model of democracy seemed to them more suitable for the future Poland than the American one. This option stemmed from their centralist leanings. In contrast to Lelewel they did not extol decentralized or federated common-wealths, the fate of Poland was for them a proof that centraliza-tion is a necessary condition of a strong and orderly republic.

Let us turn now to the constitutional monarchists. This term, I think, is the best general name for the numerous and different followers of Prince Adam. Other terms, such as 'aristocratic party' or 'conservative party', do not seem to be adequate. The old Prince, to be sure, was a scion of one of the most aristocratic families in Poland but, nevertheless, he did not set forth an aristocratic programme. Programmatic defence of the privileges of aristocracy and nobility was felt by the patriots in exile to be completely anachronistic and discredited, while the monarchical idea was still very attractive to some of them. The term 'conservative' is even more misleading, because the Great Emigration as a whole was waging a war against the conserva-tive forces in Europe. Prince Czartoryski represented the right wing of the emigration but, nevertheless, he was not a conserva-tive but a liberal, a convinced supporter of liberal constitu-tionalism against the reactionary absolutism of the Holy Alliance. His followers supporting the liberal cause in Italy proved to be further to the left than the majority of Italian liberals (see B. 193). In 1846 Prince Adam immediately recognized the revolutionary government in Cracow and publicly declared his allegiance to it. During the Springtime of the Peoples his followers, along with their democratic opponents, fought on the side of the revolution; the most famous of them, General Józef Bem, gained the admiration of the European Left as a commander-in-chief of revolutionary forces in Transylvania. Metternich was certainly right when he re-buked Prince Adam for espousing the cause of 'polonism' (identical in practice with revolutionism) and thus betraying his own class interest (cf. B. 47, II. 155 and B. 37, p. 201). There were, of course, true conservatives and true reactionaries in Poland, people no less conservative than Metternich, Russian landowners, and Prussian Junkers, but the objective logic of the political situation of their country—the simple fact that the main enemies of the independence of Poland were at the same time the main pillars of European conservatism—eliminated them from the Polish national-liberation movement.

Like the democrats, constitutional monarchists tried to deduce their political standpoint from the lessons of Polish history. The historian who provided them with the best arguments was Karol Hoffman (1798–1875), the editor of *Kronika Emigracji Polskiej*, one of the main journals of Hotel Lambert. In contrast to Lelewel, he distanced himself as far as possible from a romantic idealization of the Polish past (cf. B. 141).[15] He was a staunch Westerner, believing in the universal laws of historical development and rejecting Lelewel's thesis about the historical uniqueness and particular value of the communal institutions of ancient Slavdom. People, he maintained, are basically the same everywhere, the so-called 'national spirit' is a product of changing historical circumstances and by no means an independent, irreducible factor of historical development. Western feudalism (in the sense of a hierarchy within nobility) and absolutism were normal phases of historical evolution, while the Polish 'gentry democracy' was a historical anomaly, a deviation from the norm resulting from retarded development. When monarchy was weak in the West (i.e. during the classical feudal period) it continued to remain too strong in Poland to allow the full development of a feudal hierarchy within the nobility; later, when Western monarchies became absolute, the Polish nobility was too strong and not differentiated enough within itself to allow for a Western-type development in their country. Thus, Poland was able to skip both the phase of a full-fledged feudalism and the phase of royal absolutism. The final result of this was the beginning of the gradual dissolution of the state. Royal power had no chance to become stronger, the overwhelming domination of the nobility over all other estates killed in embryo the development of Polish cities, and the ideology of 'gentry democracy' vastly contributed to the growing anarchization of political life. Given that Poland had introduced the feudal privileges of the nobility—privileges which enabled her nobles to enslave their peasants and to liquidate the independent power of their kings—it would have been much better if a feudal hierarchy within the nobility had also been introduced. Any hierarchy, Hoffman reasoned, is better than anarchy, and anarchy within the ruling estate was especially dangerous.

The emphasis on the link between strong monarchical power and the development of cities was an important element in the ideology of the followers of Prince Adam. Because of this they were supported by people who believed that a future indepen-dent Poland would need a strong enlightened bourgeoisie of its own. The most colourful figure among them was one of the first Polish Fourierists, Jan Czyński (1801–67)—a converted Jew (from a Frankist family) who cherished the idea that Polish Jews could be transformed into patriotic Polish burghers, and propagated this belief in the columns of his journal *Echo miast polskich* (The Echo of Polish Cities). His sympathy for the monarchists harmonized perfectly with his Fourierist criticism of political democracy. True democracy, he argued, consists in the democratization of social relations and not in a republican form of government. In Polish conditions a strong royal power could promote the democratic cause much better than a demo-cratic republic ruled by the gentry.[16]

At the end of the 1830s the most militant monarchists became organized in the Monarchical and Insurrectional Party of 3 May (whose membership reached the impressive number of 1,500). The favourite idea of their leaders was to proclaim that Prince Czartoryski should be recognized as being *de facto* the king of Poland (although he himself never officially accepted this proposal). The best theoretical and historical justification of their political programme was a brochure by Janusz Woronicz entitled *On Monarchy and Dynasty in Poland* (Paris 1839). Its main arguments ran as follows.

In comparison with a republic a monarchy is not only a much more efficient form of government but also more conducive to social justice. All republics are based on exploitation and oppression, because political equality for all creates the condi-tions for an unbridled licence of the stronger. All republics are weak; ancient Rome was a republic only in its capital, its provinces were ruled by severe proconsuls. The abuse of the monarchical principle leads to despotism, but the abuse of republicanism leads to destruction. True monarchy, however, has nothing in common with 'sultanism' or 'tsarism', charac-teristic of the political system defended by the Holy Alliance. A genuine monarchy is rooted in, and draws its strength from, a genuine nation, a genuine social life. Without a nation there is no mutual agreement between the ruler and the ruled, but only the rule of sheer force. The three partitioning powers are not

national states, their populations are composed of heterogeneous elements held together by force alone. Therefore, they
cannot claim to represent monarchical principles.

In such a manner Polish monarchists in exile combined their
commitment to the idea of strong government with a belief that
'legitimism of nations' was older and more important than
dynastic legitimism, defended by the reactionary forces in
Europe.

Poland's best times, Woronicz continued, were during
periods of strong monarchy, while her republicanism resulted
in general decline. Poland's 'Golden Age' was also the result of
the efforts of her monarchs (the republican period, according to
Woronicz, began only after the extinction of the Jagellonian
dynasty). In the eighteenth century it became evident that the
return to monarchy was the only way of saving Poland. The
enthusiasm with which the nation welcomed the Constitution
of 3 May was proof that monarchical instincts remained very
strong in the Polish national character.

It was not true that republicanism had become a common
tendency in Europe. Even if it were so, however, one should
take into account Poland's specific condition. Despite Lelewel's
theory, contemporary Poland had no elements of 'republicanism from below', her republicanism was necessarily, a 'republicanism of the gentry'. Polish peasants preserved a good
memory of the Polish kings, while the word 'republic' was either
incomprehensible to them or associated with the unbridled rule
of their noble oppressors. Perhaps the November uprising could
succeed if the patriotic cause had been presented to the peasant
masses in the living person of a King of Poland and Lithuania.
Even Maurycy Mochnacki at the end of his life came to the
conclusion that the uprising was defeated because of the lack
of strong one-man leadership and, in consequence, gave his
support to the royalists in exile (see B. 82).

The last chapter of Woronicz's brochure argues that the best
candidate for the Polish throne was Prince Adam. There was
the blood of the Jagellons in his veins. In the eighteenth century
his family rendered invaluable services to the patriotic cause.
Today's Europe rightly sees in him 'the only personification of
the Polish cause'. He was, however, too moderate, and too
modest. He should have dared to proclaim himself King of
Poland during the uprising, but he refrained because of his

'selfish timidity'. It was necessary, therefore, to encourage him to proclaim himself a king and thus 'to make him infallible' (A. 107, pp. 59–61).

Needless to say, Woronicz's arguments were vehemently criticized and ridiculed in the democratic press. Even the more moderate supporters of Czartoryski's camp thought it wise not to identify themselves with these ideas. The controversy between monarchists and republicans flared up with new force.

III. The Idea of Property and the Peasant Question

1. The Changing Functions of Physiocratic Tradition

Another controversy, seen from historical hindsight as of great importance, concerned the agrarian question. The defeat of the November uprising made it absolutely clear that without an adequate solution of this question all efforts at regaining national independence were doomed to failure. Some people understood this even before the uprising, and tried to voice their opinions when it took place. In February 1831 Maurycy Mochnacki published the article 'Why do the masses not rise?', the conclusion of which was that the mobilization of the masses for the national cause was impossible without transforming political insurrection into a social revolution. The overwhelming majority of the Diet, however, insisted that the peasant question in the lands of the Congress Kingdom did not exist at all, since serfdom had been abolished there by the Napoleonic constitution of 1807. Count Jan Ledóchowski argued: 'There is no such thing as serfdom in our country. The peasants may move from place to place. They may come to agreements to compound for labour services. So there is absolutely no point in a petition for the abolition of labour services' (B. 98, p. 73). Different was the situation of peasants in the eastern parts of the old Commonwealth which were directly incorporated into the Russian Empire—there serfdom was preserved and even made more severe, close to the status of simple slavery. The leaders of the insurrection understood this and declared that one of the main aims of expanding the uprising into the former Grand Duchy of Lithuania was to emancipate its peasants. By emancipation, however, they meant only personal freedom and equality before the law, naïvely believing that Lithuanian and Belorussian peasants would be fully satisfied with obtaining the same status as the peasants of the constitutional Congress Kingdom.

In order to understand this way of thinking (and the social realities it helped to conceal) we should return for a while to the eighteenth-century Polish reformers who had embraced physiocratic ideas.[17] The most important among them, Hugo Kołłątaj, was a firm supporter of the absolute right of private property. He went so far as to proclaim that all property should belong to private persons, that no land should be public property, and that the possession of every piece of land should be secured by contract or clear title (A. 36, I. 306–11 and II. 308). He tried to persuade the Polish gentry that defence of feudal privileges by playing with the idea of conditional ownership and mutual obligations was dangerous because it could lead to questioning of the gentry's unconditional right to the soil. Accordingly, he wanted to give the peasants their personal freedom and, at the same time, to make it clear that their holdings were not their property, but the property of landlords given in usufruct to the village. He coined the slogan: 'The soil to the landlord, and free work for the peasants' (see B. 70, p. 21). It meant in practice that there should be a clear contractual basis for relations between the village and the manor: the peasants should be treated as personally free but obliged to pay the landlord for the right of using their holdings either in cash or in labour services on the manor farm. In this way compulsory labour on the manor farm (*corvée*) was to be changed into statute labour, an obligation resulting from a clearly formulated and mutually binding contract, protected by the state.

The Constitution of 3 May did not dare to proclaim the formal abolition of serfdom. It proclaimed only that peasants would be brought 'under the protection of law and of the national government', and that all agreements between landlords and peasants would henceforth be treated as 'their common and mutual obligation'. This did not achieve too much, but, on the other hand, it should be remembered that the constitution itself was regarded as a framework for future reforms (B. 70, p. 22). The article about the peasants was, perhaps, deliberately vague and left open the door for further legislation.

A step forward was made during the Kościuszko uprising. In his famous Polaniec Manifesto, Kościuszko promised the peasants full personal freedom, security of tenure, and a reduction of labour services; by the same token he directly interfered in the sphere of 'private contracts', supporting the weaker side. Personally he was in favour of granting the peasants full ownership of their holdings (cf. A. 38, p. 218). Such a move, however, would have alienated the gentry and reduced their support for the uprising.

The next step was the Constitution of the Duchy of Warsaw. It read: 'Slavery will be abolished. All citizens are equal in the eyes of the law. Personal freedom will be protected by the courts.' The author of these words, the French Emperor, did not understand, however, that the real problem in the Duchy was not that of 'slavery' (after all, there was a difference between slavery and serfdom), but that of economic bondage. The abolition of 'slavery' (i.e. serfdom) left unsolved the problem of peasants' ownership of their holdings together with that of their labour services on manorial farms. No wonder the Polish rulers of the Duchy interpreted the constitution in accordance with Kołłątaj's ideas, i.e. in the interests of the gentry as a class of landowners. Thus the peasants of the Duchy (and of the later Congress Kingdom) became emancipated without land, subject to eviction, dependent on the landlords by force of economic compulsion. Since their relations with the landlords became, in theory at least, purely economic, any governmental interference on their behalf would have been interpreted as a violation of the basic principle of liberal political economy formulated by the physiocrats in the famous words: 'Laissez faire, laissez passer.'

It was often argued that the peasants' labour services on the manor farms were in fact a simple continuation of the compulsory labour of the serfs.[18] On the other hand, however, it should be remembered that under serfdom the peasants had at least 'weak rights' to their holdings whereas with the introduction of the Napoleonic Code (which was an integral part of the Constitution of the Duchy) all kinds of 'weak property' were abolished and replaced by 'strong property', i.e. by absolute private property of the bourgeois type. If this were to be so, peasants should either be given their holdings as an unconditional property or their claims to them should be completely denied. The fact that the Polish landowners solved this question in accordance with their own class interests did not contradict the spirit of the Napoleonic Constitution of the Duchy.[19] It showed only that the bourgeois idea of property might be used for defending the property rights of the nobility. Labour services for the tenure of landlords' land were not so much a remnant of serfdom but, rather, a function of the underdevelopment of the market economy. As a rule Polish peasants had no money to pay their landlords in cash and, therefore, had to pay for the usufruct of their holding by cultivating the land belonging directly to the manor farms. Needless to say, such 'contractual' relations, no longer softened by any patriarchal ties between the manor and the village, resulted in the growing hostility of the newly emancipated serfs towards the gentry. The landlords no longer had any obligations towards their peasants. It was quite natural, therefore, that more and more peasants began to think that their holdings should belong to them as unconditional property, without any obligations for the sake of the manor.

2. From Radical Democracy to Agrarian Socialism
'The development of revolutionary thought among the Poles after 1832 [i.e. after the arrival of the Polish exiles to France] was indeed slow' (B. 99, p. 2). Although these words were written by a specialist in Polish history, it is difficult to imagine a more unjust generalization. In fact, the idea of winning national independence by means of an agrarian revolution was born during the uprising among the left wing of the Patriotic Society, and its advocates started to propagate it among the *émigrés* from the very first day after their arrival in France. In the early spring of 1832 the 'Act of Foundation' of the TDP proclaimed not only the abolition of all privileges in the future Poland but also the liquidation of all types of economic exploitation. It even contained the phrase: 'the land and its fruit common to all' (see A. 2, p. 6). Later in the same year the TDP issued a 'Proclamation to the Citizen-Soldiers' in which it solemnly declared that the peasants were entitled to the ownership of land, enlightenment, and citizenship. Soon afterwards, on the second anniversary of the uprising, Tadeusz Krępowiecki (1798–1847),[20] a co-founder of the TDP and the chief of the 'Polist tent' in the Charbonnerie Démocratique Universelle, delivered a public speech in which he painted, in the most dark colours, the whole Polish past and went as far as paying homage to the bloody Ukrainian rebellions, from Khmelnytsky's uprising to the jacquerie of 1768 which resulted

in the terrible massacre of the Poles and Jews at Humań (see A. 2, pp. 25–33). Czartoryski's followers, moderate democrats grouped around Lelewel, and even the majority of the members of the TDP were horrified at hearing these words, especially since the Polish past was condemned before a French audience. Nevertheless Krępowiecki was not alone. He was supported by such important figures as Colonel Józef Zaliwski, the radical priest Aleksander Pułaski, Jan Czyński, and others. His speech marked an important shift in the consciousness of the Polish gentry: a radical, merciless self-accusation was clearly formulated and it was difficult to forget. In spite of widespread disagreement with its excessive radicalism, it was a characteristic, although exaggerated, expression of the important process of transforming the Polish 'gentry democrats' into the guilt-conscious 'penitent gentry'.[21]

The quoted phrase about 'the land common to all' soon turned out to be liable to different interpretations. The most radical members of the TDP (Krępowiecki, Pułaski, Adam Gurowski, Zenon Świętosławski) imparted to it a more or less vague socialist meaning, while the rest understood it simply as acknowledging the peasants' right to land. One thing, however, was quite clear: the conception of property rights as something absolute—the conception embraced by eighteenth-century physiocrats and by the Napoleonic Code—was unanimously rejected. The members of the TDP agreed to see property as a social relation, subject to change by legislative acts expressing the will of a sovereign people.

In the discussion which preceded the publication of the Great Manifesto of 1836, some members of the TDP criticized the Centralization (the Central Committee) for accepting the principle of individual ownership of the land (see B. 19, pp. 29–31). Two members of the section of Reims demanded the socialization of all land. A somewhat *juste milieu* position was taken by three members of the Avignon section who postulated the abolition of the buying and selling of land and the equal distribution of all land among all members of society (i.e. the liquidation of manor farms). The most radical was the London section, influenced probably by the London Commune—a socialist organization which had split from the TDP in 1834. It voiced its opinion in the following words:

In theory you condemn inequality; in practice you uphold it. . . . We are profoundly convinced that the question of property is the question of the century. Like the question of *droit*, i.e. of [formal] justice, was the question of the 18th century, so the question of property is the question of our age. . . . In the depth of our souls we are convinced that granting to our peasants the ownership of their holdings, as you want it, will not be carried into effect. Private property must be transformed into common property, this is inevitable. (B. 19, p. 30.)

The main author of the Great Manifesto, Wiktor Heltman, wanted to unite the postulates of the eighteenth century with the postulates of the nineteenth century in a harmonious synthesis. The eighteenth-century emphasis on the *rights* of man and on the pursuit of *individual* happiness should be combined, he argued, with the nineteenth-century emphasis on the duties of man and on the pursuit of *collective* happiness.[22] The first tendency corresponds to the individual aspect of man's nature, the second expresses its social aspect. If men were purely individualistic beings, the principle of absolute private property would have been best for them; if their nature were purely social they would have established a communist system in which not only the land but also women would have been shared in common. One-sided development of the individualistic principle would lead to the struggle of all against all, but one-sided development of the opposite, socialistic principle would result in an oriental-type despotism. A careful avoidance of the absolutization of any of these two principles is, therefore, a necessary condition of sound political theory.

As a solution of the agrarian problem in Poland, the Great Manifesto put forward the idea of granting the peasants full individual ownership of their holdings without any indemnification for the gentry. Some Polish historians (especially the Marxist historians of the 1950s) have criticized this programme as not radical enough. They have rightly pointed out that the Manifesto did not demand the liquidation of the manor farms and left unsolved the problem of landless peasants.[23] However, one has to remember at least two things. First, the demand for the full expropriation of the gentry was unacceptable for the national-liberation movement, which could not have existed without the support of the patriotic gentry and could not afford to alienate them. Secondly, the conception of an entirely consistent agrarian revolution, achieving a 'bourgeois-democratic' transformation by means of total expropriation of the former ruling class, is only an 'ideal model' which was never realized in Europe. Sometimes this model is called, with reference to Lenin, 'the American way of capitalist development'; in fact, however, it has very little in common with the real agrarian development of the U.S.A. It is not true that the theorists of the TDP were too moderate to embrace the American model. Their ideal (to quote the excellent formulation of Peter Brock) was precisely 'the Jeffersonian kind of agrarian democracy, where the independent yeoman farmer predominated but in which the landed gentleman continued to exist' (B. 17, p. 77). One should add only that it was much more revolutionary to proclaim this idea as a programme for partitioned Poland than to realize it in the United States—a country in which feudal privileges never existed.

In view of all these circumstances I am glad to express my agreement with S. Kieniewicz who, in spite of the reservations quoted above, gave the following evaluation of the agrarian programme of the Democratic Society:

> . . . the manifesto of 1836 must be considered a big step in the direction of social reform, and not only by Polish standards. . . . The year 1836 was a milestone, when a clear program was formulated by an organization ready to act, to arouse a social upheaval from below in order to stir the peasants to a revolution against the established powers. . . . It was to exert a tremendous influence on the course of events—on the landlords, the peasants, and the government, both in Poland and elsewhere. These events of 1836 should be considered the first signs of an era in which the agrarian question became the major issue for a revolutionary movement—an era by no means at an end today. (B. 70, pp. 106–7.)

The agrarian programme of the TDP had its enemies both on the right and on the left. It should be stressed, however, that the right wing of the emigration refrained, as a rule, from attacking its general principles. Already in 1833 Prince Czartoryski had come to the conclusion that Polish peasants should receive full property rights to their holdings. In contrast to the TDP he thought that the reform should be carried out according to the Prussian model, i.e. in a non-revolutionary way, under the control of the nobility, favouring the wealthier peasants, and, of course, with the full indemnification of the landlords by the peasants themselves (B. 70, p. 104). For tactical reasons, however, he preferred not to embark on polemics concerning these matters. In this situation the most ferocious attack on the TDP came from the Left—from the newly emerged organizations of agrarian socialists.

The earliest of these organizations—the London Commune established in August 1834 by Krępowiecki, Pułaski, Świętosławski, Stanisław Worcell, Seweryn Dziewicki, and others—has already been mentioned above. It began its existence by proclaiming that 'property is at the centre of all the evil which oppresses mankind at present' (B. 19, p. 17). As practical measures to achieve national and social regeneration the members of the Commune proposed, first, to abolish the law of inheritance and, secondly, to ensure that 'the national society is obliged to give each of its members tools for the work to which he is trained, and to give him in addition the opportunity to work without being dependent on others' (B. 19, p. 16).

At the end of 1834 the London Commune, consisting of the 'penitent gentry', established contact with a group of emigrants of peasant origin which had recently settled in Portsmouth. This group, consisting of 212 simple soldiers and non-commissioned officers who had refused to accept tsarist amnesty and for that reason had been imprisoned for two years by the Prussian authorities who wanted to force them to return to the Congress Kingdom, proved to be susceptible to egalitarian socialist ideas. The members of the London Commune taught them to read and write, at the same time popularizing among them the ideas of Buonarroti (who was their beloved teacher), Laponneray (who represented the neo-Jacobin movement), and the Christian socialists—Lammennais and Buchez. At the end of 1835 the 'Grudziąż Commune of the Polish People' was established (named after the Prussian fortress in which the members of the Commune had been imprisoned). Its first step was a fierce condemnation of the TDP which (according to the members of the Commune) had betrayed its own initial ideas (i.e. the idea of 'land common to all') and was now a reactionary force, deeply hostile to the Polish people. At the beginning of 1836 a new Commune was founded on the island of Jersey; it was called the Humań Commune, in order to express the penitence of its gentry members for the wrongs done by their class to the peasants. Sometime afterwards the two Communes, known under the common name 'The Communes of the Polish

People' (see B. 163 and B. 143), elaborated and published a violent criticism of the project of the new manifesto of the TDP (the 'Great Manifesto') which was then being discussed in the Society's sections. The main points of this criticism, developed also in other documents of the Communes, were as follows.

The Democratic Society has based its ideology on eighteenth-century doctrines of natural law and inalienable 'human rights'. These doctrines, however, sanctify egoism, especially the divisive egoism of private property. Social justice cannot stem from the doctrine of 'rights', it needs Christian sacrifice, self-lessness, the emphasis not on one's legal 'rights' but on one's moral duties. The doctrine of the sovereignty of the people, so much extolled by the TDP, is equally treacherous: it means in fact the sovereignty of an accidental mechanical majority, whereas the true sovereignty belongs to God and to his moral laws. The abolition of all privileges, proudly proclaimed by the TDP, is a simple fraud: one cannot honestly talk about the 'abolition of privileges' if this demand does not even mean the liquidation of manor farms, let alone the liquidation of the law of inheritance. The realization of the Society's agrarian pro-gramme would be a change not for the better, but for the worse: the Society wishes to see in Poland instead of 'the small number of proprietors that are there today a much larger number. In this way tyranny and exploitation will be multiplied and Poland will be transformed from an agricultural to an industrial country. A caste of monied men will be created . . . lords of workshops and stoves, avaricious and vile, men without feeling whom Christ flogged in his holy wrath' (quoted from B. 19, p. 26). The whole programme of the TDP is an imitation of the bourgeois and Protestant West, with its materialism and idol-ization of individual reason. Nobility and Catholicism have at least a glorious past: knights, crusades, monastic orders, missionaries, and martyrs represented values incomparably higher than anything created in the bourgeois-Protestant world (cf. A. 96, p. 122). In contrast to the Western bourgeoisie the Polish peasant still believes in the value of noble disinterested-ness and Christian sacrifice; everything should be done, there-fore, to save him from bourgeoisification on the Western model.

It should be stressed that the Communities were not alone in their disappointment with the post-revolutionary bourgeois West and in their awareness that the Enlightenment had, in fact, paved the way for contemporary European capitalism with all its evident evils. The tradition of the 'Polish eighteenth-century revolution' (as it has been called by the American historian R. R. Palmer) was monopolized by the monarchists from Prince Czartoryski's camp. Lelewel always emphasized that all his attention was turned towards, and all his hopes were set on, the Slavonic East (A. 47, p. 343). The Democratic Society, initially pro-Enlightenment and pro-Western, became very disappointed both in the social realities of the West and in the capacity of the Western revolutionaries to undertake effective action against the reactionary 'old world'. As a result of this it embraced Lelewel's theory of the ancient Slavonic communalism and found solace in a romantic belief in unique features of the national character of the Slavs. Naturally enough the growing disappointment with the capitalist West led to a more or less consistent abandonment of Westernism in the interpretations of the Polish past and in the programmes for her future. It is no exaggeration to say that in the 1840s Westernism, proclaiming the need for a strong bourgeoisie in Poland, had influential followers among the liberal-conservative monarchists, but was already something almost completely alien to the democrats; an isolated exception was the Fourierist Jan Czyński, who, because of this, had no other choice but to sympathize with Prince Czartoryski's party. The other democrats were by then vying with each other in anti-Westernism. The Democratic Society cut itself off from the Westernism of the monarchists, but was in its turn accused of Westernism by the Lelewelists, who criticized it, among other things, for imitating the centralist leanings of the French Revolution, so alien to the spirit of the ancient Polish Commonwealth. Mickiewicz extolled the Slavs as people 'unspoiled by industrialization'; the Communities of the Polish People saw Western capitalism as a worse social evil than feudalism, and declared: 'We are ready to cover Poland with our corpses in order to free her from the plague of industry and trade, in the sense of the contemporary commercial exploitation' (A. 96, p. 71). The Democratic Society, accused by the Communities of a desire to westernize Poland by replacing her nobility with a 'new aristocracy of the money, of potatoes and cheese' (cf. A. 96, pp. 70 and 116), rejected this charge with indignation. It is difficult to deny that the socialists were right in indicating that the agrarian programme of the Democratic Society could lead only to 'fragmentation of individualism' and not to its liquidation; this, however, cannot change the fact that the Society's leaders were deeply convinced that the road chosen by them for Poland was in accordance with the ancient Slavonic communalism and would in no way repeat the errors of the West. The assertion that Poland needed a strong bourgeoisie of her own aroused them to vigorous resistance; General Mierosławski claimed that the lack of a native bourgeoisie was a peculiar privilege of Poland, enabling her to skip the transitional phases of development (such as property qualifications and constitutional monarchy) and to introduce at once an unlimited sovereignty of the people (A. 75). Later, under the influence of the multiple disappointments during the Springtime of the Peoples, Polish democrats became even more insistent on their unique Slavonic heritage and even more sceptical about the revolutionary, regenerative potentialities of the West.

Peter Brock, whom I so often quote in this book, set forth the thesis that the first Polish socialists, beginning with the London Commune of 1834 and the 'Communities of the Polish People', anticipated in their ideas the pattern of thought which became fully developed in later years by the Russian populists (B. 17 and B. 19). There is much to be said in support of this. The similarities are obvious: the idealization of agrarian society, the idea (as the Russian populists put it) of 'skipping the phase of capitalism', and, finally, the looking backward to the old Slavonic communes and finding in them the mainspring of the desired social regeneration. This last feature was in fact the Polish and Russian variant of 'the second reaction against the French revolution and the period of Enlightenment' described by Marx as follows: 'The first reaction against the French revolution and the period of Enlightenment bound up with it was naturally to see everything as medieval and romantic. . . . The second reaction is to look beyond the Middle Ages into the primitive age of each nation, and that corresponds to the socialist tendency.'[24] An interesting analysis of such a type of thinking, justifying the newest by referring to the oldest, was given by an early Polish Marxist, Kazimierz Kelles-Krauz, who invented for it the apt name: 'revolutionary retrospection' (see B. 68).

From the sociological point of view the importance of the

ideas of the Polish and Russian populists lies in their relevance to the problem of revolutionary ideologies in backward agrarian countries—especially such countries which in spite of their economic underdevelopment have a strong intellectual élite, fully participating in the intellectual life of more developed countries and painfully aware of their inalienable responsibility for the freedom and progress of the nation. It is not by chance that such an élite, called 'intelligentsia', emerged for the first time in the East of Europe—first in Poland and then in Russia (see B. 41). Both Polish and Russian democratic radicalism emerged and developed at a time when the purely 'bourgeois' revolutionism had already been discredited, when the 'demonstration effect' of the results of the French Revolution was felt to be deeply disappointing. This is why the Polish revolutionaries often combined Western revolutionary ideas with a more or less profound criticism of the West, anticipating the ideas of the Russian populists. This is also why Polish democrats and socialists, like the Russian populists of the second half of the century, idealized the old Slavonic communes. The vocabulary was also similar: the Polish revolutionaries spoke of the 'debt to the people', of the 'penitent gentry', and of the necessity of 'going to the people' (cf. B. 176, pp. 86–9). Polish 'penitent nobles' discussing social problems and social theories with the illiterate peasant soldiers in the 'Communities of the Polish People' provided the first and unusually successful example of a populist 'work among the people'. Even the word 'intelligentsia', widely believed to have appeared for the first time in Russia in the 1860s, was in fact used by the Polish democrats as early as the 1840s (see below, p. 177).

It should be noted, however, that the tendency to see the ancient Slavonic communes as an embryo of a socialist development was alien to the first Polish socialists. Considering themselves (in contrast to the Russian populists) as true Christians, they looked backwards to the evangelic spirit of early Christianity and were repelled by the anti-Christian leanings of the democrats, expressed, among other things, in their idealization of the pagan institutions of the ancient Slavs. Moreover, ancient Slavonic communes were seen by the democrats as a prototype of democratic self-government, and not as an embryonic form of socialism. It was only in the 1840s, when socialist tendencies began to penetrate the broad democratic movement both in the emigration (the TDP) and in Poland (Edward Dembowski, whose ideas are discussed in detail in another chapter of this book), that the ancient Slavonic commune was discovered as a form of collective ownership of the land and, by the same token, as an argument for the socialist future of Poland.

True, it was not a completely new discovery. The facts about the collective ownership of the land in the ancient Slavonic communes were more or less known thanks to the works of Lelewel, although he himself put emphasis on the 'republican' aspect of Slavonic communalism.[25] The social egalitarianism of the ancient communes and their collectivist spirit was stressed with greater force by Zorian Dołęga Chodakowski (true name: Adam Czarnocki) who was 'the first Pole to discover the folk and its culture through direct experience and the first, too, to declare his belief that the revival of Polish nationality lay in returning to its roots' (B. 20, pp. 17–18). His essay 'On Pre-Christian Slavdom' (1818) was a characteristic product of the historical and archaeological studies inspired by the slavophile atmosphere of Polish thought during the reign of Alexander I.[26] In spite of its sharp criticism of Christianity it contained many ideas surprisingly similar to those of the Russian Slavophiles of the 1840s. Ancient Slavdom was seen by Chodakowski as a unique world of free communes, united within themselves and with each other by moral unanimity and strong religious faith and, therefore, knowing neither the alienated state power nor disintegrating, atomizing individualism. In contrast to Roman Catholicism, the religion of the ancient Slavs did not create and sanction a hierarchical order in society; thanks to this, ancient Slavdom was characterized by democratic equality and by a strong social cohesion stemming from a 'unity of will and feelings'. Conversion to Roman Catholicism destroyed this harmonious state, and created a feudal hierarchy and a growing abyss between the nobility and the people. The worst results of this destructive process of 'latinization' were brought about in Poland; even the Polish peasants, although still preserving old Slavonic traditions, succumbed, partially at least, to the fatal, uprooting influence of the 'latinized' nobility and the Church. Much more optimistic was Chodakowski's view of Russia. The repartitional village commune, still existing in Russia, was for him proof of the exceptional vitality of the tradition of

Slavonic communalism among the Russian peasantry. Orthodox Christianity, unaffected by the influence of Rome, was in his eyes the most acceptable form of Christianity, the only one which was compatible with the democratic and anti-individualistic spirit of the Slavs.

The idea of Russian superiority among the Slavs was not unique in the Polish thought of the epoch. Strange to say, even some Polish political *émigrés* were fascinated by Russia, although they risked being accused of 'national apostasy'. The most drastic case was the 'national apostasy' of Adam Gurowski.[27] He was the initiator of the so-called 'coronation plot' (the unfulfilled attempt to kill Tsar Nicholas I on the day of his coronation as King of Poland), the leader of the radical Left during the insurrection and *spiritus movens* of the dethronement of the Romanovs, in exile a co-founder of the TDP and one of the first Polish followers of Saint-Simon and Fourier. On 8 September 1834, he published a statement in the *Augsburger Zeitung* saying that he was ready to accept the amnesty and to serve the Russian government. The ideological motivation for this move was presented in his pamphlet *La Verité sur la Russie et sur la révolte des provinces polonaises* (dated 12 December 1834). He declared that political and social studies had made him aware that this true fatherland was Russia—'the great total sum of Slavdom'. Only Russia represents Slavonic vitality; Poland is but a corpse which has passed through all the phases of decomposition.

A few years later, in a large book *La Civilisation et la Russie* (A. 23), Gurowski developed a peculiar social philosophy which might be defined as Saint-Simonianism reinterpreted for the use of autocracy. During the last three centuries, he argued, a spirit of criticism and negation had reigned supreme in Europe. Today, however, symptoms of a new 'organic epoch' were clearly visible: many people wanted to return to religion, to rehabilitate the principles of unity, authority, and hierarchy. The ideal embodiment of these Saint-Simonian principles was Russia, whose tsar was 'la loi vivante' and whose life was permeated by the spirit of organic unity. The Russian village commune was a perfect realization of the Saint-Simonian and Fourierist idea of 'association'. In the 1840s (i.e. after Gurowski's book) the same observation was made in the famous book of Baron von Haxthausen (see A. 26), in Mickiewicz's Paris lectures, in Herzen's Diary, and in the writings of the Russian Slavophiles.

Chodakowski's ideas, in spite of the possibility of giving them a conservative, Panslavist interpretation, exerted a considerable influence on the Polish revolutionary populists of the forties, such as the romantic poets Ryszard Berwiński and Seweryn Goszczyński, and, most notably, Edward Dembowski—a populist socialist who developed revolutionary activity in all three parts of partitioned Poland and died as the factual leader of the Cracow revolution of 1846. Thus we can say that the development of revolutionary socialist populism in Poland was preceded, as in Russia, by a kind of Slavophilism, and, ironically enough, by the discovery of the *Russian* village commune as an alleged embodiment of authentic Slavonic values.

In the Polish Democratic Society, socialist tendencies were adamantly resisted by Heltman, for whom common ownership was equivalent to 'universal theft'. Nevertheless the logic of 'revolutionary retrospection' led to the appreciation of the old Slavonic communes not only as a prototype of political democracy, but also as a model for agrarian socialism. In 1846 the Society was joined by Worcell who made it more susceptible to socialism. The events of the Springtime of the Peoples brought discredit on bourgeois radicals and, by the same token, contributed to the further popularization of socialist ideas among the Polish exiles. Characteristically enough, the TDP did not embrace the idea of the nationalization of all the land (an idea set forth in the 1830s by the 'Communities of the Polish People'), but warmly welcomed the conception of Jan Kanty Podolecki (1800–55), who propagated an agrarian socialism conceived as a federation of self-governing communes, i.e. in accordance with the prevailing image of the ancient Slavonic communalism.[28] Stanislaw Worcell (1799–1857), who had abandoned by then the crusading and millenarian spirit of the 'Communities', also strove for a synthesis of democratic and socialist values. In his articles on socialism, published in the *Polish Democrat*, he gave up the idea of liquidating all private property, insisting only on the nationalization of the means of production. In 1853 the Centralization of the TDP officially accepted his views (see B. 27, I. 489).

So, when Alexander Herzen (with the help of the TDP, and warmly welcomed by Worcell) began to proclaim and to propagate the populist creed of his 'Russian socialism', a similar ideology had already been elaborated and widely accepted by the democratic wing of the Polish emigration. With one important difference however: for the Poles the cause of socialism was closely bound up with cause of democratic nationalism. They agreed with Podolecki who saw socialism as an inevitable consequence of democracy and, at the same time, as the highest form of national life, and for whom cosmopolitan ideas were both anti-national and anti-social (see A. 84, pp. 158–72 and 178–83).

3. Millenarian Socialists

In spite of many similarities between the early Polish and Russian agrarian socialists, it is nevertheless quite clear that the *purest* type of socialist populism—i.e. of ideology opposing capitalist development and attempting to base the desired socialist transformation on the archaic collectivism of the peasant communes—appeared not in Poland but in Russia. One of the obvious reasons for this was, of course, the fact that the repartitional village commune was not preserved in the ethnically Polish lands.

The contribution of the first Polish socialists to European intellectual history should not be reduced, however, to the populist aspect of their view of the world. They are equally interesting as a perfect corroboration of the thesis about the direct links between modern utopian socialism and the old tradition of millenarian heresies (see B. 33). I would dare to say that from the point of view of a typological approach to the history of ideas, it was the Polish socialists of the 1830s and 1840s who represented the closest approximation to the ideal type of 'millenarian socialism'. I mean, of course, not the socialist tendencies which emerged within the TDP (although they also contained some millenarian motifs), but the revolutionary *Christian* socialism, represented by the 'Communities of the Polish People' and by the two interesting thinkers of peasant origin—Ludwik Królikowski (1799–1878 or 1881), the editor of the *émigré* journal *Poland For Christ* (Polska Chrystusowa, 1842–6) and the revolutionary priest, Father Piotr Ściegienny (1801–90).[29]

Already the London Commune of 1834 had elaborated a perfect fusion of religious millenarianism and socialism. Its

members shared the chiliastic expectation of the Second
Coming of Christ which was to bring about the collective
earthly salvation of mankind. According to them,

the French revolution at the end of last century was the John the Baptist of the
new faith and till now the Christ has not appeared. . . . This Christ will not be
an individual man but some great nation which, having assimilated everything truly good in the achievements of all its predecessors, and having
created from this an ordered whole, will bring to humanity a new social faith.
Why should not Slavdom be this Christ of the new faith? (B. 19, p. 17.)

A special mission assigned to the Poles would consist in spreading revolutionary French ideas among the other Slavonic
nations and in completing the social transformation of Europe.
Without such a great task, it was felt, the Polish cause would be
meaningless and not worthy of support: 'It would be unforgiv-
able nonsense to wish to raise a nation from the grave or to
create one anew without some mission for humanity' (ibid.).

There is an obvious similarity between this structure of
thought and Mickiewicz's romantic Messianism. It should be
stressed, however, that it was free both from romantic hero-
worship, so characteristic of Mickiewicz's and Słowacki's
views, and from romantic nationalism, even from that form of it
which was accepted by Edward Dembowski in Poland and by
the radical democrats in the emigration. True, in some respects
there is more romanticism in the Christian socialism of the
Communities of the Polish People than in the ideology of the
Democratic Society. The Communities accused the Democratic
Society of a bourgeois rationalism; against the 'scribblings' of
philosophers and economists they set, like Mickiewicz, teachings 'coming from the heart, from revelation' (A. 96, p. 108).
They did not hesitate to proclaim that human reason was the
source of anti-social egoism and the cause of all Poland's misfor-
tunes. Correcting the error of the Jacobins (whose tradition
they wished to continue) they rejected, as we already know, the
Enlightenment doctrine of natural law (accepted by the Democratic Society): this doctrine, they claimed, sanctified and justified social inequality, deified man, endorsed individualism and
private property, relativized morality, and denied in fact the
very notion of moral progress. However, the violent criticism of
the eighteenth century's intellectual heritage went hand in
hand with the taking over and continuation of the anti-individualistic, egalitarian tradition of eighteenth-century com-

munism—the tradition of Babeuf's 'Conspiracy of the Equals', which had its living embodiment in the person of Filippo Buonarroti. It was easier to reconcile this tradition with Christian millenarianism than with romantic individualism, including the romantic conception of a collective individuality of each nation. The peculiar features of the Christian-socialist conception of nation should not be reduced to the radical denunciation of all forms of social solidarism, to constant repetition that 'our fatherland, that is the Polish people, has always been separated from the fatherland of the gentry' (A. 96, p. 58); endorsement of such views can easily be found also in Dembowski's writings. From the theoretical point of view the most important thing was the replacement of romantic universalism—sanctifying and comprising within itself different national individualities—with a 'Christian' universalism, opposed to the rationalistic universalism of the Enlightenment, but equally insensitive to the value of differences between nations. For the Communities of the Polish People, and for Królikowski and Ściegienny as well, the moral essence of the Polish people was identical with universal Christian truth.

The 'Christianity' of the Communities was, of course, of an extremely heterodox variety. In spite of a certain sympathy towards Catholicism (which because of its opposition to Protestant individualism was so highly appreciated by Saint-Simonians and Buchez), they proclaimed that the Roman Church had betrayed the principles of Christ and that since that time Christianity had had its church and its pope in the people. According to this conception Christ was an advocate of a 'violent revolution', and the day on which Robespierre established the cult of the Supreme Being was to be celebrated as the return to true Christianity, with revolutionary Paris as the new Apostolic See.

Królikowski and Ściegienny reinterpreted Christianity in a similar spirit. Both of them—two peasants from the same poor region around Kielce—represented in their writings a classical millenarian reading of the Gospel. It seems justified even to say that millenarianism appeared in their teachings in a simpler and purer form than in the richer and more complicated theories of the Communities of the Polish People.

The sociologists of religion define millenarianism as a 'religious revolutionism', a 'religion of the oppressed', as an archaic form of social protest.[30] In the history of Christian Europe millenarian hopes, condemned by the official Church, were, as a rule, an important element in revolutionary plebeian ideologies—it suffices to recall their role in the great 'peasant war' under the leadership of Thomas Müntzer. In the nineteenth century millenarian motifs were very pronounced in the ideas of the Saint-Simonians, Fourier, Cabet, and Weitling. Królikowski and Ściegienny are interesting in this context as people who managed to interweave some socialist ideas into a genuinely archaic millenarian pattern of thought, and who expressed in their thinking the egalitarian dreams of pre-capitalist East-European peasantry. Both of them preached (using the same quotations from the Scriptures) that true salvation was collective salvation on earth, that Christ's ideals had been falsified by the official Church, and that his mission would end only with the establishment of the terrestrial Kingdom of God, that is a social order based on common ownership and universal brotherhood. Both—in sharp contrast to most of the French socialists—opted for revolution, unceasingly repeating that Christ had brought to the people not peace, but the sword. Both used the sharp, violent language of the prophets and based their preaching on a Manichean vision, sharply contrasting the redeemed with the condemned, the Kingdom of God with the Kingdom of Satan (embracing the whole of the evil 'old World').

It should be added that both thinkers were also men of action and that both represented a truly internationalist spirit. Królikowski at the beginning of the forties got in touch with Etienne Cabet and a few years later became his right-hand man in the Icarian movement. In 1842 he published in *Le Populaire* (under a pseudonym) a series of articles entitled 'Explanations of the Gospel', which exerted an important influence on Cabet's book *Le Vraie Christianisme* (1846).[31] Father Ściegienny had already at the end of the 1830s established contacts with the conspiratorial Association of the Polish People, transformed later into the Union of the Polish Nation. In 1842 he organized his own underground Union of Peasants which was to prepare for an uprising in the Lublin–Kielce area. The revolutionary priest was not a good conspirator, and the uprising, planned for October 1844, was prevented by the Russian police. Nevertheless, Ściegienny's conspiracy was remarkable as the first attempt to organize the Polish peasants for the struggle for both the national cause and social justice. As far as the propagation of ideas was concerned, the Union of Peasants was quite successful. Its members eagerly listened to the so-called 'Letter of Pope Gregory XVI'—a document in which Ściegienny expressed his ideas in the form of a pastoral letter of the pope to the Polish people. They were deeply moved by words of the final war which still remained to be fought:

It will be a war not of peasants against peasants, poor men against poor men, but of peasants against their lords, of the poor men against the rich, of the oppressed and the wretched against the oppressors living in luxury. . . . On one side there will be arrayed Polish and Russian peasants and townsfolk and, on the other, the lords and kings, Polish and Russian. (B. 19, p. 50.)

The revival of millenarian tendencies harmonized with the messianic atmosphere of Polish Romanticism. Królikowski's ideas (the ideas of Father Ściegienny were practically unknown to his contemporaries) evoked a sympathetic interest in Mickiewicz, Słowacki, and Libelt; on the other hand, both Królikowski and Ściegienny drew inspiration from Mickiewicz's *Books of the Polish Nation and of the Polish Pilgrims*.[32] Nevertheless, the ideology of the two socialist millenarians was very far from romantic Messianism. They believed in anonymous masses and not in personal Messiahs. National Messianism was also alien to them: some elements of it can be discovered in Królikowski's ideas; a closer analysis, however, makes it evident that his *Poland For Christ* had nothing in common with *historical* Poland. Finally, they had little understanding of romantic mysticism: their ardent religious faith was utterly rationalized, stripped of supra-natural mysteries, reduced to an evangelic morality transformed into a revolutionary message.

Among the most characteristic features of Królikowski's and Ściegienny's socialism, one should mention also anti-historicism, anti-individualism, and retrospectiveness. Anti-historicism, because all past history was renounced as the Kingdom of Satan, and because the radical opposition between the Kingdom of Satan and the Kingdom of God eliminated the conception of historical progress as a mediation between absolute Evil and absolute Good; Królikowski made it clear that his God 'is not the God of progress, but the God of absolute Truth' (A. 44, p. 402). Anti-individualism, because both thinkers (like the

theorists of the Communities) violently condemned all manifestations of 'separatism' (including the striving for individual
salvation), and because the beginning of the process of individualization was seen by them as the Biblical Fall, and the
process itself as one of a growing inequality among men and
their growing dependence on ungodly, arbitrary political power.
Retrospectiveness, because the desired revolutionary overturn
was to be a return—a return, to be sure, not to a pre-Christian
national past but to the primitive Christianity which, in its turn,
had been nothing other than a restoration of the original para-
disaical state of mankind.

In contradistinction to Królikowski, the theorists of the Communities of the Polish People accepted historical progress and
tried to unite an appeal to the eternal truths of the Gospel with a
conception of the laws of social evolution. Stanislaw Worcell in
his most interesting treatise *On Property* (1836)[33] set forth a
theory of the historical development of property—a development governed by laws essentially different from the laws of
nature. The institution of property, he argued, was not 'natural';
property is a relation between men, and not a relation between
men and things; it has had historical origins and has undergone
a long series of historical transformations, entailing appropriate
changes in the whole fabric of social life. Worcell himself treated
this theory as a historical and 'scientific' one. Nevertheless, he
did not commit himself to historical relativism: in value-judge-
ments he remained an absolutist, opposing 'Christian' (i.e.
common) property to 'pagan' (i.e. individual) property and
unreservedly condemning the latter.

The opposite pole of the ideology of the Communities—a
purely utopian mode of thought in quasi-religious form—was
represented by Zenon Świętosławski. His 'Statutes of the Universal Church' was a 'utopia' in the classic sense of this word—a
detailed project of a future ideal society, set against the present
nadir of human degradation (see A. 96, pp. 230–315). The
Universal Church of the future—a union of nations with its
capital near Suez, welded by one religious faith and a strong,
centralized political power—was to be a truly militant Church:
a Church unremittingly waging wars against 'pagans' and converting them by the sword. Its inner organization was to be
based upon political centralism and consistent nationalization
of all forms of property—including communal and corporate

property. Political authority was to be a religious authority as well—a new theocracy, establishing and defending the true and obligatory interpretation of the Divine Word. The Church's people were to be a paragon of the most demanding and severe morality; any transgressions of moral norms were to be punished, and open disobedience to the Church was to be atoned for by death. Economic development was to be planned in detail and to provide for not only the economic but also the aesthetic needs of the population (Świętosławski put special emphasis on building spacious and beautiful apartments). The official language of the Church was to be Polish. The Polish nation, however, was not to be privileged in any other way—all nations of the Church were to enjoy complete equality and the division into nations was to be established for the needs of an effective administration rather than for preserving cultural or ethnic differentiation. The rulers of the Church were expected to develop means of communication, build tunnels, level precipices, in a word—to remove everything which divides people. In such a manner, the Christian ideal of 'one fold and one shepherd' was to become a reality.

The 'Statutes', in 1844 officially approved (although not unanimously) by the Communities, were thus a peculiar manifesto of a revolutionary totalitarianism. It should be stressed that their totalitarian tendencies were completely alien to Worcell. Being aware of the growing danger of sectarianism, he left the Communities in 1840 and became a member of the moderate (Lelewelist) Union of the Polish Emigration. In 1846 (as I have already mentioned) he joined the Democratic Society and was appointed to work in its Centralization.

IV. The Meanings of the National Idea

1. 'Political' and 'Cultural' Nation

In the English language the term 'nation' is closely associated, sometimes even synonymous, with the term 'state'. In Poland, as in other East-European countries whose national consciousness was growing during the period when they had not yet achieved, or (as in the case of Poland) were deprived of their own statehood, the semantic difference between the two terms was felt very strongly. In France the term 'nationalité', especially when used in passports and other official documents, means simply 'citizenship of the state'; an attempt to classify French citizens according to their native language and ethnic background would be felt to be incompatible with democratic principles. In Poland state citizenship and nationality are still felt to be two different things, and an attempt to identify the two would be seen as a brutal violation of the most elementary human right. If 'nationality' and 'state citizenship' were equivalent, nineteenth-century Poles should have been considered to be Russians or Germans; needless to say, the whole of nineteenth-century Polish history was a struggle for preserving and developing Polish national identity and, therefore, nothing was more alien and horrifying to Polish patriots than the idea of identifying nation with state, nationality with citizenship, and patriotism with loyalty to the existing state.

Roman Dmowski, the Polish nationalist stateman who, on 28 June 1919, signed the treaty of Versailles in the name of the restored Poland, tried to explain to his Western colleagues the specific problems of Central and Eastern Europe in a special brochure which he published in English in July 1917. He made a crucial distinction between 'the idea of State-nationality' and 'the idea of linguistic or ethnographical nationality' (A. 16, p. 9). The first, he argued, is dominant in the West because 'in Western Europe the boundaries of the separate States were already more or less fixed during the Middle Ages, and their inhabitants—although different in race, speaking different dialects and even different languages—lived through a series of generations as members of one State, under common institutions'. The second is dominant in Central Europe because there 'the frontiers of the States were never fixed, and have gone on changing century after century up to the present moment' (A. 16, pp. 17–18). Moral links between the state and the people were in many cases very feeble or indeed, as in the case of partitioned Poland, no ties existed at all. Therefore, in this part of Europe the strongest factor in the formation of nationality became the community of language. An intermediate position, Dmowski added, was occupied by Italy and Germany: on the western border of each country the idea of state-nationality was predominant (Italian-speaking and German-speaking populations of France considered themselves to belong to the French nation), while on their eastern borders the linguistic criteria were of decisive importance.

Dmowski's distinction between the 'political' and 'linguistic' conception of nation was similar, to some extent, to the distinction made by the German scholar, F. Meinecke, in his famous *Weltbürgertum und Nationalstaat* (1907).

Despite all the obvious reservations that can be made, we can still divide nations into cultural nations and political nations, nations that are primarily based on some jointly experienced cultural heritage and nations that are primarily based on the unifying force of a common political history and constitution. A standard language, a common literature and a common religion are the most important and powerful cultural assets that create a cultural nation and hold it together. (B. 118, p. 10.)

Political nationalism, on the other hand, states Meinecke, derives from the spirit of 1789, from the idea of self-determination and sovereignty of the nation, that is, of the *political* nation that wants to form its own political constitution and to direct its own political destiny (ibid., p. 12). It is, thus, a product of the Age of Enlightenment, represented in the most classic form by the French. In contrast with this, *cultural* nationalism is a striving for national individuality, characteristic of anti-Enlightenment German thought. Very often, as it was in the case of the German romantics, purely cultural nationalism could be combined with 'cosmopolitan' political leanings.[34] Therefore (according to Meinecke) the highest form of nationalism consists of a combination of political nationalism with cultural nationalism in a culturally homogeneous and absolutely sovereign *Nationalstaat*.

In the eyes of many scholars and statesmen of the West, the rise of Nazism and World War II brought discredit on the whole tradition of German nationalism. Nationalist movements in the newly created states between Germany and Russia were also discredited ('toute proportion guardée', to be sure). All of them (with the exception of that in Czechoslovakia) were more or less anti-democratic, authoritarian, and anti-semitic. In spite of Dmowski's expectations they were not able to create a barrier against German expansionism and made no contribution to the political stabilization of Europe. On the contrary, their attitude to the problems of national minorities and the inevitable conflicts resulting from this produced in the West a growing scepticism as to the very principle of national self-determination.[35] Before and during World War II, as well as in the post-war period, the problems of East-Central Europe became an irritating nuisance for many people in the West. In order to get rid of this nuisance the easiest way was to create a theory of the political and cultural inferiority of Central- and East-European countries. A good example of such a solution is the so-called 'Hans Kohn's dichotomy', elaborated by the most prolific American specialist in the comparative history of nationalisms.[36] It claims that nationalism in Europe was divided from its very beginnings into two diametrically opposed types: Western nationalism and the nationalism of Central and Eastern Europe. The first was striving for a pluralistic and open society: the second stood for the closed society, an authoritarian uniformity of state and faith. The first was a product of the Enlightenment, 'born in a generous wave of enthusiasm for the cause of mankind'; the second was born of xenophobia, its goals were 'narrow, self-centred, antagonistic'. The first was concerned with the present, with 'national political ends', while the second 'harked back to the past, to non-political and more emotional, history conditioned factors'. The first believed 'that nations grew up as unions of citizens, by the will of individuals expressed in contracts, covenants and plebiscites'; the second conceived of a nation as 'a political unit centring around the irrational, pre-civilized folk concept'. The first accepted a legal, rational concept of citizenship and appealed to individual rights; the second appealed to collective rights and 'lent itself more easily to the exaggerations of imagination and the excitations of emotions'. The first was characterized by self-assurance resulting from rationalist optimism; the second compensated its inferiority complex by over-emphasis and over-confidence (see B. 69, pp. 234–7 and B. 150, pp. 118–20). In a word: Western nationalism was 'good', humanitarian, and progressive whereas the Eastern variety was 'bad', pathological, characteristic of backwardness, and doomed to produce the disasters of the twentieth century. But how should one classify, for instance, Italy, which in the nineteenth century was more backward than some countries of East-Central Europe (Prussia, Bohemia, even the Congress Kingdom) and which was the first to produce in our century a fascist model of nationalism? To this and similar questions the 'dichotomic' theory conveniently does not attempt an answer.

It would be easy to criticize Kohn's theory by pointing out that all the features attributed by him to the nationalisms of East-Central Europe could be found in different varieties of Western nationalism as well. It is more useful, however, to treat it as a typological conception which has much in common with the aforementioned conceptions of Meinecke and Dmowski. The common feature of Meinecke's and Dmowski's theories is the distinction between the political and the linguistic/cultural conceptions of nation and, also, the thesis that the classical model of the first conception was represented by revolutionary France (see also B. 24). Hans Kohn's dichotomy puts less emphasis on the linguistic factor, but also distinguishes between political nationalism, based upon the concept of the sovereignty of the people and sovereignty of the state, and nationalism based upon commonly shared cultural values. It seems also to agree with Dmowski in claiming that the second conception of nationalism was characteristic of East-Central Europe. This agreement, however, is more apparent than real: the Polish statesman limited himself to describing the situation which existed in 1917, and, unlike Kohn, did not indulge in sweeping generalizations.

Let us now return to the origins of Polish nationalism. If Hans Kohn is right that the 'Western' type of nationalism was bound up with the idea of the sovereignty of the people, government by consent, and a contractual, constitutional conception of the State, and that it was incompatible with an absolutist monarchy and inconceivable without the idea of political democracy (cf. B. 77 and B. 76, pp. 3 and 103), it follows therefrom that all the conditions for such a type of national consciousness were better realized in the Polish-Lithuanian Commonwealth (which covered a large part of East-Central Europe) than in the rest of Europe. The fact that the nation of Poland was represented only by the gentry does not contradict this thesis because in England (the only country with comparable political liberties, chosen by Kohn as the best example of the positive qualities of 'Western' nationalism) the number of active citizens was even smaller. Moreover: one can agree (to a certain extent at least) with Meinecke that 'the nation is always *pars pro toto* by nature', and that 'the fact that part of the nation unselfconsciously and sincerely regards itself as the core and essence of the entire nation is rooted in the very character of national life' (B. 118, p. 16).

The Polish 'nation of the gentry' was not a linguistic nation; it was a multilingual and multiethnic community, based (to quote Meinecke) 'on the unifying force of a common political history and constitution', and desiring 'to direct its own political destiny'. Cultural factors also contributed to its cohesion (after all a common political culture is also an important cultural factor), but it was undoubtedly a *political* nation. One could speak the Ruthenian language but nevertheless consider oneself, and be considered by others, as a Pole ('gente Ruthenus, natione Polonus'), because 'being a Pole' meant 'being a citizen of the Polish Commonwealth', irrespective of one's native language or ethnic background. If 'nationalism' means priority of loyalty to the nation before loyalty to the king or multiple loyalties to supra-national feudal authorities, the Polish gentry was 'nationalistic' from the beginning of 'gentry democracy', and Andrzej Frycz Modrzewski (who advocated, among other things, treating burghers and peasants as free citizens and establishing a Polish national Church) should be treated as one of the first great theorists of political nationalism. The first steps towards modernization of this political nationalism were taken, as I have tried to show, in the second half of the eighteenth century, when the 'gentry nation' became painfully aware that the sovereignty of citizens within the state was impossible without the sovereignty of their state among other states.

So, despite the theories of Hans Kohn, Polish nationalism was born as a *political* nationalism of the 'Western' type and should be treated as one of the earliest and most important manifestations of political nationalism in Europe. It continued to exist—as a distinctively *political* nationalism—after the partitions of Poland, because of the vivid memory of lost statehood and the strong will to restore it. This was the reason why both the leaders and the rank and file of the Polish national-liberation movement thought in terms of political legitimism and paid little attention to linguistic and ethnic criteria. All of them, and especially the radical democrats, wanted the future Poland to be a multilingual and multiethnic state. All of them repeatedly warned against dividing the inhabitants of the former Commonwealth according to language. Many of them warned also against identifying 'Polishness' with Catholicism, arguing that the nation should embrace all who lived within its historical boundaries and shared a common political history. All of them saw the Polish cause as a struggle of progressive revolutionary nationalism against the Holy Alliance of absolute monarchies and, therefore, were inclined to think that it would be in the interest of all-European progress if the territory of the future Poland were to be even larger than the territory of the ancient Commonwealth. This attitude had little in common with the imperialist striving for domination. As a rule, the right-wingers were much more cautious in their territorial demands than the radicals who, like the French Jacobins, sometimes too easily identified Polish territorial claims with the universal cause of liberty.[37]

For the contemporary Western reader it may be difficult to understand how it was possible to conceive of the inhabitants of the former Poland as members of a 'political nation' when the Polish state had ceased to exist. At the beginning it was difficult also for the Poles. The last partition of Poland was seen by many Polish patriots (including Kołłątaj) as the end of the Polish nation. Soon afterwards, however, a different feeling prevailed and a distinction was made between a 'mere state' and a genuine 'political nation' whose spirit can live even if its earthly body (the state) has been destroyed. A 'mere state' is an artefact, a soulless machine, while a nation is a community held together by ties of common history and by the common political will to preserve, or to regain, its independent statehood. Membership in a state is compulsory, based upon a purely territorial principle, while a political nation owes its existence to the will of its members. It was assumed, of course, that the overwhelming majority of politically conscious inhabitants of the former Commonwealth desired the restoration of the Polish state, quite irrespective of their language.

An extreme example of the difference between political nationalism and linguistic nationalism was provided by Piotr Semenenko, a polonized Ruthenian who started his political career as a member of the TDP but in later years changed his political sympathies and became Father Superior of the ultramontane Congregation of the Resurrection. In 1834, he published in a radical journal *Progress* an interesting article 'On Nationality'. In pre-partitioned Poland, he argued, the Polish nation was represented by the Polish-speaking nobility; the Poland of the future should be a people's Poland, i.e. a regenerated and resurrected Polish nation, restored in its historical boundaries, a nation in which the dominant role would be played by the common people. However, the majority of the Polish people speak Ruthenian; therefore, the Ruthenian language should be the official language of the restored Polish state and the reborn Polish nation should secure the natural predominance of the Ruthenian element in its national life (see B. 134, pp. 12–13).

What is truly remarkable in this article is the combination of the complete lack of Polish linguistic nationalism with a genuine Polish political patriotism, ardently desiring the restoration of the ancient multiethnic and multilingual Polish Commonwealth.[38]

Young Semenenko's views were, however, rather exceptional. The majority of the Poles, both at home and in exile, were becoming more and more conscious of the nation-building and nation-strengthening force of linguistic and cultural homogeneity. In contrast to Hungary, almost nobody advocated a programmatic linguistic polonization of the Ukrainian, Belorussian, Lithuanian, Latvian, and German inhabitants of the former Commonwealth. Many people, most notably Lelewel, Mickiewicz, Słowacki, and other Poles from the ethnically mixed Eastern territories, were proud of the cultural diversity of their homeland and wanted to preserve it. Nevertheless, already in the eighteenth century the reformers were beginning to think that Poland, legally and politically at least, had to become a more unified state and, therefore, that the autonomy of the provinces should be curtailed. After the November uprising only the right-wingers and moderate democratic followers of Lelewel favoured a federal constitution for the future Poland. Radicals—both democrats and socialists—were decidedly for unification and centralization. Krępowiecki developed a theory according to which centralization, as opposed to 'provincialism', was a necessary condition of nationality.[39] The radicals of the TDP were convinced that the autonomy of the provinces— especially of those provinces with a linguistically mixed population and historical traditions of their own—was incompatible with the unity of the state. Even such an innocent cultural institution as the Society of Lithuanian and of Ruthenian Lands, established in Paris by some followers of Prince Czartoryski, was seen by them as a dangerous manifestation of separatist tendencies (B. 134, pp. 9–10). They did not want to go as far as the French Revolution which had forced all inhabitants of France (except the German-speaking minority) to communicate in French. They were aware that a forcible linguistic polonization could only strengthen potential separatism and that only the idea of democratic equality of rights, including the right to speak one's native language, could win the Lithuanian, Belorussian, and Ukrainian peasantry for the Polish cause. Nevertheless, they were firmly convinced that the official language of the future Polish state should be Polish and that the laws of the country should be unified.

Thus, we can say that the Polish radical democrats of the epoch were conscious of the nation-building role of the language. Nevertheless, they were not 'linguistic nationalists'. They did not define nationality by linguistic criteria. If they emphasized the necessity of a certain linguistic unification they were following the example of the French Jacobins, that is, they wanted to use language as an instrument of *political* unification, without falling into metaphysical speculation about language as a living manifestation of the national soul. As far as the conception of nation was concerned, they were ardent supporters of the idea of 'State-nationality' (as Dmowski would have put it). All inhabitants of the former Polish Commonwealth, irrespective of their native tongue, were for them Poles, because all of them, together with the ethnic Poles, had lived for centuries in one state, shared the same historical experiences, and constituted one, undivided, collective personality. At present they had the same enemies and the same historical tasks. Therefore, according to this reasoning, even those inhabitants of the territories of pre-partition Poland who preferred to use a non-Polish language were seen as being undeniably Poles: 'From their former nationality they have preserved only the language' (see B. 17, p. 63).

It would be fair to say that the leaders of the Polish national-liberation movement, especially the radical democrats, tried to combine in their thinking the best traditions of ancient multi-ethnic Poland with the centralist leanings characteristic of the 'French conception of the nation'. At the same time many Poles were, understandably, very impressed by the 'cultural model' of a nation, represented by Germany. The Germans gave them a comforting assurance that a nation could preserve its national identity by means of its culture, without being united in one state. Polish romantics, influenced by the German idea of 'national originality and distinctiveness' (*Echtheit*), came to the conclusion that in order to survive the Poles had to prove their cultural vitality by creating a consciously national literature, philosophy, and art. Already in 1830 the achievements of Polish romantic poetry were hailed by Mochnacki as proof that Poles had finally reached the stage of self-consciousness and by means of literature 'recognized themselves in their essence'. This was, of course, not an expression of self-complacency but an appeal for more nation-building cultural efforts and, at the same time, a warning that from now on Polish literature could not abandon its national mission. The example of flourishing German philosophy created also a feeling that the cultural self-expression of the Poles could not be complete without giving birth to a truly 'national' philosophy. Thus, national ambition, the national will to survive and to take up a due place among other nations, produced an intellectual atmosphere in which a consciously 'national' philosophy was bound to appear.

A detailed analysis of the role of nationalist inspiration in the Polish philosophy of the epoch, and of the philosophical contributions to contemporary Polish nationalism, is given in another part of this book. At this point I would like only to express my opinion that Polish nationalism in the Romantic Epoch cannot be neatly classified as 'political' or 'cultural', 'French-oriented' or 'German-oriented'. Polish nationalism was by then both 'political' and 'cultural', there was no awareness of a possible contradiction between 'political' and 'cultural' conceptions of a nation. Nevertheless, each of these two aspects of national consciousness had a dialectic of its own, each of them worked differently from the other and often in different directions. The great Polish poets were deeply attached to the traditions of the multiethnic and multilingual Commonwealth but, of course, they wrote only in Polish, and therefore, quite independent of their will, their poetry in fact contributed to the increase of the importance of language in the national community, thus paving the way for a narrower, linguistic conception of nation. Political romantic nationalism, striving for the restoration of Poland within her historical boundaries, was a progressive and noble-minded movement, trying to achieve its aims by means of the emancipation of peasants in all territories of the old Polish state, and sincerely believing in its liberating mission. Nevertheless, its inner dialectics were self-destructive, because the emancipation of the non-Polish peasantry could only lead to the awakening of their own linguistic and ethnic nationalism. In conditions where non-Polish (especially Ukrainian) peasants had good reason to identify 'Polishness' with nobility, there was no chance to win them for the Polish cause. Perhaps if the Polish state had not been destroyed, if it had been able to carry out necessary social reforms in conditions of security and stabilization, it might have been otherwise. But it is an idle task to speculate about the 'might-have-beens' in history. The real historical process—history as it really was—led to the victory of the linguistic and ethnic (and in this sense 'cultural') conception of the Polish nation,[40] although the generation of 1831–48 did not desire this.

Polish revolutionary nationalists of the years 1831–48 should not be blamed for cherishing the illusion of the possibility of restoring the Polish state in its historical boundaries. We should never forget the same illusion was held by almost the entire European Left, and that Western radicals and socialists, as a rule, enthusiastically supported Polish hopes, seeing the restored, democratic Poland of the future as the best guarantee that the reactionary absolute monarchies would not be able to retard European progress.[41]

2. National Missions and Romantic Universalism

Different conceptions of nation ('political', 'linguistic', and so on) are by no means the only criteria for distinguishing different types of nationalism. Of equal importance is the general *Weltanschauung*, i.e. the style of thought and the hierarchy of values, with which a given type of nationalism is associated.

For the Polish democratic nationalists who strove to oppose 'The Holy Alliance of Monarchs' with the 'Holy Alliance of Peoples', the problem of the relationship between national and international tasks, national and universal values, was, naturally, of peculiar importance. The most widely accepted solution of this problem was the current conception of romantic progressivism. This conception was developed in many countries, but its most articulate expression is to be found in the writings of Mazzini and many Polish thinkers. The latter even made a claim that it had originated in Poland, with the famous slogan of the November uprising: 'For our freedom and yours.' While the Polish insurgents were still fighting, Kazimierz Brodziński, in an address on the anniversary of the Constitution of 3 May, credited the Poles with being the first to realize that the principle of national egoism had to be replaced by an awareness that the central position in the world of nations duly belongs to mankind:

Formerly each nation regarded itself as the goal and centre of everything in the same way as the earth was regarded as the centre of the universe . . . Copernicus discovered the system of the material universe; the Polish nation alone (I say it boldly and with a patriotic pride) could have a foreboding of the true movement of the moral universe. It has recognized that every nation is a fragment of the whole and must roll on its orbit and around the centre like the planets around theirs. (A. 4, p. 437; cf. B. 78, p. 38.)

In fact, the origins of romantic progressivism should be traced back to the emergence of romantic universalism, as opposed to the rationalistic universalism of the Enlightenment. While the latter found its ideal in the uniform, universally valid norms of enlightened reason, romantic universalism, on the contrary, professed the principle of 'diversitarianism' (Lovejoy's expression), identifying universality with variety and fullness, and thus sanctifying the pluralism of national cultures as unique and irreplaceable individualities of mankind. Romantic progressivism was simply a temporalization of romantic universalism. The Enlightenment and post-Enlightenment conception equated progress with the achievements of reason and universal civilization, measured by standards set up by the changeable 'laws of nature', and consequently, levelling the differences between nations. At the beginning of its existence the Polish Democratic Society based its programme upon such a conception and was rebuked by Lelewel for 'having abandoned the national standpoint for abstract principles' (A. 46, I. 353). The romantic conception, on the other hand, comprehended the history of mankind as a wonderful symphony with each nation representing a single sound, and, at the same time, appointed to each nation its own historical mission, thus making it serve the universal goal in accordance with its individual character. Though the national was subordinated to the universal, yet the realization of specific national tasks came to be recognized as the only possible way of attaining universal progress. The Democratic Society soon espoused this conception; after all, it perfectly harmonized with its ideological evolution from 'the foreign faith' to the 'national faith'. From that time on, nationalism of the progressivist-romantic type became the dominant ideological framework of the different currents of the Polish national-liberation movement.[42] It was rejected or significantly modified only by millenarian socialists on the one hand, and by the ultramontane right-wing of the constitutional monarchists on the other.

The main features of this pattern of thought can be summarized as follows. First, the idea of a universal historical progress inextricably involved in the conception of the nation as the individualization of mankind and the principal agent of progress; secondly, the idea of a national mission and a conviction that it is this mission, and not inherited traditions, which constitutes the true essence of the nation—hence the possibility of espousing the idea of revolution and the readiness to accept a radical break with the immediate past, if seen as a deviation from the national calling; thirdly, the ethos of activism and moral perfectionism, the recognition of the 'spirit of sacrifice' as the highest national virtue; and, finally, a belief in the active brotherhood of nations, an indignant condemnation of the egoistic principle of non-intervention—the principle of 'chacun chez soi', so much despised by Mickiewicz.

It is obvious that such a style of thought was incompatible not only with the rationalism, hedonism, and utilitarianism of the Enlightenment but also with the conservative Romanticism which saw history as a slow, organic development and condemned the very spirit of conscious, purposeful activity.[43] In the interpretation of conservative romantics, romantic universalism did not consist in the idea that each nation has its own task in the international division of labour and, consequently, that national tasks are different ways of serving the same general cause of Mankind. For conservative-romantic nationalists 'universal Mankind' was, as a rule, a dead abstraction. They would not have agreed with the famous words of Mazzini: 'Humanity is a great army moving to the conquest of unknown lands, against powerful and wary enemies. The Peoples are the different corps and divisions of that army' (A. 66, p. 55). According to them, each nation represented a unique collective personality and universalism consisted not in forcing different nations to serve the same, allegedly universal, cause of progress, but in encouraging them to cling to their unique traditions and customs, to cultivate their separateness, to accept it unreflectively, without thinking about its national justification or universal significance. Putting forward a universal norm or a universal goal, they argued, is a false universalism. True universalism consists in many-sidedness and fullness, in the clear awareness that national differences are necessary links in the 'great chain of being', and that each nation is justified in itself because humanity exists only through nations and manifests itself in the infinite diversity and richness of their cultures. Thus the conservative romantics put the emphasis not on activity but on aesthetic contemplation, not on conscious change but on plant-like growth, not on a common 'conquest of unknown lands' but on the careful preservation of the unique historical inheritance of each nation.

The crucial word for romantic conservatism was not 'national mission' but 'national uniqueness'. If the conservatives used the word 'mission' they meant not a conscious activity but a divinely assigned function which every nation fulfils without being aware of it, by means of its mere existence. 'It is the same of nations as of individuals', wrote De Maistre. 'All have a character and a mission that they fulfil *without realizing it*' (A. 56, p. 129). In contrast to this, the progressive romantics understood 'mission' as a consciously accepted and consciously realized task. General Ludwik Mierosławski put special emphasis on this by making a distinction between the 'old' and the 'new' patriotism. The 'old patriotism', he asserted, could be instinctive, traditionalist, and unreflective, but the 'new patriotism' must be conscious, critical, and future-oriented.[44]

The elaboration of this theory of national mission is usually attributed to Mazzini. 'Nationality', he wrote, 'is the role assigned by God to each people in the work of humanity; the mission and task which it ought to fulfil on earth so that the divine purpose may be attained on earth' (see B. 8, p. 49). Without denying the all-European significance of Mazzini's theories it should be stressed, however, that the invention of 'national missions' cannot be attributed to him alone. Brodziński could not have been influenced by Mazzini when he spoke in 1831 about national callings, and defined nation as 'an inborn idea which its members are trying to realize' (A. 4, p. 436). It is quite probable, on the other hand, that Mazzini was influenced by Mickiewicz's *Books of the Polish Nation and of the Polish Pilgrims* (see B. 8, pp. 19–20). The questions of priority and of influences are, however, of minor importance. What is really important is the typological, structural similarity between Mazzini's conceptions and the ideas of his Polish contemporaries. This fact can be adequately explained by historical conditions, by the similarity of tasks which the Italian Risorgimento and the Polish national-liberation movement were trying to fulfil. It is worth while to add that similar patterns of nationalist thinking were developed in France, by such writers as Philippe Buchez, Mickiewicz's friends Michelet and Quinet, Victor Hugo, and other figures of lesser importance.

To conclude: it is justified to say that in the years 1830–48 there existed in Europe a type of nationalism which could be called progressive-romantic nationalism and which should be clearly distinguished both from the so-called 'liberal nationalism' and the conservative-romantic nationalism characteristic of Germany. Thus important and influential ideology was developing mainly in the 'revolutionary countries' of contemporary Europe, i.e. in France, Italy, and Poland. In the other chapters of this book I shall try to show that its Polish variety was peculiarly rich and well-articulated, and at the same time, was differentiated into many currents within the same typological framework.

3. 'Nationalist International' and Morality in Politics

One of the main premisses of progressive-romantic nationalism was the idea of the brotherhood of nations, of their sacred duty to render help to each other in their common struggle for freedom and international justice. This idea was solemnly proclaimed in the 'Act of Foundation' of Mazzini's Young Europe—a kind of 'Nationalist International' called into being by the Italian, German, and Polish refugees in 1834.[45] One can claim, however, that *the first* powerful manifestation of the feeling of the brotherhood of nations, as well as the first powerful appeal to the international solidarity of free peoples, was provided by the November uprising in Poland.

In January 1831 the Polish Diet issued a Manifesto (written mainly by Lelewel) which explained the causes of the uprising and ended with the following words:

Yet, if Providence has appointed this land for eternal subjection, if in this last fight Poland shall lay down her freedom amid the ashes of her towns and the corpses of her defenders, the enemy will extend his dominion over but yet another desert, and the true Pole will perish with joy in his heart that, if Heaven has not permitted him to save his own freedom and his Fatherland, he has at least in mortal combat protected the liberties of the peoples in Europe. (See B. 98, p. 148.)

At the same time the Polish revolutionary press appealed to the nations of Europe: 'Our revolution should be the revolution of nations. The whole Europe, the entire world should support it. . . . Nations of all the world! You see how sacred is our cause. Support it for your own sake' (cf. B. 168, p. 290).[46]

The end of the Manifesto of the Diet contains an allusion to the historical fact of which both the Poles and the French—the main address of the appeal for support—were aware. The November uprising prevented the crusade against France which Nicholas I was preparing after the outbreak of the July Revolution and which was to be executed by the troops of the Congress Kingdom (see B. 122). Lafayette, speaking in the French Chamber of Deputies, put it as follows: 'The war had been prepared against us . . . Poland was to form the advance-guard; the advance-guard has turned against the main army . . . . It was this that saved Europe from a war which was imminent' (B. 122, p. 415). A similar statement was made on 12 February 1831, by the Polish Minister of Foreign Affairs, Gustaw Małachowski:

> Poland had a mission from God and from the peoples, a mission to resist the invasions of Europe. She was saying to the assailants as God was saying to the sea: you shall not go any further! Even a superficial knowledge of our history is enough to confirm this. Our zeal was disinterested, devoid of any calculations. Let the stronger, for whose salvation we are now dying, continue to talk about our idle wishes. Later, let them shed tears because of our destruction for their own benefit. Despite all this, we shall not retreat from our great struggle, we shall confirm the truth of the words of the noble Frenchman who understood us so well saying: let them die for us, according to their customs. (Cf. B. 168, pp. 317–18.)

The same motif, by the way, is to be found in the famous song *Varsovienne*, the words of which were written by Casimir Delavigne:

> . . . we have shed our blood for you,
> you have shed for us only tears.

It is impossible to prove that the salvation of France from the Russian invasion was from the beginning one of the aims of the Polish uprising. Nevertheless it cannot be doubted that Polish officers, many of whom had served under Napoleon, were happy to avoid fighting against France, and that the belief in the international significance of the uprising greatly contributed to the morale of the Polish insurgents.

It is truly remarkable that the insurgents were able to make a clear distinction between the Russian people and the Russian government and did everything to prove that their struggle was both for Polish and for Russian freedom. The Manifesto of the Diet proclaimed that the Poles were completely free from hateful attitudes towards the Russians and that their insurrection was not levelled against the Russian nation. The revolutionary press went even further. 'We love the people of Russia', exclaimed J. B. Ostrowski in the columns of the *New Poland*. Mochnacki, in his first article published after the outbreak of the insurrection, proposed to treat Russians as brother-Slavs, who suffered from oppression and had to be won for the Polish cause (see B. 168, pp. 284–5). Russian prisoners of war were treated with exemplary humanitarianism. The dethronement of the Romanovs was preceded by a splendid ceremony in honour of the Decembrists, organized by the Patriotic Society. Five empty coffins (symbolizing the first Decembrist leaders who had been hanged by the Tsar) were paraded in the streets of Warsaw, a religious service was conducted in the Orthodox Church, and the radical leader, Adam Gurowski, addressed the crowd from the foot of the Sigismund Column before the Royal Castle (see B. 98, p. 155).

After the defeat of the uprising, Mochnacki—one of the organizers of the ceremony in honour of the Decembrist leaders—came to the conclusion that the 'internationalist' concept of the uprising was a political error. The monarchy of Louis-Philippe was not worth defending; on the contrary, the Russian invasion of Europe would have been the best means of revolutionizing the European peoples and, at the same time, of bringing about an advantageous situation for Poland. He criticized even the slogan 'For our Freedom and yours'; in order to beat the Russians, he argued, one should hate them and not indulge in idealistic illusions (see A. 77, II. 66–81; cf. B. 107).

Mochnacki's case, however, was quite exceptional. As a rule, Polish exiles in France were firmly convinced that the alliance of free peoples was the only way to regain the independence of Poland, and that the Poles should fight for freedom everywhere in Europe. No wonder: they were greeted in Germany, Belgium, and France as heroes of universal freedom, their military songs were translated and sung by Germans as if the Polish cause were their own; the whole European Left wholeheartedly sympathized with them, the French underground organizations were proud to accept them into their ranks. In the next few years, after a series of disappointments brought about by badly prepared and abortive political actions (such as the so-called Frankfurt expedition, organized by the largest Polish carbonarist branch in France to assist the attempted revolution in Germany, and the participation of the Poles in Mazzini's unsuccessful attack upon Savoy), the belief in the imminent all-European revolution gave way to more sober moods, but none the less, the faith in the brotherhood of nations and the commitment to 'nationalist internationalism' remained as firm as before. An especially significant and deeply moving expression of this attitude was the brotherly feeling towards the Russians. One of the first actions of the Polish National Committee in Paris was to issue a friendly proclamation to the Russians (written by Lelewel with the help of Mickiewicz, on 8 December 1831): it paid homage to the memory of the Decembrists, supported their idea of a free federation of Slavonic nations, and summoned the Russians to break with the autocracy, to realize the futility of conquests, and to join the Poles in a common fight for freedom (see A. 54, pp. 50–5). In the following years the Polish exiles—alone in contemporary Europe—regularly celebrated the anniversaries of the Decembrists' uprising and the death of its five leaders. In the 1840s and later this tradition of revolutionary brotherhood with the Russians was manifested in the active help which was generously given by the Poles to the first Russian revolutionary *émigrés*—both the minor figures (Golovin and Sazonov)[47] and the great ones (Bakunin and, above all, Alexander Herzen).

The meetings organized by the Polish exiles to celebrate the memory of the Russian martyrs were attended, as a rule, by representatives of different nations. At one of them, held in 1841 in London, the most important speech was delivered by a black man, a certain Dr Linstant from Haiti. Fragments from his speech can give us a good idea of the emotional atmosphere of such meetings. The account of his words is as follows:

He will never forget the strange and moving scene which he has seen today, he will go to the other hemisphere, to his native island, and will relate this scene to his compatriots, brethren, and children. The Poles, invaded, robbed, exiled, and deprived of their fatherland by the Muscovites, invited the refugees from other nations and brotherly united with them to celebrate the memory of a few martyrs . . . the Muscovites! What has happened to national frontiers and hatreds, where is the memory of old injustices and murders destroying the unity of the human family? We see men united by love, by love for the common cause, by the reverence for the sacred martyrs, symbolizing this cause. Their graves became an altar around which representatives of all mankind gathered together to receive the Holy Communion of freedom. Italians, Germans, Spaniards are participating in this holy feast and the priests, presiding over it, are the Poles! Truly, if anybody has a right to demand enacting a law which would proclaim the reverence for martyrdom and the principle of universal brotherhood, the abhorrence of national egoism and of the doctrine of non-intervention, it is, undoubtedly, the Poles, the living examples of brotherhood and sacrifice, the victims of non-intervention and egoism. (A. 54, pp. 359–60.)

The idea of a revolutionary Polish–Russian alliance was combined, of course, with a conviction that the leading role in this alliance should belong to the Poles. Poland was seen as a natural leader of Slavonic nations, as a nation whose historical mission consisted in liberating other Slavs, including Russians, · from the yoke of political and social oppression. In the 'Act of Foundation' of the TDP this idea was formulated as follows:

Free Polish people, but only the Polish people as a whole [i.e. not reduced to the old notion of the 'nation of the nobility', but uniting in active citizenship the entire population of Poland], can inspire even the Russians with a striving for enlightenment, freedom, and true social life, because the only calling of Poland, her only duty to mankind, is to bring to the depth of the East true enlightenment and the understanding of the rights of man. This is why the existence of Poland is needed for the civilization, happiness, and peace of Europe. (A. 2, p. 7.)

This formulation is very characteristic of Polish democratic thought of the first half of the 1830s. It shows its strong roots in the tradition of the Enlightenment and, at the same time, its commitment to a secularized version of the ancient Polish idea of 'antemurale Christianitatis'. Such a conception of Poland's task was enthusiastically supported by the contemporary European Left, who saw in the Poles (as Marx has put it) 'the twenty million of heroes' defending Europe from the Asiatic despotism of tsarist Russia. It was embraced not only by the Polish Left but also by the moderates from Prince Czartoryski's camp. In fact it was the constitutional monarchists who organized an impressive network of political activists in the Hapsburg and Ottoman Empires and realized a consistent, far-reaching programme, fostering the political liberation and cultural progress of the smaller Slavonic peoples (see B. 147). Of course, it was a distinctively 'occidentalist' programme, conceived as an antidote to the growing wave of pro-tsarist sympathies among the Slavs.

For a historian of political movements it would suffice to say that Polish patriots of the Romantic Epoch saw their mission in fighting against the reactionary Holy Alliance and, thus, in promoting the cause of progress both in the West and in the Slavonic World. A historian of ideas, however, should pay attention to the fact that with the passing of time this formula of Poland's mission began to be felt by some intellectuals as not important enough and not universalistic enough. The ultimate goal began to be seen as a total regeneration of political life by establishing the rule of ethical principles in the sphere of international relations, or, in other words, by the 'Christianization of politics'. The imminent war for the freedom of Poland and other oppressed nations was to be the last war, after which the dream of eternal peace would become realized; the liberation of nations was to usher in a universal association of nations securing the rule of universal justice. These were not new ideas: different variants of them can be found in the writings of such well-known thinkers as Kant, Saint-Simon, Fourier, Mazzini, and many others. Nevertheless, it seems proper to emphasize that the idea of the rule of morality and law in politics never became as popular in any other country as it did in Poland. It was embraced not only by Christian socialists and Messianists (who interpreted it as the realization of the Kingdom of God on earth), but also by Prince Adam Czartoryski. His *Essay on Diplomacy* (A. 11), written in connection with the Greek uprising on the eve of the November insurrection, sounded the most eminent protest against the immorality of '*raison d'État*'.

In order to place Czartoryski's *Essay* in a proper historical perspective one should see it as the most important link between some eighteenth-century traditions (represented by the Abbé de St. Pierre, Rousseau, Kant, and other thinkers who were concerned with the problem of the lasting peace) and nineteenth-century romantic nationalism. In eighteenth-century Poland the awareness of the fragility of Polish independence gave birth to a rich theoretical literature dealing with the problems of the *jus gentium*, the law of nations (see B. 58). A physiocrat, Hieronim Stroynowski, put forward a theory that each nation had four natural rights: (1) the right to free and independent existence, (2) the right to defend itself by force, (3) the right to the certainty that international agreements would not be violated and, finally (4) the right to demand help from other nations, if necessary (in accordance with the physiocratic doctrine that every right had its equivalent in a corresponding duty).[48] Similar ideas were developed by many other Polish jurists of the Age of Enlightenment.[49] After the partitions of Poland the great philosopher of the Polish Enlightenment, Stanislaw Staszic, came to the conclusion that the only means of introducing the rule of law into international relations was to organize a universal Association of Nations (A. 92, I. 171–4).

Similar ideas were set forth by young Czartoryski, who as the Russian minister of foreign affairs wrote in 1803 an extensive memorandum of the 'Political system to be adopted by Russia' (see B. 91, pp. 30–1). Russia, he argued, should foster the creation of a 'Society of States' which would put an end to the 'state of nature' in relations between nations. In order to realize this goal three conditions should be fulfilled: first, the progress of civilization in backward countries must be secured; secondly, the frontiers of existing states should be redrawn in accordance with the nationality of their inhabitants and the natural, geographical boundaries between nations; thirdly, at least the most important countries should adopt liberal institutions and representative governments. If these goals were realized the idea of a lasting peace would cease to be a mere utopia.

It has been rightly noticed that Czartoryski's memorandum 'was the first to relate the idea of lasting peace to the principle of nationality'.[50] Even more important, however, seems to be his systematic elaboration of this conception in his *Essay on Diplomacy*. The significance of this book consists not only in its detailed criticism of the theory and practice of modern diplomacy but also, and above all, in relating these questions to a theory of nationality and nation. On many pages of his book Czartoryski remains faithful to the spirit of Enlightenment, but in the chapter devoted to nations he is far closer to the Romanticism of the Mazzinian type. Anticipating Mazzini he criticizes the utilitarianism and hedonism of the Enlightenment, saying that 'le but d'existence de l'homme sur la terre n'est pas d'être heureux, mais de se rendre digne du bonheur' (A. 11, p. 181). Man's true calling is to realize on earth the universal moral law, but he can fulfil this calling only through his nation. The division of mankind into different nations had been divinely constituted. Nations are necessary mediations between individuals and mankind. Human beings are too weak, too short-sighted to be able to embrace mankind as a whole; therefore 'l'association générale du genre humain' has to realize itself by means of 'des existences agglomerées, des groupes d'individus, que nous appelons nations' (ibid, p. 187). National ties (*lien de nationalité*) are in fact nothing else than the ties of universal society made practical by adjusting them to the weakness of men and the short duration of their lives. The ultimate goal of each nation, as well as each individual, is the realization of universal moral law. Therefore, no nation should be allowed to violate the moral law. On the other hand, no nation should be deprived of its independence because the independent existence of each of them is necessary for the moral order of mankind. Striving for a supra-national universal Empire is a blasphemous madness. What is really needed is a supra-national institution in which all nations will have their representatives and whose aim will consist in mediating and arbitrating in international conflicts. At the beginning one should call into being an all-European organization—L'Association Européenne. Its first task should be the liquidation of all kinds of national oppression—'d'empêcher entre les nations toute oppression, que quelque nature qu'elle soit' (ibid., pp. 413–14).

One can treat these ideas as naïve *pia desideria* and wonder how it was possible that a man with such views could be the head of the insurrectionary government of 1831 (cf. B. 168, p. 279). On the other hand one can see in them a deep understanding of the problems which were to become of topical importance for today's world. In the United States I have witnessed a growing awareness that the absolute sovereignty of nation-states is less important than effective collaboration between them, and that unbridled nationalism creates great danger for the survival of mankind. True, but one should remember that 'nationalism is plural rather than singular' (B. 51, p. 1). As I have tried to show, one of the main concerns of the Polish romantic nationalism of the first half of the nineteenth century was not how to strengthen the barriers dividing mankind but, on the contrary, how to submit nations to universal ethical (or legal) norms, how to secure their rights through supra-national institutions, and how to make them aware of their duties to support and help each other.[51]

Czartoryski's *Essay* exerted a direct influence on Mickiewicz's Messianism (see B. 73, III. 35). Quite probably it influenced also the ideas of the greatest Polish philosopher of the epoch, August Cieszkowski. In any case, the idea of morality in politics became a leit-motif in the political thinking of at least two generations of Polish patriots, active in the years 1830–64. It constituted the heart, the inner essence, of what was called later—in a positive or negative sense—the 'political Romanticism' of the Poles.

PART TWO

In Search of a 'National Philosophy'

I. Introductory Remarks

In Polish intellectual history, and in the history of Polish culture as well, the 1840s, or, to be more precise, the years 1837–48, could be characterized as a truly 'philosophical epoch'. Philosophy, conceived of in the most ambitious way, found itself by then at the very centre of the intellectual life of the country; it became expansive, striving for hegemony in Polish culture (in which, hitherto, romantic poetry had occupied the central place) or even for political leadership in the nation. It was rightly noted that 'never before, and never afterwards, did the Poles set so many hopes on philosophy—not only cognitive hopes, but moral, social and national hopes as well' (B. Baczko, B. 135, p. 10). Never before, and never afterwards, were Polish thinkers so firmly convinced of the importance of philosophy, of the possibility and desirability of the crucial role of philosophical ideas not only in science and culture, but also in the whole social praxis. Most forcefully was this conviction expressed by the most prolific philosopher of the epoch, Bronislaw Trentowski. He claimed that the spiritual leadership of the nation should be taken away from irresponsible poets and given to philosophers, that only the cultivation of philosophy could bring about the inner regeneration of the Poles and pave for them the way to national independence; only through philosophy, he reasoned, can a subjugated nation surpass its oppressors in spirit and, thereby, create a preconditon of its 'bodily resurrection' (A. 106, pp. 259–60).

To assess properly the 'philosophical epoch' of the 1840s one should never forget that the flowering of philosophical ideas took place in Poland in very peculiar conditions. After the defeat of the November uprising the institutional basis of scholarly activities had been drastically narrowed down: the Universities of Warsaw and of Wilno had been closed, the Warsaw Society of the Friends of Learning had been liquidated, its rich collections confiscated and taken to Russia. In spite of a certain liberalism of the Prussian authorities it was not conceivably possible to establish a Polish university in Poznań (Posen); outstanding Polish philosophers, such as Trentowski or Karol Libelt, who were among the best students of the aged Hegel, were refused even the position of teacher in Polish high schools in Poznania. The only Polish university was thus the Jagellonian University of the free city of Cracow.

The philosophers of Trentowski's generation did not think of themselves as belonging to one philosophical school. When we take a close look at them, analysing the place of each in the ideological conflicts of the epoch, the differences dividing them are clearly visible. On the other hand, it is understandable that already the so-called 'Warsaw Positivists' of the turn of the 1860s ignored or neglected these differences, attaching much more importance to similarities in the general style of thought— a style which was very strange or incomprehensible to the thinkers of the positivistic epoch. In spite of all the important differences, the conceptions of the philosophers of the 1840s can be given a certain common characterization which assigns them their own, well-defined place in the history of Polish thought. With a certain unavoidable over-simplification the common features of their thought can be described as follows.

The main frame of reference for the philosophical controversies in Poland was by then classical German philosophy. The post-Kantian German idealism and, even more, the post-Hegelian philosophical debates in Germany were at least as important for Polish intellectual life of the 1840s as French and British ideas had been for the culture of the Polish Enlightenment. Admittedly, the attitude of the Polish philosophers to German philosophy was programmatically critical: they wanted to overcome the idealistic one-sidedness of German philosophy or even (as it was in Cieszkowski's case) to transcend philosophy as such. Nevertheless, German philosophy was for them the highest achievement of human thought and the natural starting-point for further progress. It was to be overcome in a dialectical way which implied that in order to transcend it one had to pass through it and to learn from it. In any case it is evident that what I have called 'the philosophical epoch' in Polish intellectual history was the time when the German orientation in Polish culture was much stronger than at any other period.

This does not mean that the French orientation disappeared from the Polish cultural scene. French influence—always, to be sure, reinterpreted to suit the specific exigencies of the ideo-logical situation in Poland—remained dominant in Polish political, social, sometimes even religious, thought, and the Polish philosophers were not immune from them. On the contrary: their favourite idea was that Poland might and should create a kind of synthesis between German philosophy and French socio-political ideas, or, as it was usually put, between German 'thought' and French 'action'. In itself the idea of bringing together German philosophy and French social ideas, resulting from the French revolutionary experience, was by no means original. It was very popular in Germany where it was set forth already by Heine, himself strongly influenced by the French Saint-Simonians (B. 23), and repeated later by the young Hegelians, who proclaimed the idea of a 'Franco-German intellectual aliance'. Similar ideas were developed in Russia (young Bakunin, Belinsky, Herzen); they found also some echo in France (Edgar Quinet, Victor Cousin, and others). It was, however, not by accident that the efforts of Arnold Ruge to bring about a practical realization of the postulated 'Franco-German intellectual alliance' proved unsuccessful: German Left-Hegelians were shocked by the religious ideas of French socialists, and both sides turned out to be less open to mutual influences than had been expected. By contrast, the Poland of the Romantic Epoch was equally open to influences from both Germany and France, and the Polish philosophers, such as Cieszkowski or Dembowski, could claim to have achieved a genuine, original fusion of the most important French and German ideas of their time.

Like German idealism, Polish philosophy in the 1840s was truly 'maximalist' in its cognitive aspirations. It was interested in the Absolute, in the human self as an image of the Absolute, and in history as the manifestation of the Absolute in time. These maximalist cognitive aspirations were bound up with a conscious striving for holistic visions of the world and, at the same time, with a tendency to rationalize these visions by transforming them into skilfully constructed philosophical systems. Constructing, or at least outlining, philosophical systems became a real passion of the epoch: from this point of view the years 1837–48 were quite unique in Poland. In neighbouring Russia the 1830s and the 1840s could also be called 'the philosophical epoch' (cf. B. 180, pp. 287–8), but the intensive philosophical strivings of the Russian intellectuals of this time were not accompanied by a passion for systems-building. The Polish philosophers accused the Germans of indulging in idealistic speculations but, at the same time, wanted to compete with them in creating speculative philosophical systems. A philosophical system, it was believed, should be deduced from one basic principle and constructed 'as a circle', i.e. in such a way that its end should be a dialectical return to the beginning. True philosophy became identified with the art of constructing systems, and the inner coherence of a system was treated as an important criterion of its value. This led in practice to the under-estimation of the hitherto existing Polish philosophy, as not systematic enough to be called 'truly philosophical'. The philosophical achievements of the Polish Enlightenment were, as a rule, ignored, and the Enlightenment as such was seen as an epoch, or a style of thought, deeply inimical to the truly philosophical spirit. This view was not bound up with a negative attitude to the civilizational and cultural consequences of the Enlightenment, but it resulted, none the less, in a conspicuous lack of interest in the philosophical heritage of the great thinkers of the Polish Enlightenment, such as Stanislaw Staszic, Hugo Kołłątaj or the Brothers Śniadeckis. True, the traditions of the Enlightenment were continued by post-Enlightenment and pre-positivist thinkers. These thinkers, however, although their views were shared by a significant part of the Polish intelligentsia of the epoch, did not contribute anything of importance to Polish intellectual life of 1837–48.

One of the most important and characteristic features of the philosophical movement of the 1840s was the conscious attempt to create a 'national philosopy', i.e. a philosophy expressing and shaping the national character of the Poles. As we shall see, the demand for such a philosophy was set forth earlier, before the November uprising. Maurycy Mochnacki, in his book *On Polish Literature in the Nineteenth Century* (1830) treated philosophy, as well as literature, as a necessary component of national consciousness; the struggle for a truly national philosophy was for him a natural consequence of the struggle for a truly national literature. Mochnacki, however, did not think that his compatriots were 'a philosophical nation'; therefore, he did not expect that the Polish 'national philosophy' would have a uni-

versal significance. Such an idea was born later, in the atmosphere of messianic hopes, compensating for the defeat of the
national uprising. It can be seen as a symptom of national
megalomania, but it would be more just to interpret it as an
expression of an acute awareness that the Poles, defeated on the
battleground, should prove their strength in the sphere of
thought and that, in order to be worthy to exist as a nation, they
should contribute to the universal cause of mankind. Thus the
idea of a 'national philosophy' which would open new vistas for
all mankind was a means of combining 'nationalism' with
'universalism'. Its advocates were inimical to a narrow national
particularism; they were against 'nativism' as opposed to
'westernism' because they thought that the Poles were part and
parcel of the West and that their philosophy should start from
the highest point achieved by European thought. No wonder
that Catholic traditionalists accused them of succumbing to
foreign influences and of betraying the true national spirit.

A specifically national feature of Polish philosophy was seen
in a programmatic activism. It was to be a 'philosophy of
action', a 'philosophy of praxis', or a 'philosophy of creativity'.
What was meant by these terms was, first of all, that it would be
capable of changing the world in the desirable direction, of
contributing to the regeneration of mankind and, by the same
token, to the restoration of Poland. It was implied also that
philosophy should not be divorced from practical activity. The
biographies of the leading Polish philosophers of the epoch—
Cieszkowski, Trentowski, Libelt, Kamieński, and Dembowski—
show that this point was taken very seriously: all were active
politicians, conspirators, and/or organizers of so-called 'organic
labour', looking for the practical application of their philosophical ideas in political economy (Cieszkowski and
Kamieński), pedagogy (Trentowski and Libelt), civilizational
or revolutionary activities, and so forth. German philosophy,
seen from this perspective, seemed to be purely theoretical,
divorced from life, and because of this, always tending towards
a contemplative idealism which found its culmination in
Hegelianism.

This view was formulated for the first time by Mochnacki
who, after the defeat of the November uprising, became deeply
disappointed in German philosophy. In his splendid article 'On
the Revolution in Germany' (1833), he wrote that the Germans

'had slept away in books' the modern history of Europe. Their superiority in philosophy was the reverse side of their inefficiency in politics, of their nonage among the other nations. The creative energy of the Germans, instead of finding an external outlet in politics, had become interiorized, transferred to the sphere of pure thought. In such a way the pure thought, or imaginary Absolute, came to be considered as the only true reality. This fateful process was started by Kant who developed the art of thinking about thinking. The eyes of the German philosophers turned inwards, looking inside, at the inner life of the mind; consequently, the whole of the external world completely disappeared from their view (A. 78, p. 314).

Mochnacki concluded from this that philosophy was incompatible with action and, therefore, should be rejected. A similar idea was set forth, later, by Mickiewicz, who proclaimed that philosophy should be abandoned for the sake of revolutionary 'deed'. The leading philosophers of the 1840s did not share this view: they tried to create a *'philosophy* of action', thus implying that action itself should be based upon solid philosophical foundations. According to them, the philosophical knowledge of the Absolute was necessary for a truly wise and successful praxis. They criticized the contemplative and purely speculative character of Hegelianism, but they took for granted the necessity to pass through it. Their attitude towards German philosophy was dual: they wanted to overcome it but, at the same time, to have it planted in Polish intellectual life.

Among the other common features of the programmes of 'national philosophy' put forward by the Polish philosophers of the 1840s, the most important and most relevant to the problems of nationalism were the following:

—A critical attitude towards rationalism, putting the emphasis on non-rational, or supra-rational, faculties such as feeling, will, or imagination. This criticism, however, was directed against the Hegelian 'autocracy of Reason', and not against reason as such; therefore, one has to distinguish between this standpoint and romantic irrationalism, as represented by Mickiewicz. Rationalism was being criticized as a contemplative philosophy, good for passive onlookers, but not for men of action. At the same time it was stressed that 'action' should be rational, preceded by reflection, that philosophy should not be abandoned—on the contrary, the social praxis itself should be made 'philosophical'.

—A tendency to overcome the one-sidedness of idealism by a certain 'rehabilitation of matter' and by various attempts at reconciling idealism with realism, speculation with experience. Paraphrasing Marx's 'Theses on Feuerbach', one can say that the Polish philosophers wanted to overcome the Fichtean, purely idealistic activism, 'not knowing real, sensuous activity as such' (A. 58, V. 3). It is quite understandable: in order to fight for political independence and civilizational progress of a nation a 'real, sensuous activity' was needed.

—Opposition to Hegelian essentialism and panlogism, absolutizing the Universal and reducing the individual to the role of a tool of a supra-individual, impersonal Absolute. This characteristic 'rehabilitation of the individual' was bound up with a defence of the collective individualities of nations and with a protest against seeing nations as mere instruments of the *Weltgeist*.

—A future-oriented philosophy of history; a belief that the image of the future can be predicted, deduced from knowledge of the past. The Hegelian conception according to which history had already achieved its goal was unacceptable for a nation which could not reconcile itself with the present; on the other hand, Polish philosophers took it for granted that the goal of history did not consist in attaining self-consciousness, as Hegel chose to see it, but in the welfare and happiness of nations. Because of these reasons they had to turn their attention to French social thought, particularly rich in visions of a desired future and fired by intense hopes for an imminent regeneration of mankind.

—Last but not least, it was very characteristic of the Polish 'national philosophers' of the forties to attempt to achieve a reconciliation between philosophy and religion by means of philosophical analysis and interpretation of the revealed truths. It should be stressed that such a tendency was alien to the radical Philosophical Left, represented by Kamieński and Dembowski, who did not try to connect the problems of the earthly and the heavenly salvation. In the views of the other Polish philosophers of the epoch the tendency to create bridges between philosophy and religion was, however, of particular importance. It resulted from the maximalist cognitive aspirations of their philosophies and, also, from their conception of the 'philosophy of action'. The desire to penetrate the very essence of the Absolute was pushing them to ponder over the ultimate problems whose solution had been given in religious belief, interpreted in the official doctrine of the Church; little wonder, therefore, that this tendency of the 'national philosophers', irrespective of their intentions, did not please the Polish Catholic clergy. The programme of creating 'a philosophy of action', on the other hand, made them interested in religion as the world-view of the masses, exerting the greatest influence on their thinking and behaviour in every-day life. Cieszkowski, Trentowski, and Libelt concluded from this that a change in religious consciousness was a necessary condition of changing the world. In Poland this problem was especially complicated because of three undeniable facts: (1) the importance of religion for the spiritual survival of the partitioned nation; (2) the traditional conservatism of the Polish clergy; and (3) the disappointment of the intellectual élite in the Pope who had condemned the November insurrection. In such a situation Polish philosophers had to raise the question of the mutual relations between religion and politics and to set about the uneasy task of modernizing the religious consciousness of the nation.

From the point of view of a universal history of philosophy the conceptions of the Polish philosophers of the 1840s might be and, I think, *should be* interesting as symptoms of the general crisis of 'absolute idealism' (cf. B. 104). I shall return to this later. In the present context it seems proper to put emphasis on the differences between the 'crisis of absolute idealism' in Germany and its reflection in Polish intellectual history. In Germany the dividing line between the so-called Philosophical Left and Philosophical Right was the attitude towards religion and rationalism: the Philosophical Left moved from an utterly rationalized Protestantism, to atheism; criticism of rationalism and creating bridges between philosophy and positive religions were the monopoly of the Right, and Catholicism was closely bound up with romantic conservatism, idealizing the Middle Ages as a truly 'organic' epoch, not yet infected by the disintegrating influences of atomizing and mechanical rational thought. In Poland—a Catholic country fighting for its cultural identity and political independence—it could not be so. As in France, progressive social and political ideas very often coexisted in Poland with ardent religious feelings or, even, drew inspiration from them. Rationalism (again as in France or, even more so, Italy) was by no means a distinctive characteristic of the Left. On the contrary: very often rationalism was identified with the spirit of cowardly compromise, fear of revolution, and acceptance of the status quo. The apotheosis of a rational state, so characteristic of Hegel and of the young Hegelians, was unthinkable in Polish conditions. 'Rational States', in contrast to nations, were considered to be artefacts; and thinking in terms of non-national, bureaucratic states was treated as giving support to the reactionary political order of the Holy Alliance, in which nations, these 'living organs of mankind', were divided and oppressed. The stateless existence of the Polish nation, along with the awareness that nations, in contradistinction to states, are 'divinely constituted', i.e. alive and indivisible, was incompatible with the Hegelian apologia for the growing rationalization of social life by means of the 'rationally constituted' state. This is precisely why in Poland the romantic conception of 'progress through nations' was the dominant conceptual framework into which Hegelianism had to be fitted or in the name of which it was opposed. The prime movers of progress, according to this conception, were the nations—feeling, suffering, and loving, endowed with will and consciously fulfilling their individual callings. 'A nation suffers, therefore it is not an Idea, but an incarnation; alive and organic' (A. 79, III. 384–5) wrote the great poet, Cyprian Norwid. The glorification of the present, typical of Hegelianism, had to be replaced by concern with the future—as it was there that all hopes were invested—and with the remote past—as it was there that some thinkers, especially radicals, like Dembowski, tried to discover the primeval characteristics of the nation, which had determined the nature of its mission and its future fates. The Hegelian emphasis on the necessity of progress had to be supplemented with a heroic activism and an ethical appeal to duty, since the situation of the nation undermined the optimistic confidence in anonymous laws of history and rendered impossible any belief in self-regulating progress. Hegel's 'autocracy of Reason' had to be limited for the sake of the laws of feeling, the rational cognition of the necessity of the existing world had to be contradicted by the will to change it and actively mould the future.

It should be stressed that the romantic protest against the 'pantheistic' absolutization of the Universal stemmed in Poland not from a rejection of universalism as such, but from a different conception of universalism: a conception which sanctified the pluralism of national cultures as expressions of unique and irreplaceable individualizations of mankind. In one respect, at least, the superiority of mankind, conceived as the highest moral criterion, seems to have been much more obvious in the case of the Polish thinkers than in Hegelianism. As I have already pointed out, one of the most characteristic ideas advanced by Polish thinkers was that of introducing an ethical point of view into the sphere of politics, with the postulate of creating supra-national organs capable of justly arbitrating disputes between nations and of securing conditions for a universal brotherhood of nations in the world to ensue. This idea became widely accepted by the Polish national-liberation movement of the Romantic Epoch and by the Polish philosophers of this epoch as well. It could not be found, however, in Hegelianism. The 'Berlin sage' (as Dembowski called Hegel), considering national statehood to be the perfect revelation of the Universal Reason in social life, rampantly rejected any point of view transcending the *raison d'état* or limiting the absolute sovereignty of the State. He dissented also from Kant's belief in eternal peace, seeing it as a mere utopia.

In the above account I have used many times the adjective 'romantic', so a few words are needed to explain its meaning. The term 'Romanticism' is notorious for escaping any precise definition; it seems better to point out in concrete analyses what was, or was not, 'romantic', than to begin with sweeping generalizations about Romanticism as a whole. In the present context the adjective 'romantic' has been used as a shorter way of saying: bound up with the cultural, above all literary, trend which was dominant in Poland from 1822 (the date of the first edition of Mickiewicz's poetry) until the insurrection of 1863, and which was given the name 'Romanticism'. Because of the central position of Romanticism in the Polish culture of the epoch even the Polish Hegelians could not escape its influence, although in Germany Hegelianism was very hostile to romantic ideas. This does not mean that the Polish philosophers of the forties could be defined simply as 'romantics'. They were far from being unanimous in their attitude both to Hegelianism and to Polish Romanticism: Libelt, for instance, was less Hegelian than Cieszkowski and much more 'romantic' than Trentowski; Dembowski was much more 'romantic' and, at the same time, more Hegelian than Kamieński, and so forth. All of them, however, were influenced both by Hegel and by the romantic bloom in Polish culture; all of them adopted the conception of the nation characteristic of Polish Romanticism (which did not exclude, of course, essential disagreements within the generally accepted framework). Even if they quarrelled with the great romantic poets their ideas were meaningfully related to the romantic pattern of Polish culture. We should always remember that it was Romanticism which had paved the way for the widespread reception of German philosophy in Poland. One can say, therefore, that the ideas of the Polish 'national philosophers' were a characteristic product of 'the Romantic Epoch' in Polish culture. In this sense—and *only* in this sense—their conceptions can be called 'the philosophy of Polish Romanticism'.

II. Predecessors

1. The Beginnings of 'Philosophical Romanticism'

In the years 1815–30—i.e. during the existence of the constitutional Kingdom of Poland, created by the Congress of Vienna on the initiative of Alexander I—the conditions for the development of Polish culture were (relatively) the best in those territories of the former Polish Commonwealth which had been annexed by Russia. The Congress Kingdom was a small state, united with the Russian Empire but having its own constitutional charter, parliament, and army; its constitution, largely modelled on the constitution of the Napoleonic Duchy of Warsaw, was quite liberal, although in practice it was frequently violated by the viceroy Grand Duke Constantin and other authorities. Its intellectual life found expression in the blossoming of the periodical press, in the activities of the Society of the Friends of Learning, and in the newly opened Warsaw University. In the Lithuanian part of the former Commonwealth, incorporated into Russia, the most important centre of Polish culture was the ancient Lithuanian capital, Wilno. The University of Wilno, under the curatorship of Prince Adam Czartoryski, achieved by then the zenith of its well-deserved fame.

In the history of Polish philosophical thought it was a typically transitional period. The philosophy of the Enlightenment, passing through an evident crisis but still strongly supported by an influential part of the intellectual élite, had to coexist at that time with the growing influence of post-Kantian German idealism and with the emergence of a new philosophical formation which can be called 'Polish Schellingianism' or (because of its links with the romantic movement, both in Germany and in Poland) Polish 'philosophical Romanticism'. The most outstanding representatives of the late Enlightenment were the professors of the University of Wilno, followers of the Scottish 'philosophy of common sense', Jan and Jendrzej Śniadecki. The first of them became famous as a severe critic of Kant, whom he accused of incomprehensibility, scholasticism, and metaphysicism, extremely detrimental to the true enlightenment. Śniadecki was also an uncompromising, dogged critic of Romanticism. In his article 'On the Classical and Romantic Writings' (1819), he fiercely condemned the romantics, accusing them of mysticism, of glorification of the irrational superstitions of the country-folk, and, last but not least, of undermining the social order by proclaiming the superiority of wild imagination over enlightened reason and healthy common sense.

Śniadecki's article was an answer to the paper of Kazimierz Brodziński, entitled *On Classicism and Romanticism* (1818). Brodziński, a disciple of Herder and a popularizer of the aesthetical views of Kant and Schiller, was a chief representative of pre-romantic sentimentalism in Polish literature. He wanted to achieve a compromise between Classicism and Romanticism in which Romanticism would stand for the free expression of feelings and Classicism, in its turn, would temper the romantic 'enthusiasm and exaltation'; such a compromise, he thought, would agree with the idyllic character of the ancient Poles and of the Slavs in general.

A few years later, after the publication of the first two volumes of Mickiewicz's *Poetry* (1822–3), the controversy over Romanticism entered a new phase. Romantic publicists and literary critics, whose intellectual leader was Mochnacki, based themselves on the German idealism, setting it against the 'cold intellect' and 'empirical utilitarianism' of the Enlightenment. In such a manner both the opponents (Śniadecki) and the followers of German idealism treated it as a philosophy promoting Romanticism or, even, as a part of broadly conceived Romanticism. Such an interpretation was made easier by the fact that the highest achievement of German idealism was seen by them to be the philosophy of Schelling, who (unlike Hegel) was indeed closely interconnected with German Romanticism.

The romantic criticism of the rationalism of the Enlightenment performed different functions and had different targets in Poland. At the beginning, as in Germany, it was directed against the French Revolution and its consequences in political and social spheres. Later, however, mainly thanks to Mochnacki, the romantic attacks against the 'reasonableness' of the Enlighteners became directed primarily against the defenders of the political status quo who recommended, for the sake of sobermindedness, the relinquishing of irrational dreams about regaining national independence. Thus the 'reasonable' reconciliation with reality was contrasted with a romantic apologia for patriotic feelings and revolutionary action.

The most eminent representative of the early, conservative phase of the Polish reception of Schellingianism was Józef Kalasanty Szaniawski (1764–1843). During the Kościuszko uprising (1794) he was an active member of the 'Jacobin' Club; later, however, he cut himself from the errors of his youth and, finally, became one of the most conservative politicians of the Congress Kingdom. His contemporaries considered him to be a 'Kantian' but he himself was fully aware that his philosophical views were inspired, first of all, by the 'school of Schelling'. It should be added that he was influenced also by the French traditionalists (De Maistre, De Bonald, Lamennais in his early period) and by the conservative, Catholic thinkers of the German Romanticism (mainly by Friedrich Schlegel and Adam Müller with whom he was personally acquainted. See B. 115, pp. 35–6).

Romanticism was seen by Szaniawski as a conservative, antirevolutionary ideology, as an antidote to the disastrous influence of the Enlightenment. As the Director of the Office of Censorship in the Congress Kingdom, he used to transfer his positive judgement on the conservative German Romanticism to Polish Romanticism, paying no attention to the dangerous revolutionary tendencies of the latter.

Thus, according to the testimony of Mochnacki, a peculiar situation had emerged: the censors saw romantic writers as 'knights errant' of feudalism, and overlooked the anti-feudal implications of their thinking, including their deepest hostility to the political order of the Holy Alliance.

Szaniawski's first philosophical works, paving the way for the 'philosophical Romanticism' of the 1820s, were published at the beginning of the nineteenth century. Already in 1802, in his treatise *What is Philosophy?*, he proclaimed that philosophy should strive for knowledge of the Absolute. He interpreted the pernicious social results of the philosophy of the Enlightenment as bound up with its mechanicism and atomism; therefore, he set against it the category of 'organic wholeness' which he found in the neoplatonic and Schellingian metaphysics of 'All-Unity'. The fascination with 'organic wholeness' led him to a quest for dialectical interrelationships and to attempts at making them visible in his classifications of sciences and arts. In his book *On the Nature and Destiny of Offices in Society* (1808: see A. 93) he outlined a philosophy of the national state, conceived as a supra-individual organism mirroring in itself the hierarchical structure of the Universe. The ranks in the bureaucratic hierarchy were seen by him as having their counterparts in the hierarchy of cognitive faculties and in the structure of knowledge: from sensual knowledge (the lowest grade), through the discursive, conceptual knowledge of the intellect, to dialectical Reason, penetrating into the world of Ideas. Admiring the architectonic beauty and functional efficiency of hierarchical, bureaucratic order, he went so far as to assert that it was the means of raising the nation to the level of self-consciousness. A great official of the state was compared by him to a great artist, and his life to a great masterpiece.

The category of 'wholeness' (*Totalität*) with all its anti-Enlightenment implications is to be found also in the philosophy of Józef Gołuchowski (1797–1858). He was a disciple and a personal friend of Schelling. His best philosophical work—*Die Philosophie in ihrem Verhältnisse zum Leben ganzer Völker und einzelner Menschen* (Erlangen 1822) had been dedicated to Schelling and was highly appraised by him.

Like the Polish philosophers of the 1840s, Gołuchowski concentrated on the practical consequences of philosophy, on its bearing on individual and social life, and, characteristically, derived this concern from the character of his nation. In the Preface to his book he wrote: 'Nobody should be surprised that philosophy has been approached here from this particular viewpoint: the strength of the Polish nation lies in life, this is a characteristic feature even of its scholarly works and, therefore, no individual belonging to it should efface this feature from his thinking, if he wants to be understood by the general public' (A. 20, p. xiii).

The end of this sentence suggests that although the book was published in German it was, in fact, intended for the Poles. It was really so. Gołuchowski was the first Polish thinker who put forward the programme of a Polish 'national philosophy', consisting in making philosophy related to practice, and who tried to realize this programme in his own works. 'Each nation', he wrote, 'should have its own philosophy, irí order to keep burning its eternal fire, in order to have a domestic hearth, heating it in chilly days, a hearth which could inflame all those who have the inflammable substance in themselves' (A. 20, p. 63).

The primeval source of philosophy was seen by Gołuchowski in 'the nostalgia for an integral view of the world' (*der Sehnsucht nach einer totalen Weltanschauung*), without which the state is a dead mechanism, the sciences are devoid of a great style, and individual life is doomed to be immersed in the emptiness, vulgarity, and commonplaceness of the petty endeavours of every day. The practical task of philosophy in its relation to individuals is, thus, to enable people to experience the world as a harmonious, divine whole, to rediscover their rootedness in the mysterious primeval forces (*Urkräfte*) of divine creativeness, and, in such a way, to help them to get rid of the depressing feeling of a total meaninglessness of life. Its task in relation to the national life is to overcome painful social atomization, to cement the state by awakening common national spirit, uniting citizens by means of an inner attraction in a free organic unity, and not by external compulsion in a mechanical aggregate. Philosophy, however, should be completely autonomous, secured against any pressure from the political or religious authorities. The philosopher is an organ of national self-consciousness, but his legitimate right and moral duty is to strive for truth without making concessions to the existing national traditions or opinions of the majority.

In distinction to Szaniawski, who could be accused of a certain philosophical eclecticism, Gołuchowski was a consistent romantic and, therefore, went much further in his criticism of rationalism. The most important cognitive faculty was seen by him in divine intuitions (*göttliche Anschauungen*). The integral, intuitive vision of the world (*Totalanschauung der Welt*) was compared by him to a masterwork of art: 'ein Kunstwerk in welches sich das ganze Leben hinein bilden muss, wenn es an seiner Göttlicher Theil nehmen will' (A. 20, pp. 153–4).

In the autumn of 1823 Gołuchowski started lecturing on philosophy at the University of Wilno. His lectures, because of the emphasis on the relevance of philosophical problems to national life, were extremely popular not only among the students, but among the Polish intelligentsia of Wilno as a whole. The Russian authorities became alarmed: in the next year Gołuchowski's lectures were suspended and soon afterwards the young philosopher lost his chair. This is a very instructive case for understanding how the political functions of ideas depend on the over-all political context. In his social views Gołuchowski was closer to the conservatives than to the radicals. His philosophy, seen from an all-European perspective, was obviously a variant of *conservative* Romanticism: the categories of 'organic wholeness', 'integral vision', and so forth were typical of the romantic conservative counter-Enlightenment, combating 'mechanical changes' (i.e. revolutions) in social life and the 'atomization' of the modern bourgeois society. In spite of this the Russian authorities had good reason to fear the influence of Gołuchowski's lectures: his conception of national spirit was incompatible with the principle of political legitimism, defended by the Holy Alliance; his idea of an 'organic state', contrasted with states based on mere compulsion, could easily be interpreted as a criticism of the Russian Empire.

After the November uprising had broken out, Gołuchowski came to Warsaw and, in January 1831, delivered a public lecture on the national spirit. He defined it as a moral force cementing people into a nation, as an expression of the 'National Reason' to be found at the bottom of the seemingly irrational instincts of the masses. Such a 'national spirit' manifested itself in Poland in the spontaneous, mass support for the uprising. The audience listened to these words with enthusiasm and admiration (B. 168, pp. 302–3).

After the defeat of the uprising, Gołuchowski settled in his family estate and for many years did not try to continue his philosophical activity. His views became even more conservative than before. His attitude towards the philosophical movement of the forties was suspicious and critical: like Szaniawski, he chose to sympathize with its Catholic critics. After the Cracow uprising of 1846, the 'Galician massacre', and the Springtime of the Peoples he found himself called upon to solve the peasant question in which he saw an East-European counterpart to the proletarian question in the West. In his book devoted to this problem he criticized the agrarian programmes of the Polish democrats, along with the socialist and communist conceptions of the Western thinkers, as resulting from 'atomistic thinking', incompatible with the romantic ideal of an integrated 'organic society' (A. 22, pp. 620–4).

It seems worth while to point out that both Śniadecki's polemical articles (against German philosophy and Romanticism) and Gołuchowski's early book on the relations between philosophy and life—the book which can be seen as a declaration of faith in 'philosophical Romanticism'—were translated into Russian. Gołuchowski's Russian translator was the well-known Schellingian, Professor D. M. Vellansky, highly esteemed in Moscow philosophical circles: in the circle of the so-called 'wisdom-lovers' and, later, in the circle of Nicholas Stankevich. His translation appeared in 1834 (see A. 21). We do not know how it was received, but the very fact that Vellansky translated just this book, and not one of Schelling's original works, seems to be significant and easily explicable: in Russia, as in Poland, the interest in German idealism was not purely theoretical but 'existential', stemming from a passionate search for meaning in individual and national life.

Maurycy Mochnacki (1804–34), the main theorist of Polish literary Romanticism, was at the same time an outstanding ideologist of the 'gentry revolutionism' and, during the uprising, one of the leaders of the insurrectionary Left. This was not an accident: in his own words the romantic upheaval in Polish literature was essentially a 'literary insurrection' which had to find an outlet in a political uprising.

Mochnacki was an ardent advocate of basing literary criticism on firm philosophical foundations. He developed the idea of a 'scientific criticism', free from importunate normativism, founded on a general philosophical theory of art, that is on aesthetics. Consequently, he distinguished between normative poetics and philosophical aesthetics, demanding that the latter be constituted as a separate, autonomous discipline. Realizing this programme he popularized in Poland many important aesthetic conceptions of Schiller, the two Schlegels, and Schelling. Against the abstract universalism of Classicism he set romantic historicism. Following Schelling, he fought against the mimetic conception of art, claiming that a true artist imitates not the created nature (*natura naturata*) but the *creative* nature (*natura naturans*). As such, he is in fact not imitating but creating, in accordance with the divine laws of creation.

The most original among Mochnacki's theoretical achievements was his conception of the nation and of the nation-building role of literature. It was an attempt to see the development of nations in the light of Schelling's theory of the development of spirit from 'immediacy' to 'reflection'. Reflection is the stage in which spirit becomes divided in itself, mirrors itself, and, thanks to this, achieves a level of self-consciousness. In the development of a nation the stage of reflection, or 'self-reflection', is achieved with the emergence of a truly national literature in which the nation 'recognizes itself in its essence' (A. 78, p. 214). This means that a nation is not an 'objective' fact of nature, like a tribe or a race; neither is it purely subjective, because it becomes self-conscious through the 'objectification' of its inner essence in culture (see B. 107, p. 34). National individuality, expressed and objectified in national culture, is a unique, irreducible value. Mochnacki defended this opinion not from an ethnocentric standpoint but from the point of view of romantic universalism: national cultures are individualized manifestations of mankind; all nations are organs of mankind, supplementing each other and equally necessary for the harmonious symphony of universal human culture.

Mochnacki's political and social views were discussed in the previous chapters of this book. For the future development of Polish philosophy the most important part of his heritage was the idea that the romantic Polish literature, in which the Poles 'recognized themselves in their essence', should be followed by the expression of national individuality and national self-consciousness in the philosophical sphere. True, he became later utterly disappointed in German idealism. This disappointment, however, did not change his high appraisal of Polish philosophical Romanticism which, unlike German idealism, never turned its back on real life. In his famous history of the November uprising he did not hesitate to claim that the clandestine organizations of Polish youth, which had emerged in the 1820s, were motivated in fact by the same ideas which found scholarly expression in the lectures of Lelewel and Gołuchowski.

2. Hoene-Wroński: Discovery of the Absolute, National Missions and Eschatological Destinies of Mankind

The Polish Schellingians of the 1820s were not aware of the existence of a Polish philosopher who also treated the philo-

sophy of Schelling as the highest achievement of German idealism and who already at the beginning of the century had
espoused the philosophical maximalism of the Germans, trying
to compete with them in constructing an all-embracing system,
an 'Absolute philosophy'. This philosopher, living in France
and writing in French, saw his 'Absolute philosophy' not only
as the means of a sweeping reform of all the sciences but as the
vehicle for a universal regeneration of mankind; because of this
he chose to call it 'Messianism'. His name was Józef Maria
Hoene-Wroński (1776–1853). Although he did not aim to
create a Polish 'national philosophy', he anticipated in many
respects the ideas of the 'national philosophers' of the forties. It
is understandable, therefore, that he was discovered in Poland
at the time of the greatest bloom of 'national philosophy' and
romantic Messianism.

Wroński's life was not an ordinary one. His father was an
architect who came to Poland from Bohemia, his mother was
Polish, and he himself served in the Russian army. Because of
this, he used to say that he was a Czech on his father's side, a
Pole on his mother's side, and a Russian by service, thus
representing in his person the three most important nations of
Slavdom. As a young man of 18 he took part in Kościuszko's
uprising and, as a captain of artillery, bravely defended
Warsaw against the Russian and Prussian troops. At the battle
of Maciejowice, he was taken prisoner by the Russians and
immediately afterwards, to the stupefaction of his biographers,
joined the Russian army becoming a major in the general staff of
Surovov. In 1797 he retired from service with the right to
promotion and to wear Russian military uniform; he was proud
of this right and, later, never hesitated to ask the Russian
government for a subsidy for his works. In the years 1797–1800,
he studied philosophy in Halle and Göttingen. In 1800, he went
to France to join the Polish legions of General Jan Henryk
Dąbrowski; in the same year, however, he asked for French
citizenship, and soon after, having received a letter of recom-
mendation from the French astronomer Lalande, started to
work in the astronomical observatory in Marseille. In 1803 he
published his first philosophical work, entitled *Philosophie
critique découverte par Kant*—one of the first works on Kant in
French. When this work had already been written a sudden
change took place in his life: in a flash of illumination, on 15

August 1803, he discovered the Absolute, penetrating into the mystery of the beginning and the end. From that day on he felt himself called to promote the cause of the salvation of the world. However, in sharp contrast to Mickiewicz, who, later, borrowed from him the term 'Messianism', he did not embrace mysticism. He saw the Absolute as rational and, therefore, attempted to unveil its essence in mathematical studies. Having written several mathematical works he came to Paris to present them to the French Academy of Sciences. When the French scholars proved unable to appreciate their value he decided to appeal to a wider public and in 1811 he published his work *Introduction à la Philosophie des Mathematiques et Technique de l'Algorithme*, dedicated to Alexander I. The Russian subsidy for this book was not enough, so he plunged into debts, from which he was rescued by P. J. Arson, a banker from Nice to whom he had promised to disclose the mystery of the Absolute. At the beginning Arson was so strongly influenced by Wroński that he gave him unlimited access to his money, provided him with a beautiful apartment with a library and published his works (*Philosophie de l'Infini*, Paris 1814; *Philosophie de la technie algorithmique*, Vols. I–II, Paris 1815–17). At the edge of bankruptcy, Arson tried to recover the rest of his fortune, but the philosopher was tough: he interpreted Arson's commitment to his philosophy as a formal contract which should be kept to the end. A scandalous trial ensued in which Wroński triumphed: he asked Arson whether the teachings he had received were worth all his money, and the poor banker was not able to say that they were not.[1] In this way Wroński was given all the remaining wealth of his disciple and started to use it freely for financing his inventions (for instance, a project of new geodetic instruments) and publications. He tried even to organize his own political party and, with this intention, published two issues of a journal *Le Sphinx ou la nomothétique séhélienne* (1818–19; the term 'séhélienne' was coined from a Hebrew word denoting 'reason') and four issues of another, *L'Ultra, Archives politiques, morales, et littéraires*.

As a result of these activities he became again moneyless. He decided to enrich himself by winning a geodetic competition, announced by the British Academy of Sciences, but professional scholars disappointed him once again. He ascribed his set-back to the prejudices and ignorance of British scientists and, in revenge, published several violent pamphlets against them. He did not abandon his hopes of making a great fortune as an inventor. The next plan to which he committed himself was inventing a 'calculateur-universel' in fourteen different variants. It might have been a prototype of a modern calculator, but, unfortunately, the idea never materialized because of financial difficulties with building a model of the machine.

In the years 1814–18 Wroński wrote his first great work on the philosophy of history, entitled 'Création absolue de l'humanité'. The manuscript, dedicated to Alexander I, remained unpublished, but its main ideas were developed in a series of works which Wroński started to publish in the second half of the 1820s. The most important among them were: *Prospectus de la Philosophie absolue* (1826), *Épître aux Souverains-Pontifes sur l'urgence actuelle de l'accomplissement de la religion* (written in 1827 but published in 1847), *À sa Majesté l'Empereur Nicholas* (1831), *Prodrome du Messianisme, Révélation des destinées de l'humanité* (1831), *Metapolitique messianique, Désordre révolutionnaire du monde civilisé* (1839), *Secret politique de Napoléon comme base de l'avenir du monde* (1840), *Le Destin de la France, de l'Allemagne et de la Russie* (1842) and, finally, his *magnum opus*, entitled *Réforme absolue et par conséquent finale du Savoir humain* (Vols. I–III, Paris 1847–8). The last four works were financed by E. Thayer, a relative (through his wife) of Prince Louis Napoleon. He was interested not only in Wroński's philosophy of history, particularly in his view of the 'Napoleonic idea', but also in his inventions, especially in his project of building a vehicle with 'roues à rails mobiles'. The idea of such a project was good—it was in fact a conception of caterpillar traction—but its realization, once again, proved unsuccessful. As a result Thayer became disappointed with Wroński and broke his relations with him. In addition the philosopher had to return to him a considerable sum of money and found himself in distress. He was rescued from utter poverty by subsidies from Prince Adam Czartoryski, discreetly given to him through his disciple Leonard Niedźwiecki.

In the last years of his life Wroński found a new patron—Count Camil Durutte, a composer and musicologist who invited him to Metz and financed the publication of his works: *Les Cent Pages décisives, pour S. M. l'Empereur de la Russie* (Metz 1850), *Épître à S. M. l'Empereur de la Russie, Explication définitive de l'Univers physique et moral* (Metz 1851), and *Philosophie absolue de l'histoire ou Genèse de l'humanité* (Paris 1852).

After Wroński's death (he died on 9 September 1853, in loneliness and need), Niedźwiecki published a few other works of his teacher, among others: *Développement progressif et but final de l'humanité* (1861), *Apodictique ou Traité du Savoir-suprême* (1876), *Développement de la philosophie absolue* (1878), *Philosophie absolue, Premiers travaux, Sept manuscripts écrit de 1803 à 1806* (1879), and *Doctrine du Savoir suprême, Nomothetique messianique ou Lois suprêmes du monde* (1881). A lot of Wroński's manuscripts remained unpublished; most of them are kept in the archives of the National Library in Warsaw and in the Library of the Polish Academy of Sciences in Kórnik. Many Polish translations of Wroński's works were published in the inter-war period of our century by a group of his followers who in 1921 founded for this purpose a special Messianic Institute.

The starting point of Wroński's philosophy was Kantianism. This may seem surprising to us. As a rule, we have become accustomed to look at Kant through the prism of the reception of his philosophy in the second half of the nineteenth century, i.e. to see Kantianism as a cautious compromise between philosophical 'maximalism' and 'minimalism', much closer to minimalism because of its espousal of phenomenalism and, therefore, almost as far as possible from the unlimited cognitive optimism of the 'absolute philosophies'. Nevertheless it is a fact that the direct continuators of Kant's philosophy were the builders of all-embracing metaphysical systems. Hoene-Wroński was one of them. If Jan Śniadecki had been acquainted with his thought, he would have found in it a splendid corroboration of his idea that Kantianism could be interpreted in such a way as to make it an ally of the most 'unreasonable' metaphysics.

According to Wroński, Kant's 'Copernican revolution' in philosophy consisted in the discovery of the creativity of the mind in the cognitive process: the mind does not have to conform to its objects but the objects have to conform to the mind. Wroński accepted this thesis and went further: he accused Kant of lessening the significance of his discovery by the identification of the *a priori* forms of knowledge with the subjective forms of human mind. The *a priori* principles, he asserted, are 'the eternal laws of truth'; they are objective, because the laws of reason are identical with the laws of the universe. Thus the problem of unknowable 'things in themselves' disappeared and the idea of an unbridged gulf between the phenomenal and the noumenal worlds were replaced by a conviction that an *a priori* knowledge of the noumenal reality was possible.

Kant himself, in spite of his phenomenalism, assumed that man feels an irresistible metaphysical need, that reason necessarily aspires at reaching the unconditional, the condition of all conditions, i.e. the Absolute. Recognition of this 'striving for the Absolute' was, in Wroński's eyes, a great merit of Kantianism and, of course, of the post-Kantian German idealism. For Kant, however, the Absolute was merely a *regulative idea*, inherent in the transcendental unity of apperception, but having no 'objective' existence. Wroński disagreed with Kant that the transcendental ideas have no 'constitutive' use, and, accordingly, made the Absolute a starting point of his philosophy. The method of 'analytical retrogression', i.e. the method of descending from what is given to successive conditions of its existence, was supplemented by him with a method of 'genetic progression', i.e. a method of deducing all the existing reality from an *a priori* knowledge of the Absolute.

The possibility of such a method depends on the assumption that philosophy can have a 'genetic intuition' of the Absolute from which all reality can be deduced in the same way as (according to Kant) the whole of mathematics can be derived from the pure intuitions of time and space as categorially determined. According to Wroński, Kant rejected this possibility because he was convinced of a fundamental heterogeneity between being and knowledge. Hence the reality had to be split by Kant into the phenomenal and the noumenal worlds, and the Kantian theoretical reason had to face the insoluble antinomies (which Wroński saw as antinomies between Being and Knowledge). Wroński tried to overcome this dualism by arguing that Being and Knowledge, the constitutive elements of all reality are, to be sure, different from each other but, none the less, essentially homogeneous. Knowledge—the active, dynamic element—was endowed with ontological status; the development of reality was conceived as a process of uniting Knowledge with Being, i.e. creating conditions and endowing them with the attribute of real existence. Wroński thought that this conception enabled him to overcome Kantian antinomies, which he had reduced to the general antinomy of Reason, split by Kant into the empirical intellect (*Verstand*), closed in the sphere of the finite, and pure reason (*Vernunft*), able to penetrate the sphere of infinity.

The inspirer of the idea of overcoming the heterogeneity of cognitive faculties was Kant himself. In his *Critique of Judgement* there is the famous passage about an archetypal intellect creating objects by thinking them and thus uniting intuition (*Anschauung*) with conceptual knowledge. Such a 'seeing intellect' would have as its objects only *existing* objects, which would amount to the perfect overcoming of the heterogeneity of Knowledge and Being. For Kant, however, such an epistemological Absolute was merely a 'limiting concept' (*Grenzbegriff*), i.e. something of which we are bound to think but which is, at the same time, completely inaccessible to us. At this point Wroński, like Schelling, sharply differed from Kant: he was convinced that the highest knowledge, transcending all dualisms, became accessible to him, that it had enabled him to penetrate the inner, 'ineffable' essence of the Absolute.

This conception may seem tantamount to an extreme irrationalism. Indeed, it is beyond the range of the current usage of the term 'rationalism'; we may also add that it was consciously set against the rationalism of the Enlightenment. At the same time, however, it was a grandiose extension of the sphere of reason and an effacement of sharply defined boundary lines between human reason and the divine, Absolute Reason. Having defined the conditions of existence as the laws of reason inherent in the inner structure of knowledge, Wroński clearly implied that being is itself rational. This implied, in turn, that our knowledge should be systematized, enclosed in clear-cut intellectual schemata, expressed in mathematical formulae, shown in pedantically composed tables, and so forth. The ideal of such knowledge was, thus, maximally rationalized, explained in the most orderly, systematic way. On the one hand Wroński acknowledged that his system had originated in a flash of *intuition*, in an act of illumination; on the other, he insisted on the necessity of a total rationalization of knowledge and identified the Absolute with creative *reason*. From his point of view there was no contradiction in this. He made a crucial distinction between the 'chrematic' reason (from the Greek word 'chrema' = 'thing') and the 'achrematic' reason, the first closed in the sphere of finite things, the second attaining to the Infinite. He emphasized, however, that 'achrematic reason' is a rational faculty, having nothing in common with mysticism. The active, creative spontaneity of reason, as he saw it, was for him the opposite of mysticism, which was passive and thoughtless, striving for an irrational union with the Absolute. Contemporary scholars are justified in treating Wroński's philosophy as 'an amalgam of mysticism with rationalism' (B. 144, p. 41), or in seeing it as a conception in which there is in fact no contradiction between rationalism and mysticism. Such interpretations can refer to Paul Tillich's observation that it is wrong, historically, to place rationalism in opposition to mysticism, because 'modern rational autonomy is a child of the mystical autonomy of the doctrine of the inner light' (B. 165, p. 286). We should remember, however, and take into account, that Wroński himself did not share this view. He considered himself an intransigent enemy of mysticism, because mysticism, like empiricism, represented for him the principle of passivity, an annihilation of reason and a slavish submission to 'the given'. Because of this he became furious when Mickiewicz, in the 1840s, borrowed from him the term 'Messianism', relating it to his own mystical ideas.

The Absolute, according to Wroński, is a creative force which has in itself the ultimate condition of its existence. The essence of the Absolute consists in conditioning the world, i.e. creating it. The process of creation is not arbitrary but lawlike, governed by the law of creation. The formula of this law has two parts: the theory, or 'autothetics', concerned with the constitution of the world as the object of passive experience, and the 'technics', or 'autogenesis', concerned with what should be done, with the aims and means of activity. Both the 'autothetics' and the 'autogenesis' were subordinated to the 'pure schema' of the law of creation (cf. B. 3).[2] This schema was conceived by Wroński as a way from the 'primitive unity' to the 'crowning unity' through the successive drawing apart and drawing together of the two poles of the Absolute: Being and Knowledge.

Wroński distinguished between the law of creation and the law of progress. He defined the former as a law of creative progression, i.e. of the *physical* genesis of the universe; the latter was defined by him as a law of the *moral* genesis of the universe, i.e. of its *return* to the divine Absolute (that is why he, paradoxically, called it 'the law of progressive retrogression'). According to this conception the moral genesis of the universe was being achieved by means of man. Man, reasoned Wroński, is a created being but, at the same time, he is endowed with a potential capacity for creation and auto-creation; his reason is infinitely weaker than the Divine Reason but, nevertheless, it is reason, i.e. in its essence it is identical with the Absolute; he differs from God as a multitude of individuals, but he is identical with God as the universal Man, i.e. as the Son of God. Reinterpreting neoplatonic metaphysics in the spirit of post-Kantian, activistic idealism, Wroński saw human history as the process of 'progressive retrogression', that is to say as a process of returning to God, replacing existence in the world with existence in the Absolute. At the same time it was a movement from the 'heterothelic' stage (from the Greek word 'thelos'—aim, purpose), i.e from the aims imposed on men from without, to the 'autothelic' stage, in which men would realize their own aims and, thus, become 'like gods'. Man was to achieve this stage by his own efforts and that is why he was endowed with only a *potentiality* of divine being.

In such a manner history became part of the metaphysics of the Absolute. Human history was seen in the perspective of an absolute eschatology. The final end of history—the return of the world to God through the auto-creation of man in God—was conceived by Wroński as a complete liberation of man from the conditions of physical existence, in other words as the achievement of immortality. Through the overcoming of the 'old man'— the physical individuality being a product of the cosmic genesis—and through the 'rebirth from the spirit', mankind will vanquish death and constitute itself as the new Son of God. Wroński's 'absolute philosophy' was treated as the main means for this end, because 'scire virtutem Dei radix est immortalitatis'.

The conception of the law of creation was the philosophical foundation of Wroński's project for universal reform in the sciences. Wroński was one of the pioneers of the idea of a 'New Encyclopaedia', set against the French Encyclopaedia of the Enlightenment. Instead of a merely empirical collection of everything known, presented in alphabetical (i.e. purely accidental) order, he proposed an organic system of sciences, deduced from one principle, governed by one universal law, and integrating different branches of science in an 'absolute system of the world'. (The starting point of this great enterprise was to be the reform of mathematics by deducing all its parts from one principle—'the law of the highest algorithm'.) All the sciences were divided into three groups: (1) the sciences of the cosmic genesis; (2) the sciences of historical (moral) genesis, and (3) the sciences of man as the means of transition from the cosmic to the historical genesis. Different systems of reality, being the subjects of different sciences, were shown in their development, following in each case the general scheme of the law of creation.

Let us return, however, to Wroński's philosophy of history. The whole span of history was divided in it into three great epochs: the epoch of relative aims, the epoch of transitional aims, and the epoch of absolute aims. The first of these is the epoch of heteronomy ('heterothelic' stage), of the direct rule of Providence, and is divided within itself into four periods: (1) the period striving for physical welfare, i.e. for the satisfaction of sensuous feelings (Ancient East); (2) the period striving for justice through politics (Ancient Greece and Rome); (3) the period striving for holiness through religion (the Middle Ages), and (4) the period striving for intellectual welfare or knowledge (Reformation and Enlightenment). The second epoch (being the fifth period of history) is an epoch of transition from heteronomy to autonomy. Providence has already ceased to act, man has been left to himself, but the truth of his destinies is not yet known to him. Therefore, it is an epoch of crisis, divisions, revolutionary violence, and unbridled individualism. It has brought to light the heterogeneous character of aims which had been realized in the first epoch: sensuous consciousness (developed in the first and third period) has been set against the cognitive consciousness (elaborated in the second and fourth period). In these conditions a 'social antinomy' has emerged—an antinomy stemming from the antinomy of reason whose discovery was one of the greatest merits of Kant (although he was wrong to eternalize it). It manifests itself in the unrelenting struggle between two parties—conservatives and liberals, or the party of feeling and the party of cognition, the party of the Good and the party of the True. The former is based upon revelation and divine right, the latter on experience and human rights; each party represents a partial truth, but makes it absolute and strives for a complete annihilation of the other, which, if successful, would entail disastrous consequences for mankind. The only salvation is shown by Messianism (i.e. by Wroński's teachings), which is the absolute philosophy and the absolute religion at the same time. It makes it possible to overcome the 'social antinomy' because it proves that true autonomy (the 'autothelic' stage) does not consist in a rebellion against divine laws: it should consist in directing the creative energy of human reason (awakened and defended by the party of cognition) towards the Absolute. In the 'heterothelic' epoch, God directed his activity towards man; in his future 'autothelic' epoch man will spontaneously direct his activities towards God. Thus the aims of the two parties are not mutually incompatible; on the contrary, they have to supplement each other. Immortality (the aim of the Right) cannot be achieved without the creative spontaneity of reason (the aim of the Left), and the latter is meaningless if applied only to problems concerning merely the physical existence of man. The Absolute Good is identical in essence with the Absolute Truth (cf. B. 15, p. 179).

From the religious point of view the raising of mankind to the height of Absolute Reason was interpreted by Wroński as the fulfilment of Christ's promise about the coming of the Paraclete. The discovery of the Absolute was to be the beginning of a great religious reform, consisting in the replacement of the revealed religion, given to men as an object of faith, by a 'demonstrated religion', based upon rational proofs. This new religion—the religion of reason—was called 'Messianism' or 'sehelianism' (Wroński used these words already in his manuscript 'Création absolue de l'humanité', 1818). It was to be a kind of synthesis of all great religions hitherto revealed; the element of cult was to be represented in it by cultivating fine arts, and the activity of the church was to be reduced to promoting the 'absolute love of one's neighbour'. In later years similar ideas were developed in Cieszkowski's *Our Father*. It is quite possible that Cieszkowski was, to some extent, influenced by Wroński: his unpublished 'Diary' contains interesting information not only about his reading of Wroński's books, but also about his personal contacts with Wroński in Paris, 1837.[3]

What should be done to bring about the fulfilment of the highest destinies of mankind? Wroński set his hopes first of all on the intellectual élite, on the 'superior spirits' at both poles of the 'social antinomy'. He wanted to organize them in an association called the 'Antinomic Union', with the aim of preventing conflicts and promoting further progress. The final end of the progressive movement was defined as the Kindom of God on Earth—a social condition in which mankind would live in accordance with divine laws, distributing goods according to merits and thus realizing the ideals of universal happiness and justice. We should remember, however, that the fulfilment of the earthly destinies of man was to be only a prologue to the realization of his ultimate destiny—spiritual immortality. In such a manner a 'historical utopia' was linked to an 'existential utopia' (B. 144, p. 115). Mankind was to regain its lost union with God, to become united in the Word (in Christ) and participate in the eternal life of the Absolute.

At its initial stage this philosophy was not meaningfully related to national problems. In 'Création absolue de l'humanité', Wroński defined national feeling as a 'crude force of nature' which sometimes could be used to cement the state but, in principle, should be replaced as soon as possible by enlightened state patriotism. National individuality, he argued, is essentially incompatible with the universality of reason; by the same token, it is incompatible with the dignity of man as well (cf. A. 106, p. 123).

After the July revolution in France and November insurrection in Poland, Wroński abandoned his view, enriching his philosophy of history by a new conception of the historical role of nations. He came to the conclusion that the spiritual awakening of nations—a characteristic feature of the epoch of transitional aims—had transformed nations into prime movers of history and vehicles of universal progress. Thus, in accordance with romantic universalism, he started to write about 'national missions', concentrating, of course, on Germany, France, and Slavdom. The mission of Germany was seen by him to lie in speculative philosophy and in reforming religious life. The national mission of France he saw in politics: the highest point in the realization of this mission was for him the 'Napoleonic idea', consisting in a reconciliation of human rights with divine right, in other words in a union of democratic principles with religion. But the main role in the imminent future—the establishment of a messianic Absolute Union ushering in the new, sixth period of universal history—was assigned by him to Slavonic peoples united under the leadership of Russia. Their mission was not revolutionary because they would preserve all the achievements of their predecessors; in particular they would take over and bring together 'the speculative mission of Germany' and 'the practical mission of France'. None the less,

-their mission was eschatological because they would bring about the final synthesis and the end of history. The necessary condition for this was the reconciliation of Russia, which represented the principle of divine right, with Poland, which had always fought for the rights of man. Wroński wrote that the Russians should abandon the idea of destroying the Polish nationality and the Poles should cease to struggle against the Russian Empire. Russian tsars should restore the independent Poland and, having done this, unite all the Slavs under the banner of panslavism. A free 'confederation' of Slavonic nations, constituted in such a manner, would enable the Slavs to become a true vanguard of mankind.

Having discovered the universal, eschatological calling of the Slavs, Wroński began to emphasize the 'Slavonic' character of his philosophy. This did not prevent him from deriving its theoretical genealogy from German philosophy, and from analysing the relations between his ideas and those of the German philosophers. I have already commented upon the relationship between his philosophy and Kantianism. In post-Kantian idealism he highly appreciated the 'striving for the Absolute' and attempts at overcoming the Kantian dualism; he thought, however, that the German thinkers could not raise themselves to the 'achrematic Reason', and, therefore, could not complete their tasks. The greatest merits he ascribed to Schelling: he praised him for attempting to reconcile Fichtean idealism ('considering being on the model of knowledge') with Spinozian realism ('considering knowledge on the model of being'), but he stressed, at the same time, that this reconciliation was merely formal because Schelling had not been able to penetrate the 'inner essence' of the Absolute. Very different, almost entirely negative, was Wroński's attitude to Hegelianism. He accused Hegel of an empty 'logology', of reducing philosophy to the sterile dialectics of pure notions out of which no real, positive existence could emerge. (It is worth while to recall that the same accusation was made by Schelling, who in his Munich and Berlin lectures criticized Hegelianism as a merely 'negative' philosophy. Cf. B. 52, pp. 96–102.) In addition to this, Wroński saw Hegel as a one-sided follower of the liberal party, identifying the Absolute with the earthly life.

Polish philosophers of the 1840s found in Wroński's philosophy many arguments supporting their programmatic activism:

they liked his 'law of creation' because it was saying that
creativity is the essence of life, that passivity and inertia are
incompatible with true being, and that the chief duty of men is
to create themselves in history. Wroński's efforts to predict the
future, his criticism of one-sided idealism, especially
Hegelianism, his idea of an essential homogeneity of God with
man, his view on the mutual relationship between politics and
religion, the mediating tendency of his thought trying to
overcome the painful dualisms both in philosophy and in social
life, were also very close to their thinking. It should be
mentioned also that Wroński's interpretation of his own
philosophy as a higher synthesis of German speculation with
French politics was strikingly similar to the self-image of the
Polish philosophers of the forties (although, to be sure, he saw
his 'Messianism' as a 'Slavonic' philosophy, and not as an
expression of the Polish national spirit). It is tempting to
explain these similarities as a result of Wroński's influence on
'national philosophers', but in actual fact (with the possible
exception of Cieszkowski) it was not so. His ideas became
known in Poland rather late, at the time when Trentowski (the
most representative 'national philosopher', in some respects
especially close to Wroński) had already written his main books.

The first Pole who drew the attention of his compatriots
to Wroński's 'Messianism' was Mickiewicz, who spoke about
Wroński, and about his disciple Antoni Bukaty, in 1842, in
his lectures at the Collège de France. The correspondence of
Krasiński makes clear that he too, approximately at the same
time, devoured Wroński's books and in many points agreed
with him. The most important contributions to the popularization of Wroński's philosophy among the Poles were made,
however, not by romantic poets but by philosophers: by Trentowski, who wrote about it in a long article 'Hoene-Wroński or
Polono-French Messianism' (1844), and by Libelt, who represented a good summary of Wroński's thought in the first volume
of his *Philosophy and Criticism* (see A. 50). Trentowski, as he
himself confessed, owed his first acquaintance with Wroński's
ideas to Mickiewicz. Being committed to a struggle against
Mickiewicz's mysticism, he was inclined, initially, to neglect, or
underestimate, some important differences between Wroński
and Mickiewicz, and by the same token, to put emphasis on the
difference between his 'national philosophy' and Wroński's

'Messianism'; in spite of this, however, he did not overlook some points in Wroński's philosophy which were congenial to his own thought. As time went on, he became more and more sympathetic to Wroński, more and more aware of certain convergences between his and Wroński's ideas, and more and more inclined to draw inspiration from Wroński's philosophical heritage. His final estimation of Wroński's thought, to be found in his posthumously-published *Pantheon of Human Knowledge*, runs as follows: 'Europe and Poland have never had anything more lofty than Copernicus in ancient Poland and Wroński in contemporary Poland. They represent the two solar culminations of the human spirit.'

3. The First Polish Hegelians and the Main Centres of the Philosophical Movement of the Forties

As I have already noted, both Hoene-Wroński and the representatives of the Polish 'philosophical Romanticism' of the 1820s saw the philosophy of Schelling as the highest achievement of the German and universal philosophy of their time. The philosophers of the 1840s, as a rule, saw such an achievement in Hegelianism. They were usually very critical towards Hegel because they treated his philosophy as the culminating point of rationalistic idealism, which they themselves tried to overcome (very often with the help of Schelling). Even the outspoken anti-Hegelians could not afford to ignore Hegel and the German controversies over Hegel. In this sense we can say that all representatives of the Polish philosophical movement of the forties belonged to a post-Hegelian philosophical formation.

The Polish reception of Hegelianism began before the November uprising, in the columns of the journal *Haliczanin* (Citizen of Galicia), published in Lvov in 1830.[4] The editor of this journal, W. Chłędowski, in his article 'On Philosophy' presented the development of German idealism from Kant to Hegel as 'the noblest achievement in the history of the human mind'. More interesting—especially from the point of view of the relationship between philosophy and national problems— were two articles published in *Haliczanin* by Jan Nepomucen Kamiński: 'Is Our Language Philosophical?' and 'Argument For the Philosophical Character of Our Language'. In both of them Kamiński attempted to apply Hegelianism, especially the Hegelian concept of an immanent, dialectical reason of reality, to the philosophy of language. The true history of mankind was for him not external, political history but the history of the human spirit expressed in philosophy and in language. Philosophical categories, he argued, are closely bound up with linguistic forms; the latter preceded the former in the same way as the inflorescence of poetry precedes the development of philosophical thought. To prove that Polish is a philosophical language amounted, therefore, to proving that the Poles have in fact a philosophy of their own—a philosophy which can be found in their speech and which needs only to be translated from the language of poetry (which had already achieved its hey-day in Poland) to the language of discursive thought. This was, of course, an encouragement to embark on etymological speculations (a fancy shared by many romantic writers, East or West) and, also, to various attempts at polonizing philosophical terminology. Among the writers who indulged in these endeavours (usually with rather disappointing results) we find such important figures as Norwid, Trentowski, and Dembowski. The latter wrote about Kamiński's philosophy of language with genuine enthusiasm.

In the post-uprising period the chief role in promoting Hegelianism in Poland was played, initially, by the journal *Scientific Quarterly (Kwartalnik Naukowy)*, published in Cracow from 1835. Its editor, A. Z. Helcel and a lawyer, J. K. Rzesiński, propagated in it Hegel's views on the method of philosophy, especially on its application to the philosophy of law. But the most important Cracow Hegelian was Józef Kremer—a professional philosopher and aesthetician who had studied in Berlin under Hegel and who was to become in 1847 a professor of philosophy in the University of Cracow. His 'Philosophical Outline of Sciences', published in the *Scientific Quarterly* 1835–6, was the first systematic exposition of Hegelian philosophy in Poland.

The main fault of this exposition was, paradoxically, the omission of the whole field of aesthetics. Soon afterwards it became the domain of Kremer's special interest, but the priority in popularizing Hegel's aesthetic views fell to the lot of a young poet Gustav Ehrenberg (1819–95), an illegitimate son of Alexander I, associated with the revolutionary circles in Galicia. In 1835 he published in a Cracow journal, the *Universal Diary of Arts and Sciences*, two articles on aesthetics, entitled 'Introductory Thoughts on Aesthetics' and 'Aesthetics as a Science'. He proclaimed in them a conception of aesthetics as an autonomous philosophical discipline, emphasized its importance in national life (following in the wake of Gołuchowski), and criticized some views of Hegel, especially the idea of 'the end of art'. He popularized Hegelianism also by word of mouth, lecturing on philosophy for the Cracow students in the academic year 1835–6. We can have some idea of the spirit and content of these lectures from his manuscript 'Remarks on the Philosophy of History' (see A. 106, pp. 463–5). It testifies that Ehrenberg was the first to propagate Hegelian historicism in Poland, interpreting it in a characteristically 'leftist' way, i.e. rejecting the idea of the 'end of history', putting stress on the role of negation (and not mediation) in historical development, and so forth.

The Hegelian ideas in the columns of the two Cracow journals were the direct antecedents of the philosophical movement of the forties. Some Cracow Hegelians joined this movement—Kremer as an aesthetician, Rzesiński as a philosopher of law—but they played in it only a marginal role. Their relative unimportance in Polish intellectual history is explicable by the fact that they limited their ambitions to pure scholarship and never tried to create a philosophy bringing about national and universal regeneration. (Ehrenberg was a different case, but he was arrested in 1838 and exiled to Siberia.) Kremer, the most outstanding among them, was a philosopher of purely academic type. He did not try to create a 'national philosophy', because he thought that genuine philosophy was by definition supranational and, also, because he did not feel himself capable of building a new, truly original philosophical system. In his 'Philosophical Outline of Sciences' he simply summarized Hegelian theories, reducing his own contribution to a rather timid declaration that the speculative extremes of idealism should be curtailed by paying more attention to empirical sciences. In later years, in his *Systematic Exposition of Philosophy* (*Wykład systematyczny filozofii*, Vols. I–II, Cracow, 1849–52), he tried to reconcile Hegelianism with Catholicism: he identified the Hegelian Absolute with the Catholic personal God and replaced Hegelian 'panlogism' with a conception of parallelism between thought and Being. Even in this work, however, his attitude towards Hegel was that of a disciple, critical in some points but full of deepest respect and trying to change as little as possible in the system of his teacher. Needless to say, the idea of reforming the existing religious consciousness was completely alien to him.

The period of greatest bloom in nineteenth-century Polish philosophy was inaugurated by works published in German: Trentowski's *Grundlage der universellen Philosophie* (1837) and Cieszkowski's *Prolegomena zur Historiosophie* (1838). These works were hailed by the Polish intelligentsia of the epoch as the first books in which Polish philosophers came forward with new ideas of universal significance.

The main arena of the philosophical movement in Poland became the Grand Duchy of Poznań. The relative mildness of Prussian censorship after the enthronement of Friedrich Wilhelm IV (1840) made it the scene of an unprecedented inflorescence of Polish journalism and (along with Warsaw) the most important centre of Polish intellectual life, exerting a powerful influence on the Russian and Austrian parts of partitioned Poland. Philosophical problems were discussed on the pages of many Poznań journals, first of all in Libelt's journal *The Year (Rok)*, which opened its columns for all Polish thinkers, irrespective of their philosophical or political views. (Among its contributors we find such figures as Cieszkowski—a moderate liberal, Dembowski—a revolutionary socialist, and Feliks Kozłowski—a Catholic critic of philosophy.) Almost all the representative works of the philosophical movement of the forties were published in Poznań: all the Polish books of Trentowski, Kamieński's *Philosophy of the Material Economy of Human Society* (Vols. I–II, 1843–5), Dembowski's *Outline of Polish Literature* (1845), and, of course, all the works of Libelt.

In Warsaw the philosophical milieu was grouped around the *Scientific Review (Przegląd Naukowy*; the initial idea of its title was 'Philosophical Review'), a journal founded in 1842 and edited by H. Skimbrowicz together with Dembowski. Hegel, called 'the Berlin sage' or 'the Master of the School', was deeply revered there, although his philosophy was often revised in a rather bold manner. Hegelianism became an intellectual fashion; young Warsaw intellectuals, according to the memoirs of N. Żmichowska, debated in salons about 'spirit who knows but does not know that he knows' and 'spirit who knows and knows that he knows'. Even the moderate and deliberately eclectic journal the *Warsaw Library (Biblioteka Warszawska)* could not resist this fashion, and paid tribute to it by publishing several articles of Cieszkowski and (posthumously) three articles of a young Hegelian, a close friend of Krasiński, Konstanty Danielewicz. The growing influence of German philosophy and of the Polish 'national philosophers' caused alarm among conservative Catholic circles. In order to resist this danger a special journal was founded in 1842. Its title was *The Pilgrim (Pielgrzym)* and its editor was the first woman-philosopher in Poland, Eleonora Ziemięcka.

The interest in German philosophy appeared also in the Lithuanian part of the ancient Polish Commonwealth. A country gentleman Florian Bochwic published in Wilno several books in which he tried to reconcile German idealism with the revealed religion (making use of some ideas of the French philosopher, Victor Cousin). In 1841 the well-known novelist J. I. Kraszewski started to publish in Wilno the journal *Athenaeum*, which was not immune to philosophical fashions coming from the West. On the whole, however, the eastern borderlands of the former Commonwealth, especially the Ukraine, were a stronghold of extreme conservatism, inimical to any autonomous philosophy and fighting against it in the name of religion and national tradition. Such a standpoint was espoused by an influential group of writers called 'the coterie of Sankt-Petersburg' whose most interesting and most extreme ideologist was a magnate from the Ukraine, Count Henryk Rzewuski.

Thus, the ideological situation in Polish thought, seen from the territorial perspective, accorded to a great extent with the following generalization of Dembowski: 'In Wilno a complete obscurantism, in Galicia an awakening of some new strivings, in Warsaw—a struggle between progressive and reactionary tendencies, in the Great Poland [Poznania]—already a victory.'

We can turn now to the presentation of the five most outstanding representatives of the philosophical movement of the forties. It is useful to divide them into two groups which shared some common tendencies, especially programmatic activism and a quest for 'national philosophy', but differed from each other in the understanding of the Absolute. Cieszkowski, Trentowski, and Libelt strove for a reconciliation between the immanence and the transcendence, or between philosophy and religion, whereas Kamieński and Dembowski were concerned with the immanent Absolute only. The first three, like Hoene-

Wroński, combined activism with the neoplatonic idea of reintegration with the divine Absolute; the last two were interested only in the regeneration of life on earth and in the purely terrestrial salvation of mankind.

III. August Cieszkowski

1. Biographical Note

Count August Cieszkowski was born on 12 November 1814 on his family estate of Sucha (in Podlasie, the Congress Kingdom), as a son of a wealthy, aristocratic family. He went to a high school in Warsaw. During the November uprising, being too young to enlist in the army, he served the patriotic cause as a secretary of the Parliament. On the eve of the capitulation of Warsaw he went to Cracow and started his philosophical studies in the Jagellonian University under the tutorship of a Kantian, Professor J. E. Jankowski. In the next year he went to Berlin and continued his studies under the tutorship of an eminent representative of 'the Hegelian centre', Karl Ludwig Michelet. Soon he became his favourite pupil and, later, his life-long friend.

As an undergraduate student, Cieszkowski wrote (in Polish) the first outline of his *Prolegomena zur Historiosophie*. Having come to Poland on a holiday he showed this work to his father, who read it immediately and was so deeply stirred by it that he decided to celebrate his son's philosophical début by their praying together in the parish church in Grębków. This proved to be a significant event for the young philosopher because it made him aware that the seven petitions contained in the *Our Father* embodied all the ideas which he wanted to develop in his vision of the future.

The final German version of *Prolegomena* was completed (according to an entry in Cieszkowski's unpublished Diary) between 3 May and 30 June 1838; soon afterwards it was published. In the same year Cieszkowski defended in Heidelberg his doctoral dissertation 'De philosophiae ionicae ingenio, vi, loco' and went to Paris. He was very busy there: he became acquainted with many outstanding intellectuals, such as Ballanche, Leroux, Michel Chevalier, Lamennais, Sainte-

Beuve, the Marquis de Custine, and Hoene-Wroński; he listened to lectures at the Sorbonne and the Collège de France; he participated in the meetings of learned societies, visited factories, and observed the sessions of Parliament.

The result of these activities were two books published by Cieszkowski in French. The first, *Du crédit et de la circulation* (Paris 1839), reviewed by Michel Chevalier and discussed by Proudhon in his *Système des contradictions économiques*, established his reputation among the French economists. Cieszkowski presented himself in it as a scholar uniting a solid knowledge of liberal political economy with a skilful use of Hegelian dialectical method—a combination which was by then a novelty in France. He formulated the principle of 'organic, positive' state intervention in economic life; against the principle of 'laissez faire' he advanced the watchword: 'aidez à faire et developpez'. His ideas concerning credit and financial reform should be seen within the context of the right wing of the Fourierist movement. Cieszkowski's connections with the Fourierists are also testified to by his paper 'Du crédit agricole, mobilier et immobilier' which he presented to the 1847 Paris Agricultural Congress and which was published in the Fourierist journal, *Phalange*.

The second of Cieszkowski's French books, *De la pairie et l'aristocratie moderne* (Paris 1844), argued for the necessity of replacing hereditary nobility by an aristocracy of merit whose representation would be the senate. Cieszkowski hoped that this book would have paved the way for him to the French Parliament, thus enabling him to participate directly in French political life.

In the autumn of 1839 Cieszkowski went to Italy. He met there the poet Zygmunt Krasiński who, having read his *Prolegomena*, recognized him as the highest authority in philosophy. In spite of some ideological differences they became close friends. Krasiński's letters to Cieszkowski (Cieszkowski's letters have been lost) are among the most important and fascinating documents of Polish philosophical culture of the epoch.

Having returned to Poland (autumn 1840), Cieszkowski settled in Warsaw and started to work on the journal *Warsaw Library*, which soon became the central cultural institution of the Congress Kingdom. Regular meetings of the editors and collaborators of this journal were a good substitute for the Warsaw Society of the Friends of Learning, liquidated by the

Russian authorities after the uprising. Thanks to a subsidy from Cieszkowski, the *Warsaw Library* began to publish an excellent series of Polish translations of Western philosophical and scholarly works. Another characteristic initiative of Cieszkowski was a project to announce a contest for the best solution of the peasant question. Unfortunately, the realization of this idea was forbidden by the government.

Suspicious and petty annoyances on the part of the Russian authorities in Warsaw influenced Cieszkowski's decision to leave the Congress Kingdom and to settle in Poznania. He bought there an estate, Wierzenica, and became a citizen of the Prussian part of Poland. In 1843 he published in Libelt's journal the *Year* an article entitled 'On the Need for Uniting Intellectual Tendencies and Works in the Grand Duchy of Poznań'. It was the first philosophical justification of the liberal programme of 'organic work' in Poland. Cieszkowski set forth in it the idea of establishing a 'Society of the Friends of Progress' which would organize scholarly researchers, give scholarships to talented men of the people, and publish a journal reflecting all the currents of Polish spiritual life. According to Cieszkowski's project such a society should not strive for an impossible re-conciliation of different parties but would try, instead, to achieve their 'association', i.e. a union in which each of them could represent its own principles. In justifying this plan Cieszkowski referred to the Saint-Simonian idea of 'association' and to his own 'philosophy of action'.

In spite of his commitment to 'organic work' in Poland, Cieszkowski was very active in the intellectual life of Germany, France, and of the Polish emigration. In 1842 he published the first, 'critical' part of his treatise *Gott und Palingenesie*, in which he challenged the views of his teacher and friend, K. L. Michelet. (The second, 'positive' part of this treatise has been lost or destroyed, but its content is known from pp. 99–135 of Michelet's *Die Epiphanie der ewigen Persönlichkiet des Geistes*, Berlin 1852.) Soon afterwards he suggested to Michelet that they should publish a philosophical journal which would offer a common platform for discussion between the different Hegelian and post-Hegelian schools of thought. This proposal gave rise to the foundation of the journal *Gedanke* and of the Berlin Philo-sophical Society, of which Cieszkowski was for many years one of the most active members.[5]

In 1848 the first, introductory volume of Cieszkowski's

magnum opus, Our Father (Ojcze Nasz) was published (anonymously) in Paris. He wrote this work in Polish (some parts of it were written already at the turn of the 1830s) and never mentioned it in the Berlin Philosophical Society, being convinced that it was beyond the grasp of German philosophers. In the same year he was elected to the Prussian Diet and initiated the foundation of the Polish League—a legal organization for defending and promoting Polish interests in Prussia. The League achieved great success, became a kind of *de facto* organ of Polish self-government in Poznania, but was soon repressed by the government. In the next year, in connection with the debates concerning the political status of the Grand Duchy, Cieszkowski issued a publication drawing attention to the relevant clauses of the Congress of Vienna. Three years later (1852), he tabled a richly documented motion for the establishment of a university of Poznań. He was one of the co-founders (and for a long time, president) of the Poznań Association of the Friends of Learning. In 1860 he became the Head of the Circle of Polish Deputies and in this capacity, after the patriotic demonstrations in Warsaw in February 1861, surprised the Prussian Diet by placing on the agenda the question of changing the resolution of the Congress of Vienna in favour of Poland. During the Vatican Council I (1869–70) he went to Rome and tried to agitate behind the scenes for a more liberal interpretation of the doctrine of the church. A little later, as part of the programme of 'organic work', he established an advanced agricultural college in Poznania.

Cieszkowski died on 12 March 1894. The decision concerning the unfinished manuscripts of the other two volumes of *Our Father* was left by him to his son (who decided to publish them in 1899 and 1903). Cieszkowski himself had refrained from publishing them during his lifetime because he had thought that some of his views were too far in advance of his time and that their premature publication could bring about undesirable results: he arrived at this conclusion as the result of criticism of his views expressed by his conservative friend, Zygmunt Krasiński.

2. Philosophy of Action

Although the 'philosophical epoch' in Poland gave rise to quite a number of distinguished thinkers, Cieszkowski was the figure whose contribution to European philosophical thought can be assessed as the greatest. This opinion rests above all on his *Prolegomena zur Historiosophie*. The 'philosophy of action' (*Philosophie der Tat*) developed there was consonant with the tendencies which were becoming widespread within the German Hegelian Left at the beginning of the forties. The Polish thinker was the first to formulate the necessity of overcoming speculative philosophy, breaking with the contemplativeness of pure theory and applying philosophy to social praxis.

Cieszkowski was as much underestimated by his German contemporaries, with the exception of Moses Hess and Karl Ludwig Michelet. This fact, however, neither reduces the probability of a 'hidden' influence exerted by his thought on the significant processes occurring then in the Hegelian school, nor does it refute the thesis about his intellectual priority in formulating a number of important ideas. Cieszkowski's contribution can be fully gauged *ex post facto*, from the perspective of a comprehensive analysis of the process of disintegration of absolute idealism. The opinion that Cieszkowski's *Prolegomena* cannot be ignored in the history of the young Hegelian movement and the Hegelian Left and thus, *eo ipso*, in the history of ideas which anteceded and prepared for the rise of Marxism, is beginning to gain ground among experts on Marxism and, likewise, among historians of the post-Hegelian philosophy.[6] Some of them consider *Prolegomena* to be of crucial importance. Thus, for example, A. Cornu, a well-known Marxist historian of Marxism, came to the conclusion that the book constitutes 'the first expression of a revolutionary transformation of Hegel's philosophy', and that it was an overcoming of liberalism and bourgeois thought in general. Such an assessment was based on the contention that Cieszkowski 'treated philosophy as a branch of praxis, that is, as philosophy participating in social activity, and professed, earlier than Marx did, the decline of abstract philosophy, although he still couched his position in the terms of idealism' (B. 29, Vol. I, chap. 3). A still higher assessment of *Prolegomena* was given by a Catholic historian of philosophy, N. Lobkowicz. He devoted a whole chapter to Cieszkowski in his ambitious history of the philosophical concept of praxis, and came to the conclusion that 'at least as far as the notion of praxis is concerned' Cieszkowski's book was 'the most brilliant and the most important single text published between Hegel's death in 1831 and the *Philosophic and Economic Manuscripts* of Marx' (B. 102, p. 194).

Cornu's interpretation and all other attempts to see Cieszkowski's thought in connection with the progressive evolution of Hegelianism were resolutely opposed in the Polish Marxist literature of the 1950s. All such interpretations were accused of isolating *Prolegomena* from the total output of Cieszkowski and of ignoring the evolution of Cieszkowski's thought. The Hegelian Left, it was argued, moved towards atheism and political radicalism, whereas Cieszkowski was a religious thinker and an advocate of conservative progress, standing aloof from the ideas advanced by the German philosophical Left (cf. especially B. 88, pp. 157–227).

Who was right in this controversy? I shall try to prove that neither of the parties was right, or, in other words, that both were partially right. The common mistake underlying their opposing views consisted in considering *Prolegomena* exclusively within a German context, thus ignoring the French context of Cieszkowski's thought and, above all, its position within the Polish philosophical movement of the forties.

However, we must not look too far ahead, since the answer to the question about the place which should be allotted to *Prolegomena* in the evolution of the post-Hegelian philosophy and in Polish intellectual history has to be preceded by a presentation of the origins and content of the book.

Initially Cieszkowski's treatise was to bear the title *The Dialectics of History*, the wording of which indicates the conviction that Hegel could be defeated only by his own method. Cieszkowski's apprehension of the ambiguity contained in the word 'dialectics' seems to have been decisive in the abandonment of the original title. In a letter of 10 October 1836, he informed Michelet that he wanted to avoid his dialectics getting mixed up with the purely negative dialectics that are the 'second stage of the logical process', or with the subjective 'dialectics of the Eleatics'. He conceived true dialectics as 'objective dialectics, an inner process which unfolds the unity in diversity, the movement of the object in its organic genesis, the development of the idea perceived as a single whole'. The emphasis placed on the objective character of dialectic laws distinguished his 'philosophy of action' from the kind of activism offered by Fichte's philosophy. Cieszkowski reiterated that his philosophy, being based on Hegelianism, was immune from the pitfalls of utopianism, against the danger of which Michelet had continually warned him. Since in Hegel's system philosophy became a science, the application of its methods to the study of the future could have nothing in common with fanciful subjectivism.

The philosophy of history with which young Cieszkowski occupied himself was as much the fruit of his investigations into French social, religious, and political thought as a result of his studies of German philosophy. Characteristically, in 1836 Cieszkowski was trying to convince Michelet that the opinions of such writers as Balzac, Fourier, and George Sand should not be ignored in establishing one's own attitude towards the institution of marriage. Despite the fact that their point of view was not speculative and organic enough, he continued, it nevertheless contained 'a germ for the future possibility of enquiring into the matter thereof'. His diary discloses that his reading list for 1837 included, among others, Saint-Martin, de Maistre, Balzac, George Sand, Fourier, the Saint-Simonians, Guizot, and even Comte.

The point of departure for *Prolegomena* was Cieszkowski's criticism of Hegel's division of history. Hegel, according to his critic, ought not to have divided history into four main phases, because the very laws of dialectics discovered by him imposed a trichotomic division. Moreover, in consequence of Hegel's opinion that absolute knowledge (which Hegel considered his own philosophy to be) was able to appear after the process of development had been completed, his system included only the past and the present. Already in the introductory chapter Cieszkowski opposed Hegel on the ground that the dialectics of history ought also to include the future. Without this, he argued, the philosophy of history cannot be transformed into 'historiosophy', i.e. raised to the level of the *absolute knowledge* of history.[7] In furnishing arguments supporting the possibility of knowing the future, Cieszkowski adduced the analogy obtaining between history and nature: if Cuvier has merely needed a single tooth in order to be able to reconstruct the whole organism of an antedeluvian animal, there can be no reason why a philosopher, equipped with knowledge of the former segments of the organism of history, could stand helpless in his attempt to reconstruct its final phase.

Having rejected the Hegelian tetrachotomy, Cieszkowski proposed a division of history into three great epochs: the past, that is the ancient epoch (which he also referred to as the age of Art): the present, being the Christian epoch, lasting from Christ to Hegel (the age of Thought); and the epoch of the future, being the third and final epoch of history (the age of Action). Within this conception the first was the epoch of feeling, natural immediacy, and unreflecting unity; the second was the age of thought, reflection, and painful dualism; the third, the epoch of the future, will be the age of action and, simultaneously, of universal reintegration harmoniously uniting feeling with thought, reconciling nature with spirit, immediacy with reflection. In its embrace unconscious, unreflecting activity ('facts') will be replaced by conscious action ('acts'), in which man, no longer reduced to a merely sentient or a merely thinking being, will unfold his creative nature.

Hegel's philosophy represented for Cieszkowski the culmination of the development of pure philosophy and, by the same token, the end of the epoch of thought. Philosophy achieved with Hegel its classical expression: going further and transcending it is analogous to the movement from classical art, being the culminating point of art as pure art, to Romanticism. Having reached the climax in its development, philosophy ought to 'pass into life': 'therefore being and thought must be immersed in action while art and philosophy be instilled in social life, so that they could truly and in accordance with their utter goals emerge and flourish therein'. However, in order to effect the 'passage into life' and become an instrument of action, philosophy must no longer constitute a purpose in itself and must no longer be considered as the 'most significant centre of spirit'; it must be popularized by penetrating into the depth of social life, thus overcoming its élitist and esoteric character. It is also imperative that it be concerned with social and economic problems which it has hitherto completely disregarded, leaving them to thinkers deficient in matters of philosophy though sensitive to the urgent problems of the contemporary world. Cieszkowski shared the widespread opinion considering France to be the model country of 'sociality'. Thus, postulating his philosophy of action, he sided with the thinkers who preached the idea of conciliating the German with the French element, of combining and uniting German philosophy with French social

thought. By proclaiming action conceived as a conscious transformation of social life he rehabilitated utopian thinking—'the
passion for creating social systems and constructing society *a
priori*'—so severely condemned by Hegel; Fourier's socialist
utopia presented itself to him as the harbinger of the 'epoch of
action'.

Cieszkowski's philosophy of history was supplemented by a
'phenomenological' scheme of the development of personality.
The first stage is *being in itself*—the stage of natural, immediate
individuality; then comes the stage of *being for itself*—the stage of
thought, in which man, having renounced his 'natural immediacy', raises himself to the sphere of impersonal universal
reason; the third and final stage is *being from itself*—the stage of
free and creative action. The philosophy of Hegel was in fact the
most extreme philosophical expression of the second stage;
hence its characteristic one-sidedness, consisting in the absolutization of reason and in an extreme rationalistic idealism which
denied the rights of the individual and dissolved the material
world. The 'philosophy of action'—proclaimed Cieszkowski—
overcomes this one-sidedness by offering a dialectical mediation between feeling and thought; thus, it vindicates the rights
of the individual and rehabilitates the 'natural', physical side of
man. It is easy to see that these ideas run parallel to the
postulates of the 'rehabilitation of matter' and 'rehabilitation of
the flesh' in the religious and social doctrines of Saint-Simon,
the Saint-Simonians, and Fourier.

Closely bound up with this was the postulate of overcoming
the contemplative rationalism and 'panlogism' of Hegel's
philosophy. In Hegel's conception the world is the thought of
absolute reason and is thus identified with it; it has logic for its
ontology, while absolute knowledge—in exactly the same fashion
as being—is of a rational, conceptual, and logical nature. The
author of *Prolegomena* educed therefrom not only an absolutization of the universal, so characteristic of Hegelianism, but also
diagnosed a contemplative attitude which prevented philosophy
from participating in social practice and reduced its tasks to a
theoretical, *ex post* exegesis of the ways in which absolute spirit
unfolds itself. Hegel's was a philosophy of reason, whereas the
new philosophy was to be the philosophy of Will: for nothing
but Will alone was able to realize the idea and to secure the
transition from theory to practice. 'The Will', wrote Cieszkowski,

'ought to be elevated to the summits of speculation, which so far Reason alone was able to reach'. All the same, while strongly advocating the significance of Will and opposing the idealistic rationalism, he unequivocally indicated that he struggled to *transcend* and not to reject rationalism. He asserted that Will must be preceded by knowledge, that is, by comprehension of the laws whereby history develops, and stressed that a conscious act must issue from conscious thought. Having contrasted a pre-theoretical kind of practice, ungrounded in the achievements of theory, with its post-theoretical kind, Cieszkowski made the reservation that his concern was with rational Will in contradistinction to Will viewed in its subjectivity, particularity, and fortuitousness.

Let us now proceed to consider the relation of *Prolegomena* to the ideas advanced by the Hegelian Left—both those formulated prior to its publication and those which crystallized in the forties.

The controversy between the Young Hegelians and the Hegelian Right initially revolved around the problems of the philosophy of religion and speculative theology. A rejection of Hegel's conception of Christianity as 'absolute religion' was the basic novelty introduced by Strauss. The latter treated Christianity as one of the manifestations of the absolute which incessantly incarnates in mankind and continually attains higher stages by constantly overcoming its partial manifestations. Thus interpreted, Jesus of Nazareth was only a man, one of numerous 'religious geniuses', and the religious evolution of mankind ceased to be regarded as already fulfilled and materialized in the 'absolute religion'. The main stress was shifted from the present, in a broad sense of the word, onto the future, which was expected to reveal new and supreme manifestations of the historical process of the incarnation of God. Evidently, these ideas run parallel to the conceptions elaborated in *Prolegomena*: Cieszkowski's repudiation of Hegel's thesis holding that the progress of history had been completed, along with his own idea of including the future in the 'organism of history', were both perfectly compatible with Strauss's relativization of Christianity implying a further religious evolution of mankind.

However, there existed considerable differences between the two thinkers, and they must now be fully accounted for. First of all, while Strauss considered the process of 'God's incarnation' to be infinite (an infinite being can never be fully expressed in finite forms), Cieszkowski, whose 'epoch of action' was conceived as a fulfilment of mankind's ultimate goal, developed a finalist philosophy of history. It was analogous to the millenarian and messianist schema of the French 'social romantics', particularly to that of the Saint-Simonians, who proclaimed religious progress and simultaneously its termination in 'ultimate and complete revelation' and in the final realization of the Kingdom of God on earth. Likewise, the origins and the character ascribed to the three historical epochs distinguished by him can be traced back to Saint-Simonianism: the division of history into the epoch of 'feeling with preponderant sensuality', the 'epoch of thought with preponderant spirituality', and the future epoch of 'will in action' had been adumbrated in *La Doctrine saint-simonienne* (see A. 88).

Secondly, with Cieszkowski the relativization of Christianity never reached unequivocality and radicalism equal to Strauss's. He frequently reiterated that 'Christianity as a religion is for certain not merely an antithetic, but, undoubtedly, a synthetic moment'. Although he was positive that Christianity (in the historical sense) 'is not the ultimate and absolute stage in the development of human spirit', he, none the-less, did not deny Christ his significance by reducing him, as Strauss had done, to the status of one of the 'religious geniuses', none of which was *nec plus ultra*. In his most important work, *Our Father* (which he started writing already while he was working on *Prolegomena*), Cieszkowski outlined the vision of the future all-embracing religion of the Paraclete. At the same time, however, he made Christ the only Messiah, the caesura of history, the prophet both of the Christian epoch and of the post-Christian 'epoch of action' seen as the Kingdom of God on Earth.

Thus, a comparison of *Prolegomena* with the work of Strauss discloses substantial differences between them, which expose, none the less, a significant similarity in the general directions which their revision of Hegelianism had taken. However, when Cieszkowski is compared with Bruno Bauer, the direct continuator of Strauss's thought, both the proportions and the import of their similarities and differences change basically: the underlying incompatibility of their standpoints is brought out.

In contradistinction to Strauss, Bruno Bauer—also a theologian by education—broke with theology completely and

openly waged war against it. He replaced the Christian conception of God and Hegel's idea of the absolute with the concept of
universal self-consciousness whose essence was realized in the
world through the acts of incessant alienation. Such a conception, one which denied any absolute value to all the historically
generated and objectified manifestations of self-consciousness,
implied a certain 'philosophy of action'. Bauer sought to prove
that self-consciousness developed only by perpetually annihilating the reality which it had itself created. The annihilation is
brought about by the instrument of critical judgement, which
eliminates irrational elements from reality thus rendering it a
better expression of the developing universal self-consciousness.

The differences between Cieszkowski's and Bauer's ideas are
partially pronounced in their diametrically opposed interpretation of dialectics. Bauer, followed by other Young Hegelians,
transformed Hegel's dialectic by bringing out the concept of
negation and rejecting the mediation of the moment negated.
Cieszkowski, on the contrary, was much more faithful to Hegel
in this respect, and emphasized the mediation between the
negated and the negating element, cementing them into a unit
of a higher order and preserving the negated moment as an
element subordinated to the higher whole. His was an 'organic'
and not a 'critical' praxis, 'positive' as distinct from 'negative'
and destructive; 'action', as interpreted by him, constituted the
third level of the dialectical triad and was thus not a mere
negation but an organic synthesis, a constructive reconciliation.
The author of *Prolegomena* could never agree to reduce the
historical process to the development of a rational self-consciousness—after all, he struggled to overcome the rationalistic
one-sidedness of the 'epoch of thought'. No wonder that in his
treatise *God and Palingenesis* he opposed Bauer and stigmatized
him as the representative of 'scientific terrorism', who applied
everywhere the 'guillotine of thought'.

Now, let us digress from the main subject to consider other
implications of Cieszkowski's position. Everything in which
Cieszkowski differed from Bauer—his rejection of 'negativism',
his insistence on the organic nature of development, his critique
of rationalism—made his standpoint seemingly congenial with
that of the anti-Hegelian, conservatively romantic philosophical right wing, which found its spokesman in the elder
Schelling. The German context of Cieszkowski's thought, how-

ever, proves insufficient as evidence for his 'rightist' or 'leftist' leanings. The French Fourierists and the Saint-Simonians were equally resolute as opponents of revolutionary negation and unrelenting as critics of rationalism, while, in spite of this, they represented the French intellectual Left. Cieszkowski could endorse without hesitation the Saint-Simonian thesis that 'progress does not consist in destroying and annihilating but in developing and transforming', and that mankind is on the verge of a new 'organic' epoch which will bring about a reconciliation of conservatism with progressivism, tradition with prophecy (cf. A. 88, pp. 154–5, 175, and 293).

The conservative romantics resented Hegel's identification of God with the rational absolute, subject to logical necessity, immanent in history, capable of attaining self-consciousness only through the vehicle of man. The material to be found in Cieszkowski's Diary (part of which was published as an appendix to the second edition of *Our Father*) offers ample proof that the idea of God's close dependence on the historical world of mankind was also present, as in Hegel—though in a different guise—in the system of the Polish thinker. Cieszkowski, considering God to be a self-conscious, personal spirit, repudiated Hegel's conception which claimed that the absolute attained self-consciousness through man. He replaced it, however, with a conception linking God's harmony with that of the harmonious state of the world, thus making God dependent on the world not less than in Hegelianism, although in a different way. 'The world is the flesh of God; God is the soul of the world. In the like manner God's immanence is brought to speculative unity with His transcendence, Pantheism becomes reconciled with Personalism. All the finite things are the organs of God without constituting His essence, just as our members do not constitute us.' God, therefore, feels pain when painful disharmony reigns in the world: 'It gives pain to God and He is sick unto us as we are sick with the heart, the head, etc. It issues therefrom that with God the state of bliss and happiness is also dependent on history and only with the ascension of the harmonious society will absolute harmony be established in God.' Cieszkowski asked, 'Is not this becoming of God's happiness more probable than His becoming self-conscious in human consciousness as Hegel chose to see it?' (A. 8, II. 502–4).

The idea of a close relation between the social system and the general state of the universe and God seems to be one of the fundamental motifs of the Pantheism-tinctured philosophy of Fourier. Cieszkowski's comprehension of history as a process of attaining social happiness, in contradistinction to the attainment of self-consciousness (as it was in Hegel), was characteristically Fourierist. It is noteworthy that already in *Prolegomena* Cieszkowski defined God's ultimate goal as 'happiness in actually realized teleological fulfilment of history'. Such a definition was congenial with the spirit of the French utopians and alien to Hegelianism, which saw the purpose of history in attaining the kingdom of reason, not that of happiness.

The turning of the Hegelian Left from the critique of religion towards the critique of politics with its search for a perfect social system was propitious for the promulgation of the idea of a 'German-French intellectual alliance', attempting to reconcile German 'thought' with French 'sociality'. This change of direction brought about widespread interest in a number of ideas formulated for the first time by Cieszkowski. It is all the more curious that the representatives of the Hegelian Left centred around Arnold Ruge's periodical *Hallische Jahrbücher*, never quoted *Prolegomena*, and apparently (as is evident from a review of *Prolegomena* written by Frauenstädt) did not feel themselves to be ideologically at one with its author.[8] Strange as it seems, this is nevertheless quite comprehensible and lends itself to a full explanation. The sense of estrangement had its roots in an utterly different attitude towards action (Ruge, just like Bauer, conceived action as a revolutionary negation), as well as in the fact that Cieszkowski's works abound in ideas drawn from the social and religious traditions of French thought, alien to the spirit of the Hegelian school. It is true that the radical Young Hegelians set forth the idea of the 'Franco-German intellectual alliance', yet in practice they took up their position within the context of the controversy revolving around Hegel alone, while Cieszkowski's standpoint seems to have been quite isolated, as we have shown above. He was divorced from the Hegelian Left particularly with respect to matters of rationalism and religion: Ruge's periodical promoted consistent rationalism and secularization of consciousness, whereas Cieszkowski, together with the French Fourierists and the Saint-Simonians, criticized rationalism severely, and was a social thinker who perceived in religion 'the highest substantiality' of art, philosophy, and action.

However, there appeared a thinker among the representatives of the broadly conceived Hegelian Left who followed the ideas advanced in *Prolegomena* and considered them to be of crucial importance: Moses Hess. In his treatise entitled *European Triarchy* (composed in the period between 1839 and 1841) he recognized *Prolegomena* to have overcome not only orthodox Hegelianism, but also the Hegelian Left which, to his mind, remained at the stage of negation and was not able to proceed positively from German philosophy to action.

Hess also indicated certain points in which he differed from Cieszkowski. However, neither these differences nor the quotations from his own *Holy History of Mankind*, which can be viewed as an anticipation of some of Cieszkowski's ideas, in any way alter the impression that *Prolegomena* must have exerted a great impact on Hess and helped him to crystallize his own 'philosophy of action'. It is noteworthy that Hess's assessment of *Prolegomena* proves remarkably convergent with Cieszkowski's own evaluation of his work; he understood it as the work which had not only transcended Hegelianism and the Hegelian Left, but which, moreover, had overcome the fetters of German philosophy in general.

Such an assessment was due to the fact that Hess had never been a Left Hegelian in the narrow sense of the term and (just like Cieszkowski) was active on the borderline between different cultures. Already in his early output the close affiliation of his thought with the social and religious ideas of the French utopians is quite evident (for only having taken into consideration their influence on him, and especially that of Saint-Simonianism, can his critical attitude towards the Hegelian Left as a philosophy of pure negation, as well as his solidarity with the author of *Prolegomena* in his 'positive' and 'organic' treatment of action, find a consistent explanation). Although Cieszkowski's inspiration also lost its value to Hess when the latter became an atheist and sided with the radical wing of the Hegelian Left, his article entitled 'The Philosophy of Action' (1843) can nevertheless be understood as an attempt at reinterpreting certain ideas present in *Prolegomena* in the spirit of the materialist philosophy of Feuerbach. The possibility of such a scheme arose from a number of common points discernible in the thought of Feuerbach and Cieszkowski. Following the Fourierists and the Saint-Simonians, both thinkers favoured a rehabilitation of matter, nature and sensuality. Feuerbach's anthropology and

Cieszkowski's 'philosophy of action' were both conceived as a reconciliation of nature with logic, feeling with thought ('the heart' with 'the head'), the real with the ideal. According to both of them the ancient times were the epoch when man had not yet been divorced from nature; they both stressed, each in his own individual fashion, the connection of Hegel's idealism with Christianity; both Cieszkowski's and Feuerbach's re-habilitation of matter was meant to heal the painful dualism which was a characteristic feature, in their opinion, of the life and thought of the Christian epoch. Viewed in their totality, the conceptions of Cieszkowski and Feuerbach proved incompatible, but, nevertheless, there was a certain parallelism between them, which made them capable of supporting and comple-menting one another.

The role fulfilled by Hess in the evolution of German thought from Hegelianism to Marxism was considerable: he compelled the Hegelian Left to reinterpret, partially at least, their 'philo-sophy of action' (comprehended hitherto as a mere critique, and so as a purely intellectual act); moreover, he successfully opposed Ruge's bourgeois radicalism and thus threw a bridge between German philosophy and communist ideas. The ideo-logical relations existing between Cieszkowski and Hess ought by no means to be over-emphasized, but, on the other hand, they must not be ignored. For the historian of ideas they are a corroboration of the thesis that there existed a *possibility* of passing from the programme of the 'philosophy of action', as adumbrated in *Prolegomena*, to the current of philosophical thought which reached its climax in Marx's conception of praxis and the idea of leaping from the 'kingdom of necessity' to the 'kingdom of freedom'.

Additional confirmation of the above thesis can be found in the reception of *Prolegomena* by the Russian philosophical Left, which leant heavily towards Hegelianism.

Nicholas Stankevich, the originator of the philosophical circle which produced such eminent thinkers as, among others, Mikhail Bakunin and Vissarion Belinsky was the first Russian thinker to take an interest in Cieszkowski's 'philosophy of action'. In a letter to Bakunin (of 29 April–7 May 1840)[9] he declared himself in favour of Cieszkowski's idea of transforming philosophy into action, linking this postulate with Feuerbach's rehabilitation of feeling and sensuality. His untimely death prevented him from developing these ideas, yet they must be taken into account as an attempt at bringing together Cieszkowski's and Feuerbach's standpoints and as an anticipation of some conceptions of Herzen.

Although Alexander Herzen became acquainted with *Prolegomena* prior to his serious studies of Hegelianism, he was none the less well prepared to accept Cieszkowski's postulates because of his knowledge of French socialist thought and his capacity for confronting it with German idealism. Cieszkowski's book perfectly harmonized with his 'palingenetic' expectations of a universal regeneration. In a letter to Witberg (of 25–8 July 1839) he wrote:

Since we parted, I have been very busy working, especially in the fields of history and philosophy. Among other tasks I began writing my thesis on the subject: 'What link between the past and the future does our age constitute?' The problem seems significant and I had already done quite a lot, when one day I found out that something of a similar nature had been published in Berlin under the title *Prolegomena zur Historiosophie*. I ordered the book immediately, and, to my great joy, I agree with its author in all the main points to an astonishing degree. It signifies that all my thoughts are right and I am going to work upon them all the more. (A. 28, XXII. 38.)

Apart from informing Witberg about the existence of *Prolegomena*, Herzen made it known to Nicholas Ogarev, who, having found it excellent, circulated the book among the Moscow Hegelians connected with Stankevich's circle. In later years he mentioned the name of the Polish thinker in his article about Granovski's public lectures, the printing of which was unfortunately forbidden by censorship. In this work he attached crucial importance to *Prolegomena* as a step forward in the evolution of Hegelianism, stressing that its underlying ideas had already found universal acceptance (ibid. XXX. ii. 487–8).[10] Detailed analysis reveals Herzen to have adapted Cieszkowski's conceptions and given expression to them explicitly in his philosophical writings.[11] His essay entitled 'Buddhism and Science' (1843) and a series of essays under the collective title 'Letters Concerning the Investigation of Nature' (1845–6) are of particular importance in this context. All the essential ideas contained in *Prolegomena* are to be found therein: the division of history into three eras conceived as the epochs of feeling (natural immediacy), thought (reflection), and action respectively; the recognition of dualism as the essential feature of the second period; the assertion that the third epoch will overcome the dualism and harmonize nature with logic, immediacy with reflection, at the higher level of synthesis; the pattern of the phenomenology of spirit analogous to Cieszkowski's conception; the recognition of Hegelianism as the culmination of the development of philosophy as such and as the termination of the epoch of thought; the charge of contemplativity and predominance of the universal (logic and thought) addressed to Hegel; the main stress placed on will and the postulate of the 'philosophy of action'; the diagnosis of the present as the critical moment in history in which conscious will might control and reign over the spontaneousness of the historical process; and, eventually, the conception of action as the final stage in the development of personality. On the basis of this it can be assumed that *Prolegomena*, having been discovered by Herzen in a propitious moment, made it easier for him to adopt from the very beginning a critical attitude towards Hegelianism and to combine Hegel's philosophy with current motifs of the French Social Romanticism. In 1839 Cieszkowski's treatise helped Herzen to give final shape to his own views; these views were modified after Herzen's deeper studies of Hegelianism, but the central idea of the Polish thinker—the idea of a 'philosophy of action'—was endorsed by the development of the Hegelian Left. In his general philosophical outlook Herzen, of course, dissented from Cieszkowski's thought: in his 'Buddhism and Science' he appears as an atheist, an adherent of Feuerbach and the radical Hegelian Left, interpreting Hegel's dialectics as the 'algebra of revolution'. Nevertheless, his critique and reinterpretation of Hegelianism betrays, just as had been the case with Hess, a mutual influence and interpenetration of motifs inspired simultaneously by Feuerbach's anthropology and Cieszkowski's 'philosophy of action'.

We can now resume consideration of the two opposing interpretations of Cieszkowski's position in the controversy over the heritage of absolute idealism. The present enquiry has led to a rejection of the excessive one-sidedness of both approaches. Cieszkowski's ideas converged in certain important points with the broad movement of thought leading from Hegel to Marx; therefore they cannot be excluded from the progressive evolution of Hegel's school. On the other hand, they were not so much a link in the development of the Hegelian Left, as an attempt to indicate another alternative to orthodox Hegelianism. The author of *Prolegomena* shared with the Hegelian Left the diagnosis of the crisis of absolute idealism, so that essential convergences had to exist in their points of departure. Cieszkowski, however, considered the line adopted by the Hegelian Left to be merely negative and destructive. This, by the way, tallied with the views of the Left-Hegelians, who saw themselves as representatives of a transitional epoch whose only aim was to destroy the old. Cieszkowski, instead, wanted to find a positive, constructive solution to the crisis. Like the French socialists, particularly the Saint-Simonians, he was convinced that mankind was about to enter a new, *organic* epoch of history and that it was necessary to abandon the old revolutionary methods, born in the epoch of crisis.

In his *Gott und Palingenesie*, Cieszkowski himself made an effort to look back at the evolution his own thought had undergone and to allot to *Prolegomena* its due place in the development of post-Hegelian philosophy (A. 7, chapt. 14). This attempt proves quite revealing.

The philosopher drew a parallel between two revolutions: the French revolution against political absolutism and the German intellectual revolution against absolute philosophy. In his view the French revolution was the instrument of a great progressive change whose postponement would amount to a 'blasphemy against the objective dialectics of history'; this change, however, could have been achieved through the application of other, non-revolutionary means. He then proceeded to assess the philosophical revolution on analogous lines. A fundamental progressive transformation of science (i.e. Hegel's 'absolute philosophy') was a historical necessity, but it could have been achieved otherwise, in a non-revolutionary and non-destructive way. This alternative way for the 'translation of philosophy into life' was shown in *Prolegomena zur Historiosophie* but, unfortunately, it was ignored by the young disciples of Hegel. In Cieszkowski's eyes it was proof that Left Hegelianism was only a symptom of general crisis and not a harbinger of the organic epoch of the future.

3. Philosophy of God

In 1840, K. L. Michelet delivered a series of lectures in Berlin on the personality of God and the immortality of the soul. Two years later Cieszkowski criticized his views in the treatise *God and Palingenesis*. According to Michelet this treatise placed his Polish friend on the right wing of the German 'philosophical parliament': Cieszkowski, he wrote, 'joins Schelling, and not only because of the content of this book, like the Right [i.e. the Hegelian Right] but also because of his epistemological principle—the active intuition' (A. 69, pp. 394–5). Cieszkowski himself was fully aware that his treatise gave reasons for such a classification. In the preface to it he wrote: 'I could not deny that seemingly, especially after this critical writing, it is possible to count me among the Right Wing; this does not mean, however, that I want to remain on this standpoint.'

On the extreme Left of German philosophy was the anthropological materialism of Feuerbach; the moderate Right was represented by the orthodox Hegelians; more to the right were the so-called 'speculative theists'—I. H. Fichte ('the younger Fichte'), Ch. H. Weisse, and others; the leading figure of the extreme Right, linked with the feudalistic 'political Romanticism', was the elder Schelling, who in his Berlin lectures on the philosophy of mythology and the philosophy of revelation frontally attacked Hegelian rationalism, essentialism, and panlogism. Michelet's position was classified by Cieszkowski as that of 'Left Centre'. His Polish disciple accused him of absolutizing the Universal—a tendency characteristic of Hegelianism. Michelet wanted to defend the personal immortality of man and the personality of God, but personality as such was for him only an aspect of the Universal, i.e. an aspect of the supra-individual realm of Ideas, while the individualizing factors were conceived by him as belonging to the lower sphere of nature. Cieszkowski set against this a spiritualistic personalism, conceiving spirit as a 'concrete identity of idea and nature, the universal and the individual, soul and flesh'. According to this conception spirit represented the stage of Action ('being from itself'), containing in itself as its 'moments' (dialectical phases) both natural Being ('being in itself') and Universal Thought ('being for itself'). Michelet's distinction between 'individuality' and 'personality' was replaced by him with the trichotomy: *individuality*, representing natural Being, *subjectivity* (Michelet's 'personality'), representing Thought, and *personality*, representing Action, i.e. the self-creating activity of spirit. It followed from this that the immortality of soul is not merely the

immortality of thought; the human soul is immortal as personality; its 'individuality' and 'subjectivity' are mortal—they
can participate in immortality only as transcended phases of
personal spirit.

Cieszkowski saw this position not as a return to traditional
theism, but—on the contrary—as a true overcoming of the
'Christian epoch'. Antiquity, he maintained, was the epoch of
naturalism; its inner development consisted in a spiral movement from the *naturalistic* pantheism (the deification of substance) to the emergence of individuality (i.e. of spirit 'in itself').
The Christian epoch was the epoch of idealism, i.e. the epoch of
a spiral movement from subjectivity (individual spirit 'for itself'), whose theological counterpart was the theistic idea of a
transcendent, personal God, to the *idealist* pantheism, whose
best philosophical expression was Hegelianism. (Thanks to this
reasoning Hegel could be treated as the culmination of the
'Christian epoch'.) In his own conception of God, Cieszkowski
saw a reconciliation between, and a higher synthesis of, ancient
naturalism (or: materialism) and Christian idealism. God conceived as personality ('being from itself') could not be reduced
either to material substance or to pure thought, but had to be
seen as containing both the material and the ideal element
within himself.

In the context of the German philosophical and theological
controversies of the early forties, Cieszkowski's defence of the
personality of God, combined with a criticism of rationalistic
idealism, a 'rehabilitation of matter', and an acknowledgement
of 'the active intuition' as a mainspring of genuine philosophy,
were bound to evoke the ideas of 'speculative theists' and
'theosophical naturalism' of the elder Schelling. In spite of this
Cieszkowski was right in emphasizing that the affinity between
his ideas and the German Philosophical Right was more seeming than real. His conception of spirit as a synthesis of idea and
nature, thought and matter—an idea to be found already in
ancient Gnosticism—seems reminiscent of Schelling's 'nature
in God'; in fact, however, its connection with romantic theosophy was very loose; by contrast, it was closely bound up with
Cieszkowski's historical, political, and economic views. Schelling's conception was meant to explain the mystery of evil and
free will: man is immanent in God because if this were not so his
free will would contradict God's omnipotence; if his will leads to

evil, it can be explained only by referring to 'nature in God'—
something which is inherent in God but non-divine and, therefore, able to produce evil. The Polish thinker introduced nature
into God in order to solve quite different problems. He wanted
to attain a theological 'rehabilitation of matter', to overcome
Christian dualism setting the other-worldly Heaven against the
worthless mundane life. His conception of matter as an inalienable, constitutive part of the spirit was to be a justification
for a religious concern for earthly life, a sanctification of
the needs of the human body, a philosophical argument for a
millenarian 'terrestrialization' of the Kingdom of God. In its
light the ascetic neglect for earthly life, characteristic of historical Christianity, turned out to stem from a very one-sided
knowledge of God; instead, social and economic reforms with
the aim of establishing the Kingdom of God on Earth became a
form of truly religious activity. One can easily see from this that
Cieszkowski's conception should be analysed against the background of the religious ideas of the French socialists. It was
most closely related to the 'new religion' of the Saint-
Simonians—a religion which was to bring about a 'rehabilitation of matter' by 'introducing matter into the essence of God'.

The overcoming of Christian dualism was incompatible with
a purely transcendent conception of God. Consequently,
Cieszkowski did not replace Hegelian pantheism with traditional theism, i.e. with putting God outside the world, but with
panentheism, i.e. with a conception of the *world in God*, in
accordance with St. Paul's words: 'In Deo vivimus, et movemur,
et sumus.' He wrote in his Diary: 'God is everything and
something else in addition. The first part of this definition is
pantheistic and immanentist, the second makes room for the
personality and transcendence of God' (A. 8, II. 502). The
immanentization of God was necessary for the rehabilitation
and sanctification of the *material world*, so much neglected by
Hegel. Thus, for instance, we find in Cieszkowski's Diary
(under the date 18 November 1837) the following comment on
the discovery of new fertilizers:

We are approaching a radical reform of the world, as a result of which Nature
will be regenerated and both the moral and physical consequences of the
original sin will be effaced. The earth will become free from curse and will bear
more fruits instead of thorns. Therefore it must be enriched and the [newly
discovered] fertilizers are a means to this end.

This quotation seems to present an odd and dissonant confusion of heterogeneous dimensions of reality. If Cieszkowski were to have been accused of this he would have answered that such an impression derived from the habit of thinking in dualistic categories, and that the most urgent need of the new epoch was for a radical overcoming of the dualist of 'the profane' and 'the sacred', 'the world' and 'the other world'. He agreed at this point with many French thinkers (the Saint-Simonians, P. Leroux, J. Reynaud), and came to very radical conclusions. The so-called 'other world', he argued, is but a continuation of this world, eternity is a sum total of different epochs in time, the earth is a planet, that is a part of Heaven, because the astronomical heaven is the only Heaven which exists. This Heaven, therefore, is not outside the world, neither is it a separate part of the Universe; it is everywhere, including on earth, and this is precisely the real meaning of the omnipresence of God.

An additional proof of the affinity between Cieszkowski's thought and the religious ideas of the French 'social Romantics' is furnished by his 'palingenetic' conception of immortality which was developed in the second, more esoteric part of *Gott und Palingenesie*.[12]

The immortality of the soul, according to this conception, consists in a progressive palingenesis, i.e. in perfecting oneself through a series of successive incarnations. At the same time, like Hoene-Wroński, Cieszkowski made immortality dependent on merit: he conceded it only to those individuals who had been active enough to raise themselves, by their own merit, to the level of personality and to acquire enough strength to start their life anew. Immortality is to be won by one's own efforts: it will not fall to the lot of those who have not worked and who have achieved nothing. The striving for perfection, however, is not infinite: those who have achieved the highest possible perfection of the human spirit finish their earthly wanderings and join the Choir of the Blessed, participating in the eternal life of the Absolute.

In creating this conception Cieszkowski was inspired, or could have been inspired, by many sources. In Germany the idea of palingenesis was upheld in different variants by such thinkers as Leibniz, Herder, and Lessing: it was an attempt at a new interpretation of the dogma of the immortality of the soul—an interpretation which would overcome the dualism between Heaven and earth and which would lead to a certain 'terrestrialization' of eschatology. It should be stressed, however, that this idea was completely alien to Hegelianism and obviously uncongenial to the German post-Kantian idealism as a whole. In France, on the contrary, it was becoming widely accepted. It is no exaggeration to say that the idea of progressive palingenesis, uniting the idea of progress with the idea of reincarnation, belonged to the leit-motifs of the French 'social Romanticism' of the 1830s and 1840s. Ballanche—a thinker well known to Cieszkowski— has proclaimed that man is 'un être palingenesique', reflecting in himself the palingenetic nature of the universe. Other variants of the idea of progressive reincarnation—all of them referring to the scholarly authority of Charles Bonnet—were developed by Fourier and the Saint-Simonians, Pierre Leroux, Jean Reynand, and the naturalist-philosopher Boucher de Perthes.

As we shall see, the idea of progressive reincarnation was embraced also by the Polish romantic poets and became part and parcel of their religious and national Messianism. Among the Polish 'national philosophers', Cieszkowski was the only one to accept it. This is one of many reasons for seeing his philosophy as a kind of intellectual bridge between the philosophical movement of the 1840s and the messianic doctrines developing among the emigration and having their best exponents in the great prophetic poets of the epoch.

The peculiarity of Cieszkowski's position among the 'national philosophers' of the forties consisted also in his attitude towards the very idea of a 'national philosophy'. To put it briefly, he accepted it with much more caution than Trentowski, Dembowski, or Libelt. In a note in his *God and Palingenesis* he said, or just hinted, that the new philosophy, corresponding to the coming epoch of Action, could be called Slavonic philosophy. In the first volume of *Our Father* he gave a historical-philosophical justification of this claim by developing the conception of the leading role of the Slavonic peoples in the imminent future—without, however, putting stress on the peculiar mission of the Poles. At the same time he never ceased to emphasize that philosophy is universal by its very nature, that it should aim at solving universal, and not merely national, tasks, and that its national character is rather a fact to be recognized than a goal to be achieved by conscious efforts. In an article on the early

Ionian philosophers, published in the *Warsaw Library* (1841, Vol. 1), he argued for the view that the impact of national character is always recognizable in sciences, although the value of any scholarly achievement should be assessed from the point of view of the universal progress of knowledge. Thus, for instance, an analysis of the social and industrial development of France and Britain leads to the conclusion that Quesnay had to be a Frenchman whereas Adam Smith had to be a Britisher; this conclusion, however, is irrelevant for the assessment of the scholarly value of their works. The same is true of philosophy. Plato is a product of ancient Greece, Descartes of seventeenth-century France, and Kant of eighteenth-century Germany. Thus, they are not related to each other by blood, time or place of birth; nevertheless, they are connected by an intellectual tradition and every true philosopher sees in them his ancestors. Therefore, we should ask heroes of knowledge *what* they have produced and not *where*, or of what parents, they were born. If their contributions are valuable and belong to the organic process of universal history we should assimilate them and recognize them as our own legitimate inheritance.

Cieszkowski's philosophy of God is bound up, of course, with his philosophy of revelation, as manifested and developed in history. This philosophy, elaborated in *Our Father*, displays distinctively millenarian and messianic features. It seems proper, therefore, to discuss it in another part of this book, devoted to an analysis of the relation between the philosophical movement of the forties and the national and religious Messianism of the prophetic poets.

IV. Bronislaw Trentowski

1. Biographical Note

Bronislaw Ferdynand Trentowski was born on 21 January 1808 in the village of Opole in Podlasie region (the Congress Kingdom). His father, Leon, was a poor but educated country gentleman and reputedly one of the Polish students of Kant. The family was Catholic, although Trentowski used later to present himself as a Calvinist. As he himself confessed in a private letter, he wanted to be treated as a Protestant for tactical reasons: to have an excuse for his admiration for the historical achievement of the Reformation and to avoid disputes with Catholic theologians.

Having completed his education in Piarist schools, the future philosopher became a student at the University of Warsaw. He studied philosophy under the tutorship of Krystyn Lach Szyrma (a follower of the Scottish philosophy of 'common sense'), and the history of literature under the tutorship of Brodziński. He followed with great interest the literary controversies between Warsaw Classicists and Romanticists; under the influence of the latter he decided (already by then!) to devote his life to creating a Polish 'national philosophy'. Having graduated from the university he continued his studies in Paris, listening to the lectures of Guizot, Villemain, and Cousin. In 1829 he became a teacher in a provincial high school. When the uprising broke out, he immediately came to Warsaw—with a group of his elder pupils—and enlisted in the insurrectionary cavalry. He took part in eleven battles and was promoted to the rank of an officer. After the capitulation he decided not to emigrate to France but to settle in Prussia, in order to continue his philosophical studies. For some time, with forged documents, he studied at the University of Königsberg, but when his identity and his insurrectionary past were disclosed he had to leave Prussia and look for refuge in other German lands. In

1834 he began to study in Heidelberg, under the tutorship of the Protestant theologian and philosopher, K. Daub. In the next year he moved to Freiburg in Baden. He married a German girl, finished his doctoral thesis, and decided to settle in Freiburg for good.

Trentowski's thesis, *Grundlage der Universellen Philosophie* (1837) was rather well received in Germany, especially among the Schellingians: a positive review of it appeared in Oken's journal *Izis*. Oken himself visited Trentowski in Freiburg, and Schelling wrote him a letter. Encouraged by this, Trentowski rapidly completed his 'Habilitationsschrift', *De vita hominis aeterna* (published in Freiburg 1838), brilliantly defended it, and started to lecture—as a 'Privatdozent'—on the philosophy of nature, logics, pedagogics, and speculative theology. Of course, he wanted to have a regular, paid professorship. He thought that his nationality might be an obstacle to this end and came to the conclusion that his achievements would have been even better received if he had not declared in *Grundlage* that his philosophy was a manifestation of the Polish spirit. Therefore he published his new work—*Vorstudien zur Wissenschaft der Natur* (1840)—with an opportunistic preface in which he described himself as being spiritually germanized and deeply attached to his new homeland. These rather tactless words aroused a wave of indignation in Poland, but did not bring about the desired result in Baden. It turned out, by the way, that the decisive negative argument was not Trentowski's nationality but his critical attitude ¨towards Catholicism: liberal professors, supporting Trentowski, proved less influential than the Catholic clergy of Baden, who had their own candidate for the vacant chair of philosophy.[13]

It should be stressed that Trentowski's preface to *Vorstudien* was not only tactless but insincere as well. In fact it was written as a part of an ambitious plan to gain an influential position in German philosophy and then to use this as an argument that the spiritual leadership of mankind should fall now to the lot of the Poles.

In 1840, i.e. two years before the final decision concerning the chair of philosophy in Freiburg had been taken, Trentowski started to write philosophical works in Polish. Soon afterwards he began to receive a regular salary from the organizers of 'organic work' in the Grand Duchy of Poznań—Count Edward

Raczyński and Dr Karol Marcinkowski. This patronage enabled him to achieve a truly impressive level of activity. Within a few years he published in Poznań several works presenting different aspects of his 'national philosophy', such as ' *A System of National Pedagogics* (1842, see A. 97), *The Relation Between Philosophy and Cybernetics, or the Art of Ruling the Nation* (1843, see A. 103), and *The Art of Thought, or a System of National Logic* (1844, see A. 100). In addition he wrote many articles to Poznań journals, and in the years 1844–5 published in Paris his own journal, *The Present and the Future* (*Teraźniejszość i Przyszłość*), filling it with articles which would not pass through Prussian censorship. He even wanted to become a teacher in a Poznań high school, but did not get this job because of the hostile attitude of the clergy. In 1843 he got permission to visit Poznań, but after delivering a public lecture was immediately expelled by the Prussian authorities. The second volume of the new, enlarged and revised edition of his *System of National Pedagogics* was confiscated by Prussian censors. (After a trial in Berlin it was published but in a crippled form, with many pages cut out.) These experiences undermined his confidence in the liberalism of 'enlightened Prussia' and made him sympathize with the underground national-liberation movement.

The Cracow uprising of 1846 and the Galician massacre were for Trentowski a great shock and a turning point in his political views. He became convinced that Polish democrats were irresponsible and Polish peasants immature, and that only nobility and clergy, in spite of all their faults, represented the backbone of the Polish nation. He presented these views in *The Images of the National Soul* (1847, see A. 105), published under a pseudonym in Paris. At the same time he made friends with Zygmunt Krasiński who, soon after the death of Karol Marcinkowski, began to give him regular financial support. Krasiński even became a co-author of Trentowski's next book, *Before the Political Storm* (1848, see A. 102), although he preferred to conceal this fact.

Like Krasiński, Trentowski was afraid of a social revolution, but, unlike his conservative friend, he hoped at the same time that the Springtime of the Peoples would bring about a European war whose results would be advantageous for Poland. The complete failure of these hopes resulted in a nervous breakdown which for a few years prevented him from working. The external conditions for his work also became much worse: the increased vigilance of censorship, the decrease of interest in all-embracing philosophical systems, the unalterable hostility on the part of clerical reactionaries were all more powerful after the revolutionary years—in short, everything conspired to isolate him, leaving him with no possibility of publishing his works and, after the death of Krasiński in 1859, permanently suffering the lack of means of subsistence. His attempt to collaborate with the right wing of the emigration did not succeed because the influential figures in Czartoryski's camp, the editors of *Polish News* (*Wiadomości polskie*), W. Kalinka and J. Klaczko, wanted, as he put it 'to reform him religiously and politically'. His tragic situation was deepened by his dual attitude to Catholicism: he continued to treat the Roman faith as 'a medieval spectre, a cadaver with head cut off' but, at the same time, he clung to the view that the historical plight of Poland had made Catholicism the only mainstay of national life (see A. 99, p. 514).

Trentowski died in Freiburg on 16 June 1869. After his death two of his books, very different from each other, were published. One, *A Pantheon of Human Knowledge* (Poznań 1873–81), was an anachronistic attempt to create a philosophical system of sciences, permeated by an opportunistic, or machiavellian intention to convince its readers of the perfect compatibility of the author's philosophy with Catholicism. The other book, *Die Freimauerei in ihren Wesen und Unwesen* (Leipzig 1873), revealed that Trentowski had lived for almost thirty years and died as an active freemason. Under his leadership the Freiburg masonic lodge 'Zur edlen Aussicht' elaborated a project for radical reform of masonic organization and ritual—a project which turned out to be too liberal to be accepted by the Berlin convention of the Grand Masters of the German Freemasonry. It revealed also that Trentowski's masonic activities stemmed from his violent anticlericalism: he described freemasonry as 'true Christianity' and the legitimate successor of the Roman church which had become the main obstacle to intellectual and social progress.

Trentowski died a half-forgotten thinker because his ideas were completely out of tune with the new, positivistic trends dominating Polish intellectual life. His ideas, however, found some response abroad. Some Slovak thinkers and political leaders (J. M. Hurban, Peter Kellner, and, especially, Pavel

Hecko) saw him as the greatest Slavonic philosopher and wanted their nation to learn from him (cf. B. 137, pp. 153 and 207). Less known is the fact that three chapters from his *System of National Logic* were translated into English and published in the *American Journal of Speculative Philosophy*.[14]

2. Universal and National Philosophy

In contradistinction to Cieszkowski, Trentowski did not see Hegelianism as the highest point of philosophy and did not postulate overcoming philosophy as such. He wanted to reconcile the two elements, one-sidedly developed and (therefore) fighting with each other in contemporary European thought: the Romanic element and the Teutonic, realism (materialism) and idealism, empiricism and speculation. He found a similar tendency in Schelling whom he considered to be a greater philosopher than Hegel and whom he praised for rehabilitating nature and experience (including religious experience). His own philosophy was to be programmatically Polish, *national*, but at the same time universal, many-sided, uniting in a higher synthesis all that was true in the hitherto existing philosophical systems.

This idea was inspired, of course, by the Hegelian conception of dialectical overcoming (*Aufhebung*), that is to say, a development which consists of negation and preservation at the same time. It should be stressed, however, that Hegel's dialectical method was different from Trentowski's and that this difference was rooted in the ontological premises of their philosophies. Hegel represented a consistent idealistic monism, whereas Trentowski strove for a conception of the unity of thought with being which would, first, assume that being is ontologically prior to thought and, secondly, would not liquidate a 'relative difference' between being and thought. There was a personalistic motivation behind this: Trentowski rejected idealistic monism for the sake of human personality, defending it against being absorbed and dissolved in an undifferentiated pantheistic unity. That is why he introduced into his philosophy a certain dualism, acknowledging the difference between being and thought and emphasizing—in accordance with the 'theosophical naturalism' of Jacob Boehme and Schelling—that being (nature) is irreducible to thought. He invented for his method an untranslatable Polish term *różnojednia* by which he meant 'uniting but not dissolving, preserving the difference but making it relative'. Consequently, he attempted such a synthesis of idealism with realism as would preserve the 'relative difference' between being and thought, and not assume their identity. The world of Idealism was to be united and reconciled with the world of Realism in the divine 'third world'—the world of 'I-hood'.[15] In this way—different from Cieszkowski's—Trentowski came to the conclusion that the material element is a necessary, eternal, and inalienable part of the divine Absolute.

The method of 'uniting without dissolving differences' was applied by Trentowski to the theory of knowledge as well. He distinguished three kinds of knowledge: (1) receptive empirical knowledge, deriving from a direct contact of our senses with the external world of things and expressible in the formula: 'sentio, ergo res est, atque res sum'; (2) self-generating speculative knowledge, resulting from our contact with the ideal world and having its formula in Cartesian 'cogito, ergo sum', or 'cogito, ergo mens est, atque mens sum'; and, finally (3) a 'truly philosophical' knowledge, being a differentiated higher unity of empirical with speculative knowledge, summarized in the formula: 'sum noumen, ergo Deus est'. By contrast to the two lower stages of knowledge—the empirical knowledge *a posteriori* and the speculative knowledge *a priori*—it was to be a truly comprehensive, holistic knowledge *a totali*. The highest cognitive faculty of the empirical self is intellect (*Verstand*) which achieved its utmost development in the Enlightenment philosophy of the French; the highest cognitive faculty of the speculative self is the German reason (*Vernunft*). The higher synthesis of empirical and speculative knowledge, being the task of the Polish 'national philosophy', was to be achieved by means of an integral vision of the divine world. In his German works Trentowski called this cognitive faculty *Wahrnehmung* (a term used by Kant, although with a different meaning); in his Polish works he stressed that the potential capacity for such integral knowledge was greatest among the Slavs, particularly among the Poles. He emphasized also that *Wahrnehmung* (like Wroński's 'achrematic reason') had nothing in common with mysticism, because it was not an ecstatic annihilation of the lower cognitive faculties. On the contrary: as a higher organic synthesis of all of them—a synthesis in the sense of 'uniting without dissolving'—it presupposed the fullest autonomous development of each of them.

Without the solid base in empirical and speculative knowledge, the 'transcendental eye for the divine' could easily lead astray; therefore, it was much better to have empirical reason (or even simple common sense) without the capacity for penetrating the divine, than the other way around.

This conception enabled Trentowski to combine flattering his compatriots, by ascribing to them a potential for the highest cognitive capacity, with severe criticism of them, especially of their excessive religiosity. Philosophical truth was for him a *total* truth, that is to say, a system of partial truths dialectically inter-related and hierarchically structured; a system preventing a one-sided, isolated development of partial truths and respective cognitive faculties. It followed therefrom that the 'transcendental eye' of the religiously-minded Poles had the highest cognitive capacity only *in potentia* but not *in actu*; in actual fact it was distorted because not based on science, separated as it was from both empirical intellect and speculative reason. Moreover, Trentowski agreed with Aristotle that the distortion of the best results in the worst, from which he concluded that the distorted, one-sided development of the Polish 'transcendental eye' had brought about the victory of counter-reformation, religious fanaticism, a decline of sciences and culture, and, in consequence, the downfall of the Polish state. This diagnosis led to the conclusion that a thorough intellectual westernization of Poland was a necessary condition for the proper development of the peculiarly Polish philosophical capacity, that it was not possible to transcend French intellect and German reason without having assimilated all their achievements. Thus, Trentowski's attitude towards his nation was that of an educator who encourages and warns at the same time: if the Poles succeed in assimilating all the achievement of European thought they will be able to inaugurate the new great epoch in universal philosophy, but if they fail in learning from the West, they will never overcome their intellectual backwardness, their best qualities will change once more into the worst faults, and the final results for their national life will be as fatal as they had been before.

3. The Idea of God-Manhood in Religion, Pedagogics, and Politics

The central problem around which Trentowski's thought always revolved was the problem of the 'Individual Totality' or the 'I-hood': the absolute 'I-hood' of God and the created, God-like 'I-hood' of man. Therefore, he was concerned first of all with the philosophy of God, the philosophy of man, and the philosophy of religion, conceived as 'the nostalgia of the created I-hood for the Creator' or 'the living bridge between world and God'.

The main assumption of Trentowski's philosophy was the idea of the potential divinity of man and of the immanent presence of God in the world. In his German works he developed the idea of God being united with man by a relationship of mutual interdependence. God, he wrote in *Vorstudien*, creates and maintains man in Heaven in the same way as man creates and maintains God on earth (A. 104, I. 216). Different aspects and phases of God's self-consciousness are expressed in different philosophical systems: philosophy, therefore, is a revelation of God, and the act of philosophical thinking is divine in nature (A. 98, p. 57).

No wonder that the Catholic clergy saw Trentowski's philosophy as a revival of pagan pantheism and as an expression of a sinful pride, blasphemously proclaiming that philosophers are divine beings. In his Polish works, in order to defend himself against such accusations, Trentowski rejected pantheism and emphasized the basic agreement between his philosophy and Christianity. This agreement, as we shall see, was apparent rather than real, but the rejection of pantheism was not merely a tactical move: Trentowski rejected pantheism as a philosophy incompatible with the personality of God and man, preserving at the same time some elements of it, first of all the thesis about the essential homogeneity between God and man. The evolutionary pantheism of Hegel, maintaining that the Absolute develops in time and achieves its self-consciousness in man, was in his eyes a degradation of God and man: God was made in it much too dependent on man, and man, reduced to the role of an instrument, was deprived of his autonomy, becoming a means and not an end. Therefore, in order to save the irreducible value of personality and to defend the autonomous, responsible character of human actions, it was necessary to acknowledge the transcendence of God. On the other hand, Trentowski did not want to give up the pantheistic idea of an intimate bond uniting man with God, of the immanent presence of a divine element in human beings. He found a solution in proclaiming that the 'essential God', i.e. God as personality, exists *beyond* the world, but 'divinity' exists *in* the world, as the divine potential of human I-hood, created as the image of God. Evolutionary pantheism, i.e. the temporalization of the Absolute (cf. B. 103, pp. 320–3) was replaced with a conception of the progressive evolution of the divine element *within* the world, by means of the development of the divine attributes of the human 'I'.

The idea that men are divine *in potentia* but should become divine *in actu* as a result of their historical and individual development was central not only in Trentowski's philosophy of religion but in his historical, political, and pedagogical views as well. The fullest possible development of the divine attributes of man was conceived by him as tantamount to 'God-Manhood' (theanthropy). It followed therefrom, first, that Christ was not 'the essential God' but only the paragon of man who had raised himself to God-Manhood and, secondly, that the incarnation of God was not a unique event, something which had already been accomplished in one, historically existing individual, called Jesus of Nazareth. In Trentowski's conception 'God-Manhood' was the divine calling of all men. The development of personality, i.e. the unfolding of the divine attributes of a young man's I-hood, was conceived by him as the chief task of the educator; the raising of mankind to the heights of a 'society of gods' was seen as the final end of the historical self-education of the human species.

The absolute and the created I-hood, God and man, *existentia creatrix* and *existentia creatrix in existentia creata*, were linked in this conception by religion, inborn in the human soul and inalienable from human nature. Trentowski made a clear-cut distinction between 'religion' and 'revealed faith' (see A. 101). Religion, he argued, is one and eternal, while revealed faiths are manifold and changing; each of them is only a partial manifestation of the eternal religion, born out of and reflecting certain historical conditions, expressed through the mouth of a certain posthumously deified man, called God or the 'messenger of God'. Theologies—in contrast to 'theosophy' in the sense of a free philosophical enquiry into religion—are attempts at a quasi-theoretical dogmatic codification of particular faiths; they are, therefore, absolutizations of relative truths and as such they act as the greatest obstacles to the intellectual and moral emancipation of mankind. Man, who believes in a Holy Writ, is necessarily heteronomous and passive, whereas a truly religious man is autonomous and creative—if it were not so, he would not deserve to be called 'the image of God on Earth'. Revealed faiths are still indispensable for 'non-philosophic crowds', but the need for them is diminishing with the process of emancipation, characteristic of modern times. Philosophers, including theosophists, must sometimes make concessions to theology because mankind, as yet, is not mature enough. Nevertheless, sooner or later they will be victorious, the true eternal religion will triumph, and the revealed faiths, together with their theologies, will completely disappear.

In contradistinction to theology, theosophy, i.e. the philosophy of religion, has for its task an investigation of the historical evolution of different forms of religious consciousness and of the inner structure of each of them. Of course, it should be free from commitment to any positive religion. Modernizing the terminology, one can say, therefore, that Trentowski conceived of theosophy as a scholarly study of religions by means of historical and morphological (typological) methods.

A characteristic feature of Trentowski's view of the historical evolution of religious consciousness was the idealization of the religious beliefs on the ancient Slavs. As we know, an idealization of 'pre-Christian Slavdom' was very typical of the Slavophiles like Zorian-Dołęga Chodakowski and of the democrats like Lelewel, Dembowski, or the ideologists of the Polish Democratic Society. Trentowski was neither a Slavophile nor a democrat but, nevertheless, his views on the role of Catholicism in Polish history were strikingly similar to those of the most extreme Slavophile (Chodakowski) and democratic critics of Christianity (see A. 101, pp. 225–58). He accepted Mickiewicz's view that the ancient Slavs had known no revelation, but drew from this different conclusions. The religion of ancient Slavdom, he thought, was purely ethical, devoid of mysticism, non-institutionalized and, therefore, free from the theocratic yoke, respecting the freedom of conscience, and capable of keeping pace with historical progress. The conversion of the ancient Poles to Roman Christianity was seen from this viewpoint as a disaster: it brought about a split within the nation, dividing it into the latinized nobility and the common people who preserved in Christian form the essential content of their old pagan faith; it replaced rational ethics with a mystical belief in miracles and irrational dogmas; and finally, the Catholic counter-Reformation succeeded in subordinating Polish national interests to the interests of the Church, which resulted in the decline and downfall of Poland.

Trentowski expressed these views in his unpublished or post-humously published works—first of all in his huge, unfinished manuscript on theosophy (*Bożyca*),[16] on which he worked in the years 1844–52, and in *Die Freimauerei in ihrem Wesen und Unwesen.* In spite of this the anticlerical tendency of his thought could not escape the attention of his contemporaries. His declarations as to the alleged agreement between his philosophy and Catholicism could not convince the clergy because he made, at the same time, a sharp distinction between 'true Catholicism' (reduced to 'true theism') and 'papism'. He did not try to conceal his view that excessive devotion to 'papism' was the main reason for all the national disasters in Polish history. He made explicit his sympathies for the Reformation, seeing in it the beginning of modern times, the spiritual source of German philosophy, and the last form of institutionalized Christianity which was compatible with historical progress. He did not hesitate even to declare (in his *System of National Pedagogics*) that it would have been much better if the ancient Poles had become converted to Eastern Christianity, thus avoiding the fatal dependence on the policies of Rome.

The practical applications of Trentowski's philosophy of the 'I-hood' were shown in his *System of National Pedagogics*. As an example of a philosophical approach to pedagogics it is a truly unique work: an all-round system of a philosophy of man applied to the solution of different educational tasks. It is divided into three main parts, corresponding to the philosophical division into object, subject, and the identity of subjectivity and objectivity. The first part was a theory of educated human beings, i.e. a theory of I-hood as an object of education; the second part, which included a philosophical characterization and classification of sciences, was a theory of the educator (the active subject of the educational process); the third part, devoted to educational institutions (as forms of the unity of subjectivity and objectivity in pedagogics), contained a universal history of schools and of pedagogical doctrines, set against the background of a philosophy of historical development in which mankind evolves from childhood to maturity. The aim of pedagogics was defined as to lead young men towards maturity through awakening and developing their divine I-hood.

This formula was a summarized expression of many pedagogical and philosophical ideas. Let us mention briefly some of them.

A mature man is not an egoistic, naïve individualist; he is a personality, that is to say, he is able to recognize the divine element in other men, to acknowledge that they should be treated as ends, and not just as means, and that all persons are essentially identical in their divine substance. A prototype and the highest ideal of personality is Christ—the loftiest embodiment of 'God-manhood'.

A necessary condition of maturity is the achievement of intellectual and moral autonomy. The individual development of man should strive, therefore, for the same aim as the historical development of mankind—for emancipation from all heteronomous, unreflectively accepted norms and laws. At this point, Trentowski fully accepted Kant's definition of the Enlightenment as 'man's release from his self-incurred tutelage'.

Another precondition of maturity is universalism in the sense of many-sidedness, that is to say, equal development of all the organs and faculties of the self: body and mind, empirical intellect and speculative reason, feeling and cognitive capacity, and so forth. A one-sided development of any faculty, i.e. a development at the cost of other faculties, transforms a potential virtue into a dangerous fault and makes impossible the development of the self into a harmonious, integral personality. Each phase of the historical evolution of mankind has had for its task, heretofore, the development of a particular faculty, i.e. of a particular dialectic 'moment', of the human 'I'; at present mankind has finally entered the phase of maturity in which a many-sided, all-round development becomes possible. True universalism, however, is not possible without passing through all the phases of the historical education of humanity; therefore, the all-round development of an individual must be a recapitulation of universal history. The ideals of the successive historical epochs are norms for the education of children and young men of respective age; in other words, before entering the phase of maturity, a child and, later, a young man or woman has to pass through a series of successive stages, becoming in turn a Chinese, an Indian, a Jew, an ancient Greek, and so forth.

The highest aim of education was seen by Trentowski to be the awakening and development of the capacity for creative activity, this being the most divine attribute of man. A mature person, he argued, should resemble God in being able 'to create his own world'.

As we can see from the above, Trentowski's pedagogical ideals were *par excellence* universalist, justified by reference to the potential divinity of each man and to the general direction of universal progress. Nevertheless Trentowski emphasized the *national* character of his pedagogical system. Many of his contemporaries, especially the Catholic traditionalists, saw this as a contradiction in terms. Universalism and the emancipation of the individual, they argued, are typical of cosmopolitanism, denying the value of national traditions and of the distinctive features of national character. Their arguments seemed to be quite convincing, since Trentowski himself explicitly condemned *national education*. Cultivating national exclusiveness, he maintained, has been a pedagogical ideal of the ancient epoch, especially of the Jews; reviving this ideal would be incompatible with the whole further development of history (A. 97, II. 875–6). Nations are means, and not ends in themselves; national particularism should be transcended for the sake of the free, many-sided development of human personality.

In actual fact, however, there was no contradiction in Trentowski's attitude towards nationality. First, like other Polish thinkers of the Romantic Epoch, he combined nationalism with universalism. Nationality was for him not a given *fact* to be accepted and preserved but a *task* to be realized in order to further universal progress. He was convinced that his pedagogical ideals were in complete agreement with the true mission of the Poles, and of the Slavs in general, but in his justification of this conviction there was no place for national megalomania. He attributed to the Slavs, and especially to the Poles, the 'eagerness for deed', that is a capacity which—if properly developed—would perfectly harmonize with the ultimate task of the historical education of mankind. At the same time he severely criticized the Polish 'deeds' as devoid of reasonableness and persistence, guided by the one-sidedly developed 'oriental' imagination, i.e. by a faculty good for poetry but not for politics. The 'eagerness for deed' should result from the development of the 'creative I-hood' whose necessary precondition is the full and harmonious development of all other faculties of the I. The peculiar capacity for action, which Trentowski ascribed to his compatriots, was therefore a *conditional* virtue: it could make the Poles peculiarly capable of creativity, this being the highest manifestation of 'God-manhood', but only on condition that they have succeeded in learning from the other nations and have assimilated all the genuine values elaborated in the universal history (A. 97, II. 627).

Secondly, Trentowski made a distinction between 'national pedagogics' and 'national education'. 'National pedagogics' is a theory and an art of educating, or re-educating, one's own nation by raising it to the level of maturity, whereas 'national education' is simply education in the spirit of national exclusiveness, characteristic of the tribal childhood of the human race. For 'national pedagogics' the nation, such as it is, is not a collective teacher; it is an *object* of education, a collective pupil, whose individuality and special needs should be taken into account in the educating process. Since each national characteristic can easily degenerate into a national fault, the criticism of such faults, as manifested in national history—and not flattering one's own nation—is one of the main tasks of a 'national pedagogue'.

Another way for the 'translation of philosophy into action' was expressed in Trentowski's political philosophy. Its main principles are put forward in his *Relation Between Philosophy and Cybernetics, or the Art of Ruling the Nation*. This relatively short book (in contrast to the voluminous *National Logic*) belongs, certainly, among his best works. It should be mentioned that his excessive passion for creating neologisms achieved in this work its greatest success: it was the first book in which the word 'cybernetics' had ever been used.[17]

In his 'political philosophy' Trentowski wanted to unite—using the method of 'uniting without dissolving'—the two extreme political standpoints: 'historicism' (i.e. conservatism) and radicalism. His characterization of the struggle between historicism and radicalism was similar to Wroński's conception of the 'social antinomy'. 'Historicism' believes in a revealed, positive religion and in a personal, transcendent God; radicalism leads to the deification of the human species (Feuerbach) and, in consequence, to the deification of the individual (it is worth while to point out that Trentowski came to this conclusion before Stirner's book *Der Einzige und sein Eigentum*, 1845). 'Political philosophy' was conceived as a mediation between the two extremes: on the one hand it acknowledged the transcendence of God but, on the other hand, it ascribed the divine attributes to man.

'Historicism' defends 'historical law' (cf. Savigny and historical school of jurisprudence), condemning 'national' legislation as a violation of organic growth; radicalism represents the revolutionary 'negation' rejecting 'historicity' in the name of autonomous reason. 'Political philosophy' mediates between the two: on the one hand it defends the autonomy of man but, on the other hand, it sees the advantages of historical continuity and the dangers of revolutions. Therefore it opposes both conservatism and revolutionism, setting against them a conception of gradual, progressive reforms.

The political ideal of 'historicism' is a religiously sanctioned absolute monarchy; the ideal of radicalism is a republic based upon the fullest sovereignty of the people. As an ideal, republicanism is incomparably better than political absolutism but, unfortunately, people are still not enlightened enough, not mature enough, to live in republican freedom. Therefore, 'political philosophy' set forth the ideal of a constitutional monarchy, combining strong executive power of the king with republican freedoms.

'Political philosophy', in Trentowski's conception, was a *political theory*; as such, it was to be distinguished from the *political art* called 'cybernetics', i.e. 'the art of steering'. In contradistinction to political theory, 'cybernetics' is derived not from general philosophical principles but from political experience; it pays attention to tactical considerations, shows that everything is relative, dependent on time and place, that even the best philosophical principles cannot be applied in the same way in different conditions. Modernizing terminology we may say that Trentowski's 'cybernetics' was a kind of political 'sociotechnics' or political 'praxeology'. It was not a political doctrine but it was an early attempt at creating a theory of effective political action.

Trentowski's political position can be classified as liberalism (he himself applied this term to his political views in some of his articles), opposing radical democracy but even more hostile to feudal reaction. In philosophy, especially in his early German works, he was influenced by Schellingianism, but it should be remembered that he always resolutely rejected conservative Romanticism, characteristic of the Schellingian school, and that he agreed with young Engels in his assessment of the elder Schelling's 'philosophy of the revelation'.[18] He despised the philosophy of the Enlightenment but, on the other hand, he fully shared the men of the Enlightenment's anticlerical feelings and their commitment to the ideal of the intellectual and moral autonomy of man. His idea of 'God-manhood' was a combination of some elements of Schellingian theosophy with Kant's idea of *Aufklärung* and, even, with some aspects of Feuerbach's anthropology, claiming that men are divine beings.

4. Lessons From National History

An important part of Trentowski's political views was, of course, his programme for Poland. In the manuscript of his *Relation Between Philosophy and Cybernetics* there was a special chapter showing the application of his general political principles to the situation of a subjugated nation. However, as might be expected, this chapter could not pass through Prussian censorship; it was published later, in a modified and enlarged form, in Trentowski's *émigré* journal *The Present and the Future*, under the title 'On the Liberation of the Fatherland'. It was a political programme derived from a critical reflection on Polish history.

The first and most comprehensive outline of Trentowski's views on Polish history is to be found in his *System of National Pedagogics*. It is a synthesis of Polish history written from the standpoint of an anticlerical Enlightener. The main cause of the downfall of Poland, argued Trentowski, were the Jesuits who had dominated the Polish schools, bringing about the decline of enlightenment, and who had succeeded in subordinating Polish national interests to the narrowly conceived interests of Rome. In the sixteenth century there were chances for the victory of the Reformation in Poland or for creating a Polish national church. After the final victory of the counter-Reformation, Poland had to pass through a century of 'complete barbarism' (1650–1750) in which Poles became similar to Tartars and Turks, having earned, at the same time, a well-deserved reputation of being the most obscurantist Catholic fanatics of Europe. The middle of the eighteenth century witnessed the beginning of the process of the inner regeneration of Poland. It was started by

Stanislaw Konarski, the first important thinker of the Polish Enlightenment, whose role, although he was not a man of genius, could be compared to that of Francis Bacon, Descartes, and Thomasius in the West. The next great step forward was made by the Commission of National Education, created after the liquidation of the Jesuit Order: its reforms, however, were 'inspired by the French spirit', although it would have been much better if they had followed the example of the educational systems of the enlightened, protestant lands of Germany. The work of the Educational Commission was continued in the Congress Kingdom.

Much more severe was Trentowski's assessment of Polish political efforts tending towards the defence, or the recovery, of national independence. The Confederation of Bar, extolled by Mickiewicz and Słowacki, was for him an extreme expression of the conservative 'sarmatian' spirit, that is to say, of the Polish 'barbarianism', Catholic and Asiatic at the same time. The Constitution of 3 May 1791 and the insurrectionary Diet of 1831 were accused of leaving unsolved the peasant question. The defeat of the November uprising was a great lesson for the Polish gentry: they understood at last that it was necessary to subordinate their class egoism to the national cause. Only after this lesson did the Polish national-liberation movement become inseparable from the movement for progressive social reforms.

The general conclusion was formulated in a phrase which later became a motto of Trentowski's *The Present and the Future*: 'The new Poland will have to regenerate herself *in every* sphere.' The partitioning powers understood that her regeneration depended first of all on enlightenment, and, therefore, started to put out, one after another, the 'Polish lights'—the Society of the Friends of Learning, the University of Warsaw, the University of Wilno. The Polish patriots should counteract this by intense learning which would transform Poland into 'the Attica of Slavdom' (A. 97, II. 654).

All these ideas are to be found expressed even more forcibly in Trentowski's treatise, 'On the Liberation of the Fatherland' (see A. 106, pp. 256–72). It has placed its author among the most merciless and bitter critics of the Polish past. The downfall of Poland is explained in it as the rightful verdict of history, as a punishment for the stupid autarchy and class egoism of the Polish gentry, for its religious fanaticism, for the social and religious oppression of the Ukrainains as well as for the enslavement of the Polish peasants. For the national tragedy of the Poles nobody is to blame except themselves: they can recover their independence if they become wise, wiser than their oppressors.

The stupidity of the ancient Poles consisted, first of all, in their blind obedience to the popes. Giving vent to his anti-clerical feelings, Trentowski proclaimed the popes to be Anti-Christs, striving for the same aim as the Russian tsars—for the 'asiatization' of Europe. The cult of the pope is the same as the cult of the Dalai Lama; no wonder, therefore, that the Poles, having identified Catholicism with 'papism', turned their backs upon Europe and became susceptible to influences from the Orient. The ancient Polish commonwealth could exist only as a tolerant, multi-confessional state. The Jesuits had succeeded in persuading the Polish nobility that the defence of Roman Catholicism was their sacred universal mission—in fact, how-ever, it was a narrow religious particularism, because no posi-tive religion can legitimately identify its cause with the cause of universal progress. In order to be restored as a state, Poland has to prove that her independence is necessary for mankind; there-fore, she has to find for herself a new, truly universal mission. It is evident that her mission should consist in converting the Slavs, including the Russians, to the spirit of modern European civilization. This calling, however, cannot be realized without complete emancipation from the fatal influences of Rome.

As we can see from the above, all these views had nothing in common with the romantic idealization of the Polish past, both in the Lelewist and in the messianic versions. Trentowski resolutely rejected Lelewel's positive view of ancient Polish freedom; he was horrified by Mickiewicz's defence of free elec-tions and *liberum veto*. The constitution of the ancient Polish Commonwealth was in his eyes 'the worst, the most anarchic, and the most ridiculous in the world' (A. 97, II. 643). Pro-grammatic occidentalism, stigmatizing the weakness of royal power and the underdevelopment of the bourgeoisie in Poland, made his views similar to those of Karol Hoffman, the leading historian in Czartoryski's camp. On the other hand, he differed from the majority of Czartoryski's followers in his attitude to the Roman church; on that score his critical reflection on Polish history reflected the views of the most extreme democratic critics of Catholicism.

The anti-romantic character of Trentowski's views on the

past ran parallel with his conscious opposition to Romanticism in politics. In his *System of National Pedagogics* he advocated the 'realistic' attitude to life in general and to politics in particular, setting it against the two forms of romantic escape from reality— nostalgia for the past and dreams about the ideal future. In this respect, in spite of differences in their philosophical views, he came very close to the criticism of Romanticism in the works of Hegel.

In the Polish political context, especially important was Trentowski's criticism of the romantic cult of heroism. A mature man, he claimed, avoids both one-sided realism and one-sided idealism; he knows that noble-mindedness without realistic calculation of profits is just as bad as striving for profit without noble-mindedness. The Poles have always been enthusiastic about noble-minded, heroic deeds, but they are not aware enough of the dangers of unreasonable heroism. Therefore, the educators of Polish youth should do everything to restrain the patriotic enthusiasm of their pupils; they should teach them that an eagerness for heroic action should be controlled by reason, that everything in politics should be well calculated and well prepared, that irresponsible manifestations of patriotism, paying no attention to objective conditions and to the will of the majority of the people, are in fact a modern continuation of the anarchic spirit of *liberum veto*. A young candidate wishing to become a conspirator should always remember the maxim: 'Do for your country everything you can, but do not sacrifice yourself without need and result. If you can, kill the dangerous reptile, but don't provoke him; kill him if you have power to do that, but be quiet if you are weak and wish to preserve your own life' (A. 97, II. 575).

In his concrete political programme for Poland, Trentowski supported the liberals, i.e the party choosing the middle way between 'historicism' and radicalism. He emphasized, however, that in a subjugated country the general aims of liberalism should be subordinated to national aims. Under Polish conditions the most important task was to preserve the unity of the partitioned country and to co-ordinate the efforts aiming for its social, economic, and cultural regeneration. In order to succeed in doing this it was necessary to call into being an invisible, informally constituted 'moral government of the nation'. Such a government should be composed of the patriots who had distinguished themselves by their material wealth (being able to provide material means for patriotic activities), by their power of thought (in this category the leading role would be played by philosophers), or by their capacity for organized action. The scope of their activities should comprise the enfranchisement of the peasants, the development of industry, the defence and increase of Polish possessions in industries and agriculture, the promotion of learning and education. The organizational forms of these manifold activities should be different kinds of associations—scholarly, literary, educational, industrial, agricultural, and so forth. Different points of view should supplement each other, but the emergence of different political parties should be avoided: a struggle between political parties can be very useful for a strong and independent nation, but in a subjugated and partitioned country it would lead to waste of energy and to inner conflicts, hiding from sight the common patriotic ends.

In the history of Polish political thought the idea of a 'moral government' has become associated with the name of Jozef Szujski—a leading figure in the so-called 'Cracow School of Historiography' which emerged after the defeat of the uprising of 1863 and became famous for its criticism of Polish 'political Romanticism'. Szujski himself did not realize that the priority in setting forth this idea belonged in fact to Trentowski. In the same way the idea of organized 'organic work' has become associated with the 'Warsaw positivism' of the 1870s, whereas in fact it was set forth and implemented much earlier, already in the Congress Kingdom of 1815–30. It flourished also in the 'Romantic Epoch', especially in the 1840s; Trentowski (along with Cieszkowski and Libelt) was among its most prominent theoreticians. There was, however, an important difference between Trentowski's political programme and the later ideologies of 'organic work'. In the case of the Cracow conservatives (represented by Szujski) and of the Warsaw liberal positivists the idea of 'organic work' meant the abandonment of the idea of national independence, whereas in Trentowski's case it was conceived as a means for the recovery of independent statehood. Trentowski was a severe critic of 'political Romanticism', but he was never against national insurrection as such. On the contrary: he thought that the inner regeneration of the Polish nation through the activities directed by its 'moral government' would create conditions for a well-prepared, realistically calculated, and successful national uprising.

A few words should be added concerning Trentowski's attitude to Romanticism. He was a critic of 'political Romanticism' and a resolute opponent of romantic mysticism and Messianism; he was critical even of romantic poetry, seeing in it (like Śniadecki!) a dangerous eruption of uncontrolled emotions and unbridled, irresponsible imagination. Nevertheless, he shared the romantic view that the essence of a nation is not its language and ethnic features but its peculiar mission in the universal progress of mankind. He shared also the romantic conception of the relationship between God and the world. If Romanticism in philosophy consists (as Paul Tillich has put it) in the thesis that the infinite is present in the finite and the finite is able to penetrate the infinite (B. 165, pp. 372–5), Trentowski's philosophy of the 'I-hood' is certainly yet another variant of philosophical Romanticism.

V. Karol Libelt

1. Biographical Note

Cieszkowski and Trentowski published their first works at the same time and felt themselves neither indebted to nor particularly close to each other. Different was the case of Karol Libelt, who consciously followed their steps and presented their conceptions as different stages in the development of one powerful philosophical current which he called 'the Slavonic philosophy'.

In contrast to other 'national philosophers', Libelt was of plebeian origin. He was born in Poznań (8 April 1807), the son of a shoemaker. As a high-school boy he became a tutor in the home of an influential Polish politician of Poznania, Pantaleon Szuman. Thanks to Szuman's support, after completing his high-school education he received a stipend for university studies in Berlin. He studied mathematics, natural science, and philosophy. In his second year he was awarded a golden medal for his seminar paper on Spinoza and became one of the favourite pupils of Hegel. In 1830 he defended his doctoral thesis (*De pantheismo in philosophia*, Berlin 1830) and went to France to continue his studies in Paris. However, it was not his lot to stay there long. When the November uprising broke out he immediately returned to Poland, joined a regiment of artillery, and served in it until the end of the war. For his bravery he was awarded a silver cross of Virtuti Militari; for his skill he was promoted to the rank of a non-commissioned officer.

After the defeat of the uprising Libelt came back to Poznań and worked for some time as a teacher of mathematics in a German high school. There he gained a very good reputation but in spite of this, when his participation in the uprising was disclosed, the Prussian authorities deprived him of his right to teach. He had no other choice than to settle in the country on the estate of his wife (who was the niece of Pantaleon Szuman).

The situation changed after the enthronement of Friedrich Wilhelm IV. In May 1840 Libelt returned to Poznań and soon became one of the leading figures in what was to be called the 'golden age' of Polish culture in Poznania. He was active both in underground conspiratorial work, as a representative of the Polish Democratic Society, and in the legal 'organic work', in which he closely collaborated with Dr Karol Marcinkowski. Already in 1839 he took the lead in the conspiratorial committee which was to prepare an uprising in the Prussian part of Poland; a few years later, under the influence of General Ludwik Mierosławski, this initial conspiracy was transformed into preparation for an all-nation insurrection in the three parts of partitioned Poland. In 1841 he organized a series of public lectures in Poznań which were to be a substitute for a Polish university; he himself inaugurated it, lecturing on German literature (lectures on Polish literature were not allowed by the authorities). In the same year he was active in founding the Society For Help in Learning—an association giving scholarly stipends to talented young men from poor families. He was also a very active publicist, whose articles appeared not only in the Poznań press but also in the *Warsaw Library* and in Dembowski's *Scientific Review*. From 1843 he edited (together with the historian, J. Moraczewski) the journal *Year*. In 1845 he published the first volume of his collected philosophical writings, entitled *The Vital Question of Philosophy. On the Autocracy of Reason* (in the second edition of this book its title was changed to: *The Autocracy of Reason and the Manifestations of Slavonic Philosophy*).

On 14 February 1846—almost on the eve of the planned uprising—Libelt was arrested by the Prussian police, together with more than seventy other conspirators. Nevertheless, the uprising broke out in Cracow. The Provisional National Government in Cracow started its activities with the publication of a revolutionary manifesto written in accordance with Libelt's project.

Having spent more than a year in different Prussian prisons Libelt was transferred to the fortress of Moabit and, finally, went on trial in Berlin. His brave and dignified behaviour during the trial greatly impressed both his German judges and the other arrested Poles. He was sentenced to imprisonment for 20 years. Soon afterwards, however—on 20 March 1848—revolutionary events in Berlin forced the Prussian king to proclaim political amnesty. Libelt and Mierosławski were liberated in the atmosphere of pro-Polish revolutionary enthusiasm. Revolutionary crowds put them into a coach and dragged this coach from Moabit to the royal residence; the king had to show himself on a balcony, pay homage to the Poles, and promise to grant a constitution. After that Mierosławski and Libelt rose to speak, invoking the revolutionary brotherhood of nations and exhorting the Germans to declare a revolutionary war on Russia.

On the next day Libelt resumed his political activities. In the beginning he defended Polish interests in Berlin, but after a few days he returned to Poznań and became the leader of the Left-wing of the Polish National Committee. He collaborated with the royal commission which was to prepare a 'reorganization' of the Grand Duchy, at the same time he was a member of an underground Provisional Government which was to bring about and to lead a national uprising, in the case of lack of success in negotiations with Berlin. The situation was becoming more and more tense. Under the pretext of the imminent common war with Russia, a Polish volunteer army, composed mainly of peasants armed with scythes, was being organized, the National Committee tried to establish a Polish administration in the province, the German and Jewish population assumed a hostile attitude to the Poles, and inevitable clashes occurred. On 11 April, under the pressure of the Prussian army, Libelt signed the so-called Jaroslawiec Convention which he saw as a necessary compromise but which soon turned out to be a *de facto* capitulation. It was, as he himself put it, the darkest day in his life, since he had to witness and to resist a violent protest of patriotic scythemen. Soon afterwards he realized that the Prussians would not implement the concessions they had made to the Poles and came to the conclusion that the scythemen were right. The struggle went on: Mierosławski defeated the Prussian troops in two engagements but a firm leadership no longer existed. The National Committee dissolved itself and, at the beginning of May, the Prussians regained full control in Poznania.

When the struggles were over, Libelt tried to defend the Polish cause in the all-German Vorparlament in Frankfurt. In June 1848 he participated in the Slav Congress in Prague; he emerged there—along with Bakunin—as an acknowledged leader of the Left-wing of the Congress, rejecting the narrow, anti-revolutionary programme of Austroslavism. In October he was elected to the Frankfurt Parliament, delivered in it a speech in defence of the autonomous state of Poznania and, in view of the rejection of his proposals, ostentatiously gave up his mandate. Having returned to Poznań he took part in the activities of Cieszkowski's Polish League. In Spring 1849, he founded (together with the radical poet, Ryszard Berwiński) a newspaper—the *Polish Daily*, devoted 'to the national cause on the principles of freedom, equality, and brotherhood'. In the meantime he prepared for print further volumes of his philosophical writings: the first volume of his *Aesthetics* (1849; the second volume of this unfinished work was published in Petersburg 1854) and the two volumes of his *System of the Philosophy of Imagination* (1849–50).

In 1850, after the liquidation of the Polish League and of the *Polish Daily*, he had to withdraw, once again, to the apolitical life of a country gentleman. In 1859 he was elected to the Prussian Diet and for several years performed the function of president of the Circle of Polish Deputies in Berlin. Like Cieszkowski, he also played a leading role in the Poznań Society of the Friends of Learning. In the uprising of 1863 he lost his beloved son.

At the end of his life, in the positivistic atmosphere of the 1870s, Libelt's philosophy was felt too anachronistic, but he himself was revered as an exemplary patriot and a living bridge between 'revolutionary deed' and 'organic work'. He died on 9 June 1875.

2. The Idea of Nation and the Conception of National Philosophy

The leit-motif of Libelt's life and ideology was the idea of nation inseparably bound up with the idea of democracy. He was not a socialist; democracy meant for him *political* democracy and the liquidation of the remnants of feudalism in the relations between peasant and landlord. He sympathized, however, with socialist criticism of capitalism and—in contrast to the liberals, like Trentowski, or the ideologists of Czartoryski's camp—was convinced that 'the middle class will not save our fatherland; instead, it will engender plutocracy' (A. 51, p. 110). The roots and the basic force of the nation were seen by him in the 'common people', by which he meant, first of all, the peasantry;

the 'flower of the nation' he saw in its intelligentsia, which, in his view, had nothing in common with the middle class. In fact, despite the widespread opinion that the word 'intelligentsia' was coined in Russia in the 1870s, he used this term already in 1844, in his excellent treatise *On the Love of the Fatherland*.[19]

The word 'intelligentsia' was used also by other Polish thinkers of the 1840s. I mention this fact because of its relevance to discussion on the nature of the Polish national-liberation movement between the November uprising and the Springtime of the Peoples. Its leading force was certainly the gentry (with major exceptions like Libelt), but not the gentry as an estate; Polish democrats of the epoch were a 'penitent gentry', that is to say, they represented the *intelligentsia* of gentry origin, and not the gentry as such. Historical experience proves that the phenomenon of 'intelligentsia', i.e. of an intellectual élite alienated from the ruling class and painfully aware of its in-alienable responsibility for the freedom and progress of 'the people', emerges as a rule in backward agrarian countries, having difficult problems to solve and devoid of a social class whose prestige and whose very interests would make it the natural leader of society; in countries which, although eco-nomically backward, are not stagnant, face the problems of modernization, and want to learn from the accumulated ex-perience of more developed nations (thus, setting their hopes on the ability of the educated strata to assess this experience and to draw proper conclusions). It is understandable, therefore, that intelligentsia in the 'Russian' sense of this term should have appeared first in Poland—the biggest agrarian country in East-Central Europe, between Germany and Russia.

It should not be forgotten, of course, that in Poland, in contrast to Russia, the national problem was of paramount importance. As to the specific features of Libelt's democratism, they are explainable by the fact that he was a *moderate* democrat and represented the relatively most prosperous province of Poland, where serfdom had already been abolished; hence, his readiness to commit himself to 'organic work', so different from the uncompromising revolutionism of Dembowski.

Libelt's treatise *On the Love of the Fatherland* provides a good introduction to his understanding of national problems. Making use of the dialectical method he distinguished in it nine aspects of the idea of Fatherland, dividing them into three groups:

material aspects, spiritual aspects, and 'vital' aspects. In the first group he included the possession of the land by peasants, the abolishment of feudal estates and laws, and political freedom; the second group contained 'nationality', i.e. the customs and folkways of the people, preserved in their purest form by the peasantry, language, and literature; the third category embraced national statehood, religion, and finally, the national mission being realized in history. The kind of national mission depended on the national character, but its aim must be universal, harmonizing with the general striving for progress, freedom, and enlightenment. National mission legitimizes national being; it is 'the highest national thought' and 'the most perfect image of the Fatherland'.

It seems evident from the above that Libelt can be classified as a democratic, humanitarian nationalist of a Mazzinian type. However, two specific features of his ideology should be mentioned. First, he did not share Mazzini's anti-individualistic bias; following Trentowski, he specially emphasized that, strictly speaking, the expression 'national spirit' is 'not philosophical' because a nation is not a supra-individual whole, having a spirit different from the spirit of the individuals belonging to it (A. 50, III. 204–5); a nation is in fact a free union of individuals who share some common characteristics and realize the same historical mission. Secondly, he belonged to those Polish democrats (in the 1840s especially numerous in Poznania) who saw the Poles as a part and parcel of Slavdom and who were greatly interested in the national awakening of the smaller, Western and Southern Slavonic peoples.

Like Trentowski, whom he treated as the greatest Polish philosopher, Libelt deeply committed himself to creating a programmatically 'national' philosophy, to be at the same time a 'Slavonic philosophy'. Nevertheless, he differed from Trentowski in his general conception of 'national philosophy', especially in his understanding of its spiritual sources.

The first difference concerned the relationship between national philosophy and literature, especially poetry. According to Libelt, Polish romantic poetry was a prophetic presentiment and a 'seed' of Polish national philosophy; philosophers should, therefore, listen to the voice of poets and translate their poetic language into the language of discursive thought; even their mystical Messianism should be seen as a revelation of national spirit and as a harbinger of the great future of the Slavonic nations. Trentowski's opinion was quite different: the blossoming of romantic poetry was for him a testimony that the majority of the Poles were not mature enough to raise themselves to philosophy; he strongly opposed Mickiewicz's Messianism, calling it a *persuasio delira*, and was convinced that poets should not be seen as national prophets, let alone national leaders.

Closely bound up with this were different attitudes towards the spiritual faculty to which romantic poetry and romantic mysticism owed their existence—towards the imagination. Libelt wanted to create a 'philosophy of imagination', whereas Trentowski wrote his *System of National Logic* in order to develop among the Poles the capacity for logical thinking and to tame, in this way, their unbridled imagination, which led either to religious fanaticism or to the irrational cult of spectacular revolutionary 'deeds' (irrespective of their consequences).

Finally, there was a third difference connected with the other two. Libelt, influenced by romantic idealization of rural folk, proclaimed that a 'national philosophy' had to draw inspiration from the unphilosophical *Weltanschauung* of the common people (i.e. the peasantry); it should translate its half-mythical conceptions into a philosophical language but it should seek an essential agreement with them. Trentowski, as might be expected, strongly opposed these views. He published in Libelt's *Year* a special article, 'Can a National Philosophy Learn From the People and What Features Should Such a Philosophy Have' (1845), in which he asserted that philosophy should be developed by intellectual élites without paying attention to irrational traditions and beliefs of the people. *Vox populi*, he added, is indeed a *Vox Dei*, but only in the sphere of morality.

Trentowski's criticism was levelled against Libelt's article, 'A Characterization of Slavonic Philosophy'. Libelt formulated in this article 'a decalogue of Slavonic philosophy', in other words a list of ten principles of the *Weltanschauung* of the Polish people (and of the Slavonic peoples in general) which should lie at the foundation of 'Slavonic philosophy'. Under the influence of the Paris lectures of Mickiewicz he claimed that 'the chief dogma of the Polish nationality—and of the Slavonic nationality as a whole—is the belief in the constant action of the invisible world upon the visible' (A. 51, p. 233; cf. A. 70, XI, 113).

Mickiewicz's inspiration is to be found also in Libelt's reasonings about the Slavonic image of the spirit: unlike the impersonal German Geist, he argued, the Slavonic 'spirits' are individualized and incarnated, interfering in the daily affairs of earthly life. For Trentowski this was equivalent to 'demonomania' and 'asiaticism'. The so-called 'wisdom of the people', he maintained, has always consisted of theogony, mysticism, and magic; the first step of philosophy, as exemplified by the philosophy of Ancient Greece, consists in liberating thought from superstitious beliefs and mythological images.

In actual fact the differences between the two 'national philosophers' were not as great as one could conclude from the above. Like Trentowski, Libelt was fully aware that Slavonic philosophy, if it was to be a valuable contribution to philosophical thinking, had to assimilate all the achievements of universal philosophy, first of all its crowning achievement— German idealism. He did not want to reduce philosophy to mythology; he claimed only, in accordance with Vico, whom he highly praised in this connection, that mythology was not a mere collection of superstitions but a peculiar mode of thought and that it contained some important truths which could be translated into the language of philosophy. In his own philosophical system he utilized the formal structure of Trentowski's *National Logic*. Nevertheless, as we shall see, an important aspect of his philosophy was the conscious attempt to reconcile 'national philosophers' with prophetic poets, the truths of philosophical reason with the truths of the collective imagination of the people.

3. The German 'Autocracy of Reason' and the Slavonic 'Philosophy of Imagination'

The first volume of Libelt's philosophical writings contained a critical analysis of German philosophy, especially of the Hegelian 'absolute idealism'. Like Cieszkowski and Trentowski, Libelt accused German idealists of a one-sided rationalism, and proclaimed the necessity of defending against it the old Christian belief in a personal god and in the immortality of the human soul.

The accusations which he levelled against German philosophy can be summarized thus:

First, German philosophy was accused of establishing 'the

autocracy of reason'. Reason is undeniably very important; it has its own sphere in which its rule is fully legitimate; the human spirit, however, cannot be reduced to reason alone. The autocracy of reason leads necessarily to an extreme idealism: material substance is irreducible to rational cognition and, therefore, consistent rationalists have to claim that it does not exist at all.

Secondly, the 'philosophy of reason' is a philosophy of a critical epoch; this is its value and at the same time its limitation. It is a philosophy of pure negation since reason alone has no organic power of creating.

Thirdly, idealistic rationalism is bound to be abstract and contemplative, unable to find expression in action. It is incapable not only of creating but also of destroying anything in the real world. It can build and destroy only in the ethereal realm of pure thought.

To these three points, enumerated by Libelt at the beginning of his book, one should add another accusation, throwing additional light on the romantic criticism of rationalism. Despite his own thesis that the 'philosophy of reason' cannot influence real life Libelt maintained that there existed a close interdependence between the development of rationalism and the politics of European governments. Politics became divorced from morality and, as a result of this, began to destroy 'sacred realities', replacing free and organic societies with artificial political structures, based on mere force. The main victims of this were the nations, partitioned and suppressed for the sake of an abstract idea of the supra-national state; their life and happiness became sacrificed to different 'idols', like 'European equilibrium', 'armed peace', 'non-intervention', 'Holy Alliance', and so forth. It is important to see the difference between this reasoning and the standard argument of conservative romantics: for the latter rationalism was responsible for revolution, whereas for Libelt it was bound up with the counter-revolutionary system of the Holy Alliance, rejecting the sacred rights of nations. It is evident that Libelt was influenced in this respect by Mickiewicz, especially by his *Books of the Polish Pilgrims*.

Libelt's critical analysis of German idealism was preceded by a historical outline of the development of modern European philosophy. Especially interesting was his estimation of Spinoza. First, Libelt saw him as a thinker free from one-sided idealism, acknowledging the ontological status of matter and, therefore, much closer to truth than Hegel. Secondly, he refused to treat Spinoza as a pantheist, because (following Hegel, to whom, curiously enough, he remained faithful at this point)[20] he used the term 'pantheism' in a very narrow sense, to denote the deification of all finite things, unrelated with each other. Such an understanding of pantheism explains why Libelt himself, despite his declarations, could not escape the influence of pantheism in a more broad and more modern sense of the term.

Libelt's criticism of idealistic rationalism led to the conclusion that the most urgent task of philosophy should consist of the rehabilitation of matter, the rehabilitation of sensory images (as opposed to abstract notions)—in other words, the rehabilitation of the world of forms which are not only conceivable but imaginable as well. His own 'Slavonic philosophy' was to provide a solution to this task. It was to defend the personality of God and, at the same time, to emphasize the divine character of nature, being not an *alienation* of the Absolute (as Hegel saw it) but a *manifestation* of it, a revelation of God in the visible world. It was to be a philosophy of 'individualized, *imaginable* forms', and not a philosophy of 'shapeless, incorporeal notions'. Finally, it was to be a 'philosophy of action'—not of an action in the Fichtean sense, but in the sense of the social and historical praxis. Libelt believed that this philosophical programme reflected essential features of the pre-philosophical world-view of the Slavs—people with a rich imagination, disinclined to abstractions, eager for action, and feeling themselves intimately united with nature.

In contrast to the German 'philosophy of reason', Libelt's 'Slavonic philosophy' was to be, first of all, a 'philosophy of imagination'. Libelt defined 'imagination' as a faculty of spirit which gives shapes to ideas, forms to thoughts. He distinguished three kinds of imagination: (1) the imagination of God who creates forms out of his own being, giving images of himself; (2) the imagination of man, who can create new forms but only from the given, created material; and (3) the imagination in the objective world, i.e. the force of nature incessantly transforming all existing forms without consciousness and purpose. Forms created by God were called 'primary forms'; forms created by man, 'derivative forms'; forms called into being by natural processes were named 'transitive forms'. Each 'primary form' could have its human 'derivative' and natural 'transitory' counterpart. In such a way Libelt's system became, first of all, a complicated, sometimes very artificial, classification of all possible forms in the three 'great realms of reality'—God, Nature, and Mankind.

A detailed analysis of this system does not fall within the scope of this book. It will suffice to say a few words on Libelt's conception of God (the creative Absolute) and on his philosophy of creative man.

In his conception of the Absolute the Polish philosopher—in spite of his ambitious plan to set forth an entirely new 'Slavonic' philosophy—remained faithful to the old, great tradition of Neo-Platonism. According to Tillich, 'Neo-Platonism negates creation; in fact it has no real creation (B. 165, p. 110). It was the same in Libelt's case, irrespective of whether he was aware of it or not. The world, according to him, was a self-manifestation of God, i.e. a theophany in the Neo-Platonic sense of this term. He emphasized that it is a necessary and eternal self-manifestation, having neither beginning nor end in time; he used typically Neo-Platonic metaphors when he described the world as 'outflowing' from God or when he compared its creation, i.e. the emanative process, to the radiation of light. God, he claimed, is eternal not only in himself but also as creator; the world, therefore, is also eternal, or rather co-eternal with God. The creation of the world is a continuous process and not a unique, single act. If God had created the world in a single act, he would have become limited by it, facing, as it were, an external objectivity. God, however, as the Absolute, must be unlimited and infinite; so, the world cannot be conceived as created once in time and placed somewhere 'outside' God. God is creating the world, i.e. manifesting himself in the world, incessantly, and that is why the world can never become for him something 'external', congealed into 'objectivity'.

As we can see from the above, Libelt conceived of God as a person (in a certain sense) without conceiving of him as a transcendent being. His God was a 'person', because he was 'himself', but not in separation from the world and from mankind. God, maintained Libelt, is neither an 'ens intramundanum' nor an 'ens extramundanum', because the very distinction between the immanence and the transcendence has become untenable in the light of the conception of the creation as an incessant process. In such a way Libelt tried to avoid both the separation of God from the world (i.e. traditional theism) and the identification of the world with God (i.e pantheism). Using the term coined by K. Ch. F. Krause, one can say that this conception of the Absolute was 'panentheistic', i.e. claiming that everything exists in God although God himself exists *not only* in the world. The same classification can be applied, as I have pointed out, to the conceptions of Cieszkowski and Trentowski. However, in comparison with them, Libelt was in fact closer to broadly conceived pantheism, if only because of his explicit rejection of the very notion of the 'transcendence' of God.

Libelt's defence of the immortality of the soul also turned out to have very little in common with traditional Catholicism. He outspokenly proclaimed that immortality should not be confused with after-life: it is not life after death but the eternal existence of individualized spiritual content elaborated during one's lifetime. Following Hoene-Wroński and Cieszkowski, Libelt also maintained that such immortality is a result of merit; it is a reward for those men who have succeeded in raising their spirit to the level of a truly creative personal existence.

Libelt's philosophy of man, i.e. his philosophy of 'derivative forms', can be seen as an interesting contribution to the discussions concerning the national character of philosophy. Like Trentowski, Libelt opposed hypostatization of the 'national spirit', but, at the same time, he strongly emphasized that individuals belonging to a nation have a common national character, most pure and distinctive among the lower classes, and that this character pre-determines the products of their imagination. Seen from this perspective, the philosophy of forms created by men was a philosophy of the collective *national* imagination, objectifying itself in language, art, science, and transforming the external objectivity of nature in the process of work. Thus, all products of human creativity were derived from the deep structures of the collective imagination elaborated by the different nations, especially by their common people, who, because of their constant contact with nature, were seen as closest to the divine source of all creation.

All this applied, of course, to philosophy: as one of the 'derivative forms' it had to have its ultimate source in the national imagination of the people. Therefore, concluded Libelt, philosophy cannot escape being national. On the other hand, no nation can claim to possess an absolute, universal truth. Despite Hegel's arrogant claim, an 'absolute philosophy' cannot exist. In the development of philosophy different nations take part; each of them, in its turn, contributes something to the universal progress of thought, but none of them can claim to have reached the absolute truth. The very structure of the national imagination makes it impossible: philosophical knowledge is nationally pre-conditioned, and precisely because of this each nation can see the truth only from its own, peculiar, more or less limited perspective.

Setting his system against Hegelianism, Libelt borrowed many ideas from Schelling and his disciples (among others, from Krause). Young Schelling's 'Naturphilosophie' was almost entirely incorporated into his system, as part of his philosophy of 'transitive forms'. First of all, however, he wanted to present his philosophy as a result of the development of Polish thought and, therefore, missed no occasion to discuss, or to utilize, the ideas elaborated by his predecessors. He agreed with Krasiński that Polish 'national philosophers' and prophetic poets represented two sides of 'a great philosophical and religious movement in the bosom of Slavdom' (A. 42, II. 566); before constructing his own system he wrote a systematic exposition of the ideas of the main representatives of this movement, and included it (alongside his outline of the development of modern European philosophy) in his *Vital Question of Philosophy*. As I have already mentioned, he owed a great deal to Trentowski (although he disagreed with him on many important questions), and, at the same time, tried to translate into philosophical language the mystical and messianic ideas of Mickiewicz. On the whole, he can be described as a philosopher of mediation and reconciliation. He tried to reconcile all the ideas and intellectual currents in which he found something challenging and attractive: élitist philosophy with popular mythology, rationalism with romantic irrationalism, idealism with the 'rehabilitation of matter', autonomy of man with providentialism, pantheism with theism. He could be accused, not without reason, of syncretism and eclecticism. Nobody, however, could deny his intellectual inventiveness and erudition, his first-hand knowledge of the ancient and modern philosophy, and his capacity for a coherent and original interpretation of its development.

4. Democratic Nationalism and Aesthetics

An important field of Libelt's intellectual activity was aesthetics; his system of aesthetics was in fact an integral part of his philosophy of imagination.[21] Developing his aesthetical views he referred not to Schelling (as might be expected, taking into account the romantic tendencies of his thought), but to Hegel and the Hegelian school, especially to F. T. Vischer. His main disagreements with the Hegelian tradition in aesthetics can be reduced to the following four points.

First, Libelt disagreed with Hegel's thesis that art, in comparison with philosophy, represents a lower stage of the development of the absolute spirit and that it has no future since its development has already been completed. Such a thesis could not be accepted by representatives of the nation in which literature still performed a crucial role in developing and keeping awake national consciousness and social conscience. Therefore, Libelt replaced the Hegelian conception of the three *stages* of the absolute spirit (religion, art, and philosophy) with a conception of three parallel *ways* of the spirit. He even ascribed to art a certain superiority over both philosophy and religion. Art, he argued, is a mediation between the truth of the heart, represented by religion, and the truth of reason, represented by philosophy; therefore, it represents the human spirit in its wholeness, which can be claimed neither by religion nor by philosophy.

Secondly, Libelt modified Hegel's thesis that the task of art consists in expressing ideas in sensuous forms. Ideas, he maintained, belong to the sphere of pure thought, and the artist who gives sensual forms to them is God himself. Therefore, the task of art should be defined as the presentation of the *Ideals*, that is to say *not ideas* as pure notions, to which sensual shape should be added, but ideas in the Platonic sense, i.e. divine *archetypes* of creation. This peculiar 'platonization' of Hegelianism was supported, in addition, by a Platonic interpretation of the perception of beauty as a sudden illumination, a sudden awakening of the sleeping spirit. Libelt's intention was to defend the objective existence of beauty, to make it independent of individual perception, and, thus, to resist relativism, inherent, as he saw it, in historicism and idealistic 'negativism' of Hegel's thought.

Thirdly, in accordance with his tendency to 'rehabilitate' nature, Libelt disagreed with Hegel's view that the beauty of art, being born from the spirit, is incomparably superior to the beauty of nature, and that the latter should be excluded from the scope of philosophical aesthetics. He emphasized the great value of natural beauty as 'the aesthetical school of mankind', and, like Vischer, devoted much space to the description and philosophical analysis of different forms of beauty in the kingdom of nature.

Finally, the Polish thinker elaborated his own, original 'system of the arts', synchronic and diachronic at the same time. He divided the arts into (1) formal or plastic arts (architecture, sculpture and painting); (2) ideal arts or arts concerning the content (music, poetry, and oratory art); and (3) social arts or the arts of life. The first group consists of visual arts which are spatial; the arts belonging to the second group are sonic and temporal; in the third group, visual (spatial) and sonic (temporal) arts are united. In addition, each of the different arts was cross-divided within itself according to three criteria: (1) according to the kind of reality represented in its works (natural, human-secular and sacred); (2) according to the kind of ideal (the predominance of Beauty, Good, or Truth); and (3) according to Hegelian diachronic criterion (the symbolic, classic, and romantic stage).

The most interesting, the most relevant to the urgent national tasks—and, at the same time, very typical of the Polish aesthetics of the Romantic Epoch—was Libelt's conception of the 'social arts'. The inner classifications were as follows:

1. Idealizing the nature, moulding the ideal of Beauty:
    a. The art of gardening or embellishing nature,
    b. The art of dressing or embellishing the human body,
    c. The decorative art or embellishing life through the fusion of fine arts with crafts and industries.
2. The aesthetical education of man, moulding the ideal of Truth:
    a. Gymnastics and dance or the aesthetical education of the human body,

    b. Connoisseurship of beauty, or the aesthetical education
       of spirit,
    c. The theatrical art or education for aesthetical life.
  3. Idealizing of society, moulding the ideal of the Good:
    a. Religious cult,
    b. Political cult,
    c. National cult.

Thus, the 'social arts', the crowning achievement of all arts, were to culminate in the 'national cult' (A. 50, IV. 171–2). They were to develop fully in the future, realizing the final end of Art, i.e. the aesthetical transformation of the daily life of nations. Art, argued Libelt, has always strived for the embellishment of life; up to the present, however, this was being done privately and at random, whereas in the future it would be done in a planned, organized way by public authorities, as part of a comprehensive programme of struggle for economic and social progress. The beginnings of such an aesthetical education of nations can be traced back to the ancient Greeks and Romans who had shown a great interest in arranging public spectacles of different kinds (although only for the free people). Among other examples of a 'partial and one-sided' development of social arts in the past Libelt mentioned also the majesty of monarchal courts, knightly tournaments, religious liturgy, church and state festivals, and so on. His approach to art as a means for patriotic education was very similar to that of the Jacobin nationalists who had transformed patriotism into a kind of secularized religion with its own ritual, magic formulas, impressive symbols, and popular festivals (cf. B. 51, pp. 54, 68, and 73). His conception of introducing beauty into social life corresponded with Dembowski's dreams about an 'aesthetic social order' and with Norwid's ideas about the national function of art—consisting in the ennoblement of the every-day life and work of the people. It is worth pointing out that Libelt referred in this conception to 'the sect of the Saintsimonians', praising it for the proper understanding of beautiful ritual and ceremonies in social life.

    An interesting aspect of Libelt's conception of the application of art to social and political life is to be found in his considerations about the element of dramaturgy and theatrical art in the courts of justice and in political action. A trial, he argued, is a kind of theatrical performance, while political life as a whole (with the exception, of course, of clandestine political activities) is a kind of all-national theatre. Political leaders, in order to be successful, must show themselves to be talented actors, because the entire nation, and foreign nations as well, observe their performance on the political scene and assess them, among other things, according to their theatrical skill.

Libelt's *Aesthetics* was published too late to be widely read and influential. It belonged to the epoch of the great speculative philosophical systems and, therefore, was felt to be anachronistic in the second half of the century. One should add also that it frightened away potential readers by its lengthy and boring analyses of beauty in nature. Nevertheless, it seems justified to say that it contains some new, interesting ideas and deserves to be remembered as an attempt to show how an aesthetical theory could be applied to the needs of practical life.

VI. Henryk Kamieński

1. Biographical Note

Politically speaking, Trentowski was more to the left than Cieszkowski, and Libelt, of course, was more to the left than Trentowski. The first two represented different variants of liberalism, whereas Libelt was a moderate democrat. The other two representatives of the philosophical movement of the 1840s—Kamieński and Dembowski—were, in turn, more to the left than Libelt. Their political views were far from being identical, but, nevertheless, they shared an important common platform: both of them accepted the idea of an agrarian revolution as the only means of solving the national and social question in Poland. Dembowski was an extreme radical both in his political and in his social views; Kamieński's position can be described as an attempt at mediation between moderate and radical democratism.

Henryk Kamieński was born on his family's estate Ruda near Lublin on 25 February 1813. His father, a Napoleonic general, was killed in action during the November uprising; his mother, de domo Kochanowska, was a sister of the mother of Edward Dembowski. On the eve of the uprising he started to study at the juridical faculty of the University of Warsaw; during the uprising he fought in the famous Fourth Regiment of Uhlans and was promoted to the rank of officer. Before the capitulation he was taken prisoner by the Russian army. Taking advantage of the amnesty, he was allowed to live, under police surveillance, in Ruda; for several years he did not try to leave it (except for occasional visits to Warsaw), devoting all his time to intensive studies of German philosophy, political economy, and French social thought. At the end of the 1830s (only by then!) he began to sympathize with the *émigré* democrats, especially with their programme for the enfranchisement of the peasants. In 1842 he started to collaborate with Dembowski's *Scientific Review*. At the beginning of 1843 he got permission to go abroad. First he came to Poznań, bringing with him the manuscript of the first volume of his *Philosophy of the Material Economy of Human Society* (Poznań 1843–5; see A. 31). His next stop was Berlin; in three months he wrote there his political *magnum opus* entitled *On the Vital Truths of the Polish Nation* (see A. 32. Published under the pseudonym Filaret Prawdowski in Brussels, 1844). He dedicated this work to the leaders of the Polish Democratic Society, calling them 'the fathers of the Polish cause', but, at the same time, he criticized their emphasis on a centralized revolutionary organization and their belief in the decisive role of a revolutionary vanguard. After Berlin he came to France and Belgium where he came into contact with some activists of the Democratic Society and, also, with Joachim Lelewel. In July 1843 he was already back in Warsaw. He took part in the controversy over Hegelianism by publishing two important articles: 'A Few Words on the Philosophy of History' (in Libelt's *Year*, 1844, No. 3) and 'A Few Words on Practical Philosophy, or the Philosophy of Action' (in Dembowski's *Scientific Review*, 1845, No. 7). In order to popularize his political views he wrote a booklet *Democratic Catechism* (published in Paris in 1845 under the same pseudonym as the book *On the Vital Truths*). At the same time he began to organize a network of propagandists, seeing this as a first step towards the propagandist action on a mass scale which should precede the future revolution.

Kamieński's political books made a great impression both in Poland and among the emigration. They became the subject of an ardent versified polemic between the two prophetic poets: Krasiński and Słowacki. Krasiński, horrified by the idea of revolutionary terrorism, attacked Filaret Prawdowski in his *Psalms of the Future* (1845); Słowacki, in turn, came out with his splendid *Reply to the Psalms of the Future*, in which he expressed his solidarity with the author of *The Vital Truths*, and accused Krasiński of class egoism and faint-hearted cowardice.

In November 1845, Kamieński was arrested and put into the Citadel of Warsaw. A one-year enquiry produced no evidence against him, but in spite of this he was sentenced to three years of exile in Vyatka. He vividly described his imprisonment in the Citadel in his 'Memoires d'un prisonnier' (*Le Temps*, 1865); his trip to Vyatka and his stay there were described in his recently published *Letters From Exile*.

Being a good observer and a man of great personal charm, Kamieński was able to utilize his time in exile for making friends among the Russians and acquiring a profound knowledge of their country. As a result, he later wrote a remarkable book, *Russia and Europe. Poland: An Introduction to the Study of Russia and the Muscovites* (Paris 1854). His attitude towards the Russian people, as expressed in this book, was completely free from the current stereotypes of Russophobia; in a sense it was the attitude of a cultural anthropologist, sensitive to cultural relativism, trying to understand the distinctive features of a given culture and full of sympathetic interest towards the people representing them. He polemized with Herzen's view on the Russian village commune, seeing in it not a germ of a higher social order but an institution bound up with serfdom and peculiarly convenient for autocracy. It was not true, he argued, that the Russian peasant had raised himself above the level of private property; what was true was that he still lived at the stage of naïve 'barbarianism' and had not yet grown up enough to accept modern private ownership. The word 'barbarianism' was used in this context in a purely descriptive sense, without any derogatory meaning. Kamieński saw and criticized many negative traits of the Russian people, resulting from the corruptive influence of autocracy. On the whole, however, his judgement on the Russian national character was unexpectedly positive, not devoid of certain Slavophile overtones. The mission of the Poles in their relations with Russia was presented by him not as a defending Europe against the barbarians from the East but as disseminating humanitarian ideas among the Russians and converting them to the cause of freedom.

In 1850, Kamieński returned from exile to his estate in Poland. Soon, however, he fell ill and went for treatment to Switzerland. When he was crossing the border of the Russian Empire he experienced a sudden intoxication with the 'strange feeling of personal freedom'. No wonder that he decided to settle in Switzerland permanently. From time to time he went to treat his disease in Tunis or Algiers. He died in Algiers on 9 January 1865.

Along with his book on Russia, mentioned above, Kamieński wrote a book in Switzerland entitled *Democracy in Poland* (*Demokracja in Polszcze*, Geneva 1858). Both of these books are a telling testimony of a shift in his political views which took place after the events of 1846 and of 1848–9. Kamieński cut himself off from his former radicalism, began to glorify the ancient Polish Commonwealth with its 'democracy of the gentry', to extol the patriotism of the contemporary Polish nobility, and to advocate national unity under its moral leadership. An important change took place also in his attitude towards the West. The perfidious role played by the Austrian authorities in the Galician massacre of 1846; the betrayal of the Polish cause by the German liberals in 1848; the fact that the Western governments during the Crimean War did not dare to raise the Polish question; all these events brought him to the conclusion that the West was either hostile or, at best, indifferent towards Polish national aspirations and, therefore, that the only chance for the Poles was to become pro-Russian and to work *from within* for the inner democratization of the Russian state. Many Poles understood this position as tantamount to the espousal of Panslavism.

At the beginning of the 1860s, under the influence of the unification of Italy and of patriotic manifestations in Warsaw, Kamieński recovered his faith in the national liberation of Poland. His new political convictions found expression in a non-periodical journal *The Truth* (*Prawda*) which he edited in Geneva in 1860–1. He greeted with enthusiasm the uprising of 1863 and wanted to contribute to its cause by publishing a handbook on 'people's war', based upon the relevant chapters from *The Vital Truths* but specially adapted to the needs of the insurgents. This plan was not realized—Kamieński's handbook entitled *The People's War* (*Wojna Ludowa*) was published only in 1866, when the insurrection was already over.[22] Nevertheless, Kamieński's conviction about the possible usefulness of his theory of the 'people's war' for the Polish uprising was not groundless. Some left-wing leaders of the uprising had learned his theory from his *Vital Truths* and tried to bring it into action.

2. Political Economy and the Absolute

Like the other representatives of the Polish philosophical movement of the forties, Kamieński proclaimed the necessity of a philosophical justification for an active, creative attitude towards life. The motto of his philosophy was: 'I create, therefore, I am.' However, unlike Cieszkowski, Trentowski, and Libelt, he was not concerned with religious problems and did not try to find the infinite in the finite. In some respects he owed a great deal to Hegel; his programmatic historicism was rationalist and, therefore, much closer to Hegelianism than to Schellingian Romanticism. In spite of this, the general assumptions of his philosophy were very different not only from Hegelianism but from post-Kantian German idealism as a whole.

Kamieński's main philosophical work—*Philosophy of the Material Economy*—begins with an exposition of a theory of the Absolute. This theory, however, has little in common with Hegelianism.

First, Kamieński disagreed with the fundamental assumption of Hegelian idealism—with the thesis about the identity of thought and being. The Absolute, according to him, was the being, and not the absolute thought identical with being; thought was treated by him as a 'subsequence' of the Absolute, that is to say, as something derivative, having no power to exist from itself and by itself.

Secondly, he flatly rejected the Hegelian conception according to which the divine Absolute was seen as immanently present in the world and developing its self-consciousness by means of man. Instead, he propounded the doctrine of a radical separation between the divine world and the human world, claiming that there were two Absolutes: the 'Absolute of all things', i.e. the divine, cosmic Absolute, and the 'Absolute of all *human* things', i.e. the existence of man as a creative being. He agreed that man was not the 'Absolute of all things', because such a thesis would have amounted to the negation of the objectivity of nature; he stressed, also, that man could not have an absolute, *a priori* knowledge of the natural world, because he was not able to get in contact with the 'Absolute of nature'. Mysteries of the divine ('the Absolute of all things') can be penetrated only by divine beings; man can deal only with the finite manifestations of the cosmic Absolute, i.e. with the *phenomena* of nature.

Thus, Kamieński's opposition to the Hegelian conception of 'the universal unity of the divine with the human world' was very different from the criticism of Hegelian pantheism in the works of Cieszkowski, Trentowski, and Libelt. He rejected the doctrine of an essential homogeneity between God and man, replacing it with a conception of a complete 'otherness' of God (i.e. 'the Absolute of all things') in relation to man. The cosmic

Absolute, he claimed, cannot be known by man or united with man; it is, therefore, *alien* to man, transcendent *in relation to the human world*, although not transcendent in the sense of a transcendent personality. It is immanent *in nature*, as its inner creative source; natural things, among which man lives, are its 'subsequences'; man can know them as objects of his praxis, but their inner essence and the creative force which has called them into being are, and have to be, beyond the grasp of his knowledge. Such a conception was, of course, incompatible with philosophical systems trying to explain the world by deriving it from the divine Absolute; therefore, it was incompatible both with post-Kantian German idealism and with the Neo-Platonic tradition, so important for philosophical Romanticism.

An interesting interpretation of Kamieński's standpoint was given by a Russian revolutionary, a member of the so-called 'Petrashevsky's circle', Nicholas Speshnev. In a letter to his Polish friend, Edmund Chojecki, he compared Kamieński to Feuerbach and Proudhon, treating all of them as representatives of 'anthropotheism', the necessary final result of the development of German philosophy (A. 19, pp. 494–5). He was right in emphasizing Kamieński's axiological anthropocentrism, his essential agreement with Feuerbach's saying: *Homo homini deus est*. He failed, however, to note that the Polish thinker, unlike Feuerbach and the German young Hegelians, defended the autonomy of many not by claiming that God was immanent in mankind or identical with mankind, but on the contrary—by establishing a radical separation between God and man. Another interesting difference was that in Kamieński's conception (in contradistinction to that of Feuerbach) man was not just a part of nature—he was 'an Absolute' only in so far as he was endowed with a creative power of his own, independent from the creative power of the cosmic Absolute.

Kamieński, however, did not see man as completely independent of nature. His philosophical anthropology conceived of man as endowed with a receptive faculty of perception and with a creative power. As a receptive subject man is a part of nature; in other words, he is only one of many 'subsequences' of the cosmic Absolute and cannot exist by himself. He becomes 'an Absolute' when he starts to exercise his creative power, i.e. when he begins to exist by his own force, overcoming the resistance of external nature. The materials for his creative activity are the 'subsequences' of the cosmic Absolute with which he gets in contact, thanks to his faculty of perception; in this sense human creativity is linked to the creative power in nature. Nevertheless, as soon as man started to transform external nature in accordance with his own purposes, he ceased to be a mere 'subsequence' of nature, becoming, instead, a self-creating being, i.e. an Absolute. Thus, within the sphere of the world created by man—the sphere enlarging itself more and more in the process of history—the only Absolute is man himself.

It should be stressed that in Kamieński's conception the creative freedom of man had nothing in common with arbitrariness or licence. In this respect he remained faithful to the anti-voluntaristic spirit of Hegelianism. He was convinced that human creativity was subject to necessary, rational laws. Only because of this, he thought, the 'Absolute of all human things' (in contrast to the cosmic Absolute) was accessible to rational human knowledge. He emphasized that the laws of human creativity—the laws of progress—are immanent, intrinsic to all humanity, and not imposed upon it from without.

Kamieński wanted to cut himself off from the Fichtean, purely idealistic activism. That is why he never ceased to repeat that man was not only a self-creating being but *also* a part of material nature. For the same reason he insisted that 'the deed'—'an atom of the world created by men' (A. 31, p. 31)— had to be conceived as both spiritual and material. The true 'deed', raising man to the status of an Absolute, consisted according to him, in conquering nature, in subordinating matter to the power of the human spirit. The sum-total of human deeds was conceived as a historical and collective process of productive work. In this way the 'material economy' (i.e. political economy), studying the material productivity of man, became in Kamieński's eyes the main and most philosophical science of man. 'Material economy', he proclaimed (A. 31, pp. 347–8), was truly a *summa philosophiae* because it provided concrete answers for the most important philosophical questions, such as: how can knowledge pass into practical life? How can the human spirit conquer nature and liberate itself from servile dependence on crude matter? What are the laws of the historical progress which is being achieved through collective work? Therefore, philosophers who want to give answers to these questions should overcome romantic contempt for 'the prosaic problems of material existence' and concentrate their attention on the economic history of mankind.

Philosophical interest in political economy was not something completely new among the Polish thinkers. Hoene-Wroński's economic manuscripts of 1803–6 testify that he had seen political economy as an integral part of philosophy, dealing with the problems of 'pragmatic anthropology'. Cieszkowski, in turn, had never doubted that his book on circulation and credit was a contribution to the practical solution of essentially philosophical problems. Kamieński, however, was the first Polish thinker who claimed that political economy was of *central importance* to philosophy, that it was the main key to the proper understanding and practical solution of philosophical questions. On the one hand, he was close to Wroński because he was still concerned with the problem of the Absolute; on the other hand, he should be seen within the context of a current in post-Hegelian philosophy which can be credited with discovery of the philosophical significance of the economic activities of man. I mean, of course, the current represented by Moses Hess and, above all, by the young Marx.

3. Epistemology of History

Kamieński's philosophical activism found splendid expression in his theory of historical knowledge. The title of his article 'A Few Words on the Philosophy of History' was misleading: in fact, it dealt not with a philosophoy of history in the sense of a philosophical theory of the phases and meaning of historical process, but with an epistemology of history, i.e. with the theory of historical cognition. At the same time it was a philosophical theory of historiography—a theory surprisingly modern, 'anti-positivist', *avant le lettre*, anticipating in some respects the ideas of Marx.

Kamieński set forth the thesis about the active and multi-perspective character of historical knowledge. It is not true, he asserted, that an historian can limit his task to the description of facts. Facts are not something ready-made, 'given'; they have to be selected and endowed with meaning, which presupposes a creative activity on the part of the knower. There are no 'bare facts' in history because the so-called 'facts' are inseparable from cognitive perspective which depends, in turn, on the desire to act in a certain direction. The historian, therefore, is a 'creator'; he 'creates' the facts, even if he does not want to admit this (A. 31, p. 412).

The human spirit develops in history and each new phase of historical progress opens new vistas for the understanding of past events. The same 'facts' can be seen from different sides and interpreted differently; each of these interpretations contains a certain relative truth, but none of them claim to attain absolute truth; none of them are 'objective' because each is based on a certain *a priori* knowledge, corresponding to a certain phase in the developing self-consciousness of mankind. The meaning of history is not something 'to be found', but something 'to be created' by arranging empirical data in a meaningful order. The knowledge of history—although historians are usually not aware of this—is, thus, pre-determined by an *a priori* 'viewpoint' with which a given historian approaches his subject. Without such a viewpoint past events would present themselves as a dead, amorphous, and meaningless collection of unconnected shreds of collective memory, and history would become unreadable.

Kamieński rightly insisted that this standpoint did not sanction arbitrary interpretations and did not imply a total relativism. Historical 'viewpoints', he argued, are time-bound but not arbitrary, since all of them are predetermined by necessary and rational laws of historical progress. Each of them contains a partial truth but this does not mean that each of these truths is of the same value as the others; each 'viewpoint' is, or was, a legitimate product of history but, nevertheless, some of them are modern and some of them are obsolete; they represent the truth of the past, the truth of the present, or the truth of the future. The criterion by means of which one can distinguish between the 'less true' and 'more true' is provided by the law of progress, identical with the law of the economic development of mankind. Each new phase of historical progress has its counterpart in a new historical 'viewpoint', and each new 'viewpoint'— if not influenced by particularism but really expressing the truth of the epoch—contains in itself, and unites in a higher synthesis, all the partial truths of the past (A. 31, pp. 418–19). The *a priori* element in historical knowledge is a product of historical development, and can be explained as such from the vantage point offered by a higher stage of progress. Thus, although all historical interpretations are time-bound, there is a progress in historical knowledge, and its laws are the same as the laws of the historical process itself.

In contrast to Hegel, Kamieński did not envision the possibility of an absolute knowledge of history. He assumed that the absolute truth ('the ideal moment of knowledge') had to exist but, at the same time, was convinced that men could never attain it, although they had to strive for it and were able to make progress in approaching it. It followed therefrom that all attempts at creating an all-embracing system of a philosophy of history, pretending to provide a definitive and final explanation of the meaning of historical process, were doomed to failure. This was, perhaps, the reason why Kamieński, unlike Cieszkowski or Dembowski, did not try to create such a system himself.

4. Social Philosophy, Revolution, and the Conception of Nation

Kamieński treated his philosophy of the Absolute as a necessary introduction to the social sciences through which philosophy could be translated into action. He divided them into 'moral economy' or 'the psychology of human society', 'political economy' (in a special sense, denoting a science of political activities and institutions), and 'material economy', dealing with 'the progress of human activity in its struggle with matter' (A. 31, pp. 39–50). The latter, as we already know, was for him a study of the universal, objective progress of mankind and, therefore, the most important science of human deeds and the key to the understanding of history.

A distinctive feature of Kamieński's philosophy of man was a pronounced sociologism and historicism. In this respect he was a disciple not only of Hegel but also of some French thinkers, especially Saint-Simon and Pierre Leroux who set themselves against the atomistic conception of society typical of the Enlightenment. Praising man's creativity he meant not the individual but collective man. For him society was 'a collective entity in mankind, living a complete and perfect life'; in contrast to this, the individual was seen as only 'a particle, an atom, incomplete in itself and having no significance of its own' (A. 31, p. 37). It followed from this that the conception of a 'social contract' was sheer nonsense, because men had never lived in a pre-social 'state of nature'. At the pre-social stage the ancestors of man had not yet become human beings capable of communicating with each other. The true nature of man is social; therefore, the process of socialization is not something unnatural but, on the contrary, is a gradual unfolding of human nature.

Kamieński's political philosophy, and his political practice as well, was based on the assumption that man's creative activity was governed by laws, inherent in it and independent of individual desires. A violation of these laws, he thought, was possible but always harmful for genuine progress. Truly important progressive changes, even revolutionary changes, could be achieved without violence. Developing this thought Kamieński insisted that revolution was not necessarily a romantic struggle on barricades, that the name 'revolution' should be given to important, qualitative changes in economic relations quite irrespective of how much revolutionary violence was involved. Revolution, he asserted, was 'an organic social function which the nation exercises within itself in order to recast its inner organism; everything which fulfils this condition is a revolution, irrespective of the superficial forms which it may assume and of the source from which the change takes its beginning' (A. 32, p. 62).

Another consequence was the question of timing. Progress, as it was pointed out by the Saint-Simonians, consists in growing unity among men. This unity, however, must correspond to man's successes in the struggle with matter. In other words: the goals of revolution should be in accordance with the achieved level of economic development. Small wonder, therefore, that, in contradistinction to Dembowski, Kamieński highly appreciated the progressiveness of capitalist development, and dismissed socialist teachings—as applied to Polish conditions—as mere utopias. He was fully aware of the fact that the prime mover of capitalist progress is 'individual interest', but did not see in this anything morally wrong. 'Individual interest' was not identified by him with antisocial egoism; on the contrary— it was seen by him as a socializing factor. Interest, he wrote, 'is a social tie, and not a dissolvent'; it is 'an expression of man's individuality, and this expression cannot be antisocial since the individuality itself is a creation of society' (A. 31, p. 109). Exploitation of men by men is a by-product of the social division of labour and, therefore, cannot be completely eliminated. It should be limited, but not at the cost of hampering economic progress and, by the same token, of weakening mankind in its struggle with matter.

In the second volume of Kamieński's *Philosophy of the Material Economy* we find a certain modification of this standpoint. Kamieński recognized that there is a theoretical possibility of such an 'ideal moment' in social development in which the phenomenon of exploitation would disappear: private interest as a stimulus to work would then give way to work conceived of as a calling; wealth would be distributed according to needs, and the necessary division of labour would be based not on a social hierarchy but on free choice motivated by a universal desire to be useful. However, Kamieński placed emphasis on an important reservation: the only way to this social ideal should be a spontaneous evolutionary process in which 'interest itself gives way to higher motives'. It was to be a *natural* process—not 'a violation of the principle of interest by means incapable of replacing it', but 'its natural disappearance'. Any artificial acceleration of this process by a centralized political power could only result 'in destroying human society, and not in bringing about its progress' (A. 31, pp. 324–5).

Kamieński's theory of the revolution should be seen against the background of the theory of revolutionary dictatorship, elaborated by the Polish Democratic Society and presented in the most consistent form by General Ludwik Mierosławski.

During the revolution—Mierosławski argued—the principle of the sovereignty of the people must be suspended; the people can exercise their sovereignty only as the result of a victorious revolution, and not before it, i.e. before their physical and moral emancipation. The only true plenipotentiary of the general will is the successful revolutionary organization—its very success is the best proof that the revolutionary conspirators have acted in accordance with the authentic general will of their nation. Therefore, the revolutionary executive—either collective (if possible in the existing conditions) or exercised by one man—should be given unlimited power. The revolutionary government must have all rights, the nation—only unlimited duties. No freedom of the press, no activities of revolutionary clubs can be tolerated, since final victory depends solely on discipline, on 'blind obedience' (see A. 54, pp. 538–47).

Kamieński's book *On the Vital Truths of the Polish Nation* set forth a very different theory. Its basic assumption is the historicist conviction that the 'universal reason' of the masses is more worthy of trust than the reason of a revolutionary élite. In the theory and practice of revolutionary conspiracies Kamieński saw the danger of voluntarism: conspirators, he asserted, always want to impose upon society their own will, not taking into account that society, 'like the physical world, is subject to inevitable and unflinching laws' (A. 32, p. 21). In a similar way he criticized different variants of the 'faith in persons', such as Mochnacki's 'revolutionary absolutism', the hero-worship of Mickiewicz, and the exaggerated hopes which many democrats began to put in Mierosławski. He went so far as to deny the *émigrés'* claim to leadership: emigration, he argued, is necessarily a detachment from the concrete, real conditions of national life, exposing people to the danger of an uncritical acceptance of foreign theories and thus giving birth to illusions and 'impractical' solutions.

The same theoretical assumptions served as a justification of a broad programme of propagandist activity, seen by Kamieński as a necessary preparation for revolution. The masses, he maintained, must be *prepared* to understand the revolution. The revolutionaries, on the other hand, must have the opportunity for an unceasing confrontation of their ideas with the real needs and strivings of the masses. Thus, the emphasis put on propaganda was, in Kamieński's case, not a testimony to an idealistic belief in the magic power of words, but, rather, the result of clear awareness of the dangers of revolutionary élitism, stemming from an absolutization of conspiratorial methods of struggle.

Very interesting in this respect is Kamieński's account of his discussions with Tomasz Malinowski, an emissary of the 'Centralization' (Central Committee) of the Democratic Society (A. 33, chapt. 3). Malinowski accused Kamieński of 'anarchy', arguing that the success of revolution depended, first of all, on good conspiratorial organization, based upon the principles of centralization, hierarchy, and unconditional obedience. Kamieński, in his turn, accused the Centralization of a patronizing attitude towards the patriotic majority of the nation, neglecting 'universal reason' and pushing the country to actions which would increase sacrifices and repressive measures without real benefit for the cause. Revolution, he claimed, must have time to ripen; conspiracy can achieve its aim only if *the masses* are prepared and willing to act. One should try to accelerate revolutionary maturity, but not strive for unripe fruits.

The book *On the Vital Truths* contained a whole chapter devoted to the problem of revolutionary terrorism. However, in spite of Krasiński's exaggerated reaction. Kamieński's advocacy of terror was rather moderate, more moderate than the position of the 'Jacobin' Left Wing of the Democratic Society. True, he did not hesitate to state bluntly that terror, i.e. revolutionary justice, will be turned not only against individuals but against whole classes as well, if they choose to behave like a counter-revolutionary mass. Nevertheless, at the same time he expressed his deep conviction that the Polish revolution would entail only very little bloodshed. He based this conviction on the educative influence of the Polish tragedy which, as he thought, had cured the Polish gentry of their class egoism, thus making them capable of understanding and fulfilling their patriotic duty.

Kamieński's optimism as to the possibility of avoiding a civil war in the future revolutionary insurrection in Poland enabled him to develop in detail (in a separate part of *On the Vital Truths*) an interesting theory of the 'People's War'—a war in which the peasant masses were expected to take part together with the revolutionary gentry. This war, as Kamieński saw it, was to be waged by a mass guerrilla army of the peasants, organized by militarily trained revolutionaries and gradually transforming itself into a more regular army. Looking for historical precedents, Kamieński paid particular attention to the war waged against the Poles by Ukrainian peasants and Cossacks under the leadership of Khmelnytsky, and to the guerrilla warfare waged by the Spaniards against the Napoleonic invasion. He discussed also the role of the revolutionary clubs which he saw (in contradistinction to Mierosławski) as necessary instruments for shaping an adequate revolutionary consciousness.

It seems to be no exaggeration to say that Kamieński's theory of the 'People's War' was an important achievement in Polish revolutionary thought, anticipating to some extent the phenomenon of the so-called 'militarized mass insurrection'—a phenomenon fully developed only in the twentieth century (cf.

B. 62, pp. 56–7). It should be added that in developing this theory Kamieński was not alone. As Walter Laqueur has rightly noted, the theory of the 'People's War' and guerilla warfare 'was first described and analysed in quite surprising detail' by Polish and Italian radical democrats of the 1830s and 1840s—'one hundred years before Mao Tse-tung' (B. 96, p. 23. Cf. B. 95, pp. 115–18 and pp. 135–8).

The importance of Kamieński's theory was fully recognized by Polish Marxist historians in the 1950s. Because no serious attempt at a reinterpretation has appeared since that time, I would like to add a few words concerning the relation between Kamieński's and Mierosławski's views. According to the interpretation of the 1950s, Mierosławski's opinion that the revolutionary process should be totally controlled by a centralized revolutionary government and that the revolutionary war should resemble as much as possible regular war, waged by regular, disciplined army units, was simply an expression of fear of peasant masses and of the wish to exercise the 'revolutionary dictatorship' in the interests of the gentry (cf. Introduction to A. 54, p. lxxviii. This interpretation, however, is to me not entirely convincing. It can easily be reversed—as was shown, by the way, in Mierosławski's polemic with Kamieński. Mierosławski claimed that 'revolutionary dictatorship' was necessary to prevent the counter-revolutionary activities of the gentry and, also, its growing influence within the revolutionary movement; it was Kamieński's conception, he maintained, which in practice would give the gentry too much freedom of action. The theory of the educative influence of the bitter experience of Poland was for him an illusion, since no social class could reasonably be expected to commit collective suicide (see A. 76, p. 12).

The actual meeting of the two views on the methods of revolutionary struggle can be grasped, I think, not by trying to establish which of them was 'more to the Left', but, rather, by classifying them from the point of view of the classic problem of 'spontaneity versus organization' in the revolutionary movement. Seen from this perspective, the revolutionary General represented a combination of blanquism (revolutionary élitism, absolutization of centralized political power) with the traditional attitudes of a professional soldier; Kamieński's views, in their turn, appear as an attempt at vindication of the legitimate role of spontaneity—not 'anarchic' spontaneity, as his opponents claimed, but law-governed spontaneity of the 'universal reason' of society, more worthy of confidence than 'the reason of Centralization'. It was remarkable that in his struggle against revolutionary voluntarism he drew his main arguments from Hegelian historicism, anticipating, as it were, Plekhanov's usage of Hegelianism in the struggle against blanquism in the Russian revolutionary movement (cf. B. 176, pp. 155–6).

One should remember, of course, that in Kamieński's view social revolution was not an end in itself but part of a programme of national liberation. It seems justified, therefore, to maintain that this revolutionary strategy should not be separated from his conception of nation and from his views on the revolutionary calling of Poland.

Kamieński's social philosophy, permeated, as it was, by the spirit of rationalism and universalism, left no place for romantic anti-rationalism, which we could find in Libelt's views and, in a more pronounced form, in the Messianism of the romantic poets. His *Philosophy of the Material Economy*, except for a few introductory remarks on the relation between philosophy and the national character of the Poles, did not deal with peculiarly national problems at all. Nevertheless, it was intended to contribute to a better understanding of some general conditions for the correct solution to the national question. This followed from a general principle: like the other Polish thinkers of his epoch, Kamieński was convinced that one should work for the benefit of mankind through one's own nation; cosmopolitans were for him nothing else than 'hideous egoists', trying to find an excuse for getting rid of their moral debt to their motherland and, thus, not deserving to be called 'men'.

In accordance with his historicism, Kamieński did not think that the division of mankind into nations was something natural and eternal. On the contrary, he was keenly aware that the national bond, i.e. a moral tie uniting all the people of a given country, was a historical phenomenon of relatively recent origin, that its emergence would have been impossible without a considerable weakening of the rigid barriers dividing society into separate feudal estates. In his *Vital Truths* he pointed out that the downfall of the Polish state should be explained by the fact that feudalism and feudal interests had proved to be stronger in eighteenth-century Poland than national consciousness and the feeling of all-national solidarity in the face of an external enemy. He stressed that the ancient Poles had no idea of the true 'love of the fatherland' because they had identified the nation with one class only—with the gentry. 'Love of the fatherland', conceived as the love of all children for a common country, was for him the chief article of the 'people's faith'. In his *Democratic Catechism* he wrote: 'To love one's fatherland means to love its freedom, and freedom is nothing else than the welfare of the people. No country can be free if its people are oppressed; in such conditions the word "freedom" is meaningless, although it can serve as a convenient cloak for concealing the exploitation of the people.'

The ideal of national solidarity had, of course, two sides: on the one hand, it provided arguments for the criticism of feudal privileges and of the egoism of the ruling class; on the other hand, it exerted a moderating influence on revolutionary thinking, shifting the emphasis from class antagonisms to the necessity of attaining and maintaining national unity. Thus, the main practical problem of democratic nationalism was: how to win peasants to the national cause without alienating the gentry? As I have already pointed out, Kamieński believed (not without good reason) that the gentry, especially the middle and the petty, landless gentry, was the most patriotic social force in Poland and, consequently, he saw no alternative to the gentry's leadership in the national-liberation movement. His theory of the educative influence of the Polish national disasters provided a rationale for hoping that at least the best part of the Polish gentry would readily sacrifice their privileges for the benefit of a common national cause. This hope enabled him to accept the widespread view—shared, among others, by Marx and Engels— that Poland was revolutionary as a whole, because her restoration depended on the victory of progressive forces over the forces of reaction. Therefore, he proudly proclaimed that the Poles were, and had to be, the vanguard of mankind: 'The initiative will belong to us. Poles should not rely on anybody, because they are destined to be followed by others, to lead the universal movement, and not to lag behind it' (A. 32, p. 53).

VII. Edward Dembowski

1. Biographical Note

Kamieński's cousin, Edward Dembowski, was born in Warsaw on 25 April 1822. His father, Leon Dembowski, had the title of castellan and was a senator in the parliament of the Congress Kingdom. The future philosopher and revolutionary spent the first years of his life on his family's estate, Klementowice (Lublin voivodship). He was carefully educated under the tutorship of Adrian Krzyżanowski, a historian and publicist who, incidentally, became later the first Polish popularizer of the ideas of August Comte. In 1840 he took a trip abroad during which he got acquainted with the German romantic poet, Ludwig Tieck. Having returned to Poland, he joined the milieu of the progressive literary youth of Warsaw—the so-called 'Enthusiasts' (a female group) and the 'Warsaw Bohemia'. In the autumn of 1841 he married one of the leading 'Enthusiasts', Aniela Chlędowska. In January 1842 he embarked on editing a new journal—the *Scientific Review*. The title of this journal is a little misleading because its editors (Dembowski and Skimbrowicz) used the word 'science' as a synonym for 'philosophy'. Dembowski himself was particularly concerned with philosophy and literary criticism; the great majority of the philosophical and literary articles published in the *Scientific Review* were written by him. He also wrote a few poems, interesting as a document of the epoch but without genuine artistic value.

The year 1842 marked also the beginning of Dembowski's revolutionary activity. He became active in the radical wing of the conspiratorial 'Association of the Polish People' and tried to pull his elder cousin, Kamieński, into it. It is probable that he was in contact with the conspiracy of Father Piotr Ściegienny as well. In the summer of 1843 the Russian police discovered the existence of the Warsaw revolutionary organization and he had to save himself by escaping to Poznań. The Prussian authorities kept him for a month in a military working brigade; after that he was released but put under police surveillance. In spite of this, he immediately included himself in the conspiratorial activities of the Poznań National Committee (supporting its Left Wing, represented by Libelt) and, above all, joined the radical 'Union of Plebeians', a clandestine organization founded by a bookseller, Walenty Stefański. His underground work did not prevent him from writing a large number of philosophical and critical studies which he published mainly in the radical *Literary Weekly* (*Tygodnik Literacki*) and in Libelt's *Year*. By now he had written a book entitled *An Outline of Polish Literature* (Poznań 1845) and a series of important philosophical articles. His philosophical testament—'Thoughts on the Future of Philosophy', published in the *Year*, April 1845—was, probably, also written in Poznań.

In October 1844, Dembowski was accused of 'spreading communist propaganda' and ordered to leave at once the territory of the Prussian state. He came first to the West, to get in contact with the democratic wing of the Polish emigration (among others, he visited Lelewel in his hermitage in Brussels). In January 1845, he arrived in Galicia and, in consultation with the Centralization of the TDP and with the Poznań Committee, resumed his underground revolutionary work. Among the organizers of the uprising he represented the most radical current, trying to transform the national-liberation struggle into an agrarian revolution. Therefore, anticipating the Russian 'go to the people' movement of the 1870s, he often dressed himself in a peasant's russet overcoat and went to the countryside to preach the revolutionary gospel.

The outbreak of the Cracow uprising found him in Lvov. He immediately returned to Cracow, heading an insurrectionary detachment composed of 200 miners of Wieliczka. Formally he was given the post of secretary to J. Tyssowski, who had been proclaimed the 'dictator'. In fact, however, he became from the first day the virtual leader of the insurrection. Soon it turned out that, in spite of his efforts, the peasants were not prepared to join the uprising; on the contrary, the Austrian officials succeeded in spreading rumours that the uprising was aimed at strengthening nobility's control over the peasants and preventing their enfranchisement by the benevolent Kaiser. Nevertheless, when the peasant *jacquerie* broke out and when the first terrifying news of the massacre of the gentry in the Tarnow region became known in Cracow, the revolutionary 'castellan's son' did not despair but undertook a bold attempt at winning over the riotous peasants to the side of the patriotic insurgents. To this end he organized a big procession which on 27 February, carrying crosses and church standards, marched out from Cracow in the direction of Wieliczka. This procession, headed by himself, with a cross in his hand and a pistol girded on his belt, was soon attacked by Austrian troops. He tried to organize armed resistance and was killed fighting.

Despite the 'Galician massacre' one should not say that Dembowski's efforts to win the peasants to the national cause were a complete failure. Some peasants and shepherds in the Tatra mountains reacted to the Cracow uprising by coming out against the Austrians (the so-called Chocholów uprising). After his death Dembowski became a legendary hero—the mountaineers believed that he was hiding somewhere and would re-emerge sometime to lead the struggle against domestic oppression and the foreign yoke.

2. The Philosophy of Creativity

At the beginning of his activity—in 1842—Dembowski was an enthusiastic Hegelian. According to Kamieński's ironical account of his views he did not see by then a greater man than Hegel and a more important task than popularizing his philosophy in Poland (A. 33, p. 74).

In his first major philosophical work—a long treatise entitled *An Outline of the Development of Philosophy in Germany* (1842)—Dembowski made an appraisal of the contemporary state of philosophical knowledge. In England, he claimed, true philosophy did not exist at all, and even the idea of what philosophy should be was entirely forgotten. The Slavonic contributions to philosophy, as testified by the names of Cieszkowski and Trentowski, were much higher than the English. Nevertheless the time for a Slavonic philosophy had not yet come and the leadership in philosophy still belonged to Germany (developing its theoretical side) and to France (developing its 'practical' side). In the realm of pure theory the highest, unsurpassed achievement was seen by the young Polish thinker in Hegelianism. This did not mean that he was unaware of the recent, post-Hegelian developments in philosophy; on the contrary, he paid due attention to the ideas of the Hegelian Left, to Feuerbach's *Essence of Christianity* and to Cieszkowski's 'philosophy of action'. He acknowledged their contributions but, at the same time, he insisted that, in spite of their claims, they *did not go beyond* Hegelianism. Thus, he was ready to accept Cieszkowski's postulate of 'translating philosophy into action', but disagreed with the idea that the 'philosophy of action' was *overcoming* Hegelianism and *transcending* philosophy as such. Action, he asserted, should be conceived as a realization of philosophy and not as something higher than philosophy; action, according to this argument, represented the sphere of empirical reality which by definition had to be lower than the sphere of Absolute truth, represented by philosophy.

Dembowski's first doubts as to the validity of Hegel's system concerned the problem of the stages of the Absolute Spirit. His attempt at correcting Hegel on this point was, in intention and meaning, diametrically opposite to the analogical attempt of Cieszkowski. The author of *Prolegomena* replaced the Hegelian triad 'art-religion-philosophy' with the triad 'art-philosophy-action', whereas Dembowski's triad was: 'philosophy (knowledge)-history (passing of knowledge into action)-art'. As we see, both thinkers refused to consider religion as a stage of the Absolute Spirit, but they did so for different reasons. For Cieszkowski religion was not a stage of the Absolute Spirit but the very *substance* of it, *inseparable* from each of its stages; for Dembowski religion was only the first step of knowledge—the most primitive, misty form of knowledge, *not deserving* to be treated as a separate stage of the Absolute Spirit.

Considering art as the highest stage of the development of the Absolute Spirit also demands an explanation. In Dembowski's case this had nothing in common with aestheticism. True, it was bound up with a romantic cult of art and with a romantic protest against the Hegelian thesis that the historical mission of art had already been completed. One could argue, not without good reasons, that it was also a form of *pan-aestheticism* in the sense of striving for a form of life in which everything, including daily work, would be beautiful and reminiscent of art (cf. B. 121, pp. 229–30). However, a striving for transforming the world by making it beautiful was the opposite of aestheticism in the sense of escaping from the real world into the realm of pure art. Another fundamental difference was the fact that in Dembowski's eyes art was a means and not an end in itself, the highest value being the 'welfare of the people'. Art, reasoned Dembowski, was a prototype of self-dependent creativity, and the main passion of a true artist was a 'boundless love of mankind'; creativity, conceived as a higher synthesis of thought and feeling, was the precondition and the essence of the 'absolute (i.e. perfect) social life'. People should be made self-dependent and creative; therefore, the realization of the Absolute in the social life should be preceded by the fullest possible development of the Absolute Spirit whose highest and crowning stage was represented by art. It followed therefrom that the highest value for which all men, including the artists, should strive was the 'absolute social life'. On the other hand, however, it was made clear that without the fullest possible development of artistic creativity the 'absolute social life' could be conceivable neither in the Idea (i.e. in philosophy) nor in history (i.e. in action).

Dembowski's ardent commitment to revolutionary activities made him even more critical of the 'absolute philosophy' of Hegel and, at the same time, more confident of the philosophical mission of the Poles. Like the other Polish philosophers of the 1840s, although in a different way, he began to criticize Hegelian panlogism and contemplativeness, setting against Hegelian universalism the rehabilitation of the individual and against Hegelian rationalism the vindication of the great role of strong, passionate feelings in history. He came also to the conclusion that Hegelianism could be accused of tolerating and even justifying the existence of evil in society. At the end of 1842 he read young Engels's pamphlet *Schelling und die Offenbarung* and fully agreed with its author that the main task of philosophy should be paving the way for the social progress of mankind (cf. A. 13, II. 289–96). However, he allotted this task not to the Germans but to the Polish national philosophers. The idea of a Polish 'national philosophy' became a leit-motif of his thinking. At the beginning of 1843 he went so far as to accuse Cieszkowski and Libelt of 'imitating' German philosophy and, therefore, of not being 'national' enough.

The writings of Henryk Rzewuski and of the Catholic critics of philosophy (see below) made Dembowski acutely aware that the idea of the 'national character' of philosophy could be interpreted in a conservative way. Therefore, he took care to make it clear that by 'national philosophy' he did not mean a philosophy steeped in traditionalist thinking or implied in national customs. He criticized Libelt for putting too much emphasis on the religious beliefs of the peasantry, tainted, as they were, by superstitions and by the Roman faith of the ruling class; he was even more critical, of course, of the writers who identified the national character of the Poles with the traditional attitudes of the Polish gentry. According to him the Polish national character was an inborn quality of the common people of Poland and should not be identified with the external features of their beliefs or customs, elaborated under the corrupting influence of the 'latinized' culture of the gentry. He saw such a quality in the 'briskness and dash' (dziarskość), and concluded from this that the Poles were destined to develop the philosophy of the future, i.e. the 'philosophy of creativity'. He drew attention to the fact that already Hoene-Wroński had tried to develop a philosophy of creativity and that the Polish word 'twórczość' (creativity), as used in the philosophical works of Kamieński, was, allegedly, much better for expressing the idea of creative activity than the French 'force créatice' or the German 'das Schaffen' (A. 13, IV. 365). He was also convinced that the historical task of the Poles consisted in the practical implementation of philosophy, i.e. in bringing about the 'absolute (perfect) social life'.

The most important part of Dembowski's 'philosophy of creativity' was the philosophy of history (he was using Cieszkowski's term 'historiosophy'), that is 'the knowledge of social progress and the philosophy of social sciences' (A. 13, IV. 67), interpreting the past in order to deduce from it an image of the future. In his article 'On the Progresses in the Philosophical Understanding of Being' (1844), he presented an outline of an interesting theory of 'creativity in history', consisting of the process of 'individualization', i.e. the movement from the primitive, undifferentiated unity through its disintegration into autonomous ('individualized') and conflicting elements into a new higher unity, complicated enough to comprise—and to transcend—all the positive results of 'individualization'. According to this theory the first stage in the development of society was theocracy, i.e. a state in which the primitive unity, based upon common faith embodied in the person of a theocratic ruler, made no room for an autonomous ('individualized') existence in any sphere of social life. The next stage—royal absolutism—was a great advance because it was limited to the political sphere; absolutist rulers did not pretend to be autocrats in the religious sphere and allowed the existence of private ('individualized') property. Further 'individualization' was achieved in a constitutional monarchy, because the political power became divided ('individualized') by being transferred from the hands of one man to the hands of many (the king and the members of the ruling class). Still further advances along the road of 'individualization' were represented by elective monarchy and by the republican government of the privileged. The final goal of this process was conceived as the fullest possible democracy, in which every individual would be autonomous, self-dependent, and having the same share in political and social life as the others. Thus, the democratic ideal of the sovereignty of the people was seen by Dembowski as the highest stage of 'individualization'. At the same time, however, it was to be a dialectical return to unity: free people, ruling themselves, were expected to overcome conflicting centrifugal tendencies, to abolish all kinds of divisions, and to develop a free unity in political, social, and intellectual spheres.

The most original and valuable among Dembowski's contributions to philosophy is, probably, his conception of development through the struggle of opposites, set forth in the article entitled 'A Few Thoughts on Eclecticism' (1843). Following the radical Hegelian Left, especially Bruno Bauer and Michael Bakunin (whose article 'Reaction in Deutschland' was known to him),[23] the young Polish thinker postulated a revolutionary reinterpretation of Hegelian dialectics, bringing out the concept of negation and rejecting the idea of mediation between the two opposites in the name of their higher synthesis. The other Polish philosophers—Cieszkowski, Trentowski, and even Libelt, more faithful in this respect to the orthodox interpretation of Hegelian notions of 'Vermittelung' and 'Aufhebung', put emphasis just on the mediation between the negating and the negated, on their reconciliation in a higher unity, preserving the 'truth' of the negated moment as an inalienable, although subordinated component of a new dialectical totality. Practice, they postulated, was not to be 'negative' and 'critical', but 'positive' and 'organic'. For Dembowski such a conception was tantamount to a philosophical justification of the 'eclectic' posi-

tion of the *juste milieu* liberals, trying to reconcile the irreconcil-
able. In the struggle of opposites, he maintained, only the
negating force represents the truth of the future; all attempts at
softening the struggle by an 'eclectic' mediation between the
opposite principles can only weaken the dynamics of progress,
thus playing into the hands of reaction more effectively than the
extreme reactionaries, who, unconsciously, help the revolution
by bringing about a clear-cut polarization of social forces.

Dembowski did not imply that all 'eclectics' were conscious
enemies of progress. He made a distinction between three types
of eclecticism. The first type was the eclecticism having no
self-consciousness, i.e. stemming from ignorance. The second,
exemplified by the Polish Constitution of 3 May 1791, was
classified as eclecticism stemming from the lack of force and the
feeling of timidity bound up with it. Only the third type—the
'deliberate eclecticism'—was seen as representing the position
of the most sophisticated reactionaries, hiding themselves
behind 'progressive' phrases and, at the same time, combating
genuine progress in the most efficient way.

The last word of Dembowski's 'philosophy of creativity' was
his 'Thoughts on the Future of Philosophy' (1845), setting forth
a programme for a Polish 'national philosophy' which would
unite the German 'science of thought' (i.e. speculative philosophy) with the French 'science of action' (i.e. social theories,
especially socialism). In fact what this article proposed was not
a revision and a further development, but rather a radical
transcendence of Hegelianism. 'Creativity' became identified
with 'creating', which, in turn, was presented as the process of
development in the 'sensual substance', i.e. in material reality.
Hegelianism was discussed as a philosophy developing the idea
only in the sphere of logic, thus making it 'only the law of life
and not the living law' (A. 13, IV. 336, note). The inspiration
behind these thoughts was obviously Feuerbach's criticism of
Hegel—his 'rehabilitation of matter', leading, consequently, to
a rehabilitation of 'sensuality', 'heart', and 'passions', and, in
this respect, easily harmonizing with a romantic criticism of
Hegelian rationalism. From the point of view of the problem of
revolution the importance of Feuerbachian inspiration consisted in the fact that it gave Dembowski a theoretical justification for seeing dialectics—interpreted by him in a revolutionary
way—as an immanent living law of *material* reality (cf. B. 157,

pp. 268–72), and not only as a dialectics of the absolute mind (Hegel) or of the human mind (B. Bauer).

In the article *On the Tendencies of Our Time* (1845), Dembowski expressed his views on the religious question. He distinguished four phases of the negation of Catholicism: (1) Protestantism, (2) neo-Catholicism, i.e. Catholicism concentrating on ethical issues and consciously avoiding political commitments, (3) neo-Christianism, represented by the Saint-Simonians and by different messianic sects, including the followers of Towiański and, finally (4) the Hegelian Left, representing the most consistent religious radicalism, leading to a complete dissolving of religion in political and social life. As an avowed enemy of all forms of 'eclecticism' he espoused, of course, the Left-Hegelian standpoint. There were, as we can see, many other reasons for treating his philosophy as very close to some tendencies in Left-Hegelianism. In a loose sense of this term he can be classified, together with Michael Bakunin and Moses Hess, as a representative figure of the 'second generation of young Hegelians, continuing the work of the first generation to its logical revolutionary conclusions' (B. 16, p. 268). There was, however, an important difference between the classical, German variety of Left-Hegelianism and the Polish Left-Hegelianism, represented by his 'philosophy of creativity'. The German Left-Hegelians waged a war against Romanticism, which was to them an ideology of feudal reaction, whereas in Dembowski's philosophy Left-Hegelian motifs were interwoven with a populist Romanticism, glorifying exalted feelings, the simple life of uncorrupted peasants, and the prophetic power of inspired poets. Such a combination of ideas was inconceivable in Germany, but very natural in Poland.

Dembowski's commitment to Romanticism was especially pronounced in his literary criticism and aesthetics, closely bound up with his 'philosophy of creativity'. As a revolutionary populist, he rejected the idea of 'art for art's sake', but, unlike the later Russian populists, without embracing the conception of literature as a faithful description and critical analysis of existing social reality. On the contrary, he defended the romantic conception of art as an expression of spontaneous creativity and set a much higher value on poetry, especially prophetic poetry, than on descriptive realistic prose. Romantic 'loftiness' was the central category in his aesthetics, and the highest literary genre was for him (as for many other romantics) the drama—a literary form which he thought to be best suited for showing the struggle or antagonistic forces in history. He rejected literary realism not only for aesthetical reasons but, and above all, as a method of implying a reconciliation with, or even a capitulation to, the empirically given social reality. Against 'objective' descriptions of reality he set a romantic 'subjectivism', bound up with an active, creative attitude towards the existing world. In the name of such 'subjectivism' he condemned the novel, seeing it as a mere description of unimportant, prosaic facets of social life, expressing a contemplative and mean-spirited attitude towards the world. It is worth noting that in Cieszkowski's case programmatic activism did not lead to such conclusions: in his article *On the Contemporary Novel*[24] Cieszkowski praised Balzac and treated the novel, especially the realistic novel, as the literary genre best suited for the needs of his time. This difference between Cieszkowski and Dembowski can be explained by their respective political attitudes: the realistic novel harmonized with the spirit of 'organic work' but not with the spirit of *romantic* revolutionism.[25]

3. Socialism and Agrarian Revolution

As I have pointed out, by the French 'science of action', which should be combined with, and enriched by, the German philosophy, Dembowski meant first of all the theories of the French utopian socialists (Saint-Simon and the Saint-Simonians, Fourier, Leroux, Proudhon) and communists (Babeuf, Cabet). Already in 1842, at the very beginning of his revolutionary activity in the Association of the Polish People, he did not want to limit his tasks to democratic radicalism. In a conversation with Kamieński he stated bluntly: 'We have abolished hereditament and replaced it with common property' (A. 33, p. 22).

Dembowski's social ideas were strongly influenced by his Romanticism. He opposed private property because, unlike Kamieński, he saw it as a disintegrating, atomizing factor and not as a form of social bond. Cold calculation, utilitarianism, and rational egoism, characteristic of the bourgeois societies of the West, were repellent to him. He could not conceive of true social life without lofty ideals, passionate love, and sacrifice. He emphasized that individual 'love for mankind' was not enough because the principle of love should be embodied in social institutions. The inevitable conclusion was, of course, that a social order based upon love was incompatible with the divisive egoism inherent in the principles of private interest and private property.

In his article 'Creativity in Social Life' (1843) Dembowski set forth a theory of three types of subjugation of the people. The first type, called 'physical subjugation', was based upon sheer force; the second type—'economic subjugation'—was based upon unequal division of property; the third type—'intellectual subjugation'—stemmed from unequal access to education. In all these cases, however, the subjugation was rooted in the principle of private property, as opposed to mutual love, disinterestedness, and sacrifice. Not only 'economic subjugation' but 'physical' and 'intellectual' subjugations as well had been called into being by the material interests of the stronger. It followed therefrom that private property necessarily engendered subjugation and, therefore, was incompatible with freedom. 'Freedom of the people', concluded Dembowski, 'is based upon the liquidation of property because only then no form of subjugation will hamper people's development' (A. 13, III. 238).

'The community of ownership' should be 'absolute': 'the people as a whole will have property but individuals will have no property at all' (ibid.). No wonder, therefore, that Dembowski was not satisfied with the theories of French socialists who in their attitude towards property represented, in his view, a typical 'eclecticism'. He was especially indignant at Fourier's idea that the income of the phalansteries should be divided not only in accordance with the work and needs of their members but also in proportion to the amount of invested capital. The existence of capitalists and private capital, he argued, would be a glaring contradiction to the principles of the 'absolute society'. Otherwise the idea of a phalanstery was very attractive to him, mainly as a means of avoiding the enslaving effects of the division of labour. The division of labour in society, he thought, should be replaced with the principle of the division of each individual's daily work into different occupations: each man should occupy himself, successively, with all kinds of labour, thus exercising all his capacities and preventing the situation in which especially hard or unpleasant work is being done by a special category of people. The working day should be as short as possible, in order to give everybody enough time for artistic creativity and philosophical thinking. The social income—not the income of each community taken separately, but the income of society as a whole—should be divided not according to work and talent (as Saint-Simon wanted it to be) but in accordance with the formula: 'chacun selon sa capacité, à chacun selon ses besoins' (A. 13, IV. 80).

As we can see from the above, Dembowski's views on the ideal social order were unambiguous: it was not without reason that he was considered to be a 'communist'. It should be added that he was not a 'peaceful' communist but an ardent revolutionary, deeply convinced (in contradistinction to Kamieński) that an overwhelming majority of the Polish gentry were conscious enemies of the emancipation of peasants and, therefore, did not deserve to be treated as part of the Polish nation. Nevertheless, in his practical activity he did not strive for a socialist revolution and did not refuse to co-operate with the moderate wing of the national liberation movement. Instead of a socialist, or communist, programme he put forward the idea of an agrarian revolution which would give the peasants the full (*private!*) ownership of their holdings, without indemnification for the gentry. He fully supported the Manifesto of the Cracow uprising, issued on 22 February 1846, which announced the abolition of privileges, unconditional enfranchisement of the peasants, giving land from the crown estates to the landless peasants who would join the national cause, equal rights for the Jews, and so forth. True, it was a very progressive, revolutionary programme, enthusiastically approved by the whole European Left, including Marx and Engels who declared their solidarity with the Cracow revolutionaries in a special paragraph of the *Manifesto of the Communist Party*. In spite of this, however, no socialist or communist ideas could be found in it (cf. B. 157). Thus, the differences between Dembowski's and Kamieński's political views seem to be much more pronounced in theory than in practice.

If so, was there a contradiction between Dembowski's socialist theories and his political practice? Not at all. On a theoretical plane he did not contradict himself because he had espoused, although not without reservations, an historicist view on the development of society. In his article 'On the Progresses in the Philosophical Understanding of Being' he clearly stated that each form of social structure was necessary and, therefore, good for its time; if it was not, it would have been rejected and changed by the 'general will of society'. He was convinced that the 'general will' of the Polish people was fully prepared for the rejection of all remnants of feudal relationships, but he was aware (which was to his credit) that it was too early to demand acceptance of a direct transition to the 'absolute form of social-ization'.

On a practical plane the most important problem was how to carry out the agrarian revolution in a truly radical, consistent way. Unlike the Marxist historians of the 1950s, I do not share the conviction that a radical peasant revolution could have been successful as a solution to the national and social question in Poland. A revolution proclaiming a total expropriation of the landowners would have alienated the Polish gentry, who, un-deniably, were by then the most conscious and most active patriotic force, and it would, at the same time, have created a panic, mobilizing against itself all the forces of the three parti-tioning powers; even the European liberal Left, very Polono-phile at that time, would not have sympathized with such an ultra-radical movement. Kamieński, I think, was essentially right in advocating moderation in revolutionism; by the same token, it was, in my view, to Dembowski's credit that in the critical moment he refrained from setting forth and propagating ultra-radical slogans. Nevertheless, irrespective of different views on 'what might have happened' in history, a careful study of Dembowski's revolutionary activity (in conjunction with his thought) leads to the conclusion that the Polish Marxists of the 1950s were right in claiming that despite his seeming solidarity with the political programme of the Polish Democratic Society (shared also by Libelt and other moderate democrats), he represented, in fact, the most extreme left wing of the Polish political spectrum. He believed that the most important thing was to bring about a revolutionary explosion, and he knew that this was impossible without mobilizing the revolutionary potential of the patriotic gentry. He hoped, however, that once the revolution had started the peasants would join it, making it more and more radical and, finally, emancipating themselves from the leadership of the patriots from the gentry. Thus, unlike Kamieński, he believed that the Polish national-liberation movement would, and should, become transformed into a genuine peasant revolution. He did not succeed in preventing the bloody pro-Habsburg *jacquerie*, but, none the less, he came as close as possible to the identification of the 'national cause' with the 'peasants' cause'. A moving testimony to this were the words from his revolutionary appeal, 'To All Poles Who Can Read', written two days before his tragic death: 'We, the people; we, the peasants; we, the Poles' (A. 13, IV. 405).

4. The Idea of Nation and the Philosophy of Polish History

The identification of 'Polishness' with 'peasantness' was a leit-motif of Dembowski's romantic populism. He went so far as to reverse the traditionalist notion of the 'nation of the gentry' by claiming that the Polish gentry was not part of the Polish nation because it had betrayed the true national spirit whose sole repository was by now the Polish peasantry. Following the early Polish Slavophiles, especially Chodakowski, he saw the Polish gentry as embodying the principle of 'latinism', alien and hostile to the truly Slavonic spirit of the Polish peasants. He thought also that national community was incompatible with the oppression and exploitation of the people and, on this ground, accused the oppressors of splitting the nation, destroying it, and, in consequence, putting themselves outside it. Thus, for instance, in one of his poetic compositions he wrote:

> How can I not suffer, if the people are oppressed
> By Polish nobles, or, rather, by infernal nobles,
> Because what is Polish—oh, God!—is of the people
> And not of the nobility (A. 13, III. 108.)

In many of his articles Dembowski tried to elaborate a comprehensive philosophy of Polish history. His thinking on this topic exemplified the phenomenon of 'revolutionary retrospection' typical of the Polish democrats of the Romantic Epoch. Paraphrasing Marx's words we can say that he was 'looking beyond the Middle Ages' into the primitive age of Polish history, in order 'to find what is newest in what is oldest'.[26] In doing this he was inspired by Lelewel's theory of the ancient Slavonic communalism, by Chodakowski's Slavophilism, contrasting the Slavonic principles with the principles of 'latinism', and by the growing number of studies of Polish folklore, which emphasized its artistic value and its significance for the knowledge of history.

Dembowski's first attempt at periodization of Polish history was presented at the end of 1842. He divided it into three great epochs: (1) the primitive, Slavo-Polish epoch, (2) the epoch of struggle between the Slavonic and the Latin cultures, resulting in the victory of the latter, and (3) the epoch of the decline of Latino-Polish culture, and of the birth of the truly Polish, consciously national culture, being a dialectical 'return on a higher level' to the first, Slavo-Polish epoch (A. 13, II. 339).

In his later articles Dembowski preserved this schema enriching it with new nuances of thought. Thus, in his 'General view on the Education of Individuals and Peoples' (1843) he put forward an interesting theory of the role of great prophetic poets in awakening the dormant national consciousness of the common people. In the first, pre-Christian epoch of Polish history, he maintained, the 'socialization' of the Polish people was democratic and, therefore, national; it was, however, a *theocratic* democracy, leaving no room for the development of critical, reflective thought and, therefore, not allowing the people to raise themselves to the level of self-consciousness. In the next epoch the influence of 'Latinism', which had appeared in Poland together with the Roman Church, brought about a deep distortion of the truly Polish, democratic principles, splitting the nation into the common people, who remained faithful to their Slavonic inheritance, and the 'latinized' gentry. This very split, however, having destroyed the primitive theocratic unity, made the most sensitive members of the gentry aware of the contrast between their culture and the culture of the people, thus creating conditions for the emergence of national self-consciousness. The decline of 'Latino-Polish socialization' and the resulting downfall of the Polish state precipitated the process of national self-awakening and opened up the third, nationally-conscious epoch of Polish history. The uncontaminated, truly Polish element, preserved in latency by the common people, was at this stage rediscovered and was sung by poets, whose poems, in turn, began to penetrate into the countryside awakening the peasants to *conscious* national existence (A. 13, III. 83–4).

A characteristic feature of Dembowski's conception of Polish history is his negative view of the Polish Enlightenment. The most comprehensive presentation of this view is to be found in his article 'A Few Thoughts Concerning the Historical and Social Development of Poland' (1843). In France, he argued, the epoch of Enlightenment had many sides: a 'courtly' side, a scientific side, and a 'popular' side. It was the culmination of a courtly, aristocratic culture, resulting in the utter demoralization of the upper class and of 'polite society' as a whole; from this point of view it was, therefore, an epoch of degeneration and decline. From the 'scientific' point of view, the French Enlightenment was, on the one hand, an epoch of a shallow, superficial philosophy but, on the other hand, an epoch of great progress in the exact sciences as well. Finally, the French Enlightenment had its 'popular' side which found expression in the struggle against the Catholic Church (although not in the theoretical criticism of religion which, in Dembowski's view, lacked the profundity of Left-Hegelianism) and, of course, in the French Revolution. The aristocratic intrigues compelled the Jacobins to make use of terror which resulted in spoiling the image of revolution; nevertheless, the revolutionary upheaval in France was a magnificent event and an important watershed in universal history. In Poland, however, the upper classes were immune to revolutionary ideas, and the common people, being unable to read, identified everything French with the 'latinism' of the gentry. Therefore, the Polish Enlightenment, with its characteristic gallomania and 'courtliness' (both equally repellent from the point of view of democratic, romantic nationalism) was only the final stage of the decadence of the 'latinized' Polish civilization. It weakened the morale of the ruling class, killed its former vigour and robustness, destroyed the ancient equality among the gentry by furthering aristocratic tendencies, and, consequently, paved the way for national disaster.

The one-sidedness of this judgement is striking. The great intellectual upheaval brought about by the Polish Enlightenment was reduced to aping everything French, and important reforms initiated and carried out by the Enlighteners, including the Constitution of 1791, were not even mentioned. To be more precise, these reforms were mentioned in an indirect way and in a negative context. French influence, according to Dembowski, was destructive for Poland because, among other things, it led to the replacement of the republican form of government with a consitutional monarchy. As we know, in Dembowski's historical typology elective monarchy or, in other words, an aristocratic republic, represented a higher form of government than a hereditary constitutional monarchy. Seen from this point of

view the Constitution of the 3rd of May looked like a retrogression. In such a way Dembowski's ardent republicanism
made him blind to the fact that in eighteenth-century Poland
'gentry republicanism' was bound up with social and cultural
conservatism, whereas the introduction of a constitutional
monarchy was an attempt at strengthening the state while
preserving, at the same time, as much as possible, the ancient
Polish freedom.

In another article, entitled 'The Polish Devil' (1843), Dembowski made his position even more clear. He defined the
republican (democratic) form of government as peculiar to the
Slavs and as representing the truly Polish element in the
Latino-Polish epoch of Polish history. Unlike the Latin
countries, he maintained, Poland had never developed political
feudalism (in the sense of a hierarchy within the nobility) and
royal absolutism; her 'democracy of the gentry' was a *latinized*
form of government, because it denied citizenship to the people,
but it was Slavonic in so far as it preserved republican freedom
and democratic equality, although this was limited to the ruling
class. So it was a very bad form of 'socialization', but, nevertheless, better than the purely Latin 'socialization' of the West.

In the same article Dembowski took up Chodakowski's
theme of 'pre-Christian Slavdom'. For the Polish peasants, he
claimed, Roman Catholicism became firmly associated with the
foreign influence which had destroyed the ancient Slavonic
communalism. Therefore, the peasants had returned in fact to
their native pagan faith while clinging, at the same time, to the
external forms of the Catholic religion. Externalities, however,
should not be taken for essentials. The folklore of the Polish
peasantry, its legends and customs, its animistic cult of nature,
its belief in magic and in the existence of water-nymphs and
other miraculous creatures—all these things were in Dembowski's eyes a telling testimony to the strength of pre-
Christian, pagan elements in the genuine world-view of the
Polish people.

All these motifs reappear in Dembowski's *Outline of Polish
Literature*. The whole span of the history of Polish literature was
divided into three periods: (1) the pre-Christian period
(although there was no written literature at that time), (2) the
period of latinized culture, lasting until 1820, and (3) the period
of a consciously national culture. The second period was

divided, in turn, into four sub-periods, the second of which, embracing the years 1500–1600, was called 'the epoch of splendour'. The splendid development of Renaissance culture in Poland was explained as a result of the victory of the Slavonic (democratic) tendency *within* the latinized culture, i.e. as the result of establishing the 'democracy of the gentry' which had changed the Polish state into a republic headed by a king. In the religious sphere, maintained Dembowski, the anti-Latin and, therefore, more national tendency was embodied in Protestantism, especially in the radical Reformation, represented by the Socinians or 'Polish Brethren'. The victory of the Jesuit counter-Reformation (at this point Dembowski fully agreed with Trentowski) brought about a cultural and political decline which lasted until 1770, to be replaced by another form of decline, represented by the sub-period of 'courtliness' and gallomania (1770–1820). Having passed this lowest point of decline and self-denial, the Polish national spirit, as expressed in Polish literature, awoke and began to return to itself, recovering its inner essence and raising it to the level of self-awareness. In the beginning (sub-period 1820–25) it was a nostalgic awakening of national feelings in the poetry of Kazimierz Brodziński and Antoni Malczewski. In the next short sub-period (1825–30), thanks to the romantic poetry of Mickiewicz and the romantic literary criticism of Mochnacki, Polish literature reached the stage of full national consciousness. The task of the last sub-period—from the November uprising until 1844— was the development of a truly national political and philosophical thought, stemming from love of the people. Thus, the development of Polish literature was conceived as a great dialectical process of self-estrangement of the dormant national spirit and, later, of its awakening and returning to itself on a higher level—i.e. on the level of self-consciousness.

It should be stressed that this process was presented by Dembowski not only as a struggle of abstract 'principles' but also, and primarily, as the struggle of the social forces embodying them. Dembowski's sympathies were always on the side of the common people in whom he saw the only bearers of the truly national spirit; in spite of this, however, the departure from national (Slavonic) principles and the self-estrangement of the national spirit in the process of 'latinization' were treated as a necessary stage of development, and not as mere retrogression.

One could say that the whole of the second period of Polish literature (1000–1820) was in Dembowski's eyes a retrogression and a progression at the same time. It was a retrogression from the point of view of the democratic, egalitarian principles inherent, as he saw it, in the Polish national spirit; it was a progression because the destruction of the primitive, stagnant unity was necessary for civilizational and cultural development, and because national self-denial was a necessary condition of national self-consciousness. Thus, in the dialectical development of the national spirit the whole period of 'latinized' culture represented the necessary phase of 'negation'. Passing through this phase, Dembowski thought, had enabled the Poles to replace 'negative progress' with 'positive progress', i.e. with a type of progress in which there was no contradiction between the welfare of the people and the demands of civilizational and cultural growth, in which social antagonisms were no longer necessary for the historical development of the nation.

VIII. Conservative Critics of Philosophy

1. In Defence of the Church

The striving for the modernization of religious life, characteristic of Cieszkowski, Trentowski, and Libelt, was actively resisted by the defenders of the traditional Catholic faith. Curiously enough, they did not pay much attention to the representatives of the philosophical Left. In Kamieński's case this could be explained by his deliberate avoidance of religious questions; Dembowski's case was more complicated: his hostility towards the Roman Church was too explicit to be ignored, but, on the other hand, his indifference towards religion combined with outspokenly atheistic leanings could be considered as less dangerous to clerical conservatism than the attempts to modernize the religious consciousness of the Poles by making it more 'philosophical' and, by the same token, less dependent on the authority of the Church. In other words, the main danger was seen not in religious agnosticism, or even atheism, but in philosophical speculations about Christianity, which, it was felt, could bring about a new Reformation. There was some justification for this feeling. After all, the younger disciples of Hegel frequently referred to themselves as representing 'the Reformation of the nineteenth century' (see B. 16, p. 7).

One of the first symptoms of the increased vigilance of the defenders of traditional Catholicism was an article by the woman philosopher Eleonora Ziemięcka published in the *Warsaw Library* (1841) in response to Cieszkowski's article praising the philosophy of Hegel.[27] It condemned the 'pantheism' and rationalism of Hegel, setting against them not only the revealed faith but also the philosophy of Kant. In contrast to the post-Kantian German philosophers, argued Ziemięcka, Kant himself rejected the 'pride of reason' by demonstrating the incompetence of theoretical reason in the sphere of metaphysical problems. Such a position was acceptable for the defenders of the Church because it put limits on the ambitions of rational philosophy and thus made room for religious faith. What was unacceptable was the boundless cognitive optimism of post-Kantian philosophers who tried to penetrate and rationally explain all the mysteries of the Absolute, openly challenging the Church as the only legitimate interpreter of the highest truths. In spite of their criticism of the 'one-sided rationalism' of Hegel, the same was true of Cieszkowski, Trentowski, and Libelt: their philosophical maximalism was based on the assumption that autonomous human reason was capable of understanding the Absolute and, therefore, that the content of the revealed religion should be submitted to philosophical analysis in order to be reinterpreted and modernized.

Conservative Catholics, understandably enough, saw this attitude as tantamount to embracing the principle of 'free inquiry' characteristic of the Protestant Reformation. They set against it a new version of the old theory of 'two truths': the scientific truth, limited to the sphere of earthly things, on the one hand, and the revealed knowledge of divine things whose only legitimate interpreter was the Church, on the other. From this point of view the programmatically anti-metaphysical position of the late Enlighteners, especially of Jan Śniadecki, was praised by them as an example of philosophical modesty and as a desirable antidote to the German 'metaphysical infection' (see A. 82).

Understandably, the greatest danger was seen in the philosophy of Trentowski who, unlike Cieszkowski and Libelt, did not refrain from direct attacks on the Catholic Church and openly proclaimed his sympathies for the Reformation. The polemical campaign waged by the Polish clerical conservatives against the usurpations of autonomous reason concentrated almost entirely on his ideas. The main (part) was played in it by Feliks Kozłowski (1803–72), a former personal friend of Trentowski and the author of an enthusiastic review of his *Grundlage*. At the beginning of the 1840s he became aware of the dangerous implications of Trentowski's philosophy, and devoted all his efforts to the struggle against it. His crowning achievement was a work in two big volumes entitled *The Beginnings of Christian Philosophy, Including the Criticism of the Philosophy of B. F. Trentowski* (see A. 39). This was a systematic exposition of the doctrine of the Church, confronted in each point with Trentowski's philosophical views. The final result of all these confrontations was unequivocal: Trentowski's philosophy was proclaimed to be anti-Christian and, by the same token, antinational, more anti-Christian than German idealism, and, worst of all, hypocritically pretending to express in philosophical form the highest truths of Christianity.

Invoking the authority of the Catholic philosopher Franz von Baader, Kozłowski accused his former friend of identifying the created personality of man with the absolute personality of God. Trentowski's philosophy of the 'I-hood' was, in his view, a return to ancient pagan pantheism—a form of pantheism which sanctified matter and was, therefore, much worse than the purely idealistic pantheism of Hegel. Trentowski's idea of 'Godmanhood', in turn, appeared to him to be an attempt to present eminent men—above all philosophers who had raised themselves to the knowledge of divine things—as divine beings. As such, argued Kozłowski, Trentowski's philosophy resulted in a deification of man, i.e. in a peculiarly dangerous form of idolatry—more dangerous even than the idolatry of Strauss, because the latter deified mankind as a whole, and not its élite only, thus avoiding the mortal sin of pride. In such a manner, Trentowski's philosophy was accused, in addition, of an élitist tendency motivated by personal ambitions: Trentowski, according to his critics, engaged himself in slandering the theologians and the clergy in order to pave the way for replacing them with a new aristocracy—an aristocracy of science headed by philosophers who wanted to be 'like gods'.

Kozłowski was particularly indignant about Trentowski's claim to have created a Polish 'national philosophy'. National philosophy should stem from the national tradition, that is, above all, from the traditional religion of the nation. How could a man call himself a 'national philosopher' if he did everything to slander and defame the religion and historical past of his nation? The Germans, whom Trentowski praised so much, had no national philosophy—their philosophy was a philosophy of scholars, and scholars had never been true representatives of any nation. In contrast with this, the Poles, uncorrupted by Protestant intellectual individualism, had their national philosophy in their Catholic faith. Their philosophy was not élitist but truly national, i.e. 'popular'. Writing books is not necessary to be a mouthpiece of 'national philosophy'; every man can be a 'national philosopher' if he is faithful to the religious beliefs of his ancestors.

Similar, if not the same, accusations were levelled against Trentowski by other clerical conservatives. The most important among them was the Bishop Ignacy Hołowiński (1807–55), an influential member of the 'coterie of Sankt-Petersburg'. In a series of articles entitled 'On the Relation of the Immediate Philosophy to Our Religion and Civilization' (see A. 29), he treated Trentowski as the most dangerous Polish representative of the so-called 'immediate philosophy', i.e. the philosophy of autonomous individual reason trying to attain knowledge of the divine without the mediation of the Church.

The intellectual level of the writings of the clerical conservatives was rather low. They were interesting not in themselves but as a background against which the Polish 'national philosophy' of the epoch should be seen. Much more interesting was another variant of conservative criticism of philosophy: the aristocratic variant, represented by the 'Polish de Maistre', Count Henryk Rzewuski.

2. Count Henryk Rzewuski and the Paradoxes of Traditionalism

Count Henryk Rzewuski (1791–1866), born on his family estate in Volhynia, was the scion of a family of Polish magnates from the Ukraine—a family which in the eighteenth century had become well known for its stubborn clinging to the traditions of the ancient Polish Commonwealth, and for its fierce resistance to all kinds of innovations. His close relative, Seweryn Rzewuski, was an ardent advocate of the four 'cardinal principles' of ancient Poland: the Catholic faith, free elections of kings, *liberum veto*, and the strong power of the Hetmans. The logic of his life and, indeed, the logic of his family tradition, led Seweryn Rzewuski to oppose the Constitution of 3 May 1791, and to join the Russian-sponsored Targowica Confederation.

By strange accident, Henryk Rzewuski was born on the same day on which the Constitution of the third of May was proclaimed. A combination of circumstances decided that during the first years of his life the person responsible for his upbringing was his grandmother, the sister of Tadeusz Rejtan.[28] Thus the future's most outspoken opponent of the Polish national-liberation movement was educated in his early childhood by the sister of the man who became a symbol of the inflexibility of the Polish will for independence.

As a young boy, Rzewuski went to a Carmelite school in a small Ukrainian town called Berdyczow; as a teenager he was educated in a French boarding-school in Sankt-Petersburg. In 1807 he enlisted in the army of the Grand Duchy of Warsaw. His general world view began to crystallize after the Vienna settlement, under the influence of the main ideologists of the European feudal reaction, such as de Maistre, de Bonald, and K. L. Haller, with whom he became personally acquainted during his many travels in Europe.

During his visit to Rome in 1830 he entered into friendly relations with Mickiewicz (whom he had met for the first time in Odessa in 1825). Mickiewicz discovered in him great narrative talents and induced him to write down his stories. Such was the origin of Rzewuski's first and best literary work— a series of sketches from the life of the eighteenth-century, old-fashioned Polish gentry, entitled *The Memoirs of Sophlica* (1839).

In 1832 Rzewuski returned to his homeland, settled in Volhynia and soon became one of the leaders of the conservative movement in the eastern borderlands of the ancient Polish Commonwealth. In 1841 a group of conservative writers— among them the well-known literary critic Michał Grabowski, Bishop Ignacy Hołowiński, and the editor of a Polish weekly published in Petersburg (*Tygodnik Petersburski*), J. E. Przecławski—met at his estate and constituted the 'coterie of Sankt-Petersburg', whose aim was to propagate among the Polish nobility the idea of a necessary reconciliation with the Russian Empire. Rzewuski carried this idea to extremes. In his *Miscellanea of Jarosz Bejla* (A. 86) he proclaimed that Poland had ceased to be a nation, that her tradition and culture could survive only as a part, or a regional form, of an all-Slavonic culture developing under the sceptre of the Russian Emperor. He compared Poland to a corpse eaten by worms, making clear that by 'worms' he meant the patriotic conspiratorial organizations. Of course, the book did not contribute to his popularity in Poland. Even the members of the 'coterie of Sankt-Petersburg' preferred to treat it as an expression not of their common standpoint but of the private views of its author.

Miscellanea was the first in the series of books and articles in which Rzewuski formulated his views on philosophical and social questions, especially on the relationship between philosophy and historical tradition. The most important among them were *Voice in the Wilderness* (1847), 'Civilization and Religion' (*The Warsaw Daily*, 1851), and *Intellectual Wanderings* (1851). Philosophical and social ideas set forth in these works were given an artistic form in Rzewuski's novels and literary sketches, like *November* (1845–6), *Polish Teophrast* (1851), and *The Memoirs of Bartlomiej Michalowski* (1857). The last of these books contained a sharp criticism of the Four Years' Diet and an apotheosis of the Targowica Confederation.

In 1850 the Tsarist government, appalled by the revolutionary events of the Springtime of the Peoples, decided to make use of Rzewuski's willingness to combat the influence of liberal and radical ideas. The Polish aristocrat was made an official for special tasks in the Congress Kingdom and a personal aide of its vice-regent, Prince Paskevich. Soon afterwards he received a government subsidy for publishing the newspaper the *Warsaw Daily*. At the beginning this newspaper was quite successful, but collapsed when its reactionary extremism became apparent. One of the main causes of its downfall was Rzewuski's article 'Civilization and Religion' after which several hundred copies of the newspaper were ostentatiously returned to its editor.

A few years later Rzewuski left Warsaw, returned to Volhynia, and retired from public activities.

In the history of Polish thought Rzewuski occupies a peculiar place of his own. Unlike the case of some Polish Slavophiles or Panslavists his pro-Russian feelings did not stem from a critical appraisal of Polish history. On the contrary, he was in love with the ancient Polish traditions, with the colourful 'sarmatian'· culture of the gentry and with the republican institutions of the ancient Polish Commonwealth. And yet he decided to opt for tsarist Russia whose cultural tradition and political structure were very different from everything he loved.

In fact there was a logic in this seeming paradox. Rzewuski was in love with the tradition which, according to his own diagnosis, had been irrevocably lost, disrupted, dissolved. He loved the Polish past, while fully aware that it could not be restored. Each national civilization, he thought, had its 'vital form', divinely constituted and inseparable from national existence. The vital form of the Polish nation was the collective sovereignty of the gentry who ceded a small part of their power to the elected king. With the rejection of this form, that is, with the introduction of the Constitution of 3 May, the Polish nation voluntarily dissolved itself and, in consequence, became the victim of its neighbours on the one hand, and the prey of revolutionary Western ideas on the other. Now the Poles are a nation which is cut off from its past, deprived of its collective soul, and fully participating in the general crisis of post-revolutionary Europe. They are not worthy of independence because their political existence could be regained only as a result of an all-European revolution, that is to say, at the cost of the triumph of disintegrating evil forces in the whole of Christendom. The only part of Christendom which is still young, vital, and determined to resist the universal evil is Russia. Her cultural and political traditions are very different from the old (and lost) traditions of Poland but, after all, every nation stems from a divine revelation of its own, has its own protective angel, and, therefore, necessarily differs from others. What is really important is that national existence should be based on divine Christian principles and not on the calculations of emancipated human reason. Russia is undoubtedly a Christian state: instead of believing in infinite progress she believes in the essential corruption of fallen man. Instead of embracing industrialism and utilitarianism she is aware of the irreplaceable value of poverty and sacrifice; against the disintegrating individualism of the West she sets the obedience to divine law embodied in her ruler. Therefore, she fully deserves the loyalty of the Poles for whom Christianity is more important than national independence and who want to avoid the fate of the rapidly declining West.

In such a manner Rzewuski opposed the national aspirations of his compatriots in the name of a kind of universalism—the universalism of the Holy Alliance. Consequently, he opposed also the principle of national self-determination and of the sovereignty of the people. Absolute sovereignty and self-determination, he argued, are incompatible with divine, moral laws: once a nation has begun to believe that its own will is the supreme law, it becomes a wild beast for whom nothing is sacred and everything is allowed. The executions of kings in the

English and French revolutions provided a good illustration of this.

If the principle of national self-determination is defined as the very essence and condition *sine qua non* of nationalism, Rzewuski should be placed, of course, on the antipodes of nationalism. Nevertheless, like his teacher, de Maistre, he combined his rejection of the secular, democratic variant of nationalism with a strong belief that nations, created by God, were the most genuine and organic forms of human existence, that society based on rational principles and deprived of a divinely created national spirit was a dead artefact, and that both supranational mankind and individuals devoid of national characteristics were mere abstractions, not to be found in real life. Like de Maistre he condemned the false pride of individual reason and set against it the collective national reason which expressed itself in the national tradition, in national legends and prejudices, and, last but not least, in the national laws—on condition, to be sure, that they were a product of organic growth and not an arbitrary rational invention. True national life, he argued, is governed not by the syllogisms of human logic but by a divine intuitive logic whose instruments are not philosophers and rational reformers but great lawgivers, powerful warriors, and inspired poets (A. 87, I. 71–3). National self-consciousness, expressed in a deliberately national literature, is by no means a precondition of healthy national existence; on the contrary, the sudden appearance of a rich literature permeated by exalted national feelings (as was the case with Polish romantic poetry) is usually a symptom of the imminent death of the nation (A. 86, II. 58–60)—a symptom of entering the stage of the final decline in which national values cease to be accepted unreflectively, instinctively, becoming instead an object of aesthetic contemplation. Even more evident symptoms of the nation's death were seen by Rzewuski in the emergence of autonomous speculative philosophy, divorced from the traditional beliefs of the nation and trying to attain the highest truths not by a virtuous life but by means of a rational discussion. In his estimation this was precisely the case of the Polish 'national philosophers'. The very attempt to *create* a national philosophy by means of individual reasoning, imitating foreign examples, instead of trying *to find* it in the national legends, prejudices, and laws, was for him irrefutable proof that the collective national mind of the Poles had entered the stage of disintegration and destruction. By contrast, the lack of philosophical systems in Russia was in his eyes an additional testimony to the healthy state of Russian national consciousness.[29]

In his view of the destructive role of rationalism in social life, in the emphasis put on intuition and inspiration, represented by the great lawgivers, warriors, and poets and, especially, in his criticism of philosophy, Rzewuski came very close to Mickiewicz. In his *Intellectual Wanderings* he called Mickiewicz 'the greatest mind of Slavdom' and quoted with reverence from his Paris lectures (A. 87, I. 9–12). In spite of this, however, Rzewuski's conception of a nation was very different from Mickiewicz's. The poet saw the nation as a community of individual spirits striving for perfection, a community whose main components were charismatic leaders, embodying the divine revelation, and the people inspired by them. For Rzewuski purely spiritual hierarchy was not enough. The common people, in his view, were doomed to be always immature and passive while the higher men, representing the true national spirit, should be organized into a closed estate or, as he put it, into a caste. Only a caste, he thought, can develop a truly corporate spirit, a sense of honour, warlike virtues, strong, inflexible will, and an ability to sacrifice individual interests for the sake of collective glory (see A. 87, III. 135–43). He fully shared Mickiewicz's contempt for the bourgeoisie but, in contrast to him, he was inclined to think that no nation would escape 'embourgeoisement' if its ruling caste were dissolved. Therefore, he fully, unequivocally committed himself to the defence of the old feudal world and, in contrast to Mickiewicz, could not set his hopes on a popular revolution led by a 'new Napoleon'.

The problem of the relationship between Rzewuski's ideas and nationalism can be approached from different points of view, depending on the definition of 'nationalism'. From the point of view of a political scientist for whom nationalism means a legitimizing device, consisting of putting forward the principles of popular sovereignty and national self-determination, the author of *Miscellanea* should be classified as a resolute adversary of nationalism. A historian of political and social movements, defining nationalism as a technique of mobilizing mass support for political actions, would fully share this view: indeed, nothing was more alien to Rzewuski's thought than the idea of a political mobilization of the masses. A historian of ideas, however, should adopt a different standpoint. In the intellectual history of the broadly conceived nationalism there was a school of thought in which Rzewuski fits very well—a school extolling the national community as an organic product of history, and setting national tradition against revolutionary blueprints, rationally devised constitutions, bourgeois individualism and utilitarianism, and so forth. Carlton J. H. Hayes has called it 'traditional nationalism' (B. 51, chapt. 4); it would be better, I think, to call it '*traditionalist* nationalism', because it represented not a traditional attitude, inherited from the past, but a modern traditionalism, i.e. a post-revolutionary current of thought which emerged as a reaction against the political and social changes brought about by the French Revolution. This was an important and influential stream of thought whose impact on the history of the national idea should not be ignored. In France it was represented by Rzewuski's teachers, de Maistre and de Bonald; in Germany by nationalistic romantic conservatives like Görres or the Schlegels; in England (with some reservations) by Burke; in Russia by the Slavophiles, who exerted an important formative influence on the subsequent forms of Russian nationalism. The views of all these thinkers, to be sure, were far from identical: they differed, for instance, in their respective attitudes towards Romanticism, towards royal absolutism and aristocracy, or even towards the common people (Russian Slavophiles, for instance, represented, so to speak, the most 'populist' variant of traditionalist nationalism).[30] Nevertheless, from the point of view of a general typology of nationalisms, their similarities are more important than their differences. All of them set a living, organic, 'divinely constituted' nation against mechanical artefacts resulting from revolutions; all of them put the highest value on the national tradition and on the continuity of national history; all of them defended historical laws, the products of organic growth, against rational legislation; all of them, in a word, discovered the possibility of using the idea of a national community—an idea which was anti-feudal in origin—not as an argument for popular sovereignty, but in defence of the feudal national tradition, as a means of combating all forms of political and economic modernization. In this sense all of them were nationalists—

anti-bourgeois, anti-democratic nationalists, but nationalists none the less.

Rzewuski was the only major representative of traditionalist nationalism in Poland. The weakness of this type of nationalism in Poland was due to the obvious fact that the victory of the Polish national cause was dependent on the breakdown of the reactionary system of the Holy Alliance, i.e. on the breakdown of the main stronghold of European feudal conservatism. Torn between the interests of his own country and the supra-national interests of European reaction, Rzewuski chose to sacrifice the former for the sake of the latter, justifying his decision by the thesis that Poland herself had abandoned her 'vital form' and, in consequence, ceased to be a living organic nation. 'Poland must either be revolutionary or perish', wrote Engels (A. 65, XVIII. 526). In the face of such an alternative Rzewuski, consistent to the end, proclaimed that Poland had already perished, and found for himself a new fatherland in tsarist Russia.

PART THREE

National and Religious Messianism

I. Introductory Remarks. The Native and the Foreign Sources of Polish Romantic Messianism

In Polish intellectual history the 1840s were not only a 'philosophical epoch', but also the period of the greatest flowering of Polish Romantic Messianism. It was then that the most articulate expressions of Polish messianic consciousness, such as Mickiewicz's Paris lectures on Slavonic literature, the mystic works of Słowacki, Krasiński's poem *The Dawn* and 'Treatise on the Trinity' or 'On the Position of Poland for Divine and Human Reasons', made their appearance. It should be stressed that 'national philosophy' and romantic Messianism were inter-related, not only because of the mutual influences, but also—and above all—as two approaches to the same problems of religious and national regeneration. Krasiński's view on 'national philosophers' and prophetic poets as representing two sides of one 'philosophical and religious movement' was essentially right.

First of all, I should define what I mean by 'Messianism'. In the Polish literature on the subject there is a widespread tendency to use this term in a very broad sense, that is to apply it to everybody who believed in the important mission of the Poles in defending the West against Turks and Russians or in spreading the light of Latin civilization in the Slavonic East. From this point of view both the old, traditional idea of Poland as 'antemurale Christianitatis' and the nineteenth-century beliefs in the important, revolutionary mission of Poland, so widespread among the emigration, should be included in the history of Polish Messianism.

It seems evident, however, that the 'broad' definition of Messianism is *too* broad to be of scholarly value. Almost every Polish patriot of the Romantic Epoch believed in the important historical mission of his nation, but it would be rather strange to say that this amounted to 'national Messianism'. Certainly, such a terminological decision *is possible*, but it would obscure the tremendous, ideological and practical, differences between, for instance, the 'messianically-tinged' patriotism of the Polish Democratic Society and the fully-fledged, religious and national Messianism of Mickiewicz, so sharply criticized and ridiculed by the members of the Democratic Society. It *is* possible to use the term 'Messianism' as a common name for all the ideologies predicting, and striving for, an imminent regeneration of mankind. This is, in fact, what Jacob Talmon did in his book on nineteenth-century 'political Messianism' (B. 159). In spite of all its merits however, Talmon's book is not a convincing justification for such a broadening of the term: if both Mickiewicz and Marx are labelled 'Messianists', this can only mean that the word 'Messianism' is used as a polemical device rather than as a scholarly, descriptive term.

As far as *national* Messianism is concerned, it seems more justified to apply the term 'Messianism' to such thinkers who claimed that the mission of their nation was not only important in the international division of incomparable, *messianic* mission fringing about the *univeral* historical tasks, but more than that— that it was a *unique* salvation of mankind. In this sense it is proper to say that Stanisław Orzechowski, a sixteenth-century Polish writer of Ukrainian origin ('gente Ruthenus, natione Polonus'), who claimed that the Poles were a God-chosen nation, or Wojciech Debołęcki, a seventeenth-century priest who maintained that the Polish language was the only original and unmixed language in the world (a theory reminiscent of Fichte's conception of 'Ursprache') and that the Poles would rule over other nations in the final, apocalyptic epoch of history, represented a conservative, Catholic variant of Polish national Messianism. In a similar sense Mickiewicz's friend and colleague in the College de France, Jules Michelet, who spoke with fervour about the 'saint bayonets' of the French army, can be classified as a representative of a democratic, secularized variant of the French national Messianism.

The definition of Messianism which I am using in this book is, however, even narrower. Messianism, according to this definition, is, first of all, a type of *religious* consciousness closely bound up with millenarism, i.e. with the 'quest for total, imminent, ultimate, this-worldly, collective salvation' (B. 160, p. 350). It is a belief in a redeemer, individual or collective, mediating between the human and the divine in the soteriological process of history. It implies that the process of salvation has not been completed, that in addition to individual salvation in an other-worldly Heaven one can expect the second coming of the Messiah and the second salvation—this time a *collective* and *terrestrial* salvation of mankind. Therefore, from the point of view of traditional, post-Augustinian Catholicism, Messianism is necessarily a form of *heterodox* religious consciousness (cf. B. 105); usually (although not necessarily) it is a more or less outspoken heresy, bound up with social revolutionism, since the belief in an earthly salvation is typical of the 'religions of the oppressed' (cf. B. 94). It is clear, I hope, that from *this* point of view neither Orzechowski and Debołęcki nor Michelet could be classified as archetypal 'Messianists'—the first two because they were orthodox Catholics, the latter because he was not a religious thinker at all. By contrast, Mickiewicz's Messianism, especially his Messianism of the 1840s, was very close to the ideal type of Messianism in the narrow and *proper* sense of this term.

The same is true, I think, about the other prophetic poets of Polish Romanticism. From the point of view of the history of ideas—especially in the light of the contemporary increase of interest in millenarian patterns in religious and political thinking—Polish Messianism would seem to be an extremely rewarding, although still much neglected, field of study. It was not a form of religious sectarianism, nor yet an 'archaic form of social movement' (in E. J. Hobsbawm's sense of the expression); on the other hand, it should not be reduced to 'political Messianism' in the broadest and, necessarily, rather vague meaning of this term. Polish romantic thinkers were, rather, Messianists in a narrower and more precise sense than were the other nineteenth-century thinkers whom Talmon characterized as 'political Messianists'. Polish Messianism was in fact a form of modern social utopianism—a form, however, which was religiously inspired, and which consciously adopted the old millenarian patterns. It was not a survival of a genuinely archaic structure of thought, nor was it a relic of pre-political and pre-philosophical thinking; on the contrary, it was rather a deliberate romantic attempt at a peculiar 'millenarization' of some modern political and philosophical ideas (particularly of the idea of progress). This 'millenarization', moreover, was not a literary exercise, not an external stylization. As an expression of the human predicament it was no less authentic than its pre-political chiliastic model, and its social causes were essentially the same.

Polish romantic Messianism was a product of the national catastrophe of 1831—of the defeat in the insurrection against Russia—and of the tragedy of the political emigration which followed. We may define it in more general terms as a hope born out of despair; as a result of multiple deprivation; as an expression of an increased feeling of self-importance combined with a sense of enforced rootlessness and isolation in an alien world (emigration); as an ardent search for religious consolation combined with a bitter sense of having been let down by the traditional religious authority (the condemnation of the Polish insurrection by Pope Gregory XVI). These normal explanations for millenarism can and, indeed, should be applied to Polish Messianism too; it would even to some extent be correct to interpret the circle of Towiański, in which Mickiewicz had been active, as a genuinely millenarian religious sect. Yet the Messianism of Mickiewicz, Słowacki, and Krasiński was not a direct continuation of religious millenarism —it was part and parcel of the culture of nineteenth-century European Romanticism, and represented a peculiar recrudescence of millenarian tendencies within a secularized cultural and political setting. The European importance of Polish romantic Messianism lies in the fact that in it those millenarian or quasi-millenarian tendencies which were inherent or patent in most nineteenth-century social thought were most distinctly expressed, and approached most nearly to their religious prototype. Karl Mannheim said that Germany achieved for the ideology of romantic conservatism what France did for the Enlightenment—'she exploited it to the fullest extent of its logical conclusions' (B. 113, p. 82). It seems justified to say, paraphrasing these words, that it was Polish Messianism which 'exploited to the fullest extent of their logical conclusions' the messianic-millenarian tendencies of European romantic thought.

This interpretation does not imply that the Polish Messianism of the 1830s and 1840s was so peculiar to the atmosphere of the Great Emigration that to look for its antecedents in earlier periods of Polish history would be in vain. On the contrary, Józef Ujejski has written a whole book on

Polish Messianism before the Emigration (B. 168), and I do not deny that most of the ideas discussed in this book are relevant to the understanding of the Messianism of the Polish prophetic poets. I would like only to put emphasis on the new quality of the latter. It is true that the idea of Poland as a chosen nation can be traced back to Orzechowski, that it became central in seventeenth-century 'Sarmatism'; nevertheless it was not bound at that time with a truly chiliastic (millenarian) pattern of thought. It is true, on the other hand, that some chiliastic motifs can easily be found in the tradition of Polish Free-masonry (although they were usually the same as in all-European Freemasonry, i.e. not centred around the specific destiny of Poland); it is true also that the Polish literature of the past was full of prophetic insights, and that the element of prophecy concerning the future role of France, Poland, and Russia was very important even in Polish political thought, especially in the epoch of the French Revolution, the Kościuszko uprising, and the Napoleonic wars (cf. B. 162, B. 45, and B. 168). Nevertheless, a *full-fledged* Messianism, national and religious at the same time, striving for an imminent and total regeneration of earthly life, was born in Poland *after* the defeat of the November uprising. Many of its motifs were, to be sure, not exclusively messianic; even its central political idea, demanding the rule of ethics to be established in the sphere of politics, was elaborated earlier by non-messianic currents of Polish thought. The really new element in it—an element from which the entire structure of messianic thought could be derived—was the conviction that traditional faith was not enough, that Christianity should be rejuvenated or reborn, and that the fate of Poland depended on the universal religious regeneration of mankind.

Among the factors to which Polish romantic Messianism owed its existence, an important place was occupied by cultural contact with France. The Polish exiles reached France at a time when French social utopianism was at its peak and when a religious regeneration of mankind was believed to be round the corner. Such a climate of thought was very favourable to millennial dreams, and it is understandable that messianic and millenarian motifs are to be found in the writings of many French thinkers of that time. They were never as pronounced as in the case of Polish thinkers but, nevertheless, some of the principal ideas of Polish Messianism were in fact Polish reinterpretations of similar ideas in French thought. This applies particularly to the idea of expiation—of the purifying, redemptive force of suffering, and to the idea of the 'new revelation' which would bring about the Christianization of social life and the rule of moral principles in international relations.

The idea of expiation was used by French religious thinkers to explain and justify the French Revolution. For the great reactionary, Joseph de Maistre, the Revolution was a terrible national catastrophe—a catastrophe, nevertheless, for which justification had to be found, if belief in the rule of Divine Providence in history were to be maintained; following Saint Martin, he accordingly interpreted the Revolution in terms of a mystical blood sacrifice of purification and salvation through the shedding of blood (A. 55, pp. 165–6). These ideas of Saint Martin and de Maistre were reinterpreted by Ballanche, who tried to combine them with the idea of progress: he saw in history a series of ordeals (*épreuves*), and interpreted progress as perfection through suffering, as a process of collective expiation and the rehabilitation of fallen man. This kind of theodicy was of great value for the Poles—it enabled them to explain the national catastrophe of Poland, and made them believe that her sufferings were not in vain, since, like the sufferings of Christ, they served as a purifying force for the general redemption and regeneration of mankind.

The second idea—the idea of a 'new revelation', of a 'new explosion of Christianity'—was also held by de Maistre. The victory of the Revolution had meant for him the total destruction of all he held sacred, and it was precisely this that led him to believe in the need for supra-natural aid for fallen humanity, in a 'nouvelle effusion de l'Esprit'. The situation of the Polish exiles was in this respect very similar. With the defeat of their insurrection they had lost everything, and this led them to the intense and desperate belief that the existing state of affairs could not last long, that a radical and sudden change was imminent, and that the period of the greatest disasters was only a prologue to the Kingdom of God on earth.

The motif of a 'new revelation', of a '*Révélation de la Révélation*', was to be found also in the writings of French utopian socialists, especially in those of the Saint-Simonians (who quoted and commented on the relevant passages from de Maistre), and of

Fourier (cf. A. 80, pp. 170–5 and B. 33). The Saint-Simonians saw in their Master a 'new Messiah'; in themselves, instruments of the Holy Ghost; and in history, a series of successive 'revelations', culminating in the 'last and final' Saint-Simonian revelation. The message of this 'new Revelation' was conceived as the final solution of the 'social question' and as the Christianization of political life. The revelation of Christ, it was argued, was confined to the sphere of *private* life, whereas the new revelation would bring about the Christianization of *social* and *political* relationships; this idea was formulated not only by Saint-Simon but also, strangely enough, by de Maistre, who had expressed the hope that the 'société des individus' would be elevated to the 'société des nations'. For Polish Messianism this conception was of paramount importance. It was probably the source of the parallel between the crucifixion of Christ and the sufferings of Poland: as the sacrifice of an individual man— Jesus of Nazareth—had been necessary for the redemption of individual souls, so the sacrifice of a whole nation—Poland— was believed to be a pre-condition for collective, social and *political* salvation on earth.

It is worth while to point out that the parallel between the crucifixion of Christ and the martyrdom of a nation sacrificing itself for the benefit of mankind was also to be found in Saint-Simonianism. In *Le Globe* of 29 January 1832, Mickiewicz could read: 'La France a bu le calice révolutionnaire: elle l'a avalé d'un trait; la France a monté sur la croix. La France a été le Christ de nations' (see B. 83, pp. 57–8). A few years later an ex-Saint-Simonian, Philippe Buchez, proclaimed on behalf of France: 'La nation française declare que son but est de realiser socialement la morale enseignée par Jésus Christ' (B. 59, p. 108).

Buchez, however, was an exception. On the whole, the Saint-Simonian school was not very interested in national problems and did not develop its millenarian ideas into a kind of French national Messianism. This was probably the reason why Mickiewicz, although he had read *La Doctrine saint-simonienne*, did not feel himself to be particularly close, or indebted, to Saint-Simonianism. The idea of France as the Christ among nations was taken up later—in his exile after the coup d'état of Louis Napoleon—by Victor Hugo who, like Mickiewicz, was an ardent romantic nationalist (see A. 30, VIII, 531–2).

Very close to the spirit of Polish romantic Messianism—

especially the Messianism of Mickiewicz—were in fact the
ideas of Mazzini (who was, by the way, an admirer of
Mickiewicz's genius and even called him 'the first poet of the
age').[1] Mazzini's ardent belief in the unifying mission of the
'third Rome' was bound up with the firm conviction that
nations, although 'sacred and divinely constituted', are never
ends in themselves, that the egoistic principle of non-
intervention should be rejected in the name of a Holy Alliance
of the Peoples. Like the Polish romantics, he condemned the
rationalism, utilitarianism, and hedonism of the Enlightenment, and replaced the individualistic ethos of the eighteenth-
century 'declarations of rights' with the ethos of supreme
duties, extolling the spirit of heroism and self-sacrifice. His
Messianism was not merely national, but religious as well—he
deeply felt that 'every true revolution is essentially religious',
that 'only faith, Authoritative Truth, can regenerate the
peoples' (A. 66, pp. 146 and 314), and that historical
Christianity—the *'second* Rome'—must give way to a new
religion of earthly collective salvation—a religion of the *'third*
Rome' which will transform earthly life into a true image of the
Kingdom of God and liquidate the painful dualism between the
sacred and the profane. On the other hand, however, one has to
admit that, in comparison with Mickiewicz, Mazzini's
'religion' seems to be rather a quasi-religion—a *secularized*
religion, devoid of a supra-natural element, lacking the
authentic irreducible experience of 'the sacred'. Thus we can
say that—from the point of view of the ideal model of
Messianism—Mazzini was a more genuine Messianist than
Michelet, but a less genuine Messianist than the Polish poet.

Let us now examine the main motifs of the Messianism of
Mickiewicz (1798–1855), Słowacki (1809–49), and Krasiński
(1812–59). Unlike the case of the Polish 'national philosophers',
biographical and bibliographical data concerning these three
poets are more or less easily available in English.[2] Therefore, I
shall not try to present here a full account of their lives and
works; I shall limit my task to the discussion of their Messianic
ideas, against the background of only those events from their
lives which were most relevant.

II. Adam Mickiewicz

1. The Books of the Polish Pilgrims
The first articulated expression of Mickiewicz's Messianism is
Part III of his lyric drama *Forefathers' Eve*, written in Dresden in
early spring 1832. The hero of the poem, Konrad, an
embodiment of Promethean heroism, challenges God accusing
Him of being not the Father of the world but its Tsar. In doing
this he feels himself speaking on behalf of his nation:

> I challenge Thee.
> I and a nation's mighty heart are one
> . . . .
> My fatherland and I are one great whole.
> My name is million, for I love as millions. (A. 73, p. 277.)

Thus, a rebellious romantic individualism becomes transcended in a powerful feeling of belonging to a living and
suffering national community. Nevertheless, Konrad's heroism
is a rebellion against God, permeated by satanic pride and,
therefore, self-defeating. It needs the element of Christian
humility, represented by a Catholic priest, Father Peter, and
expressed by him in the words: 'Lord, what am I before Thy
countenance? Dust and naught.' Human spirit draws its
strength from God; great heroes are God's elect; therefore, they
should break their human pride and act as instruments of a
higher, Divine Will. The salvation for Poland will come, it will
be brought about by a great, divinely-inspired man, uniting in
himself Konrad's heroism with Father Peter's obedience to
God. In the 'vision of Father Peter' this future redeemer,
impatiently awaited by the suffering nation, is described as
follows:

> Born of a foreign mother, in his veins
> The blood of ancient warriors—and his name
> Shall be forty and four (A. 73, p. 294).[3]

From Dresden Mickiewicz went to Paris, and found himself in the middle of the political and intellectual life of the emigration. He was shocked by its disunity—the struggle between different parties and 'communities' was in his eyes a disastrous wasting of moral forces. In order to reunite the *émigrés* and to warn them against imitating the party-struggles in France he wrote *The Books of the Polish Nation and of the Polish Pilgrims* (1832)—a splendid piece of biblical prose in which he extolled the great universal mission of Poland in general and of the Polish exiles in particular. Messianism—this time a *collective* Messianism—became thus a metapolitical means to a distinctively political aim.

A revolutionary hatred of tottering thrones was curiously combined in the *Books* with the mysticism of Saint Martin and with an openly conservative, backward-looking criticism of contemporary European civilization (see B. 133 and B. 185–6); retrospective, 'reactionary' ideals (a conservative-romantic idealization of the Middle Ages and an apologia for the Polish 'gentry-democracy') rubbed shoulders with revolutionary prophecy, with a catastrophic vision of history, and with chiliastic expectations of the total and imminent regeneration of mankind. The unilinear Enlightenment conception of progress was replaced in the *Books* by a vision of history as a series of descents, followed by sudden upward surges which were achieved by means of sacrifice and regenerative grace. The primitive golden age—an epoch of monotheism and freedom —had been followed by a descent whose climax was the crucifixion of Christ; the sacrifice of Christ raised up fallen humanity, but the mission of Christ was non-political, and Christianization was confined to the sphere of private, individual life; hence the new descent, whose nadirs were the partitions of Poland and the suppression of the insurrection of 1830. In both cases the instrument of evil was despotic secular power (the Roman Empire and the three partitioning powers, Russia, Austria, and Prussia); in both cases the descent consisted in a drawing away from faith and freedom. The mission of the Poles—the nation whose political crucifixion, like the crucifixion of Christ, was in fact the fulfilment of the providential plan of salvation—was seen in the overthrow of the 'pagan idols' of European politics (Domination, Honour, Commerce, Welfare, etc.), in the regeneration of the spirit of faith and sacrifice, and finally, in the Christianization of political life. This mission was to be fulfilled by the sword, by means of a revolutionary crusade against the corrupt old world. In 'The Pilgrim's Litany' (at the end of the *Books*) Mickiewicz wrote:

> For,a universal war for the freedom of the Peoples,
> We beseech Thee, O Lord. (A. 73, p. 415.)

The millenarian features of the *Books* are sufficiently obvious. The division of history into three epochs, separated by two great upward surges—the coming of the Messiah and his *parousia* in the form of the collective Christ (Poland); the prophetic interpretation and sanctification of historical events, the expectation of an imminent earthly collective salvation; a peculiar combination of traditionalism and revolutionism, making it possible to link the invoked future with the idealized past—in all this the parallel between Mickiewicz's thought and primitive millenarianism is close and overt.

The *Books* were to impress their readers as a sacral, prophetic text. Therefore, they were written in biblical style and their structure was that of a 'figurative exposition', i.e. such a narrative in which one event refers to, and is explained by, another event: 'One event forecasts the other, the other completes the first; both have something transitory and incomplete in themselves and both point to the future perfect fulfilment of the prophecy' (B. 152, p. 43). Thus the crucifixion of Christ was seen as a 'figure' of the martyrdom of Poland, and the latter was interpreted as a 'completion' of the sacrifice of Christ; the Christian crusades were presented as a 'figure' of the imminent revolutionary crusade for the freedom of nations, and the union between Poland and Lithuania was treated as a harbinger of the brotherly union of all nations.

It followed therefrom that Poland was a 'Christ among nations' and that her downfall, along with the martyrdom of Christ, was the most important watershed in universal history. However, this should not be interpreted too literally. Mickiewicz did not mean a mystical identification of Poland with Christ; he was satisfied with drawing a parallel between the redemptive meaning of the sufferings of Christ and the sufferings of Poland and with the conclusion that Poland's mission was to destroy immoral politics, replacing it with politics based on Christian ethics. Nevertheless, it is significant that the meaning of universal history was explained by the poet in religious categories of the fall, redemption and salvation. This was very typical of millenarianism as a structure of thought building bridges between religion and politics and making no clear distinction between the secular and the sacred.

In the interpretation of the mission of Poland, represented by the Polish *émigrés*, there was a tension between universalism and a pronounced contempt for everything foreign. It seems justified to conclude that Mickiewicz wanted the *émigrés* to unite on the basis of commonly shared xenophobic feelings. He did not hesitate to say: 'Be mindful that ye are in the midst of strangers as a flock among wolves and as a camp in an enemy country, and there will be concord among you. . . . Ye are not equally good, but he who is worse among you is better than the good stranger, for each one of you hath the spirit of self-sacrifice. . . . Ye are on your pilgrimage in a strange land, as was God's people in the wilderness. . . . Ye are among strangers as were the Apostles among idolaters' (A. 73, pp. 390 and 403–5).

On the other hand, however, this xenophobic attitude was bound up in the *Books* not with national egoism but, on the contrary, with a programmatic internationalism, demanding sacrifices for the common cause of all nations. The Poles were extolled as an élite of heroism and selfless sacrifice, as 'knights of universal freedom'. Let us quote again:

Ye hear that the Jews and the Gipsies say, and men with the souls of Jews and Gipsies: 'There is the Fatherland where it is well'; but the Pole saith to the nations: 'There is the Fatherland where it is ill'; for wherever in Europe freedom is downtrodden and there is a struggle over it, there is the struggle for the Fatherland, and to fight in that struggle is the duty of all.

They said of old to the nations: 'Lay not down your arms so long as the enemy holdeth one foot of your land'; but say ye to the nations: 'Lay not down your arms so long as despotism holdeth one foot of a free land.' (A. 73, pp. 409–10.)

Mickiewicz really meant what he wrote. He was among the most consistent 'internationalists' among the emigration, much more consistent than the ideologists of the Democratic Society who advocated caution in shedding Polish blood. He wholeheartedly supported the march of 500 Polish exiles, organized in a Carbonarist branch at Besançon, to assist the attempted revolution in Frankfurt in 1833; he welcomed also the Poles who joined Mazzini in his attack upon Savoy on 31 January/1

February 1834 (the so-called Savoy expedition). These and similar acts on the part of the Poles amounted, in his view, to laying foundations for the future international system based upon the principle of 'mutual help in the struggle for freedom' (A. 70. VI, 120). He rejected 'reasonable' arguments in favour of caution and avoiding unnecessary bloodshed. Heroic deeds, he argued, were valuable irrespective of success, and the shedding of blood was always useful, because it was necessary to throw more blood onto the scale of Providence in order to overweigh it and change God's verdicts. In his journal *Pilgrim* he wrote a special article on 'reasonable people' and 'mad people' supporting 'madness' against 'reasonableness' (A. 70, VI. 133–6). Too much 'reasonableness' among the Polish patriots, he maintained, was the main cause of the downfall of Poland. 'Reasonableness' is good for the daily life of an individual but it is not enough in times of national emergency. In such times one should be obedient to a higher reason—a supra-individual national reason—whose voices are the so-called 'mad men': the men of feeling and of duty.

Shortly after the Polish edition of the *Books* was published, a French translation of them appeared. A number of French liberals and democrats, who had been accustomed to associate religion with the *ancien régime* and the cause of freedom with the cause of secular philosophy, were deeply impressed by a way of thinking which joined the cause of faith with the cause of freedom and opposed them to secular philosophy and secular despotism. The liberal Catholic, Count Montalembert, wrote in his preface to the French edition of the *Books* that they expressed the ancient spirit of Christianity, which had survived in Poland while it had been suppressed elsewhere in Europe by godless philosophy and despotism. Lamennais, formerly a theocratic traditionalist, called Mickiewicz's work 'a book of the whole human race' and, to some extent, tried to follow Mickiewicz's example in his *Paroles d'un croyant* (cf. B. 85, B. 87). Among the enthusiastic admirers of Mickiewicz's *Books* we also find Mazzini, who believed that Italy, united 'in the name of God and the People', would perform the historical mission of leading mankind to the realization of the universal brotherhood of nations. Thus, the Messianism of the *Books* was not a completely isolated phenomenon; it was rather an extreme expression of some characteristic trends in the European thought of the period.

It is interesting to note that Mickiewicz's *Books* played some role in the awakening of the Ukrainian national consciousness. Mickiewicz himself would not have welcomed this. For him Ukrainians, Lithuanians, and other ethnic elements of the ancient Polish Commonwealth were parts of the Polish nation; *mutatis mutandis* he could say about the Ukrainians what he said about the Lithuanians: 'The Lithuanian and the Masovian are brothers: do brothers quarrel because one hath for a name Władyslaw, another Witowt? Their last name is the same, the name of the Poles' (A. 73, p. 396). The Ukrainians, however, began to think about it differently. The Ukrainian historian, Nicholas Kostomarov, a member of the secret society of St. Cyril and St. Methodius (in which the great Ukrainian poet Taras Shevchenko was also active), was very impressed by Mickiewicz's *Books* and decided to write something similar for his people. He called his composition *The Books of the Genesis of the Ukrainian Nation* (see B. 106). Following Mickiewicz, sometimes consciously paraphrasing him, he presented the beginning of history as an epoch of monotheism and freedom, destroyed later by monarchs and by the cult of the Golden Calf, proclaimed once more by Christ and betrayed again by idolaters. The Slavs embraced the teaching of Christ in a purer form than other nations but they too betrayed its spirit in their later history. Poland, so proud of her freedom, enslaved her peasants; Russia developed into an autocracy in which everybody was a slave. Only the Ukraine remained faithful to the truly Slavonic and Christian spiritual heritage and embodied it in the free fraternities of Cossacks, living in accordance with divine law. She always strived for a free union of Slavonic peoples; therefore, following Lithuania, she voluntarily united with Poland but was betrayed by the Polish nobility who wanted to subjugate her and to turn her people into serfs. Having risen against the Polish yoke she joined Russia but soon was betrayed and partitioned (in 1667) between Russia and Poland. After the downfall of Poland the whole Ukraine became a province of Russia and reached the nadir of her national existence. Nevertheless, in spite of double (political and social) oppression, the Ukrainians—they alone!—preserved the ancient Slavonic spirit of freedom and equality, consonant to true Christianity and incompatible with both nobility and autocracy. Therefore a great historical mission fell to their lot:

they were to awaken the ancient democratic spirit both in Poland and in Russia, to put an end to Polish-Russian strife, and to unite all Slavonic peoples in a free republic, knowing neither tsar nor landlords.

2. From National to Religious Messianism

In 1840 the French government established a chair of Slavonic literature at the Collège de France and offered it to Mickiewicz, who was widely recognized by then as the greatest poet of Slavdom. Mickiewicz's lectures at the Collège de France (1840–4) became the most important document of Polish romantic Messianism. In many respects it was a different Messianism than Mickiewicz's Messianism of the 1830s. Because of the clear awareness of its inevitable clash with institutionalized Catholicism (although combined with the hope of reforming the Church from within) it was a more mature, more self-conscious Messianism. The last two courses of Mickiewicz's lectures, published under the titles *L'Eglise officielle et le messianisme* and *L'Eglise et le Messie* (1845),[4] were put by the Vatican on the 'index librorum prohibitorum'. The same was the lot of Mickiewicz's *Books*, but nobody could deny that in the case of Mickiewicz's Paris lectures the Vatican's verdict was much more justified.

I cannot trace here in detail the evolution of Mickiewicz's Messianism during the years which elapsed between his *Books* and his Paris lectures. It is necessary, however, to discuss briefly the role which was played in this evolution by Andrzej Towiański (1799–1878)—the Lithuanian mystic who came to France in December 1840 (when Napoleon's body was conveyed to Paris for re-burial), and who in the following year, on 27 September 1841, delivered a speech at Notre Dame in Paris proclaiming the inauguration of a new, higher epoch in the development of Christianity.

Mickiewicz met Towiański on 30 July 1841; a week later he became fully converted to his 'Divine cause', and in the next year was instrumental in establishing a circle of Towiański's followers in which he himself was to play a leading role. This sudden conversion was usually attributed to Towiański's 'miraculous cure' of Mickiewicz's half-insane wife, Celina. Towiański's skilful play on Mickiewicz's prophetic inclinations should also be mentioned; in his esoteric work *The Banquet*,

Towiański referred even to Mickiewicz's prophecy about the coming redeemer whose name would be 'forty and four'. The decisive influence, however, was the irresistible charismatic power of Towiański's personality. He was truly a magnetic, awe-inspiring man. A member of his circle, who had served as an officer under Grand Duke Constantine, confessed once that his fear of Constantine's famous attacks of fury was nothing in comparison with the holy fear which he experienced in the presence of Towiański, although the latter never raised his voice (see A. 71, p. 290). At the same time 'Master Andrzej' had a unique capacity of inspiring hope. In a letter to his old friend, Mickiewicz wrote about it as follows:

> Since I met him [Towiański] the exile became finished for me, because I firmly hope that very soon God will raise us by means of this strange cause. . . . I repeat, a great cause will start in the world, and everybody who wants to serve it must first purify and sanctify himself. . . . God will overthrow the order of the ancient Europe and in the new order Poland will be restored. You remember that I always expected this; now I have a scientific certainty that this change will come (A. 70, XV. 467–8).

The same feeling infected everybody who succumbed to the influence of the Lithuanian prophet. Some people began even to liquidate their affairs in France, preparing themselves for a speedy return to Poland.

As we know, the 'great change' did not come. Towiański claimed that it was accomplished in the spiritual sphere, but this was not enough for his followers. Their circle which was to be a germ of a 'new, immaculate fatherland' for the Poles and a mainspring of regeneration for the entire world became, like many other millenarian sects, a scene of scandalous conflicts between those who blindly followed their Master and those who rebelled against his despotism. Their striving for a collective holiness, their incessant 'spiritual labour', bound up with the conviction that higher spirits should lead the lower ones, resulted in a horrible system of constant moral pressure, penetrating into the most intimate spheres, leaving no place for rest and privacy. Many people could not stand it; many episodes from the history of the circle were testimonies of human frailty or of the inevitable pathology of a small and closed sectarian community. Nevertheless, even the people who, like Słowacki, consciously broke from the circle, never denied that there was a peculiar greatness in Towiański's personality and in his 'cause'.

Towiański's mystical teaching revolved around a spiritualistic conception of development, conceived as the increasing perfection of spirits and their advance to God through exaltation and inner concentration.[5] In contradistinction to Saint-Martin, Towiański saw this path to God as a progressive evolution (parallel to organic evolution) and not as a return to the blessed state of man before the Fall. Spirits perfect themselves in a long series of successive incarnations; the precondition of progress is divine grace, which descends on men through 'the column of bright spirits'. From time to time there appear in history great individuals who, thanks to their peculiar spiritual power, can disperse the clouds of dark spirits which hover over our planet, and—standing at the head of the 'bright column'—bring supra-natural aid to their nation and, through it, to the whole of mankind. The final destiny of Christianity—the establishment of the Kingdom of God on earth[6]—will be brought about through 'the Seven Men of God'; the mission of the first of these (i.e. of Towiański himself) is to inaugurate the epoch of the Christianization of political life. This great task will be accomplished by the Slavs (in the first place, by the Poles) and by France (the country of Napoleon, who, according to Towiański, was the immediate precursor and harbinger of the 'new Christian epoch'). However, in order to perform her mission Poland must renounce her hatred towards Russia and give up the revolutionary means of struggle.

In Mickiewicz's Paris lectures we find many ideas which differ from his earlier Messianism and which share many points in common with Towiański's teachings. However, Mickiewicz was never an orthodox disciple of Towiański and his intellectual debt to him was in fact much smaller than might appear at first sight.

The Messianism of the *Books* was exclusively Polish; France was condemned in them, together with the rest of Europe, as materialistic, cowardly, and corrupt. In the Paris lectures Mickiewicz's Messianism has become Slavophile and Francophile. This significant shift was in harmony with the teaching of Towiański, but cannot be ascribed to his influence: a Franco-Slavonic orientation was already very marked in Mickiewicz's first course of lectures, at a time when the ideas of

Towiański were still unknown to him. The same is true of Mickiewicz's cult of Napoleon: although it exactly parallels the doctrine of Towiański, Mickiewicz in fact arrived at it independently of his future 'Master'.

On closer examination it turns out that even those ideas which Mickiewicz apparently shared with Towiański were in fact often interpreted by him in a different way. The most important difference—one which changed the meaning of almost every element in Towiański's teaching—concerned the interpretation of the coming revolution. Towiański preached non-violent resistance to evil, whereas Mickiewicz expected and invoked a messianic warrior, a divinely-inspired leader who would liberate the oppressed peoples by means of a revolutionary struggle against the old, evil order.

On the whole, it is justified to say that in the evolution of Mickiewicz's Messianism Towiański performed a catalytic function—he accelerated its development, but without changing its direction. This catalytic function, however, should not be underestimated, especially as far as the problem of the nation is concerned. Mickiewicz saw in Towiański a messenger from Heaven and this very fact helped him to transform his *national* Messianism into a *religious* Messianism, subordinating national aims to the universal, religious aims. Towiański violenty *condemned* any striving for national independence *as such*, for its own sake. He repeated: 'Let the Emigration feel in their souls that thinking of a terrestrial fatherland incompatible with God's will is a crime, and that we are scoundrels if we desire that' (see A. 108, II. 30). He deeply felt that the national existence was not an end in itself, that Poland had to prove that her restoration was necessary for mankind. Following his example Mickiewicz was able to say: 'Poland must inchoate a new (better) world, otherwise it makes no sense to struggle for her restoration' (A. 71, p. 341).

In interpreting these pronouncements we must remember that for Towiański and Mickiewicz nations were not empirically existing ethnic communities but 'associations of kindred individual spirits'. This idea, to be properly understood, has to be related to the conception of progressive reincarnation, to be found in Towiański's mystical doctrine. The belief in progressive reincarnation was also very characteristic of such French thinkers as Fourier and the Saint-

Simonians (who took it over from Lessing), Pierre Leroux and Ballanche (who transformed it into a theory of 'social palingenesis'). The importance of the romantic rediscovery of this ancient belief consisted in the fact that it enabled the reconciliation of the millenarian idea of a collective salvation with romantic individualism, claiming immortality for the individual. The future Kingdom of God on earth was thus made open for each individual spirit, who through the long chain of his incarnations had achieved the highest level of perfection. This is why the theory of reincarnation was so attractive to Polish prophetic poets. All of them thought about reincarnation before they became acquainted with Towiański's doctrine. Nevertheless, the centrality of the idea of reincarnation in their respective messianic ideologies has to be attributed, partially at least, to the influence of Towiański. This is true even in the case of Krasiński, although he was never a member of Towiański's circle.

The idea of progressive reincarnation had far-reaching consequences for the romantic conception of the nation. It prevented an absolutization of nations by subordinating them in the hierarchy of values to the supreme cause of individual spiritual perfection and, equally strongly, to the idea of mankind as—to quote Krasiński—'the common labour of all the human individual spirits' (see B. 40, p. 214). For Mickiewicz a nation was nothing else than 'a set of aids given to man to help him to apply the truth' which had been revealed to him by God (A. 70, XI. 186). By force of this argument a nation was given a religious sanction but, on the other hand, it came to be conceived as a means, and not as an end in itself.

3. Tradition, Prophecy and Charismatic Power
Let us now examine—as briefly as possible—the main ideas of Mickiewicz's Messianism as expressed in his Paris lectures. Philosophically speaking, his general vision of the world may be classified as 'spiritualistic universal perfectionism' combined with romantic anti-rationalism and hero-worship. It was based on a belief in a hierarchy of spirits formed as a result of their inner labour in their present and former incarnations.

By 'Messianism' Mickiewicz meant a conception of progress interpreted as a series of 'revelations' given to mankind from above through the medium of chosen individuals. 'The most developed spirit', he wrote, 'has a natural duty to lead the less developed ones. This is the chief dogma of Messianism' (A. 70, XI. 18). The great heroes 'whom the astonished masses immediately recognize as their legitimate rulers' (ibid., p. 36) were seen by him as 'intuition incarnate', as the embodiment of anti-rationalism; progress, which was accomplished through them, was conceived not as a progress of reason but as a sequence of sudden upward surges, of inspired lungeings, which break the chains of all 'established forms'—both rational and traditional. This irrationalist progressivism was elevated above the usual, conservative-romantic antithesis of 'reason' and 'tradition' (or 'reason' and 'history'); this antithesis was replaced by that of 'spirit' and 'routine', in which the spirit— this 'eternal revolutionary', as Słowacki put it—was opposed both to rational doctrines and to ossified tradition. Tradition, of course, was much closer to the poet's heart than reason—after all, traditions stem from divine revelation and are the instrument of the spirit. But 'living' tradition, the tradition of the spirit, was to be distinguished from traditional routine. Mickiewicz criticized the Catholic traditionalism of Chateaubriand from this point of view, saying that the 'spirit' should not be identified with any of its historically established forms.

This assertion has, however, to be qualified. In the first two courses of the Paris lectures, conservative-romantic motifs of thought were more prominent than messianic ones; thus, for instance, in the second course of lectures, Mickiewicz condemned the Great Diet (of 1788–92) and the Constitution of 3 May 1791 in the name of the 'historical wisdom of the people' (A. 70, X. 219). But with the intensification of Mickiewicz's Messianic yearnings, these conservative motifs were abandoned: the notion of tradition underwent a process of spiritualization and, finally, became identified with the element of continuity in an unceasing progress. Progress—proclaimed the poet—is the very essence of the spirit; on the other hand, true progress is to be found only in the realm of the spirit—it is the development of our inner being, its march to God (A. 70, XI. 468).

The man whose spirit has been most intensively working and which has raised itself to the highest level throws open 'the channel to heaven' (an expression of Towiański) through which the divine revelation streams forth from above and rains down on mankind. Such a *revelator* is, thus, not a passive and accidental instrument of God; he is one of the elect because of his own 'spiritual labour' and 'spiritual sacrifice'—because he has proved to be most active, and because he has put aside 'his own cause, his individuality, his ego'. The fundamental, Christian, universal human revelation—the Word—has exploded twice in the history of mankind: once in the 'primitive revelation' and, again, in the revelation of Christ. Apart from these general revelations, there have also been 'partial', national revelations: 'Each nationality is based upon a distinct revelation. Each of the great nations has been founded by one man, each of them has sprung from one thought and lived to realize this thought' (A. 70, XI. 19). The revelation of Christ is not the final one: there are many indications that a new religious climax is imminent: 'even the people who were the most attached to the old tradition, like Joseph de Maistre, foresaw and expected the possibility of what they have called "the third explosion of Christianity"' (ibid., p. 196). It was surely not in vain that Cieszkowski began and ended his book (*Gott und Palingenesie*) with the words: *Veni Creator Spiritus*; it was surely not in vain that Krasiński and Schelling announced 'the coming of the epoch of St. John, the epoch of enthusiasm and love'. In this coming epoch Christian morality will extend its rule over the sphere of politics; the nations will recognize in each other members of humanity and put an end to these political crimes which have achieved their culmination in the martyrdom of Poland. But the victory of love must be preceded by a catastrophic period of revolutionary wars. The new Messiah, so ardently summoned by the Poles, will be 'not a Christ before Pilate, but a Christ risen, Christ transfigured, armed with all the attributes of power, Christ *the Avenger* and Christ *the Redresser*, the Christ of the Apocalypse and of Michelangelo' (A. 70, XI. 494). He will be the new and higher incarnation of the spirit of Napoleon—the greatest genius of war, who possessed the compelling, magic power of command.

It is important to note that Mickiewicz's Messianism was consciously and aggressively anti-philosophical. Philosophy, defined by the poet as the product of reason which thinks that truth can be attained by means of reasoning and discussion, without sacrifice and 'spiritual labour', was in his eyes 'merely an imitation or, rather, a counterfeit of revelation' (ibid., p. 19). This general attitude towards philosophy determined Mickiewicz's assessment of Cieszkowski's book *Gott und Palingenesie*, to which he devoted a whole lecture. He found in it a great deal to praise: the defence of the personality of God and of the immortality of the human soul; the criticism of Hegelian rationalism and the conception of 'active intuition'; finally, the progressivist and activist spiritualism, which he thought very similar to his own. Nevertheless, he accused Cieszkowski of criticizing rationalism from within rather than from without, and of believing in the possibility of the salvation of the 'Hegelian dynasty' and the German 'philosophical parliament'. Cieszkowski was in his eyes the most promising of the philosophers but, none the less, a philosopher; he was the man who had completed the development of the 'German Scholastic philosophy', but who had proved unable to break with it in a radical manner. His final judgement was very severe: Cieszkowski, at least for the time being, was still a 'denationalized Slav', a prisoner of German philosophical thought.

There was, however, at least one German philosopher whom Mickiewicz himself treated with reverence, and whose teaching seemed to him to resemble the ideas of the Polish Messianists. This was the aged Schelling, who, when Mickiewicz was lecturing in Paris, was preaching in Berlin his anti-Hegelian 'philosophy of revelation'.

In contrast to Krasiński and Cieszkowski, who were influenced by Schelling's 'historiosophy' and speculative theosophy, Mickiewicz did not pay much attention to the systematic and speculative aspects of Schelling's thought. He was impressed mainly by Schelling's conception of 'intellectual vision', as opposed to rational knowledge, especially by his assertion that this 'organ of truth' is by no means accessible to all. Schelling, according to Mickiewicz, understood that the capacity for attaining truth depends on a man's moral value and is distributed very unequally among individuals and nations. This characteristic élitist element in Schelling's theory of knowledge was seen by the poet—quite rightly—as a corollary to his conception of the spiritual hierarchy, the 'chief dogma of Messianism'.

Mickiewicz combined an aristocratic theory of knowledge

with a mystical conception of the *heterogeneity of time*. The segments of time, of which human life is composed, are of very different value; the higher truths are revealed to men only in rare moments of ecstasy, and not in the humdrum routine of everyday life. In confirmation of this view Mickiewicz quoted Emerson, though at the same time he accused the American transcendentalist of 'isolating' men, of not taking into account 'the epoch, the nation, and the land'. 'Emerson's man', he wrote, 'is a man suspended in a void' (A. 70, XI. 183–4).[7] Cieszkowski was closer to the truth, 'since he was aware of the importance of nations'. Moreover, he remained in Mickiewicz's estimation the first philosopher who had understood that the precondition of both true knowledge and 'moral certitude' was to be found in the elevation of the spirit, in 'spiritual labour'. But even Cieszkowski, like Emerson, did not realize that 'not all people and all nations are equally prepared for this labour'.

This assessment of Cieszkowski was quite accurate: in contrast to Mickiewicz, he was a firm believer in cognitive egalitarianism. We may even say that the differences between Mickiewicz and Cieszkowski were in fact greater than Mickiewicz thought. He was wrong when he identified Cieszkowski's conception of truth as 'the fruit of spiritual labour' with 'grace' in the teaching of the Church, and with the aristocratic 'organ of truth' in the philosophy of Schelling. In fact, as we shall see, there was much less irrationalism and mysticism in the philosophy of Cieszkowski than in the philosophies of Emerson and Schelling; intuition was for him not a criterion of truth but only a necessary component in essentially rational philosophical speculation. The 'third epoch', in Cieszkowski's interpretation, was the epoch of *exoteric* truths, of truths that are accessible to all; the 'final revelation' was conceived by him as a revelation without mysteries, a revelation which does not 'explode' from above but reveals itself gradually in the successive achievements of philosophy and science.

Though Mickiewicz's Messianism was born of the national tragedy of the Poles, it also reflected the widespread sense of a general European crisis. One of the main symptoms of this crisis was seen by the poet in rationalism—in knowledge divorced from morality, in the loss of the 'gifts of the Holy Ghost', in the replacement of 'living' and 'total' truths by 'dead' and 'partial' truths, accessible to all and morally indifferent. The nations of

Western Europe (apart from France), he felt, had exhausted
their vitality. They had lost their enthusiasm and the feeling of
veneration. After the great God-inspired lawgivers had come
legitimists and lawyers; 'spiritual power' had been replaced by
parliamentary discussion, bearing witness to a lack of inner
strength; the bureaucratized Church had ceased to have
contact with Heaven. After the apostles and miracle-workers
had come the theologians and casuists; after the great warriors
had come the people who proclaimed the doctrine of people and
non-intervention: '. . . such a generation is always a sign of the
decline of the human spirit. In this manner the Greek world
came to an end, and the Western world is now declining' (A. 70,
XI. 336–7).

Mickiewicz's protest against the rationalization of social life
was to a certain extent paralleled by the ideas of the German
conservative romantics—especially by those of Franz von
Baader, Friedrich Schlegel, and Adam Müller, all of whom he
often quoted in his lectures. His ideals were often backward-
looking—hence the possibility of significant similarities
between some of his ideas and the conservative-romantic
criticism of modern bourgeois civilization. But the scope of
these similarities was limited. Conservative romanticism was
not compatible with the cult of revolutionary France, nor with
the cult of Napoleon. It was characteristic of the German
romantics to turn from Protestantism to the Catholic Church,
in which they saw the oldest and the most thoroughly
institutionalized Christian tradition; Mickiewicz, by contrast,
proclaimed the coming of a 'new revelation' and violently
attacked the official Catholic Church. He echoed the conservative romantics in his criticism of the French Convention,
which he accused of dependence on secularized autonomous
reason, but he parted company with them when he recognized
in the Jacobins 'a spark of the true Christian spirit' (A. 70, X.
372) and when he adumbrated the following ideal of man: 'This
man will have the zeal of the apostles, the devotion of the
martyrs, the simplicity of the monks, the audacity of the men of
1793, the firm unshakable and overwhelming valour of the
soldiers of the *Grande Armée*, and the genius of their leader' (A.
70, XI. 477).

A closer similarity exists between Mickiewicz and Thomas
Carlyle, although the Polish poet was not influenced by the

classical English representative of hero-worship. Carlyle, like Mickiewicz, proclaimed that great God-inspired men—the 'heroes'—were the founders of societies, that hero-worship is the basis of the social bond and the ark of salvation in times of crisis; like Mickiewicz, he despised rationalism, liberalism, and the parliamentary system, arguing that only a great charismatic leader could really solve existing problems; both agreed that such a leader was the most urgent need of their epoch. In spite of this, however, Mickiewicz's dream of a Messianic leader who would combine 'the spirit of Christ' with 'the spirit of Napoleon' was different from Carlyle's call for a hero who would restrain and suppress the revolutionary forces of Europe. Mickiewicz called for a great leader because he thought (like many other Polish exiles) that the lack of strong leadership was the principal cause of the defeat of the Polish insurrection; he desired a leadership which would discipline the revolutionary forces, give them impetus, and bring their cause to a victorious end. His Messianism was a harbinger of revolution, a strange but symptomatic prognostication of the revolutionary year of 1848.

Mickiewicz's revolutionism enabled him to be an even more consistent ideologist of charismatic power than was Carlyle. The English author made some concessions to rationalism: he stated, for instance, that the 'hero as prophet', as a direct messenger of God, was a product of an earlier age, who would not recur in the new age of scientific progress. Mickiewicz would have assessed this qualification as sheer pusillanimity. In spite of his hero-worship, Carlyle was a conservative, whereas charisma is in general a revolutionary force—charismatic leadership is 'the product of enthusiasm and crisis', it legitimizes itself by a *mission* which often breaks down the established political order (see B. 10, p. 303). This was precisely what Mickiewicz wanted and that was why he was not afraid of the revolutionary potentiality of charismatic leadership.

For Mickiewicz, the idea of charismatic leadership was also a peculiar solution of the problems arising from the experience of the insurrection of 1830 on the one hand, and from the romantic interpretation of Polish history, on the other. On the one hand, Mickiewicz fully shared the prevailing feeling that the insurrection had been defeated because of the lack of strong and able personal leadership; on the other hand, he idealized the ancient Polish 'republicanism' and disagreed with the thinkers of the Polish Enlightenment and their contemporary followers, who claimed that Poland had fallen because of the lack of a hereditary monarchy of the Western type. The idea of charismatic authority enabled him to recognize the need for the strongest leadership without making any concessions to rationalist, Enlightenment-inspired criticism of the Polish 'anarchy'. Strong leadership, Mickiewicz argues, does not consist in dynastic principle, enlightened absolutism, or 'majority rule', in the Diet. The ancient Poles, like other Slavonic nations, lacked great divinely-inspired leaders: *this* was their misfortune, but they were *right* in rejecting the doctrines of the West. They were right in striving for a society based entirely and exclusively upon enthusiasm and exaltation (A. 70, X. 44). If they had had a great inspired leader, they would have obeyed him with enthusiasm and their republican freedoms, including free elections and *liberum veto*, would have been perfectly compatible with strong executive power.

The idea of a *personal* Messiah—of a great leader incarnating the new revelation—was combined in Mickiewicz's lectures with that of a *collective, national* Messiah. Nationality was seen by the poet as an element essential to the performance of a divinely imparted mission. Not only individuals but nations, too, are the instruments of the Word: the human spirit must pass through nationality in order to attain the universal.

The role of chosen instruments of universal regeneration was allotted by the poet to two peoples: to the Slavs and to the French. The first are a virgin people, uninfected with rationalism, unspoiled by industrialization, unburdened with a great historic past; the second are the people of action, a people which as a result of its unceasing 'spiritual labour' has accumulated the greatest reserve of the 'holy fire' while, at the same time, retaining its barbarian freshness. Leadership among the Slavs will fall to Poland—the most faithful ally of France, the nation which has suffered the most (like Christ) and has, at the same time, 'married' the militant spirit of Napoleon. This Franco-Slavonic orientation was a great step forward in comparison with Mickiewicz's Messianism of the thirties—it signified an awareness of the inseparability of the Polish cause from the cause of European revolution. 'Polish Messianism', proclaimed Mickiewicz, 'must not remain outside the European movement, must not be independent of France . . . the whole power of the future is in France and nowhere else than in France' (A. 70, X. 423). Thus, from a *political* point of view, Mickiewicz's Messianism was tantamount to the idea of an alliance between the two most revolutionary nations of Europe—the French and the Poles—plus the bringing into the revolutionary movement of the oppressed Slavonic nations. The supremacy in this 'Holy Alliance of the Peoples' was given to France—the country of Napoleon and 'the elder daughter of the Church'.

According to Mickiewicz, each nationality was founded by a single man. Naturally, the common people afford the material from which a nation is shaped. The nation emerges only when the revealed truth transferred to the people by inspired heroes calls forth a response in the people, infuses them with God's breath, and focuses their activity on the realization of a great goal. Thus, the great inspired men perform a crucial function in the process of nation-building. The 'holy fire' kindled by them and preserved by the people is the measure of national maturity. Therefore France, the country of Charlemagne and Napoleon, possessed of the greatest amount of 'holy fire', was called by Mickiewicz 'the arch-nation'.

In sharp contrast to the overwhelming majority of Polish, Czech, and Russian Slavophiles, Mickiewicz did not praise the 'idyllic' features of the national character of the Slavonic peoples. The docility and peacefulness of the Slavs were, in his eyes, a source of weakness, something which had to be overcome with the help of the militant and military spirit of the French. Not only the Poles, but the Slavs in general had always lacked great divinely-inspired leaders; the only exceptions were the Russian tsars, who had inherited charismatic power from the great Mongol chieftains, and had later managed to combine it with the 'most rationalistic' system of running the state (A. 70, X. 231–2). The Slavs were a chosen people because they were 'new barbarians', people without heritage, with a virgin soul ready to accept a 'new revelation', possessing nothing and, thus, having nothing to lose in the imminent cataclysm. Therefore, Mickiewicz thought, the new revelation had to be proclaimed by a Slav; its practical realization, however, depended on the French who were still the initiator-people, a people whose mission was to awaken the Slavs and to unite them, with the help of the Poles, under the strong and inspired leadership of a new Napoleon.

A few words should be added concerning the role of Jews in

Mickiewicz's messianic vision. In his *Books of the Polish Pilgrims* he wrote about Jews with scorn; later, however, when his Messianism became centred around religious problems, his attitude towards Jews underwent a significant change. He began to use the word 'Israelite' as a synonym of 'chosen' and proclaimed that there were three 'Israelite nations' in universal history: the Jews, the French, and the Slavs, each of them representing a necessary phase in the progressive unfolding of religious truth (cf. B. 35). Moreover, he presented religious progress not as a process in which lower phases are transcended by higher, preserving only a historial significance, but as a process of building a many-storeyed temple, in which Judaism is the third storey, the Roman Church is the second, and Towianism the third. Thus, Judaism was, in Mickiewicz's view, not the 'lowest phase' of a process but the foundation of a building. The poet drew from this three important conclusions. First, he developed a notion of Jews and Poles as two parallel nations in exile, and of a mysterious link between Jewish and Polish Messianism; it was not accidental, he claimed, that Poland was 'the main seat of the oldest and the most mysterious of all the nations', the nation which 'from the depth of its synagogues has not ceased for centuries to draw out of itself cries with which nothing in the world can enter into comparison; calls, which human memory has already forgotten' (A. 70, XI. 343). Secondly, he concluded that not only the Poles and other Slavs but the French and the Jews as well should lead mankind into the new epoch of the Holy Ghost and, therefore, that it was utterly important to pull some Jews into Towiański's circle. Thirdly, he became convinced that Jews should not be converted by abandoning Judaism, but that Judaism, as the foundation of the whole edifice of Messianism, should be preserved, although, at the same time, lit up by light coming from the higher storeys of the Temple. In accordance with this he held in contempt the Jews who became acculturated in Western cultures, betraying their spiritual heritage. Instead, he highly esteemed orthodox Jews and wanted the Towianists to share 'the sorrow of Israel'. A deeply symbolic expression of this attitude was Mickiewicz's participation in the synagogue service in Paris, on the anniversary of the destruction of both Jerusalem Temples (11 August 1845). There he raised his voice, speaking 'in the name of the Synagogues of the Orient', condemning the prosperous, religiously indifferent Jews and praising the poor, orthodox Jewry, unrivalled in suffering and in hope.

It is quite possible, as has been pointed out by a Jewish-American scholar (B. 35, pp. 55–7), that Mickiewicz's views on the Jewish-Polish problem were influenced by Frankists—the followers of the eighteenth-century Jewish prophet Jacob Frank who embraced the truth of Catholicism without abandoning Judaism, and who proclaimed Poland to be a chosen nation. There are many arguments for such a hypothesis: Mickiewicz's wife, Celina (née Szymanowska), was of Frankist ancestry; it is probable (although not definitely established) that Mickiewicz's mother was also of Frankist background; finally, Mickiewicz himself mentioned in one of his lectures (in connection with Hoene-Wroński's Messianism) 'a numerous Israelite sect, half Christian, half Jewish, which also looked forward to Messianism and saw in Napoleon the Messiah, at least his predecessor' (A. 70, X. 369). The most important argument, however, is, in my view, the striking similarity between Frank's conception of the stages of religious development and Mickiewicz's image of the relationships between Judaism, Catholicism, and Towiański's teachings.

4. Mickiewicz's Messianism Seen From the French and Russian Perspectives

Mickiewicz was not alone in proclaiming from the Collège de France the great, holy mission of the French nation. He was one of the 'three Anabaptists from the Collège de France' (B. 46) whose lectures called forth a most vivid response among the audience and, in a sense, paved the way for the revolutionary events of 1848. The other two were his colleagues and friends, Edgar Quinet and Jules Michelet.[8] They deeply felt the greatness of the Polish poet, admired and tried to imitate (unsuccessfully) his inspired improvisations. In their writings of that time one can find many traces of Mickiewicz's influence. This example kindled their religious feelings, his attacks against the 'official Church' were interpreted by them (mistakenly) as consonant with their own anticlericalism. Quinet was so fascinated by the prophetic poet that for some time he balanced on the edge of Towianist conversion.[9]

Many motifs in Quinet's thought made him peculiarly

susceptible to messianic ideas. His belief that historical progress followed the pattern of successive 'religious revolutions' was similar to Mickiewicz's view of history as a series of revelations; his glorification of great, inspired men, especially of Christ and Napoleon, as well as his explanation of the religious meaning of the French Revolution, differed very little from the corresponding ideas in Mickiewicz's Messianism. The main difference was to be found in the intensity and quality of religious feeling behind their ideas: Mickiewicz was an ardent believer and an authentic prophet, whereas Quinet was a secular thinker fascinated by the phenomenon of religiosity. Nevertheless, it is truly remarkable that both of them saw the way to the imminent religious regeneration not in a philosophical explanation of religion or in a return to the original spirit of the Gospel but in the rekindling of enthusiasm and exaltation and in the restoration of the miraculous, charismatic leadership of Christ. Christ, proclaimed Mickiewicz, was not a legislator, his only book of laws was the words: 'Follow me!' We find the same view in Quinet: like Mickiewicz (and under his influence) he condemned theories, theological dogmas, and written laws asserting that the essence of Christianity could be summarized in Christ's words: 'Sequere me!' (cf. B. 191, pp. 104–6).

Michelet, even more than Quinet, was deeply impressed by Mickiewicz's powerful encouragement of French national Messianism. In his Diary he wrote about his Polish friend as follows: 'How do I thank a man whose heart is more French than France? Nobody ever had a deeper feeling for France' (cf. A. 68, pp. 267–73). He was equally impressed by Mickiewicz's eulogies about the common people with pure hearts, unmistakable knowledge of the good, and a capacity for foreseeing the future. In spite of this, however, when he saw Mickiewicz's lectures in print he was shocked by finding in them many ideas with which he could not agree. He rejected Mickiewicz's hero-worship as well as his religious fervour, militant anti-rationalism, and glorification of unreflective action. He did not cease to love and admire Mickiewicz, but ceased to feel unanimous with him. Instead, he began to see Mickiewicz as his greatest opponent, the only one to be taken seriously, the only one worthy of a discussion which would imply the existence of a certain common platform in the sphere of the highest values. He expressed this dialectical attitude in the words: 'Notre seul adversaire, notre cher adversaire, à nous autres philosophes, c'est Mickiewicz, il nous est moins adverse que correspondant et symétrique' (A. 68, p. 267).

In order to complete this brief sketch of the French reception of Mickiewicz's ideas it is worth while to add that Towiański's mystical doctrine, preached by Mickiewicz and rejected by Michelet as an expression of the 'Eastern' view of the world, had called forth an enthusiastic response among the followers of the French visionary and prophet, P. M. Vintras. In a letter addressed to Mickiewicz they 'fell to their knees before the New Poland' and unconditionally accepted Towiański's leadership (see B. 110, p. 453).[10]

Equally interesting was the reception of Mickiewicz's lectures in Russia, concentrating, naturally, on the 'Slavophile' motifs in his Messianism. To understand peculiar features of the 'Slavophile' dimension of Mickiewicz's thought it is necessary, I think, to look at it through the prism of the Russian ideological controversies of the 1840s (cf. B. 179 and B. 178, chapt. IV).

At the beginning of 1844 Alexander Herzen wrote in his *Diary*:

The lectures of Mickiewicz in Collège de France 1840–2. Mickiewicz is a Slavophile like Khomyakov and Co., the difference consisting in the fact that he is a Pole and not a Muscovite, that he lives in Europe, and not in Moscow, that he speaks not only about Russia but also about Czechs, Illyrians, etc. (A. 28, II. 333.)

Very similar was the opinion of the Slavophiles themselves. Samarin, the future ideologist of the chauvinistic, anti-Polish campaign of the 1860s, interpreted the last two courses of Mickiewicz's lectures as a search for the 'true Slavonic principles' which had been betrayed by Poland but preserved in Russia and made conscious in Russian Slavophilism. Sometime or other, Samarin wrote, the history of the Polish emigration would be recognized as one of the most interesting chapters in the history of nineteenth-century Europe. Emigration was the necessary and final solution of the historical tragedy of Poland. Poland had always been a vassal of the West; she was the only Slavonic country which had really accepted and deeply assimilated 'western principles'. But now the Polish exiles, like

Jews who had been converted to the New Testament, became the first Europeans who dared to raise their voice against the falsity of European civilization. Doubly uprooted, torn away from both their native and from western soil, they proved able to look at their western heritage from without and to condemn it. 'The purifying force of suffering and the pain with which nothing can be compared in the whole of modern history made their vision clearer and their thought more sober' (Mickiewicz's mysticism was interpreted as a symptom of this 'sobering'). It is not the Poles, however, who are destined to build the new world, embodying principles in the name of which they condemned contemporary Europe: 'Their condemnation of the West was equivalent to passing sentence upon Poland' (A. 89, I. 351–2).

Thus, both the Russian Westernizers (Herzen) and the Russian Slavophiles (Samarin) agreed that Mickiewicz's lectures on Slavonic literature were relevant to contemporary controversies in Russia, and that some of the Polish poet's ideas might be used to support the standpoint of 'Khomyakov and Co.'. Comparative analysis of Mickiewicz's lectures and Russian Slavophilism shows that there were deep reasons for such a view; nevertheless, it shows also that Mickiewicz's romantic Messianism and Slavophile romantic conservatism represented two different types of romantic *Weltanschauung*. The opinion of Hans Kohn that 'the Polish messianists resembled most closely the Russian Slavophiles of the same period' is, I think, a crude exaggeration (B. 78, p. 31).

Slavophile romanticism was a 'romanticism of tradition' whereas Mickiewicz represented a typical 'romanticism of charisma'. The Russian thinkers and the Polish poet were unanimous in condemning rationalism, both in philosophy and in social life, but they differed in their final conclusions. The Slavophiles were guardians of the purity of the Orthodox Christian faith, while Messianism was a religious heresy of a chiliastic type. Such notions as 'religious progress', 'the new revelation', 'the religion of the Holy Ghost', were completely alien to Slavophile thought. Messianism was a prophecy turned towards the future—although this future could be interpreted as a vindication of some values of the past. The Slavophiles were the prophets of the past, harking back to the past which had been lost and trying to build upon the relics of this past which were still alive in some of the traditions of the Russian peasantry and in the Orthodox Church. They created a kind of a 'conservative utopia', and not a 'chiliastic utopia', as did the Polish Messianist.

Let us illustrate this by a few concrete examples of similarities and dissimilarities between Mickiewicz's and the Slavophiles' thought.

Both Mickiewicz and the Russian Slavophiles set against all kinds of rationalism the concept of 'living', 'immediate' knowledge. Mickiewicz called it 'intuition', while Kireevsky and Khomyakov preferred to call it 'faith'; Mickiewicz spoke about 'second sight', 'the vision of the spirit', and Kireevsky meant the same when he wrote about 'intellectual vision', the 'vision of the mind'. This similarity was noticed by Samarin, who stated in one of his letters that the most precise definition of 'living knowledge' might be found in Schelling and Mickiewicz (A. 89, XII. 175–6). The word 'intuition' was derived by the poet (of course, wrongly) from *intus itio*—entering into oneself: 'The more deeply one enters into one's own essence, the more truths one attains, because after this manner one draws nearer to the focus whereby man communicates with God' (A. 70, XI. 174). The same view was expressed by Kireevsky, who asserted that true, integral knowledge was attainable only through religious concentration of the spirit, through the bringing of all spiritual forces into an 'inner focus', hidden in the depth of the human soul and inaccessible to rational cognition. A special capacity for such spiritual concentration was ascribed, of course, to the Slavonic nations, unspoiled by Western rationalism: Mickiewicz ascribed it in the first place to the Poles; the Slavophiles, to the Orthodox Russians.

The common features of Mickiewicz's and the Slavophiles' criticism of rationalism might be summed up in three points:

First, rationalism was criticized as the main source of the disintegration, the internal dissolution, of the spirit (cf. A. 35, I. 276, A. 70, X. 384);

Secondly, rationalism was criticized as knowledge independent of, and separated from, morality (cf. A. 35, I. 159, A. 70, XI. 426);

Thirdly, rationalism was accused of being tantamount to cognitive egalitarianism, setting forth the ideal of knowledge accessible to all, irrespective of God's grace and the inner value of the cognizing subjects (cf. A. 35, I. 229–30, A. 70, XI. 184).

As we see, the agreement between Mickiewicz and the Slavophiles was large and significant. Nevertheless, it did not embrace the whole of their respective ideologies. The Slavophiles put forward against reason the ideal of love, and by love they meant a conservative force of solidarity and concord; Mickiewicz also talked much about love, but laid emphasis primarily on such emotional states as exaltation, enthusiasm, and inspiration. The Slavophiles saw the main uniting force in tradition; Mickiewicz also appreciated tradition, called it a truth which unfolds in time, and defended it against 'rationally contrived doctrines'. But the highest uniting force, able to discipline enthusiasm and to transform it into action, was seen by the poet in the great heroes, instruments of a higher Revelation, who possessed 'tone'—the compelling power of command. In contradistinction to the Slavophiles, who were lacking in a genuine prophetic element (cf. B. 11, p. 48), Mickiewicz was a typical prophet and, we are told, 'history shows that the revolutionary character of prophecy prevails over conservative features, which, however, are not entirely absent from the prophetic character and activity' (B. 174, p. 356). The Slavophiles might call themselves 'guardians of Revelation'—of the *old* Revelation, preserved, in their opinion, in the tradition of the Orthodox Church. None of them could subscribe to Mickiewicz's words: 'I stand before the face of God as a living witness of the *new* revelation . . . I am a spark shot forth from the torch' (A. 70, XI. 453).

Mickiewicz's and the Slavophiles' protest against rationalism was not only, and not even primarily, motivated by philosophical reasons. It was above all a protest against the bourgeois rationalization of social life, so magnificently described by Max Weber. The defence of 'living', 'immediate' and 'integral' knowledge was equivalent to the defence of 'immediate', unreflective and emotional social ties, which were endangered by the progressive rationalization of economic production, human behaviour, and social institutions.

Especially significant was the position which Mickiewicz and the Slavophiles alike represented in the great all-European controversy about the essence of legislation. Opposing so-called 'juridical rationalism' (Weber), they emphasized (in accordance with the general spirit of conservative social philosophy—from De Maistre to the German 'historical school of law') that laws could not simply be 'devised', but had to 'grow' from traditions and folkways and that this growth should be spontaneous and 'organic', free from any 'mechanical' interference from above. In a word, both Mickiewicz and the Slavophiles took the side of 'historical law' and sharply attacked 'rational' or 'theoretical' law. One of the main reasons for the contrast between the Old Russia and western Europe was seen by the Slavophiles in the fact that the West, under the fatal influence of its Roman heritage, had espoused the cause of 'rational law'. The same conservative understanding of historical continuity found expression in Mickiewicz's negative judgement upon the Polish Great Diet and the Constitution of 3 May 1791. According to the poet, the reformers in the Diet were 'split off from national history'; they were trying 'to deduce from rational principles' the whole constitution of a great nation, instead of confiding in 'the historical wisdom of the people' (A. 70, X. 219–21).

The similarity between some ideas of the Polish poet and of the Russian Slavophiles is especially conspicuous in Mickiewicz's estimation of the reforms of Peter the Great. Sharp criticism of the methods and results of these reforms, together with an idealization of pre-Petrine Russian life, is, as we know, the essential feature of Russian Slavophilism; the very word Slavophilism originally meant not 'love of Slavs' but love of the 'purely Slavonic' and Christian principles of pre-Petrine, non-westernized Russian life. In the eyes of Slavophile thinkers Peter was the embodiment of the most ruthless rationalism in action. Their criticism of his violent reforms paralleled the criticism of the French Revolution by conservative thinkers of the West. Mickiewicz, being unconstrained by censorship, made this parallel explicit. He said that the rule of Peter the Great in Russia corresponded to the rule of the revolutionary Convention in France: 'Both these events: the Russian reform and the terrorist Frence revolution, explain each other. I would say even that they are essentially the same single event: in both of them we see the eighteenth century becoming a legislator' (A. 70, X. 94).

In some of his utterances Mickiewicz went even further, rejecting not only 'juridical rationalism' but also written laws as such. The ancient Poles, he thought, strove to transform Poland into a society basing itself exclusively upon the inner impulses and good will of its members. A very similar attitude towards law was taken by Konstantin Aksakov, the most ardent and extreme Russian Slavophile, for whom law as such was but 'external justice', an effort to replace human conscience by an outward apparatus of institutions (see B. 180, p. 259).

Criticism of rationalist theories of law was closely linked by the Slavophiles to the criticism of bourgeois forms of property, to which they opposed the peasant commune. We find the same motifs interwoven in Mickiewicz's thought. According to him, the ancient Slavonic communes provided a better solution to the problem of property than the socialist theories of the nine-teenth century; their principles were similar to the ideal of Fourier, but more consistent, practical, and realizable (A. 70, VIII. 82, XI. 308).

The idealization of the ancient communal principles on account of their similarity to socialism later became part and parcel of the 'Russian socialism' of Herzen and of the different ideologies of Russian Populism. But the first Russian thinkers who played with the idea of an analogy between the peasant commune and modern socialism were the Slavophiles, and in doing this they were echoing Mickiewicz's lectures. Samarin, polemizing with a liberal Westernizer, K. D. Kavelin, indicated that 'the Slavonic people gave a living answer to the last query of the western world' and, to confirm this, referred directly to Mickiewicz (cf. A. 89, I. 37–40). This and other utterances of the kind provoked Belinsky to state that the Slavophiles 'had imbibed their ideas from the socialists' (A. 3, XII. 468). A few years later they inclined Herzen to believe that socialism was a bridge on which he and the Slavophiles could meet and join hands (see A. 28, VII. 118).

It is interesting to note that the development of Herzen's thought, his transition from Westernism to 'Russian socialism', was to some extent directly influenced by Mickiewicz's lectures. Not Haxthausen, as is still widely believed, but the Slavophiles and Mickiewicz gave Herzen the first stimulus to ponder over the peasant commune and the destiny of the Slavonic world. Herzen's *Diary* of 1843–4 bears sufficient testimony to this (A. 28, II. 333–6).

The negative attitude towards bourgeois forms of property was yet another factor linking the ideas of Mickiewicz to those of

Russian Slavophilism. Both he and the Slavophiles treated 'absolute', individual property as something alien to their peoples, characteristic of the rationalistic and corrupted West. In both cases criticism of economic individualism was bound up with rejection of bourgeois individualism as such. In the reforms of Peter the Great and in the French Convention, Mickiewicz condemned the false pride of the individual who dared to act in accordance with his own narrow individual reason. He hated or, rather, despised calculating rationalistic individualism no less than the Slavophiles.

In spite of this, however, Mickiewicz—in contrast to the Slavophiles—was an individualist, and not a collectivist. Unlike the Slavophiles, he conceived of a nation not as a supra-individual community but as an association of individual spirits, striving for individual perfection. His anti-rationalism was bound up with a longing for a divine revelation which would effuse from above through the medium of a chosen heroic individual, and not (as in the case of the Slavophiles) with the notion of a supra-individual, closely-knit community, *preserving* in its tradition the original gifts of the Holy Ghost. Needless to say, his spiritualistic, romantic individualism of hero-worship was very different from rationalistic individualism, let alone from the utilitarian individualism of a Bentham. Nevertheless, it was very different from romantic traditionalism as well.

The opposition between the romanticism of tradition and the romanticism of charisma, is, of course, relative: both were antithetic to rationalism and both remained equally 'reactionary' from the standpoint of the conventional values of bourgeois progress.[11] Max Weber used the words 'traditional' and 'charismatic' to denote the two ideal types of domination and of social cohesion, but he treated both of them as characteristic of the pre-rational model of society. Charisma, having undergone a process of routinization, becomes tradition, and tradition, on the other hand, is valued, as a rule, for the sake of the divine inspiration which still shines through it. Rationalism is the common enemy of charisma and tradition; this accounts for the fact that in the ideologies expressing the romantic protest against rationalism, the 'romanticism of charisma' often coexisted with, and sometimes even merged into, the 'romanticism of tradition'. Nevertheless, the case of Mickiewicz is a brilliant confirmation of Max Weber's assertion that 'the difference between charisma and tradition is more important than the similarity' (see B. 10, p. 303). The cult of revolutionary France and the Napoleonic idea were utterly incompatible with romantic traditionalism, but perfectly compatible with the romanticism of charisma. That is why Mickiewicz's Messianism and Russian Slavophilism resulted, and *had* to result, in different actions: at the decisive moment, in 1848, Mickiewicz and the Slavophiles found themselves on the opposite sides of the barricade.

III. Juliusz Słowacki and Zygmunt Krasiński

1. The Metaphysics of Revolutionary Heroism

Juliusz Słowacki, the greatest rival of Mickiewicz, became a Messianist only in the 1840s, under the influence of Towiański's teaching. He was prepared to accept this teaching by the writings of Swedenborg, whom he had read already in his early youth; in a sense, as in Mickiewicz's case, his entire intellectual evolution led him to his mystical conversion. Nevertheless, the acceptance of Towiański's doctrine was a most important fact in his intellectual biography, quite irrespective of his changing attitudes to Master Andrzej and his circle. All his so-called philosophical works—a gnostic poem in prose entitled *Genesis From the Spirit*, 'Conversations About Genesis', 'Apostolic Letter', and others—are closely related to Towiański's ideas, although interpreted and developed in an original way. The same holds true of his mystical dramatic poems and, above all, his poem *King Spirit* (1847), the story of the successive incarnations of a powerful, 'kingly' spirit in Polish history.

Słowacki became acquainted with Towiański's teaching in the autumn of 1841. From the very beginning he noticed and highly appreciated its heretical character—Towiański appeared to his eyes as the incarnation of Perun, an ancient Slavonic deity, resurrected and shaking the dome of the basilica of Saint Peter. After his talk with Towiański—on 12 July 1842—he became his follower and joined his circle. However, he remained in it for a very short time, because he was shocked and disgusted by the 'Russian tendency' represented by Towiański and Mickiewicz. This tendency, inherent in the Slavophile notion of a common mission of all the Slavs, found expression in Towiański's idea of a necessary reconciliation between Poland and Russia; in Mickiewicz's lectures it was combined even with a certain admiration for the charismatic power of Russian tsars, for the unsurpassed endurance of Russian peasants and soldiers, and for the commanding 'tone' of Russian officers. A collective manifestation of this tendency was the participation of Towiański's circle in the Mass for the soul of Alexander I, organized by the French mystic, Vintras. On 1 November 1843, Słowacki put his veto on this (he called it a 'veto from the Polish spirit') and parted company with the circle. He had not changed by then his basic attitude to Towiański as a man and to his teaching; in the summer of 1844 he wrote his *Genesis From the Spirit* and dedicated it to his former Master. Soon afterwards, however, Towiański and Mickiewicz, cherishing a hope that Nicholas I might be converted to their ideas, included Alexander Chodźko, a member of the circle and a former Russian diplomat, to send a letter to the Tsar, explaining the content of the 'new revelation' and expressing a conviction that its acceptance by the Russian monarch would make him the spiritual leader of all Slavs and 'the most powerful instrument of God'. For Słowacki this was too much. He removed from his *Genesis* its dedication to Towiański, replacing it with the dedication to Colonel Mikołaj Kamieński who protested against Chodźko's letter and broke with the circle.

Słowacki's Messianism was convergent in many points with the Messianism of Mickiewicz.[12] The philosophical basis of both of them was spiritualistic universal perfectionism bound up with the idea of progressive reincarnation; in both cases spiritual progress was to be achieved by means of inner labour, pain, and sacrifice; finally, in both cases national Messianism was inseparable from the cult of great heroic individuals and from the belief in a spiritual hierarchy among individuals and among nations. Like Mickiewicz, Słowacki was convinced that the higher spirits—the 'kingly spirits', as he called them—had a moral right and a duty to lead the inferior ones. The most conspicuous difference was the cosmogonical and quasi-naturalistic character of Słowacki's conception of universal genesis. Spiritualistic universal evolutionism, typical of Towiański's doctrine which proclaimed the essential unity of the human spirit with the entire, even inorganic, nature, was to be found also in Mickiewicz's lectures, but only Słowacki—with the help of philosophical naturalists like Charles Bonnet and Boucher de Perthes—developed it into an all-embracing system of cosmic genesis.[13] The world was conceived in this system as a great spiritual organism ('the world spirit') composed of

individual spirits which—not satisfied with a passive participation in the Absolute—started to create from themselves their
visible shapes, more and more perfect, in order to achieve in this
way the highest possible perfection—the 'angelification'—and
to become reunited with the Absolute by means of an active
participation in its eternal life. This 'genesis from the spirit'
was, thus, a *creative* evolution (as opposed to mechanistic
evolutionism), that is, a progressive development by means of
one's own heroic efforts. Cosmic genesis turned out to be a
process of self-creation. Laziness and love of comfort,
unwillingness to progress at the cost of increasing sacrifices,
were defined as the greatest sin against the spirit.

It followed from this that the 'world spirit'—identical in
substance with the individual spirits and existing only in
them—was autonomous, independent from the transcendent
Absolute. In contrast to Towiański and Mickiewicz, Słowacki
conceived progress as being accomplished by means of
individual merits, without divine grace or other forms of supra-
natural help. In Mickiewicz's synthesis of heroism and humility
he accepted only heroism. He did not agree to put aside his
individuality in order to become an empty vessel, ready to
receive the grace streaming forth from Heaven; in Mickiewicz's
Messianism he discovered the 'resignation of a Lithuanian
peasant' passively accepting the will of God (see A. 90, X. 568).
Consequently, he denied the necessity of the Church as a
mediator between God and men and as an institutionalized
repository of grace. Another consequence was a more positive
(than in Mickiewicz's case) attitude towards individual reason:
according to Słowacki, the truths attained by means of mystical
inspiration should be investigated by reason, because the
inuitive knowledge—'the seeing faith'—was only a first step to a
truly spiritual knowledge (A. 90, X. 280–1).

Another important difference between Mickiewicz's and
Słowacki's Messianism was the absence of conservative-
romantic motifs in the latter. Słowacki, to be sure, also referred
to tradition; he had to refer to it because he believed that the
value of man depended on the merits of his ancestors and that
spiritual superiority, in the case of both individuals and nations,
was a result of self-creating efforts in a long series of incarnations. Nevertheless, Słowacki reduced tradition to its purely
spiritual dimension, thus liberating it from emotional commit-

ment to any concrete form of social life. The spirit was for him an 'eternal revolutionary'; he demanded, therefore, that all given forms of life should be destroyed incessantly, and not only (as Mickiewicz saw it) in special, critical moments of historical time. His ideal was the 'holy anarchy'—the unlimited freedom of the most developed, i.e. the strongest and most holy, spirits, breaking without scruples all existing traditions, laws, and, even, ordinary moral rules. For the 'King-Spirits', standing in the van of universal progress, everything was allowed. Słowacki extolled them in a way which might remind us of the Nietzschean super-man.

Słowacki's philosophy of history was an apotheosis of the 'torture of bodies' perfecting the spirit, an apotheosis of bloody revolutions and, even, of great crimes, devoid of any moral justification but, nevertheless, furthering mysteriously the cause of progress. At the same time it was a splendid illustration of the Nietzschean distinction between the love of what is close to us (*Nächstenliebe*) and the love of what is afar (*Fernstenliebe*): Słowacki's 'King-Spirit' loves mankind, is the most powerful instrument of progress, but, none the less, commits the most cruel crimes and sadistically enjoys their monstrosity.

The poet believed that the laws of progress *must* be cruel, because suffering and oppression are the most effective means of mastering the energy of the spirit. He agreed with Saint Martin that the way to Salvation leads through sacrifice, through the shedding of blood. It was only through the ordeals, through the formidable sufferings, which hardened and strengthened the Polish spirit, that the Polish nation allegedly surpassed others in heroism and holiness and assumed the 'papacy of spirit'. Especially beneficial for the Poles was the massacre at Humań—the famous eighteenth-century slaughtering of Polish nobles by Ukrainian Cossacks and peasants. Now the Poles are the New Israel, the King-Spirits among the nations, fighting for the New Jerusalem. In order not to relent from fulfilling its mission, the revolutionary heroism of the Polish nation should never abate, even at the cost of suffering and defeats, which might ensue as the result of heroic actions.

I should add that Słowacki's Messianism was exclusively Polish; unlike Mickiewicz, he despised the French and indignantly refused any partnership with them (let alone their leadership).

Because of its exaltedly Polonocentric character, Słowacki's Messianism seems to be much more nationalistic than the Franco-Slavonic Messianism of Mickiewicz. It is important, however, to point out that both Mickiewicz and Słowacki were very far from nationalism in the sense of pursuing the egoistic interests of the Polish nation as an empirically existing community. The greatness and weakness, the sublime and utopian nature of their Messianism lay precisely in the fact that 'Polishness' was for them a lofty idea and the Polish nation was conceived as an association of spirits realizing it. 'The Fatherland', professed Mickiewicz in his Paris lectures, 'is not a mere piece of land bound by frontiers which limit the national existence and activity of the Pole' (A. 70, VIII. 36). Social reformers who believe that the 'fatherland signifies the future social order which should be achieved' are much closer to the truth. As liberty, power, and happiness are constitutive elements of the concept of fatherland, it is 'no wonder that this concept, conceived in this manner, had never been fulfilled in reality', since the empirically existing Poland never comprised all the conditions requisite for the existence of the ideal fatherland (ibid., p. 35). The example of Słowacki bears witness to what extent the *idea* of the nation and its spiritual essence could be opposed to the realities of national life. In his view, a nation as a spiritual category was in principle independent of a 'nation's body': 'When the body of a nation has aged and the spiritual greatness no longer finds its abode therein, then the spirits commence their great migration in search of better, brighter houses, better endowed to serve them.' In such a way, after the republican liberty had been suppressed in Pskov and Novgorod, the souls of the inhabitants of these cities 'stole away from their enslaved bodies to become Poles' (A. 91, XII. 287-8). In a similar way all the nations will become Poles in the future, this being the ineluctable stage of the universal progress leading to the 'new, sunny Jerusalem'. 'Polishness', identified with the ideal 'republicanism from the spirit', was thus elevated to the rank of the guiding principle of mankind, though it was only attainable at the cost of attenuating its connection with the reality of Polish national existence. The pitfall lurking in this conception did not consist in the danger of national particularism. Quite the contrary: it was rather the pitfall of messianic universalism, disregarding too easily the actual situation and the actual needs of the concrete, living people, over-disposed to sacrifice the immediate and the real at the altar of an ideological Absolute.

Like Mickiewicz, Słowacki saw the Poles as a chosen nation not only because of their present sufferings but also, to some extent, because of their past. Mickiewicz's lectures presented a vision of the Poland of the olden times as a country without 'reasoned-out' institutions, in which everything good resulted from free patriotic zeal. The ancient Poles were considered to be a unique people endeavouring to make the 'inner impulse and good will' the only basis of its national life; their free elections and their ideal of unanimity (and thus *liberum veto*) were an expression of a religious conviction that any significant political decision must rely on a miracle—the inspiration of the Holy Ghost—if it were to be conceived as free and morally binding. The author of *King Spirit* carried this messianic idealization of Poland's past still further. From his point of view the famous *liberum veto* was a precious device, by means of which the true spiritual hierarchy was able to defend itself against the false, artificial, material hierarchy. In sharp contrast to the Western bourgeois republicanism, in the ancient Polish republic the inferior spirits, although they constituted, of course, a majority, could not hold sway over the superior ones, but, quite on the contrary, the superior spirits were secured the right of opposing the will of the majority with their *liberum veto*. It is evident that this kind of idealization of the veto, and, consequently, of the principle of unanimity as opposed to the principle of majority, had very little in common with the views of the Russian Slavophiles, who also held the 'principle of unanimity' to be an inalienable part of the Slavonic ideal of society. The Slavophiles had set the Slavonic unanimity against the individualism and social atomism of the West; they interpreted this principle as a recognition that the individual should accept his moral dependence on the community by giving up his separate views in the name of unity and concord. Słowacki's position was, of course, on the other extreme. For him, the principle of unanimity was, first of all, a recognition of the *liberum veto*, that is, as he saw it, of the special privilege of the superior spirits to disagree with the mechanical majority, to rise above existing traditions and laws and to destroy them for the sake of spiritual progress. In opposition to Lelewel and other Polish democrats, who saw the ancient Polish republic as a prototype of modern democracy, Słowacki glorified the ancient Poland from an entirely different point of view: as a society most favourable for the spiritual élite, least resistant to the legitimate rights of spiritual superiority.[14] In Poland alone Christ would not have been crucified for professing his gospel.

The belief in spiritual hierarchy was a common feature of both Słowacki's and Mickiewicz's Messianism. It seems relevant to remind ourselves in this connection that such a belief was typical of the world-view of aristocracy and nobility. In the system of values of the two prophetic poets—in their uncompromising rejection of bourgeois utilitarianism, in their glorification of heroism, honour, and sacrifice, in their demand to combine the teaching of Christ with the powerful 'tone' of great warriors—a sublimation of knightly ethos can easily be found. This aspect of their Messianism can be interpreted as an attempt to bring back to life the warlike spirit of the ancient Polish nobility and to set it against the 'idyllic', home-loving ethos of the emasculated landowning gentry. This does not mean, however, that it is justified to see them as 'ideologists' of nobility: the values characteristic of the *Weltanschauung* of nobility were so much sublimated in their Messianism that they had lost any tangible connection with the interests of the nobility as a really existing social class. The idea of 'spiritual superiority' could easily be directed against the privileged classes; in fact it was taken for granted that revolutionaries, and not conservatives, represented the spiritual élite. Therefore, Słowacki's spiritual aristocratism was perfectly compatible with his revolutionism. Knowing that the defence of historical privileges contradicted the 'eternal revolutionism' of the spirit, being aware that Polish magnates were not ready 'to shake the ancient mold off themselves' and to 'inflame the holy revolt', he unhesitatingly set his hopes on the revolutionary people. In his poetical answer to Krasiński's *Psalms of the Future* he warned his conservative friend in the following words:

> Polish people, it's your own father—
> From it, like from a thorny shrub,
> God is ready to flare out,
> To weave winds into his cloak
> And to advance on you—and to move on,
> Having blown you away, like a candle.[15]

The bloody slaughter of the Galician gentry in 1846, skilfully encouraged by Metternich's administration, was interpreted by Krasiński as the decisive proof of the correctness of his conservative position. Słowacki, however, remained faithful to his belief in the revolutionary upheaval from below. In his 'Voice From Exile to the Brethren in Poland', he wrote:

> Ye are standing now on the edge of the abyss, people of noble stock, death and hell are under your feet, and up there, overhead, God and Poland.
>
> ***
>
> Recognize God's hand in your punishment and thank the Father in Heaven who sent it for your improvement.
>
> You measure the peasant by the stick of your own reason but he is superior to you by his faith.
>
> Have regard for the crude russet coat because this is the dress of the future soldiers who will win Poland's freedom.

2. Messianism and Counter-Revolution

The third prophetic poet, Count Zygmunt Krasiński, was an aristocratic conservative and did not share Mickiewicz's and Słowacki's enthusiasm for the revolution. He idealized Poland's past in a rather conventional manner. He glorified the religious piety of the ancient Polish nobility along with their tolerance and love of freedom, emphasized the dignity and knightly generosity of the nation which, abhorring pillage, spread through voluntary unions. It is interesting to note, however, that before his conversion to Messianism his views on the Polish past were extremely critical, comparable to Chaadaev's criticism of Russia. In his famous letter to his father (a former Napoleonic general and a dignitary of the Congress Kingdom) of 26 January 1836, he described the ancient Poles as a nation in whose history there was nothing truly 'whole' and organic, whose culture was purely imitative, whose only stable tradition was that of anarchy and whose freedom, of which they were so boastful, was nothing else than lack of discipline and laziness. Even the famous religious tolerance of ancient Poland was explained as stemming from a lazy indifference towards great spiritual issues of universal significance (see B. 65, II. 290–2).

The greatest and most difficult problem of Krasiński's *Weltanschauung* (a problem which for Słowacki did not exist at all) was how to reconcile messianic longings with the traditional Catholic faith. He was aware that the idea of a 'religious progress' and a chiliastic expectation of the new 'aeon' of the sacred history of mankind, in which the Church of Saint Peter would be replaced with the Church of Saint John or of the Holy Ghost, ran counter to the teaching of the Roman Church. In his *Legend* (1840) he made an attempt at a reconciliation between Catholic traditionalism and messianic hope: according to the eschatological vision presented in his work, in the coming epoch of Saint John Poland would be redeemed not because of her revolutionism but, on the contrary, because 'the remnants of the Polish nobility' had chosen to fulfil their duty to the end and died under the ruins of the basilica of Saint Peter, defending the Pope and the 'old Church'. As we can see, it was a rather ambiguous position: a moral option for faithfulness to the old, Catholic Church was bound up with the conviction that Catholicism was doomed and that the future, better world would emerge from its ruins. Soon afterwards Krasiński became committed to even more heterodox ideas. More and more was he immersed in the 'waves of revelations', more and more he identified himself with those who were 'waiting for something, longing for something', 'seeing the future behind the shapes of the present' (A.42, I. 440). At Christmas 1841 he experienced a state of rapture in which a vision of a new Christianity, regenerated and 'supplemented' thanks to the martyrdom of Poland, was revealed to him. After this spiritual upheaval he began to preach a religion of 'Polishness', superior, as he saw it, to traditional Catholicism although inseparably bound up with it, supplementing, and not negating, its truth. He sang it in his prophetic poem *The Dawn* (1843) and gave it a philosophical justification in his treatise 'On the Position of Poland for Divine and Human Reasons'.

Like Słowacki, Krasiński was indebted in his philosophical conceptions to some French thinkers—especially to Pierre Leroux, whose religious philosophy of history was based upon the idea of progressive reincarnation, and to the philosophical naturalist Boucher de Perthes who developed the idea of an 'extramundane progress'. However, in contradistinction to Mickiewicz and Słowacki, Krasiński was also a disciple of the German speculative idealists. Of course, he *had* to oppose Hegelianism: not only because of its rationalism, but also, and first of all, because Hegel saw the historical development as already accomplished in the 'absolute religion' (i.e. historical Christianity) and his own 'absolute philosophy', thus leaving

no room for messianic speculations about the future. The most
messianic among the German philosophers was Schelling in the
last phase of his development, i.e. in his 'philosophy of the
revelation'. No wonder his philosophy of the Trinity, together
with his chiliastic vision of the coming Church of Saint John
and the earthly Kingdom of the Holy Ghost, exerted a deep
influence on Krasiński's thought (see B. 84). Of course
Krasiński was deeply influenced by Polish philosophers as well:
by Hoene-Wroński, Trentowski, and, above all, by
Cieszkowski. The latter, his close personal friend, was for him
the greatest authority in philosophy and a providential man for
Poland.

In elaborating the religious side of Messianism, Krasiński
was greatly indebted to Towiański and Mickiewicz. He was
suspicious of all sects and never became a Towianist, but,
nevertheless, he was fascinated by Towiański's ideas and by the
charismatic power of his personality. The teaching of Master
Andrzej seemed to him 'crazy in details', but deeply true and
surprisingly similar to Cieszkowski's philosophy in its essential
content. In 1843 he reproached Cieszkowski with not paying
enough attention to the 'Paris movement' (i.e. Towianism). In
the same year he defined his *Dawn* as a 'disclosure' of the
mysteries of Towiański's doctrine; his friend, Konstanty
Gaszyński, added to this that the idea of writing the *Dawn* was
born under the profound influence exerted on Krasiński by the
second course of the Paris lectures of Mickiewicz (see B. 110,
pp. 430 and 497). The next two courses impressed Krasiński
even more. He reacted with enthusiasm to Mickiewicz's lecture
on Cieszkowski. In a letter to Cieszkowski he wrote:

You have read, probably, Mickiewicz's forecast about you. Nobody can
deceive such a spirit like Adam's. He has surmised your future from a few
words of yours. Towiański is a messenger who kindles flame in others—
nothing more, but this flame will become a great fire. This flame has all of us as
its stakes. (A. 41, p. 80).

It seemed to him by then that the contact and collaboration
between Adam and August would be, perhaps, of decisive
influence for the future fate of Poland and of all mankind.

It is interesting to see how Krasiński transformed
Towiański's idea of progressive reincarnation and of the
'hierarchy of spirits'. The 'superior spirits' came to be identified

with aristocracy as a social class, while progressivism furnished, by way of a paradox, an argument for traditionalism. The argument was as follows: the most perfect is always that which had a chance of the longest historical perfectioning; the existing social inequality is the result of the inequality of merits attained in previous incarnations. In this way Mickiewicz's 'superior spirits', endowed with the capacity of transferring the gifts of the Holy Ghost to the people, became identified with the social aristocracy. Thus the dividing line easily fits the classic typology of Max Weber: on the one hand a non-institutional individual charisma glorified by Mickiewicz and Słowacki, on the other hand a 'routinized', inherited charisma professed by Krasiński—in this respect a typical conservative.

The first part of the treatise 'On the Position of Poland' contained many ideas which could be found in Cieszkowski's *Our Father* as well. Krasiński, however, developed them in a somewhat different way—putting more emphasis on the 'absolute eschatology', i.e. on the future deification of man and the ultimate victory over death (see B. 196). In Cieszkowski's book the three hypostases of the Holy Trinity corresponded to three great *historical* epochs: the epoch of ancient paganism, the Christian epoch, and the future epoch of the Kingdom of God on earth. In Krasiński's treatise, instead, the entire span of history, conceived as the epoch of acquiring merits through pain and labour, corresponded to the second person of the Trinity, symbolized by Christ as the incarnation of Logos; thus, history as a whole was seen as a transitional period between the pre-historical unconscious Paradise (the epoch of Grace) and the future post-historical, or supra-historical, epoch of the Holy Ghost (the epoch of Love) in which further progress would be undisturbed by death. The Kingdom of God on earth, i.e. the epoch of the 'Christianization of politics', was conceived as the last phase of the second, historical epoch and, at the same time, as a kind of vestibule to the supra-mundane Kingdom of the Holy Ghost.

In all this process the individual spirits, immortal as spirits although changing their incarnations, were seen as continuing the divine work of creation by growing up to God and, finally, becoming 'gods' themselves. In this way the prophecy of the snake, 'Eritis sicut Deus' would be fulfilled and the original sin would turn out to be a 'felix culpa'. In developing these ideas

Krasiński made a clear distinction between God (the Absolute) and 'gods' as divinized human spirits. He insisted on this difference not only to avoid the equalization of created spirits with God but also to save their personal existence by preventing their fusion with the divine Absolute. God's likeness, he wrote, 'consists in the strange capacity for understanding and feeling one's own personality, that is to say, its difference from the personality of God; thus, one's *closeness* to God consists in the capacity for understanding and feeling one's *distance* from Him' (A. 43, VII. 60).

In the next part of Krasiński's treatise, entitled 'On the Trinity in Time and Space', the philosophy of God and the philosophy of universal progress passed into a philosophical interpretation of the meaning of Polish history. Each of the great ideas steering universal history, argued the poet, had to incarnate itself, that is to manifest itself in a visible, spatio-temporal form. Christ was the incarnation, the archetype, of the idea of inviolability and immortality of an individual person, while Poland was the archetype of the idea of inviolability of a nation (i.e. a historically developed and indestructible association of spirits). The martyrdom of Poland was of the same significance to nations as Christ's martyrdom to individuals. Christ's crucifixion was followed by his resurrection and ascension, tantamount to opening the door to Heaven to individual spirits; the political death of Poland would equally be followed by her resurrection, tantamount to the collective salvation of all the nations in the Kingdom of God on earth. However, the earthly Millennium was not seen by the poet as the final end of the progressive movement; having passed through this, i.e. having finished their earthly history, the created spirits would become immortal angels and would recover the memory of all their previous incarnations; they would progress further towards God, but knowing no death and enjoying the 'fullness of spirit'.

In the third part of the treatise, entitled 'The Position of Poland Among the Slavonic Peoples', Krasiński tried to show that the entire historical past of Poland prepared her for fulfilling her messianic mission. In his image of ancient Poland he was inspired mainly by Mickiewicz's *Books of the Polish Nation and of the Polish Pilgrims*. Thus, for instance, he followed Mickiewicz in interpreting the union between Poland and

Lithuania as a 'figure' of the future voluntary union of all nations.

As we can see from the above, Krasiński's treatise was a kind of synthesis of the ideas of the Polish prophetic poets and the 'national philosophers' of the Romantic Epoch. But this was precisely the reason why it could not escape condemnation by the representatives of the 'official Church'. After Krasiński's death—and according to his own will—the priests of the Polish congregation of the Resurrection, H. Kajsiewicz and P. Semenenko, examined his treatise from the point of view of orthodox Catholicism and found it incompatible with Christianity, leading to 'self-deification, the main error of the German philosophy' (see A. 43, VII. 199–20). Because of this negative verdict—also in accordance with the author's last will—the heretical work remained unpublished. A part of it was published in 1903 by Krasiński's grandson, and the whole text was given to the public only in 1912, in the Jubilee edition of Krasiński's works.

Among the texts published by Krasiński during his lifetime the most important philosophical credo was his preface to *The Dawn*. It was devoted almost entirely to the national question. Humanity, the poet argued, 'is the entirety and the unity of all the powers of the spirit of man, expressed visibly on this earth by concord and love of its members, that is, of nationalities'. In contrast to governments which are 'a human creation', nations are 'the Divine creation'. The division between 'what is God's' and 'what is Caesar's' cannot be eternal because essentially everything is 'God's': 'What was yesterday considered as owing to Caesar, today must be counted as belonging to God until the government of God shall be nought and God's kingdom all' (see B. 40, 277–8). The logic of this reasoning led to the conclusion that the Kingdom of God on earth would ensue from the replacement of the un-divine, man-created multi-national states with a brotherly union of free, God-created nations.

A few years later, in a letter to Trentowski of 2 January 1847, Krasiński wrote:

The true goal of Poland consists in realizing the Kingdom of God on Earth, in fusing politics with religion, in laying the foundation of the future Church of universal mankind, as well as in demonstrating to the whole world that sovereignty does not rest with the king or the people but with the nation alone. This is so because every nation constitutes one of the senses in the organism of mankind, and the constitution of this organism on our planet is the goal and end of terrestrial history and, at the same time, the beginning of a superior, more vital, more spiritual, extramundane progress. Verily, the new Covenant of mankind with God, the third one and the last one, breathes in the womb of Poland. (A. 40, III. 184.)

The words concerning the fusion of politics and religion found in this quotation touch upon the central idea of Polish Messianism: the idea of the Christianization of politics, of introducing ethical considerations into international relations and abolishing the rule of sheer force. This idea inspired Krasiński and Mickiewicz equally strongly despite the fact that their political convictions and their attitude towards the events of the Springtime of the Peoples were diametrically opposite. Mickiewicz expected and invoked a 'universal war for the freedom of the peoples', believing that the Christianization of politics would come as a result of it. Krasiński, on the contrary, expected a bloody social revolution, a terrible catastrophe which would unfetter infernal forces and bring about the reign of Anti-Christ: a period of revolutionary chaos after which tsarist Russia, representing the principle of the tyranny of matter over spirit, would intervene and establish her rule over Europe. Only after this period of disasters would Poland re-emerge from her ashes and lead other nations to the Kingdom of God on earth. Thus, the mission of Poland would consist not in leading the revolutionary struggle but, on the contrary, in calling forth a spiritual counter-revolution, replacing revolutionary hate with Christian love.

From the point of view of modern theories of nationalism Krasiński provides a very interesting and instructive case. 'The rise of nationalism', we are told by an eminent specialist in the field, 'is closely linked with the origins of popular sovereignty. . . . Nationalism has from the beginning been a politically revolutionary movement' (B. 77, p. 64). Krasiński, however, was an aristocratic conservative deeply opposed to revolution, defending social inequality by referring to the inequality of merits in previous incarnations, i.e. in the same way as the Indians defended their caste system. On the other hand, he was for changing the map of Europe by replacing 'artificial' empires by national states, and saw this change as tantamount to the establishing of the rule of God on earth. At the same time, however, he made a distinction between popular sovereignty, which he rejected, and national sovereignty, which he treated as the only source of a truly legitimate government. So he was certainly a 'nationalist' (in the sense of supporting the principle of the national state), but he did not fit the widespread generalization about the close connection between nationalism and democracy.

It seems to me that Krasiński's case, as well as the case of many other Polish thinkers, provides an argument for a certain modification of this theoretical thesis. It is true that the struggle for national sovereignty can be identified with a struggle for popular sovereignty—Polish democrats of the Romantic Epoch are a good illustration of this. It is no less true that democracy, even (as I have pointed out) a democracy of the gentry, increases the number of politically active citizens and thus contributes to the development of national consciousness. Nevertheless, the essence of broadly conceived 'nationalism' should not be reduced to the principle of self-determination by means of a democratic voting—'one man, one vote'. Krasiński rejected this principle because he believed that 'inferior spirits'—the masses—should be led by 'superior spirits', i.e. by 'historical classes' embodying national traditions and aware of the national mission. His example shows that it was perfectly possible to support national self-determination without supporting popular sovereignty. A nation, in his view, was a spiritual community, a free unity stemming from commonly shared traditions and values, striving (although sometimes unconsciously) for a common goal, endowed by God with a common mission to be performed for the sake of humanity. As such, a nation should not be partitioned or subjected to foreign domination; it should have its own state, expressing its own spiritual essence. Whether this state should be democratic, and to what degree, was a quite different question.

IV. Messianism versus Philosophy

1. Cybernetics Against Prophecy

As I have already pointed out, the Messianism of the prophetic poets—a characteristic product of the emigration, and the 'national philosophy'—a characteristic product of the intellectual life of the Congress Kingdom and, above all, of Poznania, were interestingly related to each other and influenced by each other. Among the poets the most philosophical was Krasiński; among the philosophers a conscious effort to assimilate some elements of Mickiewicz's and Krasiński's thought was made by Libelt; even more important was an attempt to bring together speculative philosophy and religious Messianism was, as we shall see, provided by Cieszkowski.

Quite different the case of Trentowski: a thinker firmly believing that Polish intelligentsia should follow its philosophers and not its 'irresponsible romantic poets'.[16] At the beginning of his philosophical career Trentowski made an attempt to gain Mickiewicz's support for his ideas and, towards this end, sent him his *Grundlage* and his *De vita hominis aeterna*. Mickiewicz's reaction to these works was quite interesting. In a letter to Trentowski of 9 September 1839, he paid tribute to Trentowski's philosophical erudition and to the merits of his style but, at the same time, gave him several suggestions clearly implying a critical attitude to his philosophy. He indicated, first of all, that a national Polish philosophy should be expressed in the Polish language; this advice Trentowski was prepared to accept, but the other recommendations and critical remarks were more difficult for him to swallow. True philosophy, argued Mickiewicz, should not be arbitrarily 'reasoned out' but deduced from the legends and myths of the people; it should not be a merely intellectual endeavour but an expression of a certain practical, moral attitude towards life; it should not neglect mysticism and the great heritage of the Middle Ages; finally, it should not replace the living God, to whom man could pray, with an abstract Absolute. A truly universal philosophy should be able to explain the universal phenomenon of prayer.

Trentowski's answer was very polite but firm. He drew a contrast between a philosopher and a poet, a believing Christian and a man committed to truth alone. In addition he styled himself as a Protestant, describing Protestantism as 'a philosophy within Christianity', as opposed to Catholicism, which he considered a 'poetical' religion.

During the following year Trentowski started to write his *System of National Pedagogics* and Mickiewicz began to lecture at the Collège de France. After the first two courses of Mickiewicz's lectures, Trentowski came to the conclusion that the poet had become an instrument of the fanatical Catholic clergy and that philosophers should do everything to resist his dangerous influence. A little later the heterodox character of Mickiewicz's lectures, in which the poet set his mystical teaching against philosophy in general and Trentowski's philosophy in particular, deeply hurt him and convinced him of the necessity to launch a systematic, organized counter-attack against Messianism. His journal *The Present and the Future* was devoted almost exclusively to this purpose. In Trentowski's eyes his struggle against 'Mickiewiczanism' was a real crusade, a defence of European civilization against the dark, demonic spirit of 'Asiaticism'.

Let us first look at this controversy from the point of view of Mickiewicz. Philosophy, he thought, was not a proper way to attain the truth. Truth is a 'daughter of pain and suffering' and not the result of writing books and empty discussions. The 'living truths' pertain not so much to our judgements as to the mode of our existence: 'to possess truth' means 'to be true'. In contradistinction to this kind of truth, rational truths are always partial and morally indifferent: 'They do not oblige a man to do anything; nobody feels obliged to let himself be crucified in order to prove the truth of a scientific or mathematical thesis' (A. 70, XI. 426). Philosophy, i.e. *autonomous* philosophy, identified with rationalism, does not demand any effort to achieve 'elevation of spirit' and thus corrupts men by offering them too comfortable a way of attaining the truth. It deceives them by making them believe that truth can be attained by reason alone, without moral commitment engaging the whole man's being.

The condemnation of empty philosophical discussions was, as we know, a characteristic feature of the world-view of the French traditionalists (De Maistre, De Bonald, Lamennais in his early period) who saw philosophy as a factor and symptom of social disintegration. Therefore it was easy for Trentowski to believe that his struggle against Mickiewicz was tantamount to combating the extreme Right. From Mickiewicz's point of view it looked quite different: the most dangerous conservatives were for him the philosophers, because they were satisfied with a rational analysis of the existing social realities instead of trying to change them. The most typical expression of a philosophical attitude towards the world was Hegel's thesis that everything real was rational.

The philosophy of Trentowski was in Mickiewicz's eyes an exemplification of all the faults of philosophy as such and of the German philosophy in particular. Together with Cieszkowski, Trentowski was classified by the poet as a 'denationalized Slav, enslaved by the German thought' (A. 70, XI. 150). In spite of this characterization in common, Mickiewicz was able to see great merits in Cieszkowski's thought, whereas his attitude to Trentowski was much more severe. He was deeply irritated by Trentowski's belief in the beneficial effects of philosophical education, by his eulogizing of modern European civilization, and by his attempts at rationalizing the mysteries of the faith. He was particularly offended by Trentowski's conception of God-manhood and by his view that philosophical knowledge was the means of awakening and developing the divine potential of man. This view, he claimed, was shameless blasphemy because it made German philosophers equal to Christ or even superior to Him. From Christ's life one should draw a lesson that God-manhood and the salvation of mankind had nothing in common with writing and reading philosophical books.

Trentowski was appalled by these arguments. He saw in Mickiewicz a spokesman of Asiatic mysticism, hostile to philosophical lucidity, or a prophet of the 'new barbarians' who would destroy libraries and overthrow the whole edifice of European civilization. He hesitated as how to classify Mickiewicz politically. At the beginning he treated him as a reactionary and compared him to the aged Schelling lecturing in Berlin on the philosophy of revelation; very soon, however, he became aware of the revolutionary implications of messianic hope and accused Mickiewicz of a dangerous radicalism. Finally, he seemed to have arrived at the conclusion that Mickiewicz was a reactionary and a revolutionary, an advocate of 'historicism' and an advocate of radicalism, at the same time. This paradox, he thought, was possible because extremists and fanatics were similar to each other independently of whether they hated the present in the name of the ideal future or in the name of an idealized past. It was especially true, he asserted, in the case of romantic thinkers, because romantic irrationalism and wild romantic imagination made them equally susceptible to reactionary and revolutionary daydreams—both equally 'poetical' and equally opposed to the prosaic present. Therefore, in his *Relation Between Philosophy and Cybernetics* Trentowski set against such a frame of mind his 'political philosophy', carefully avoiding all kinds of extremes, and his 'cybernetics', trying to elaborate the rules of a purely pragmatic, expedient political action.

Trentowski's observations about Mickiewicz's romantic Messianism can be applied, to some extent, to all kinds of millenarian and messianic ideological structures. A peculiar feature of millenarism is an unclear demarcation line between the dreams of a restoration and the dreams of a radical renovation; this is, in fact, one of the reasons for the wide appeal of millenarian ideologies in certain historical situations. It seems justified to add that this holds true in the case of some secularized versions of millenarian patterns of thought: George Sorel with his fierce anti-intellectualism, glorification of myth, and chiliastic expectations of the catastrophe of the corrupt old world, followed by the 'new beginnings', is a good example of an ideological ambiguity, comparable to that which was discovered by Trentowski in Mickiewicz's Messianism.

2. Cieszkowski's Philosophy of Revelation

In Cieszkowski's magnum opus—*Our Father*—the encounter between philosophy and Messianism brought about different results than in Trentowski's case. This philosophical interpretation of the Lord's Prayer can be seen as an attempt at a comprehensive synthesis of the messianic ideas of the romantic poets with the historiosophical speculations of the Polish systematic philosophers, disciples of Schelling and Hegel. In his *Russian Idea* Nicolas Berdyaev compared it to the messianic philosophy of Vladimir Solovyev:

It is interesting to place Russian messianic and eschatological ideas side by side with those of the greatest philosopher of Polish Messianism, Cieszkowski, who has not hitherto been sufficiently appreciated. ... The similarity is apparently one which is due to the nature of Slav thought in general. In certain respects I am prepared to place the thought of Cieszkowski higher than Solovyev's, although the personality of the latter was more complex and richer, and it contained more inconsistencies. (B. 11, pp. 212–14.)

The way to this synthesis was paved by Cieszkowski's first philosophical work, *Prolegomena zur Historiosophie*. Orthodox Hegelianism was a deeply anti-messianic philosophy: it had to reject messianic hopes because it claimed that the Spirit had already completed its development in history and that historical Christianity was an 'absolute religion' after which there would be no 'new revelation' (cf. B. 170, p. 122). Philosophy, in Hegel's view, was not a harbinger of the future and could not predict future events; it was compared by him to the owl of Minerva which took flight only as the shades of dusk were falling. In Cieszkowski's book, however, Hegelianism was transformed in such a manner as to reconcile it with the future-oriented millenarian and messianic thinking. It is not an exaggeration to state that in order to disclose the old millenarian pattern, which lay behind Cieszkowski's *Prolegomena*, it was necessary only to give his three epochs of history the classic names of the age of the Father, the Son, and the Holy Ghost.

The main idea of *Our Father* was the interpretation of the Lord's Prayer as a *prophetic* prayer—as a series of requests to be fulfilled in the final, *post-Christian* epoch of history. As I have already pointed out, this idea occurred to Cieszkowski before the publication of the *Prolegomena*. When he wrote *Our Father* he felt himself inspired from above, although, of course, in a different way than Towiański or Mickiewicz. He wished to give in this work the fullest possible explication of the last and final revelation—'the revelation of the revelation'.

The 'millenarization' of Cieszkowski's philosophy of history was accomplished with direct reference to Joachim of Fiore and medieval chiliasm. The chiliasts—argued Cieszkowski—were quite right when they interpreted St. John's Gospel as a promise of the Kingdom of God on earth; their hopes were not unfounded but only *impatient*, ahead of their time, and thus out of tune with the 'economy of revelation'. But the Paraclete will fulfil what Christ has promised; the hope which in the Christian epoch had to be recognized as a heresy will be realized in the third epoch—the epoch of consolation and fulfilment.

The old millenarian framework was rounded out by Cieszkowski with a multitude of modern ideas, for the most part not very original, taken from German and French thinkers, e.g. Lessing,[17] Schiller, Schelling, and Hegel among the Germans, the Saint-Simonians, Fourier, and Ballanche among the French. All of them were, however, skilfully adapted to fit in with each other and to form a new, beautifully constructed architectonics of thought. The division of history into the ages of the Father, the Son, and the Holy Ghost was given a dialectical Hegelian interpretation in terms of a thesis, antithesis, and synthesis; the epoch of the Holy Ghost, which Joachim of Fiore had interpreted as an epoch of contemplation, was presented as the epoch of action, an epoch in which grace would be replaced by merit, and heteronomy by autonomy. The final result of Cieszkowski's 'historiosophical' speculations was analogous to his philosophical theology: the attempt to reconcile the transcendent concept of God with the immanent one was paralleled by a philosophy of history which tried to reconcile theistic providentialism (seeing the historical process as directed from above by a transcendent God) with the conception of immanent historical reason (interpreting history as a progressive process of human emancipation). Hence the characteristic and deliberate ambiguity in Cieszkowski's views: on the one hand, his historiosophy was a 'millenarization' and sacralization of the modern idea of progress; on the other hand—seen within the context of religious consciousness—it represented a far-reaching secularization and a thorough-going philosophical reinterpretation of millennial dreams.

Another characteristic feature of Cieszkowski's philosophical millennialism was its lack of 'catastrophism', which sharply distinguished it from the revolutionary Messianism of Mickiewicz. The transition to the epoch of the Holy Ghost, argued Cieszkowski, will be different from the transition to the

Christian epoch; the victory of Christianity was preceded by the destruction of the ancient world, but the victory of the religion of the Holy Ghost will be accomplished without 'new barbarians', without great wars and revolutions. This difference was explained as deriving from the dialectical rhythm of history: the Christian epoch represented an antithesis, that is a *negation* of the ancient world, whereas the third epoch will be an epoch of *synthesis*—an age of constructive work and universal reconciliation.

No wonder that Cieszkowski's attitude towards the Catholic Church bore no resemblance to the militant spirit of the revolutionary chiliasts. It was obvious to him that 'the faith of our fathers has evaporated or rotted' (A. 8, III. 92). At the same time, however, he emphasized that *historical* Christianity was the only authentic Christianity, that the 'official' Catholic Church had been the 'figure' of the Kingdom of God and the harbinger of the future Church of Humanity, that the new religion, which would issue from its womb, would be not a 'negation' but a 'consummation' of the old Catholic faith.

In spite of this, it was improbable that the 'official Church' could accept Cieszkowski's views, and the author of *Our Father* was deeply aware of this. He conceded that his work was a heresy; he even proudly called it 'an arch-heresy, an ultra-heresy', a rehabilitation, fulfilment, and dissolution of all heresies (A. 8, II. 431–4). But he claimed that this 'arch-heresy' was a legitimate continuation of the main stream of the religious tradition of mankind.

'Christianity', wrote Cieszkowski, 'is by no means the final and absolute sphere in the development of the human spirit' (A. 8, III. 279). It is only the second, antithetic 'moment' (in Hegel's sense of a 'dialectical phase') in the great triad of history. Despite this, Cieszkowski's view of history remained Christocentric. Christ, according to him, was not only the founder of Christianity; as the author of the Lord's Prayer he was also the prophet and the teacher of the epoch of the Holy Ghost. The Lord's Prayer, in Cieszkowski's interpretation, is seen as an exhortation to the Paraclete to come and bring deliverance to suffering humanity, symbolized by the suffering Messiah. During the Christian epoch it had been *verbum absconditum*, now it was becoming *verbum patefactum*: the mystery of the revelation would soon be revealed to all. To prove this,

Cieszkowski—following the Saint-Simonians and Fourier—pointed to the achievements of science and scholarship, which were successive 'revelations of the revelation' and were constantly reducing the number of existing mysteries.

Like every 'antithetic moment' of development, Christianity was both a progress and a regression. It was (and still is) an epoch of 'internally split and dismembered man'; an epoch of painful dualism in which God was separated from the world, heaven from earth, spirit from flesh; an epoch of the greatest sufferings and of the ascetic 'abnegation of the world', which was bound up with the fatal neglect of earthly life. This characterization of Christianity was taken mainly from the Saint-Simonians, but it also resembled some Hegelian motifs (cf. Hegel's analysis of the internally split 'unhappy consciousness') and some ideas of Schelling's (cf. his view of the Christian epoch as an epoch of disharmony and divorce from nature). There was also an interesting, though partial, coincidence with Feuerbach—another thinker who was much concerned with the problem of overcoming Christian dualism. According to Cieszkowski, the other-worldly orientation of Christianity brought about a regression in social affairs: 'all truth, all good, and all order has been transferred to heaven; our earth, humiliated and condemned, has become a prey to disorder' (A. 8, I. 72–3). The same idea was expressed by Feuerbach, who thought that Christianity had divorced from man his best generic features, ascribing them to an other-worldly God, and had thus made earthly life a prey to utter egoism and evil. Cieszkowski was aware of this coincidence and he conceded that Feuerbach's criticism of Christianity was basically right. Feuerbach was wrong, however, when he saw Christian dualism as the essence of religion as such. Christianity is not the 'full essence' of the 'great and eternal religion', but only a stage in its development. This stage will be transcended in the religion of the Holy Ghost, which will become the main instrument of 'absolute reintegration'.

In accordance with Fourier's 'great law of analogy' Cieszkowski saw a prefiguration of this 'reintegration' in great scientific discoveries: in the system of Copernicus, who discovered that the earth was in fact an organic part of the heavens, and—following Saint-Simon and Fourier—in Newton's law of gravitation, this 'physical law of association' which binds material objects in the same way as religion binds spiritual beings

As the religion of God-man, Christianity has confined its task to the moral education of the *individual* man; the new religion of the Paraclete, being a religion of God-mankind, will aim at the moral education of *collective* man. The epoch of the Holy Ghost will bring about a 'socialization of societies' and international brotherhood. People of different races will recognize that they belong to one 'organic Humanity'. Nations, however, will not be dissolved; 'organic humanity' was conceived by Cieszkowski as *plenitudo gentium*, unity in diversity. The backward, barbarian nations will be liberated, civilized, and accepted as equal members of the general human family. The moral union of mankind will be preceded by its physical union, which will be achieved by the rapid development of means of communication. The development of military technology will enormously increase the destructiveness of war and, by the same token, will necessitate the renunciation of military solutions, thus inaugurating the long-awaited epoch of 'everlasting peace'. Regenerated humanity will organize itself: all nations and states will recognize the authority of the Central Government of Mankind, the Universal International Tribunal, and the Universal Council of the Peoples.

The spiritual belief of this new world—the religion of the Paraclete—will be the first religion of a truly universal and social significance. It will be possible to preserve the traditions of the great and ancient monotheistic religions—Christianity, Judaism, Buddhism, Mohammedanism, and Confucianism—as distinctive elements within the new, internally differentiated, unity. The new dispensation will make it clear that the 'dead ceremonials and superstitious rites' of today are only symbols of the true ritual of the spirit. Concern about the other world will be transformed into concern about the future of this world; the liturgy of the new religion will be art; its dogmatics—science; its sacraments—the cultivation and diffusion of culture; monastic orders will be replaced by leagues, trade unions, and other associations; piety will consist in purposeful, devoted action comprising 'the whole field of social life, the whole organism of social functions and duties' (A. 8, II. 464). The clergy as a separate caste will cease to exist; the priesthood of the Holy Ghost will be composed of all men of goodwill who contribute to society's material and spiritual welfare. In this respect Cieszkowski was inspired by the Saint-Simonians, although he differed from them in rejecting the need of a hierarchical order. He tried to cut himself off from Saint-Simonianism as a religious movement, but stated, none the less, that he saw in it a harbinger of 'the great Spring of the spirit' (A. 8, III. 455).

Like Fourier and the Saint-Simonians, Cieszkowski conceived of the new religion as overcoming the Christian 'abnegation of the world', rehabilitating the material, and, consequently, showing the greatest concern about the physical needs of men. The 'sanctification of the material' found its justification in the chief dogma of Saint-Simonian religion, which claimed that God is not a pure spirit, that the material element is an inseparable part of his essence. This was accompanied by an appropriate 'terrestrialization' of the image of the Kingdom of God: it was conceived as an earthly millennium in which the fourth petition of the Lord's Prayer— 'give us this day our daily bread'—will be at last fulfilled for the whole of the human race. The main role in managing the affairs of society will be performed by the 'industrial class'; the class of proletarians, 'the people without bread', will cease to exist, since everybody will be given a 'proportional minimum' for their subsistence (Fourier's expression). The economy of the Kingdom of God will combine the institution of private property and (to some extent) economic liberalism with the principles of universal insurance, universal guaranty, and universal association; work will become pleasure and constantly increasing needs will be satisfied by even more rapidly increasing production. This great reform, according to Cieszkowski, has been adumbrated by two prophets who, in spite of their errors, will soon be canonized by mankind: Saint-Simon and Fourier (A. 8, III. 206).

It is proper to add at this point that Cieszkowski put emphasis on the anti-revolutionary aspect of Saint-Simon's and Fourier's teachings. Revolutionary socialists were, in his eyes, socialists who had become anti-social, who had betrayed their own ideal. Revolutionary means, he thought, were incompatible with the 'economy of the revelation'; socialist revolution would only defeat itself by plunging humanity into a new dark age.

In view of Cieszkowski's close connections with the Fourierist movement it seems proper to stress that his economic ideal placed him among the most moderate followers of Fourier, among those who substituted for the socialist utopia of their teacher the programme of an internal reform of capitalist society. Cieszkowski was so far from the utopian fantasies of Fourier that even the struggle of conflicting interests was not incompatible, in his view, with the realization of the Kingdom of God: harmony without conflict—he argued—would be dead and stagnant; one must not try to eliminate conflict but to make the conflict itself 'harmonious', devoid of brutality, and contributory to the general welfare of society. Even more striking is the contrast between the moderation and soberness of Cieszkowski's vision and the chiliastic dreams of a new Jerusalem in which 'there shall be no more death, neither sorrow, nor crying, neither shall there be any more pain: for the former things are passed away' (Rev. 21:4). And yet it is significant that Cieszkowski himself interpreted his vision in millenarian terms, presented his Kingdom of God as the age of total regeneration, as the 'new heaven and the new earth', as the epoch in which God will 'marry' mankind, and the world, being God's flesh, will become permeated by the immediate and sanctifying presence of the Holy Ghost.

The fifth and sixth petition of the Lord's Prayer—'forgive us our sins . . . and lead us not into temptation'—gave Cieszkowski an opportunity to tackle Ballanche's favourite problem: the problem of sin, punishment, and expiation as conditions of human progress. Original Sin—the prototype of all evil—was 'the most felicitous fault', *felicissima culpa*. Without the Fall we would have had a vegetable, natural Paradise; thanks to the Fall we shall win a *human* Paradise, the Paradise of the spirit, in which man, conscious and creative, will become a true image of God. 'Ye shall be as gods', said the serpent and it was not a lie; in the third epoch the serpent will be rehabilitated, and we shall see the truth of his words. But for the regeneration of mankind, and for the regeneration of nature, a purifying expiation is needed. The means of expiation depend on the stage of progress: the ancient form of expiation was sacrifice (objective expiation), the Christian form is penance (subjective expiation); the epoch of the Holy Ghost will be ushered in by a 'universal amnesty of the world'. Peoples and nations, having realized that no one is without fault, will forgive each other all wrongs and offences. It will be the completion of the process of expiation and the second salvation of mankind.

And what will happen after the fulfilment of all the promises of the Lord's Prayer? The author of *Our Father* acknowledged an unwillingness to deal with 'absolute eschatology' but, as a result of Krasiński's influence, he none the less devoted a few pages of his work to speculations about 'the last things'. In his eschatology he developed one of the favourite ideas of Krasiński and Słowacki: the idea of evolution beyond man, transcending the human species and transforming men into higher, angel-like beings. Like the Messianic Polish poets, he combined this idea with the conception of the progressive evolution of individual souls, achieved through successive reincarnations. All these ideas had their sources or parallels in contemporary French thought: the belief in reincarnation and the idea of *'progression extraterrestre'* were shared, among others, by Fourier, Ballanche, Stoffels (*Résurrection*, 1840), and Boucher de Perthes. On the other hand, some of his ideas concerning the cosmic evolution are strikingly similar to conceptions set forth some hundred years later by Teilhard de Chardin.[18]

Let us turn now to a comparison of Cieszkowski's and Mickiewicz's messianic views. Such a comparison, I think, will throw additional light on some peculiarities of Cieszkowski's thought; above all, however, it will contribute to a better understanding of the relations between Messianism and systematic philosophy in the Polish thought of the epoch.

In contrast to Cieszkowski, Mickiewicz did not try to visualize the details of the future social order. The Word, he claimed, 'never says in advance what is to be realized; it speaks and realizes itself simultaneously'. His Messianism was a messianic *utopian consciousness without utopian doctrine*; the poet saw in socialism a symptom of crisis and the germ of the new 'social dogma', but he was not interested in its social and economic theories. Like the revolutionary chiliasts, he did not describe the coming Kingdom of God because *he felt it as present* in ecstatic upsurges of the spirit (cf. B. 114, p. 216).

This difference between Mickiewicz and Cieszkowski stemmed like other differences dividing them, from their different attitudes towards philosophy and rational thought as such. Mickiewicz's revolutionism was bound up with an extreme and uncompromising anti-rationalism; Cieszkowski's moderation and gradualism were in part the result of his quite conspicuous rationalist leanings. Mickiewicz flatly rejected the autonomy of human reason, whereas Cieszkowski made it clear that the emancipation of reason and philosophy was a necessary phase in the development of the spirit, that the future *restitutio ad integrum* would be by no means a return to immediate, unreflective intuition. Mickiewicz treated with contempt all systems and doctrines, whereas Cieszkowski created a new system, a skilfully constructed religious philosophy of history, mercilessly rationalizing the mysterious content of religious symbols. The poet-mystic vehemently attacked the 'official Church', accusing it of having lost the prophetic gift and divine foreknowledge, of an inability to work miracles, and of a low-spirited, abashed avoidance of any mention of the miraculous; in contrast to this, the author of *Our Father* proclaimed that the 'new revelation' was being revealed to men by means of the progress of science and that there would be no more miracles: Christ was a thaumaturge because he lived among men who could be convinced only by the evidence of their senses; today, however, after humanity has passed through the epoch of thought, the 'new revelation' can dispense with such obsolete means. An apology for charismatic leadership was completely alien to Cieszkowski's thought. Mickiewicz set against 'ecclesiastical bureaucracy' a consistently charismatic conception of the Church, whereas Cieszkowski espoused the ideal of universal priesthood. The heterodoxy of Mickiewicz was the heterodoxy of a mystical prophet; Cieszkowski, although as a philosopher he opposed the 'one-sidedness' of rationalism, as a religious thinker represented a heterodoxy of a markedly rationalistic kind.

In contrast to many superficial generalizations about the nature of Polish romantic Messianism, neither Mickiewicz nor Cieszkowski were *merely national* Messianists; both of them subordinated national cause to the cause of a universal regeneration of mankind. Nevertheless even in this respect their ideas were not the same: Mickiewicz believed that universal tasks should be realized by means of chosen nations and chosen individuals, whereas Cieszkowski did not share this view. A closer examination of his thought makes it evident that, strictly speaking, it left no place for either a personal Messiah or a national Messianism. In his philosophical millenarism the agent of deliverance was conceived of as *impersonal* and *general to mankind;* it was in fact a 'messianization' of historical progress, especially the progress of science, and—as in the case of Hoene-Wroński—a Messianism of philosophy, becoming a new religion and revealing 'the ultimate destinies of mankind'. It could not accept the concepts of 'chosen individuals' and 'chosen nations' (in Mickiewicz's sense of these words), since it denied the necessity and possibility of supra-natural aid for mankind. In accordance with the will of God—maintained Cieszkowski—humanity has finally come of age and grown up to become autonomous: 'The age of Grace has come to an end, the age of Merit has come to pass' (A. 8, I. 3).

Equally significant are the contrasting attitudes of Mickiewicz and Cieszkowski towards the bourgeois civilization of the West. Cieszkowski fully accepted capitalist development, highly appreciated English liberalism, the rule of law, and the rationalization of economic life; his programme for Poland recommended peaceful economic and social progress, which would improve the situation of the people without, or with the least possible, prejudice to the possessing classes. Mickiewicz's position was diametrically opposite: in the rationalization of social life he saw the mark of decay; he waxed eloquent at the sight of the 'moving relics' of the Middle Ages and uncompromisingly rejected capitalist civilization, setting against it a vision of a society which would be based entirely upon the spirit of sacrifice, enthusiasm, and exaltation. Cieszkowski opposed revolutionary change but accepted the general direction of social development in modern Europe; Mickiewicz dreamed of a great revolutionary war for the liberation of all peoples, but his revolutionism was combined with many elements of backward-looking, conservative-romantic thought. The irrationalistic and revolutionary Messianism of Mickiewicz had some truly archaic chiliastic features—it was the Messianism of a prophet expecting and summoning up the 'new revelation', believing that the great, imminent change would happen suddenly and explosively. The Messianism of Cieszkowski was thoroughly rationalized, philosophically reinterpreted, stripped of revolutionism and 'catastrophism', and in harmony with the conception of peaceful 'organic progress'. As an ideological construction it was more skilful and rich, but from the point of view of the intensity of 'Messianic consciousness' it could not match the Messianism of the poet.

The most striking contrast emerges from a comparison of the

attitudes of Mickiewicz and Cieszkowski towards industrialism. The author of the *Paris Lectures* saw in industrialism the mark of a 'society in decay'. He despised the commercial spirit of the France of Louis-Philippe, and proclaimed that the 'holy fire' of France was preserved only among the French workers and in the French army: the Slavs needed French military leaders but they had no need of French industrialists, engineers, and tradesmen (A. 70, XI. 338–9). Cieszkowski, instead, seeing in industry a powerful means for the 'liberation of the spirit', quoted the parable of the talents (Matt. 25), interpreting it in terms of praise of 'honest work and diligent earnings'. His comment on evangelical morality ran as follows: 'Thus, growing rich and making money, turning over one's capital in the most profitable way, never relaxing but always *progressing* along all the different paths of the spirit, is not only a just thing—it is the mark of the "good and faithful servant"' (A. 8, I. xix).

In this way the Polish aristocrat and Messianist introduced into his religious philosophy that Puritan element which Max Weber saw as the most important component of the 'spirit of capitalism'. But we must not think that he made it dominant in his conception of man. Cieszkowski's acceptance of the spirit of rational economic calculation was, in fact, only relative: it should be treated as part of his attempt at a complete transformation of the Catholic religious consciousness through the sanctification of an active 'this-worldly' life—'the sanctification of all the essential activities and capacities of man' (A. 8, II. 472). His idea of the *integrality* of spirit implied a certain autonomy for each of the spirit's different 'paths' (art, science, industry, etc.), but at the same time postulated their subordination to the common, pre-ordained goal of human history. None of the 'paths of the spirit' is an end in itself, but all of them are acceptable *if* they lead to the Kingdom of God.

This was exactly what Cieszkowski meant by 'the deed' (or 'action'). Activity within the Polish League, educational and scientific work, social philanthropy, the organizing of various 'associations', and so on, acquire the significance of 'deeds' if they are not 'ends in themselves', but are conscious contributions to the building of the Kingdom of God on earth—a Kingdom which cannot come by itself, which must be *created*, but which has been planned by Providence, and promised to men in the Lord's Prayer. These 'deeds' are not necessarily heroic and great. Even 'small deeds', every-day activities, can be invested with a higher, historical and, at the same time, suprahistorical significance—a significance which derives from conscious participation in the great process of the deification of humanity and the humanization of God, of the ascent of earth to Heaven and the descent of the Heavenly Kingdom to earth.

By comparison with the Mickiewicz brand, Cieszkowski's Messianism seems very attenuated, but this does not mean it was a quasi-Messianism. Devoid of ebullition and exaltation, it offered a sanctifying experience for everybody, without the mediation of 'higher spirits'. It was the Messianism of an *exoteric* revelation, accessible to all, to those without special charismatic qualities. It would be unfair to call it a reduction of Messianic dreams to the prosaic programme of 'organic progress'; it was rather an attempt to raise 'organic progress' to messianic heights.

Thus, the difference between Mickiewicz's and Cieszkowski's Messianisms reflected the difference between the two basic trends in nineteenth-century Polish political life: the insurrectionary or (if the social emphasis was strong enough) revolutionary trend, and the trend which saw the way to national regeneration in legal 'organic progress'. Seen in the broadest perspective, the two Messianisms were in fact two solutions to the characteristically Polish dilemma of heroism and anti-heroism (cf. B. 21).

3. The Springtime of the Peoples: Test and Watershed

The revolutionary events of 1848–9 are known as the *Volkerfrühling*, the Springtime of the Peoples. This name indicates the inseparability of the social question from the national question. As such, it fits better, perhaps, the events in East-Central Europe than the events in France, whose revolutionary movement, although sympathetic to the cause of oppressed nations, did not belong, of course, to the category of national movements. As far as East-Central Europe is concerned, there is no doubt that the national question was of paramount importance there. Therefore, in studying the revolutionary events in this part of Europe one should concentrate on different state-less nationalities, forgetting, for a while at least, about the existing political boundaries. This is especially important in the case of partitioned Poland. If a scholar tries to present revolutionary events in Polish lands not as a part of the history of the Polish nation but as a margin of the history of Prussia, Russia, and the Habsburg Empire, the meaning of one of the most important national questions in Europe (i.e. the Polish question) and the role of Poland as a counterpart of revolutionary France east of the Elbe (as—to quote Engels—'a revolutionary part of Russia, Austria, and Prussia') necessarily escapes his attention. The results of such studies deserve, sometimes, to be called scandalous. Is it possible to write a book about the Springtime of the Peoples in which the revolutionary role of the Poles everywhere in Europe is not even mentioned—in which the uprising in Poznania is put by in a few phrases, as a minor event in Prussian history, completely unconnected with the revolutionary activities in the other parts of Poland and in the Great Emigration; in which the agrarian question in the Habsburg Empire in 1848 is discussed without reference to the Cracow uprising of 1846 and the Galician massacre? Unfortunately, it is possible (see B. 151. Cf. also B. 138). In spite of the widespread and well-grounded opinion that the year 1848 was the moment of the most ardent belief in the revolutionary brotherhood of nations, it is possible, and, indeed, normal, to write books ignoring the deeply symbolic fact that Poland's greatest poet had organized by then a legion of Polish exiles fighting for the freedom and unification of Italy. Polish history does not exist in such books, and the role of Poles in the history of other nations is played down or, even, completely ignored. In the light of such books the exalted pro-Polish feelings of the European Left seem to be an inexplicable phenomenon, completely irrelevant to the under-standing of real history. No wonder, therefore, that the authors of these books do not care, as a rule, even to point out that enthusiasm for the Polish cause among the broadly conceived Left—from liberals to communists—was a characteristic feature of the European intellectual history of the epoch. They seem not to realize that even illusions, if important enough, belong to history and should not be passed over in silence.

Fortunately, there is at least one important exception to this general rule—Lewis Namier's book on *The Revolution of the Intellectuals*. It cannot be accused of a pro-Polish bias, on the contrary, but one can obtain from it an understanding of the crucial role of the Polish question in the history of European nationalism; it is sceptical about the very principle of national self-determination, but it comes to grips with the real problems connected with this principle and presents the events of the Springtime of the Peoples in East-Central Europe as most important for the proper understanding of later European history, including World War II. One can disagree with Namier that the liberals from 'the much belauded Frankfort Parliament' were in reality 'forerunners of Hitler' (B. 123, p. 38), but, I think, one has to agree with him that the disappointing results of the revolutions and national movements of 1848 were meaningfully related to the gloomy experience of our times.

The biographies of the Polish philosophers and messianic poets of the Romantic Epoch provide a good argument for the thesis that the Springtime of the Peoples was indeed a 'revolution of intellectuals'. Their respective philosophical, religious, and political viewpoints were applied then and tested by practice, confronted with each other in action, and brought to ultimate consequences. It seems worth while, therefore, to analyse, as briefly as possible, their experience of the revolutionary years and its meaning for Polish intellectual history.

Let us begin with Cieszkowski. As a resolute opponent of revolutionary methods he might be expected to have taken an anti-revolutionary stand; however, as a patriotic Pole, he welcomed the revolutionary ferment in East-Central Europe, seeing it as a movement for reforms, very far from a revolutionary apocalypse, and utilizing it for his own political aims. In the spring of 1848 he was elected to the Prussian Diet. Soon afterwards, in May of the same year, he went to Wroclaw (Breslau) to take part in a conference of Polish politicians from all parts of the partitioned country. Using Cobden's Anti-Corn Law League as a model, he proposed the organization of a League which would defend Polish national interests by co-ordinating legal, political, and social activities in Prussian, Austrian, and Russian Poland; a partial realization of this ambitious project was manifested in the Polish League of Poznania. In addition to this, Cieszkowski, on behalf of the conference, wrote a Manifesto in which he appealed to the members of European parliaments to demand the restoration of Poland and to take measures to introduce the rule of ethical principles in politics. In particular, in accordance with the ideas set forth in *Our Father*, he demanded the convocation of a Universal Tribunal of Nations which would be able to solve on legal grounds the international problems, and effectively defend the oppressed nations against their oppressors.

The Polish League in Poznania achieved great organizational successes: after one year's existence it had almost 40,000 members and became *de facto* a second government of the province. Cieszkowski's part in its activities was very important: he was responsible for the department of national rights and for outgoing correspondence (that is, in fact, for the 'foreign policy' of the League). In spite of ideological differences he closely collaborated with Libelt. Together with him, he resolutely resisted opportunistic tendencies within the League, emphasizing that its ultimate goal was the independence of Poland and not merely the defence of the apolitical, cultural, and economic interests of the Prussian Poles.

The League was short-lived (its headquarters had to dissolve themselves in April 1850), but the long-distance effects of its activities could hardly be over-estimated. It was a good education for a whole generation of Polish patriots in Poznania—not only for the patriotic members of the upper and middle classes, but for the peasants and artisans as well. In the second half of the century the people who had passed through this school were capable of a stubborn and effective resistance against the increasing pressure of the Germanizing policies of the Prussian government.

As a member of the Prussian Diet, Cieszkowski supported the German liberal Left. Unlike the revolutionaries he set his hopes on piecemeal reforms and legal legislative institutions; on the other hand, however, in sharp contrast to Krasiński, he was not horrified by revolutionary events and saw the Springtime of the Peoples not as a catastrophe, but as a prologue to the Kingdom of God on earth.

The two leaders of the radical wing of the Polish philosophical movement of the 1840s—Kamieński (exiled to Vyatka) and Dembowski (killed in the Cracow revolution)—could not take part in the political events of 1848–9. Therefore, the Polish democratic Left had by then only one philosopher in its ranks: Karol Libelt. His indefatigable political activity during the revolutionary period was sufficiently described in his biographical note. The meaning of his actions, however, will be clearer if we pay more attention to two aspects of his activities and experience of that time.

First, Libelt's role in the Slav Congress in Prague. In Namier's words, he 'pulled off a coup which altered the character of the Congress' (B. 123, p. 137. See also B. 197, II. 142–57). Thanks to him it abandoned the narrowly conceived Austro-Slav programme and, instead, put forward a programme for all Slavs and for Europe as a whole. He was the main author of the 'Manifesto to the Nations of Europe' suggesting the convocation of a Universal Congress of European Nations to settle all important international problems. In its original version, for which Libelt was solely responsible,[19] the Manifesto proclaimed the ideas of 'Christian socialism' and of the 'christianization of politics', of the rule of law in international relations, of respect for the rights of all national minorities and, finally, of creating a free federation of all Slavonic nations. Thus, if the ethos of the Springtime of the Peoples consisted in belief in the brotherhood of nations, in the essential identity of their true interests, and in the possibility of the rule of moral principles in international politics, there can be little doubt that Libelt was one of the best and most influential representatives of this ethos at the Slav Congress. The same ethos was represented by Cieszkowski's 'Manifesto', by Mickiewicz's legion, and by other Poles fighting everywhere against the immoral 'old world'. It was represented as well by General Józef Bem who in 1849, as Commander-in-Chief of the Hungarian insurrectionary troops in Transylvania, did everything to prevent or, at least, to weaken the growing antagonisms between the Magyars and the Slavs. It seems justified to claim that Poles of Libelt's generation believed in supra-national justice more ardently than any other nation and that their contribution to the ethos of the brotherhood of nations was then of particular importance. On the other hand, it can be pointed out that this was due to certain romantic illusions, stemming from the fact that they had nothing to lose but their chains. However, this was not entirely true. The Ruthenian (Ukrainian) delegation to the Congress was aware of the antagonism between their national aspirations and the interests of the Polish landlords in Galicia and, therefore, resolutely opposed the idea of the restoration of historical, multi-ethnic

Poland. For Libelt this was a real shock: it opened his eyes to the fact that Polish interests might not be identical with the common cause of all oppressed peoples. In the atmosphere of exaggerated hopes it was possible, through Czech mediation, to reach a compromise: the Poles accepted 'a most liberal programme securing real equality of rights for the Ruthenians in Galicia, while the question of dividing the province in accordance with nationality was referred to its future Constituent Diet' (B. 123, p. 138). In reality, however, it turned out that the Polish population in Galicia were not prepared to accept the Prague agreement.

Another aspect of Libelt's political experience was much more optimistic. The insurrection in Poznania was defeated, but it had proved at the same time that the idea championed by the Polish democrats—the idea of winning the peasants to the national cause—was not an illusion. Two years before Dembowski had suffered a heroic death witnessing a tragic divorce between the Cracow revolution and the rebellious peasants, for whom the Polish cause was the cause of their landlords. Libelt suffered humiliation by signing the Jaroslawiec Agreement, but he saw the Polish cause wholeheartedly embraced by the peasantry of Poznania. True, this was not only due to the influence of Polish democrats, like himself; it was also a result of the prosaic fact that social antagonisms between the Polish peasants and Polish gentry of the province were less acute than in Galicia because the peasants had already been enfranchised by the Prussian government in the 1820s. Irrespective of its reasons, however, the patriotic attitude of the peasants of Poznania was a real watershed whose importance could hardly be exaggerated. An *émigré* democrat with socialist leanings, Edmund Chojecki, attributed to it a deeply symbolic significance: Great Poland (i.e. the territory of Poznania) was the place where Polish statehood had been born; future historians would recognize that the same land, in 1848, became a birthplace of the modern Polish nation (A. 6, pp. 244–55).

Trentowski's experience of the revolutionary events was very different from Libelt's, although not less instructive for the understanding of some turning points in Polish intellectual history.

As we already know, the abortive uprising of 1846 and the

Galician massacre, which followed, pushed Trentowski to the right wing of the Polish political spectrum. In his *Images of National Soul* (1847), he set forth the view that Polish nobility and clergy, whom he had so severely criticized before, had to be supported as the only stronghold of Polish national tradition and national consciousness. It was, for him, a sad truth, a truth which made him unhappy as a European liberal, but which he had to acknowledge as a Polish patriot: 'A European must generally condemn nobility as a rotten body belonging to the grave of past centuries; a Pole, however, should defend our gentry at least as the head and heart of his own nation' (A. 105, p. viii). Thus, the widespread opinion about the essential identity of the Polish cause with the cause of the European Left was brutally reversed, and the other side of the coin—the obsolete structure of Polish society—was brought to light.

A peculiar feature of Trentowski's book was the messianic motifs which unexpectedly appeared on its pages. Merciless criticism of Messianism, so characteristic of Trentowski's former views, was replaced by lyrical passages about Poland as the Christ among nations, about the moral superiority of Poles over the other nations of Europe, and about their great redemptive mission. It is probable that these passages were written by Krasiński, but even if this was the case, it was symptomatic that Trentowski did not hesitate to include them in his book.

In order to be precise, one should point out that the *Images* were published under a pseudonym and that Trentowski pretended to express in them not his own, individual opinions but—allegedly—'the common voice of the country'. The book—as stated in the 'Editor's preface'—had no individual author because it was to be merely a faithful recording of the prevalent opinions among the Poles. By means of such a 'cybernetic' manoeuvre Trentowski wanted to preserve the freedom to dissociate himself from the opinions expressed in his book without being accused of inconsistency.

This was wise indeed: very soon political events pushed him once more to change his views, to recover some of his old hopes. Unlike Krasiński, he greeted the February Revolution in France with enthusiasm. Hoping for a revolutionary war which would bring about the restoration of Poland, he went (in April 1848) to Cracow and revealed himself (another 'cybernetic' move!) on the pages of the newspaper *Poland*, in the role of a convinced democrat and republican. Expelled from Cracow, he arrived, with a mandate from the Cracow democratic Committee, in Frankfurt, in order to watch and influence the debates in the Frankfurt Parliament concerning the Polish question. At the same time he was writing *Before the Political Storm* (A. 102). It was a strange and important document: a book full of paradoxes, harshly condemning the June insurrection of the proletariat of Paris but, at the same time, severely criticizing the cowardly foreign policy of Lamartine's government and the lack of revolutionary boldness in the Frankfurt Parliament; hostile to violent social revolutions but, simultaneously, expressing the cherished hope of the Polish *émigrés*—the hope that local revolutions would be followed (to quote Mickiewicz) by a 'universal war for the freedom of the Peoples'.

An important aspect of the changes in Trentowski's views was his utter disappointment in German liberals and a complete abandonment of his pro-German intellectual orientation. His indignation at the perfidious role of Austria in the events of 1846 was the catalyst for this change. The Austrian Germans, however, were backward Catholics; so, he could still set his hopes on the enlightened, Protestant Prussia. The events in Poznania in 1848 and the decisions of the Frankfurt Parliament to incorporate Polish provinces into Prussia cruelly disappointed these hopes. The attitude of the Prussian members of the Frankfurt Parliament towards the Polish question were for Trentowski a terrible shock, in spite of the fact that he was otherwise a sober thinker, devoid of romantic illusions, and very sceptical about the possibility of 'moral politics'.

After this painful experience Trentowski's new view of the Germans became settled for good. In 1848 they appeared to him as a nation of infamous and hypocritical egoists, deeply hostile to all Slavs and in all respects—even in philosophy!— much inferior to Frenchmen. In contradistinction to French thought, Trentowski argued, German philosophy was completely divorced from practice and that was why its extreme idealism was perfectly compatible with the ignoble, selfish 'realism' of German politics, as it manifested itself in 1848.

The other side of Trentowski's disappointment in Germany was his newly acquired national Messianism. Of course, he embraced the anti-revolutionary version of Messianism, represented by his friend and patron, Zygmunt Krasiński; however, even this form of messianic thought was vulgarized by him, stripped of a deep, religious motivation, and reduced to an uncritical eulogy of everything Polish. Moreover: Trentowski's messianic exaltation did not seem to be sincere and authentic. It was, obviously, not an organic product of his thought but, rather, a sad symptom of its disintegration.

Politically, the defeat of the Springtime of the Peoples confirmed Trentowski in the conviction—put forward in 1846 —that the nobility and the Catholic clergy were still, whether one liked it or not, the only stronghold of 'Polishness'. He was convinced, also, that the victory of reactionary forces was definite for a long time, and that it was necessary to find a way of accommodating to them. In fact, however, he was not able to satisfy the clerical circles whose influence, indeed, became dominant in Poland (although, of course, not among the emigration). It should be added that the interest in philosophical speculations suddenly disappeared at that time not only in Poland but in Germany as well: revolutionary events, as Engels put it, 'thrust the whole of philosophy aside' (A. 18, p. 18). Thus, Trentowski found himself in tragic isolation and—in spite of his desire to accommodate himself to the victorious conservative Catholicism—attributed all his adversities to the intrigues of Catholic obscurantists (see B. 25).

Let us turn now to the messianic poets. The most simple and unambiguous was Krasiński's standpoint. The revolutionary years broke down his former belief that Adam and August (Mickiewicz and Cieszkowski) should join their efforts in order to save the world. The Springtime of the Peoples was for him the work of dark, infernal forces, the apocalyptic catastrophe, the temporary triumph of Evil, which had to precede the final triumph of Good. He was deeply hurt by the fact that Cieszkowski, as a member of the Prussian Diet, associated himself with the liberal Left and voted for the abolition of aristocratic titles. Bewildered and upset by his friend's unshakeable optimism and by his willingness to co-operate with the democrats in the Polish League, he hesitated: 'August is great, but from whom does his greatness derive—from the Holy Ghost or from the Antichrist?' (A. 41, II. 67).

As to Mickiewicz, Krasiński had no doubts: he saw him in

1848 as a powerful tool of 'infernal mystical bands' whose sinister activities were described in the works of Hoene-Wrónski.

Słowacki, as might be expected, adopted a diametrically opposite stand. When the revolution broke out in France, his first thought was to organize the *émigrés* in a 'confederation', revolutionary and traditional at the same time, modelled on the confederations of the ancient Polish Commonwealth and acting in the spirit of the future republic of Poland. This idea could not be successful, since the *émigrés* had been organized into well-established political camps. Nevertheless, it was meaningful as an attempt at creating a symbolic bridge between Poland's past and Poland's future.

Soon afterwards, Słowacki came to Poznań in order to take part in the revolutionary events in Poland. A group of his followers, who came with him, enlisted in the insurrectionary detachments; he himself could not do that because of illness (tuberculosis) but, instead, joined the leadership of the movement. He spoke at the meetings of the Poznań National Committee, supporting, to be sure, its left wing, represented by Libelt and Stefański. In accordance with his belief in the omnipotence of the spirit he neglected the material means of struggle and proclaimed the ushering in of the epoch of a 'holy anarchy'. He tried to convince the members of the National Committee that they should rely not on guns and numerous troops but on the divine energy of the spirit. If the Poles in Poznania, he thought, were able to come out without any weapons and forcefully demand the keys to the fortress of Poznań, the Prussians would have to surrender and to withdraw from the Polish lands. Thus, the real struggle was seen by him as a kind of spiritual duel: he hoped that the Poles would win it because of the spiritual force which he saw growing among the peasant soldiers of the insurrection.

Another important aspect of Słowacki's attitude to the Springtime of the Peoples was his keen interest in Italian affairs and in the role of the Church. When the liberal pope, Pius IX (who, at the beginning, was expected to join the Italian national cause), chose to adopt an anti-revolutionary stand and had consequently to leave Rome and ask for the protection of the King of Naples (who was an ally of Austria), the Polish poet was wholeheartedly on the side of the revolutionaries. The Pope's escape from Rome was for him the final corroboration of his negative view of the 'official Church', and a symbolic proof that the Roman papacy had collapsed to make room for a new, Slavonic (i.e. Polish) spiritual leadership. He wrote a poem about the coming 'Slavonic pope' who, unlike Pius IX, would not be afraid of swords and would be 'a brother of the people' (see A. 90, I. 253–4).

On 3 April 1849, Słowacki died of tuberculosis, believing enthusiastically, until the end of his days, in the imminent universal regeneration. Shortly before his death he wrote a poem in which he set his hopes not only on the Polish peasants but on the revolutionary proletariat of Europe as well. The defeat of the revolutionary and Polish national cause did not drive him to despair because he believed that suffering and oppression were necessary for mustering the power of the spirit. He was obedient to the call from his poetical 'Testament':

> I implore the living not to lose hope,
> But, when the time comes, to go forth to their death,
> Like stones thrown by God upon a great rampart.

The most active, most tragic, and most complicated in his ideological commitments in the revolutionary years was Mickiewicz. Already in 1846, when Towiański explicitly forbade his followers to take part in revolutionary events, 'brother Adam' brought about a split in the Circle establishing a separate Circle of his own, which, although acknowledging Towiański's 'revelation', disagreed with Master Andrzej as to its practical application, demanding not only 'the sacrifice of the spirit' but also 'the sacrifice of flesh and blood', i.e. revolutionary activity. At the very beginning of the Springtime of the Peoples Mickiewicz went to Italy to organize a Polish legion which would fight for Italian freedom. He wrote 'the Set of Principles' for it which was to be an extract of the Polish spirit and an embryo of the future Polish constitution. In it, he proclaimed the principles of democratic self-government and of communal ownership of the land, full emancipation of Jews (whom he called 'Israel, our elder brother') and of women, the solidarity of all Slavs (including Russians), and the international duty of 'Christian help' for all nations in need. In spring 1848, he demanded a papal blessing for his legion and violently urged Pius IX to realize that the Holy Ghost dwelt under the blouses of the revolutionary workers of Paris. The following year he founded *La Tribune des Peuples*—a quite unique international newspaper whose collaborators were not only Frenchmen and Poles but also three Russians (Ivan Golovin, Nicholas Sazonov, and Ivan Voinov), two Italians (Frapolli and Ricciardi), three Roumanians (Nicholas Bălcescu, Ion Brătianu, and S. Galcescu), one German (Herman Ewerbeck), one Spaniard (Ramon de La Sagra), one Croat (A. Brlić), one Belgian (Jean Colins), and even one Chilean (F. Bilbao). He preached in it his belief in the 'initiative mission' of France and even espoused the cause of socialism, trying to combine it with the 'Napoleonic idea' and with the messianic prophecy of a 'new revelation'. At the same time he supported, for the sake of the 'Napoleonic idea', the President of the French Republic, Louis Napoleon (which antagonized many collaborators of the *Tribune*). The irony of history proved to be bitter indeed. Mickiewicz's legion, enthusiastically welcomed by Italian patriots, sided, of course, with the Italian revolutionary republicans and distinguished itself in defending republican Rome against pro-papal French troops sent to Italy by Louis Napoleon; thus, the Poles had to fight against the Pope whose blessing they had demanded, against France in whose liberating mission they deeply believed, and against Louis Napoleon in whom their spiritual leader saw a Providential Man. Pius IX, whom Mickiewicz wanted to be a reformer of Christianity and rescuer of nations, had good reasons to agree with the Polish Resurrectionists who zealously combated Towianist heresy. Almost at the same time that Mickiewicz pressed the Pope to declare himself for the freedom of peoples, the Sanctum Officium decided to put the last two courses of his Paris lectures on the index of prohibited books.

In the preface to the new French edition of his Paris lectures, dated 31 May 1849, Mickiewicz stated that he had almost nothing to change in their content and that his political activity was nothing other than a practical realization of his Messianism (A. 70, VIII. 9). It meant that his lectures at the Collège de France were the key to the understanding of his articles in the *Tribune*. It was really so; if mysticism and Messianism were not so pronounced in Mickiewicz's articles in the *Tribune* as in his lectures, this should be attributed mainly to tactical reasons (after all, it was a political newspaper, whose contributors and readers were, as a rule, not mystics). During the revolutionary years Mickiewicz remained a Messianist approaching politics from a *metapolitical*, mystical standpoint (see B. 185).

Of course, as the editor of the *Tribune* he had to face some new problems of which only the revolution made him fully aware. The most important among them was, probably, the problem of socialism.

Socialism, according to Mickiewicz, was one of the 'sacramental words of the epoch' and a sentence upon the old world. The founders of socialism—Saint-Simon and Fourier—claimed to have received their call from Heaven; this distinguished them favourably from the revolutionaries who still clung to the conception of the 'social contract' and believed that social ideas could be 'devised' by reasoning. In one respect, however, the socialists could not match the revolutionaries: they could not sanction their ideas by acts of force. They were merely theoreticians, and not men of action; they were apostles, and not law-givers. The same attitude characterized their current disciples, who, like Victor Considerant, thought that it was possible to solve the problems of mankind 'in a peaceful way, without harming anyone' (A. 70, XII. 115). Socialism must become revolutionary and practical; if it remained theoretical and peaceful it would be nothing more than a 'pure utopia'.

To become 'practical' and fulfil its mission, socialism should emphasize its 'religious sanction' and embrace 'the idea of nationality'. Religious and national feelings were, in fact, the true source of socialism. Socialist theoreticians, however, surrendered to the pedestrian, huckstering spirit of the French bourgeoisie: they persuaded themselves to believe that people acted mainly from material motives, that the workers of Paris took up arms to have more food in their dishes. In reality the French people rebelled against their rulers because the latter were unable to combine material power, which was in their hands, with spiritual leadership, drawing strength from truly Christian and national strivings for disinterested sacrifice, greatness, and glory. The destinies of mankind are realized through nations; France is now the leading nation of Christendom; therefore, in order to fulfil its universal task, socialism should become national, permeated by French national feelings.

Mickiewicz's further conclusion was that socialism should

also embrace 'the Napoleonic idea'. Militant democracy must have a powerful leader, a new Napoleon who would be able to discipline revolutionary enthusiasm. France 'should find the man'.

Similar ideas were propagated in France by Napoleon's nephew, Louis Napoleon, who saw himself as a providential man, called upon by God to continue the work of his great paternal uncle. Revolutionary events gave him a chance: in December 1848 he was elected President of the Republic. Mickiewicz, possessed by the 'Napoleonic idea', interpreted this as a sign from Heaven. In his articles in the *Tribune* he criticized the politics of the French government, condemned its counter-revolutionary intervention in Italy, but never attacked the French President. He welcomed the President's *coup d'état*; when he was informed (wrongly) that Louis Napoleon wanted to exile him to Cayenne, he reacted by saying that he would humbly accept this verdict. He welcomed also the proclamation of the Empire, and in a special memorandum warned the new Emperor, Napoleon III, against the 'artificial nation' surrounding him—a nation composed of 'legitimists, orleanists, and republicans'. He was to be disappointed in his hopes, but his illusions were stubborn indeed (see B. 185, pp. 173–5).

It would be easy to throw discredit on Mickiewicz's 'Napoleonism'. We should remember, however, that he was a prophet, and not a politician, and that it would be unjust to apply to him the usual political criteria. The real meaning of his actions was symbolic, and not *merely* political.

It is fully justified to say that Mickiewicz's activities during the Springtime of the Peoples symbolized, above all, the ethos of revolutionary internationalism. In his Italian legion and in *La Tribune des Peuples* the romantic belief in the brotherhood of nations, in the essential identity of their struggle, in the power of the spirit which would secure the victory of justice, reached the point of culmination. Mickiewicz's legionnaires, like other Poles of that time, truly believed that 'the fatherland of the Poles lives and is active wherever pulsate the faithful hearts of her sons' (A. 70, VIII. 36).

The events of 1848–9 strongly shook the belief. They uncovered the brutal fact that nations are driven not by ideals but by interests, that they violently antagonize one another, and that sheer force, not the right cause, is victorious in the conflicts. They seemed to corroborate the views of Wilhelm Jordan, a member of the Frankfurt Parliament, who frankly stated that the only right which counted was 'that of the stronger', and that it was necessary 'to awaken a healthy national egoism without which no people can grow into a nation' (see B. 123, p. 108).

Thus, the events of the Springtime of the Peoples marked, on the one hand, the culmination of the romantic ideology of the brotherhood of nations, with Polish revolutionary Messianism as one of its extreme expressions, and the breakdown of this ideology, on the other. This breakdown was the starting point for the development of a different type of nationalism—an ideology consciously cultivating national egoism, strictly separating politics and ethics, and professing that the severe laws of the struggle for survival reigned supreme in the sphere of international relations.

V. A Critic of Messianism: Cyprian Norwid

The last great philosophizing poet of Polish romanticism was Cyprian Norwid (1821–83). His ideas crystallized in the revolutionary year 1848, in a sharp conflict with revolutionary Messianism.

At the end of March 1848, Mickiewicz spoke in Rome to a meeting of Poles who were helping him to organize the Polish Legion in Italy. He asserted that the commander of the Legion should represent the future, not the past, and, therefore, should not be of aristocratic background. Norwid vehemently protested against this: he professed that breaking with the past was not his intention, and he struck his name from the list of legionaires. Soon afterwards he declared himself against Mickiewicz's 'Set of Principles'. After the famous allocution of Pius IX (of 29 April 1848), in which the Pope refused to support the Italian national cause, he hurried to the Vatican City to defend the head of the Church against the fury of the patriotic masses. As a reward for this, he was personally presented to Pius IX and received from him a 'sealed apostolic letter' which was to be the object of his greatest pride until the end of his days.

In his letter to General Skrzynecki (of 15 April 1848), Norwid said about Mickiewicz: 'This man is horrible for Poland' (A. 79, VII. 60). In another letter (of 24 April, to the poet J. B. Zaleski), he defined Mickiewicz's views as 'mystical radicalism and a gnostic spiritual aristocratism of the chosen' (ibid., p. 62). His criticism of Mickiewicz was the starting point for a series of works—articles and also poems—in which he set himself against the general assumptions and practical implications of romantic revolutionary Messianism. He scrutinized it—and rejected it—from three points of view: (1) religious, (2) historiosophical, and (3) national.[20]

Religiously, Messianism and millenarism were for him a

dangerous heresy. As a convinced orthodox Catholic, Norwid could not accept the concepts of a 'new revelation' and of the Kingdom of God on earth. His conception of the Kingdom of God was vertical, and not horizontal; the Kingdom of God is in Heaven, that is, *above* history, and not at the end of the historical process. The Church should be concerned with the salvation of human souls and not with the solution of historical conflicts. Such was the meaning of Norwid's words:

> Church is above History;
> Tribes or races are under History,
> And only nations are in History. (A. 79, VII. 36.)

This did not mean that God, according to Norwid, was not present in history. The Kingdom of God penetrates into human history from above and shines through it; in this sense it is *constantly* present in history. But precisely because of this one should not expect a sudden change after which earth will become Heaven. The fundamental dualism between *Civitas Dei* and *Civitas terrena* will be abolished after the end of the world, not earlier.

There was yet another reason behind Norwid's rejection of the idea of the terrestrialization of the Kingdom of God. In his view the Kingdom of God was by definition the sphere of absolute values, while everything historical was by definition time-bound, relative. Placing the Kingdom of God in earthly history was tantamount, therefore, to the absolutization of a certain form of time-bound human existence. In his poem *Slavery* (1849), Norwid pointed out the dangerous consequences of this: striving for absolute perfection on earth, instead of striving for constant relative progress, would inevitably result in a terrible retrogression. Absolutized values would become transformed into their opposite, and instead of the expected universal regeneration a degeneration of mankind would follow (A. 79, III. 391).

Norwid's criticism was levelled against all forms of messianic and millenarian thinking. Nevertheless, it was obvious that Krasiński's and Cieszkowski's messianic ideas were in his eyes relatively harmless (almost acceptable) in comparison with the revolutionary Messianism of Mickiewicz.[21] This was especially clear in his criticism of Messianism from the point of view of the philosophy of history. Seen from this angle Messianism appeared to Norwid as a revolutionary eschatology. He would have agreed with the thesis that millenarism (and Messianism as a particular form of it) was in fact a 'religious revolutionism'. In *Slavery* he drew a parallel between the messianic belief in the imminent regenerating miracle, and revolutionary belief in the miraculous power of the revolutionary deed. Miracles, he wrote, are 'heavenly revolutions' and revolutions are 'earthly miracles' (ibid., p. 391).

Against messianic expectations of a sudden miraculous change, Norwid set his evolutionary historicism and the rehabilitation of ordinary, everyday life; against the romantic cult of heroism he put forward an apotheosis of perseverance in collective, civilizing, and constructive work. The Polish word 'czyn' (deed) was derived by him from the Tartar language and associated with bloodshed. The romantic cult of heroic deeds appeared thus as the opposite of the greatest value of European civilization: the Prometheanism of work. Peaceful work was conceived as the only means of rehabilitating and regenerating the fallen man. This view was a conscious polemic against messianic belief (characteristic of Mickiewicz and Słowacki) in the soteriological meaning of the shedding of blood. In his poem *Promethidion* (1851), Norwid wrote:

> Not the Tartar deed, a blood-stained bridge
> Thrown on a scaffold glowing with flames
> . But daily work by love relieved
> Until the toil of toils is achieved. (A. 79, III. 446.)

'Promethidion' means 'the scion of Prometheus'. The title of Norwid's poem suggested that its author interpreted the difference between Mickiewicz's Prometheanism (the Prometheanism of romantic rebellion) and his own Prometheanism (the Prometheanism of work) as a difference between the older and the younger generation. Of course, Norwid referred also to the sphere of associations much older than Romanticism: to the ancient image of Prometheus as a 'hero of culture' who had taught people different crafts and symbolized the unceasing, creative efforts of civilization (cf. B. 117, VIII). However, unlike the later Positivists, Norwid did not see the civilizing work as an end in itself: he saw it as a means of redemption—although very different from the bloody sacrifices extolled by revolutionary Messianists. True progress, he thought, consisted in 'making martyrdom unnecessary' (A. 79, III. 466). This could be done through work, but work itself should be redeemed, 'relieved by love', liberated from the degrading stamp of automatism and compulsion. A means to this end was seen by the poet in art. According to his conception, physical work was to be transformed into creative art, and art, on the other hand, was to descend from Olympus to become united with industry and thus to ennoble the daily life of the people (see B. 132).

From the national point of view Norwid criticized Messianism as a false form of patriotism, detrimental to the true interests of the Polish nation. He saw it as an expression of 'impatience' and illusory hopes; as a glorification of spectacular heroic deeds combined with the neglect for organic work which was for him the only way of making patriotism 'organized and organic'; finally, as a form of abstract universalism, dreaming about the general regeneration of mankind and disregarding the concrete, actual needs of the Poles.

The last point does not harmonize with the widespread opinion that Norwid was a Christian universalist who accused other Polish poets of paying too much attention to the particular problems of their nation. In reality, his attitude towards Polish Messianism was more complicated than that. True, he was against mixing religious feelings with national fervour—in this sense one can say that he criticized national Messianism from a universalist standpoint. Nevertheless, it is no less true that he treated 'mankind' as a mere abstraction, necessary and holy as an idea but having no real existence. In contrast to 'mankind', nations are the real subjects of history whereas 'mankind' is an unhistorical notion, 'inspiring, but not binding' (A. 79, VII. 31–2). One can serve mankind only through the mediation of a nation. The so-called 'love of mankind' is a characteristic feature of ideological fanaticism sacrificing the real at the altar of the ideal. Seen from this perspective, the messianic idea of a universal regeneration to which the Polish cause should be subordinated appeared to Norwid as chimerical and very dangerous from the point of view of the legitimate national interests of Poland.

The word 'legitimate' should be stressed because Norwid, in

sharp contrast to integral nationalism, never thought in terms of the naked material interests of his nation. Like the Messianists, he wanted politics to be moral, and rejected the formula: 'my country, right or wrong'.

Let us turn now to Norwid's conception of nation.

In *Slavery* Norwid declared himself against the 'old political world' disregarding the holy rights of nations. A nation, unlike an abstract idea, is a 'living, organic incarnation'; therefore, it cannot be articificially shaped or 'carved out'. National unity is based on patriotism, that is, on love; therefore it cannot be formalized and institutionalized. In this sense Norwid defined nationhood as the 'eternal anti-formalism' (A. 79, III. 384–5). Nations, in his view, existed prior to states; the latter, if developed in a normal, organic way, were seen by him as created by nations, and not the other way round. A nation deprived of its own statehood could nevertheless live a genuine life, but a state not based upon a genuine national feeling was a soulless form, a dead artefact.

Does this mean that Norwid declared himself in favour of the principle of the national state? An affirmative and negative answer can be given at the same time. Yes, because he whole-heartedly supported the view that states should be national; no, because he rejected the view that national states should be monolingual and monoethnic. Linguistic and ethnic criteria belonged in his conception to the 'subhistorical', racial and tribal sphere, whereas nations were the products and active agents of history. The nation, argued Norwid, is a free, inner union of kindred tribes in the name of their common historical calling, while the state (if divorced from the nation) is a territorial political organization imposed on different people, based on external compulsion, and disregarding the will of the population (A. 79, VII. 27 and 34). In contrast to tribes and races, nations are defined not only by their particular, distinctive, and differentiating features but also by their common features, by their belonging to a higher civilizational unity. As might be expected, Norwid's favourite example of a 'free union of kindred tribes' was the union between Poland and Lithuania—a union which gave birth to a new, Polono-Lithuanian nation, being part and parcel of the Catholic civilization of Europe.

Let us confront this conception with Norwid's criticism of the followers of Mickiewicz:

Their understanding of nation places them near the *political communism* end of the spectrum; in other words, near panslavism. For them there are no fatherlands as yet. They identify nations with tribes. Such a notion can bring us back to barbarian hordes. . . . This is a return *from the flower to its roots, from nationhood to tribalism.* It would be interesting to know what the Italians, Spaniards and Frenchmen would have said if somebody advised them to create of themselves one Romanic nation. (Λ. 79, VIII. 60–2.)

To accuse Mickiewicz of panslavism was, of course, a great exaggeration—especially if 'panslavism' was understood as the desire to unite all Slavonic peoples into one nation. Norwid's intention, however, is quite clear: like Mickiewicz, Lelewel, and many other Polish romantics, he accepted the traditional Polish conception of the multi-ethnic nation, rejecting at the same time their slavophile leanings. Slavophilism—both as the emphasis on linguistic criteria and as the idealization of pre-Christian (i.e. pre-national) Slavdom—was, in his eyes, a betrayal of historical, civilizational heritage, a dangerous relapse into 'sub-historical' layers of consciousness.

Closely connected with this was Norwid's conception of the mutual relationship between spontaneity and reflection, spirit and form, 'word' and 'letter', immediate and mediated social ties.

In comparison with the artificiality of supra-national states, nations, according to Norwid, represented the principle of 'eternal anti-formalism'. Nevertheless, in their own inner constitution nations were held together not only by spontaneity but by certain forms, elaborated in history, as well. In Norwid's eyes the principle of non-formalized 'inner truth' was embodied in the ancient tradition of Slavonic communalism (A. 79, III. 387).[22] Without such 'inner truth', binding men together from within, it would have been impossible to create genuine, free nations. On the other hand, Norwid repeatedly emphasized that the 'inner truth' was only a *precondition* of national life, and not a *sufficient* condition of it; Mickiewicz's espousal of the idea of democratic communal self-government and of the communal ownership of the land was to him yet another example of a dangerous unhistoricism. Nations, he thought, are products of history, that is to say, of the process of reifying, objectifying the 'inner truth', of creating forms stabilizing uncontrolled and unpredictable spontaneity. As such, forms are not bad; on the contrary, they are a *conditio sine qua non* of history. The source of slavery is not form as such, but form as an end in itself; true freedom, on the other hand, is not formless, it expresses itself as 'form permeated by end' (A. 79, III. 376–7). Therefore, the neglect of all forms in the name of free spirit—a common feature of Slavonic communalism and of romantic Messianism—was seen by Norwid as a dangerous tendency, destroying the European heritage and the results of the historical, national development of the Poles.

In order to cut himself off from this tendency Norwid went so far as to declare that he himself was not a Slav but a Norman by origin and a citizen of Rome. In contrast both to the Slavophiles, condemning the 'latinization' of Poland, and to the Messianists, feeling themselves to be the instruments of the divine 'word', he defended 'letter' against the 'word' and accused the Slavs of neglecting the nation-building role of historical forms, as represented, among other things, by the great aristocratic families. Unlike Mickiewicz, he did not set his hopes on 'new barbarians'. His proud words, 'civis Romanus sum' (A. 79, IX. 64), were an expression of solidarity with the 'formalistic', juridical tradition of Rome—both the ancient and the Catholic Rome. By the same token they expressed his solidarity with the historical institutionalized Church of Saint Peter, as opposed to the messianic dream about the future Church of Saint John.

Another characteristic aspect of the anti-tribal conception of the nation was the rejection of all kinds of unreflective, uncritical identification with people of one's own stock. 'Socratical victory over one's own nation' (A. 79, III. 446) was, in Norwid's view, a necessary condition of a truly national consciousness. Nationality, he maintained, does not consist in exclusiveness; fatherland is not a 'sect'; true patriotism has nothing in common with 'le sentiment végétal du filo-paysme' (A. 79, VIII. 200).[23]

In the epilogue to *Promethidion* Norwid set forth an interesting conception of the national calling of the intelligentsia. Each nation, he argued, consists of two parts: the uneducated people who are the bearers of the distinctive features of the given nation, and the educated stratum, the so-called 'polite society', whose duty is to unite their nation (not themselves only!) with other nations (A. 79, III. 468). The people from the 'polite society' should resist national particularism by drawing their nation into 'intercourse with the moral unity of Europe'; on the other hand, however, they should not split off from their nation by taking care of only their own intercourse with the cultural élites of other nations. Such a split should be avoided because no nation can maintain itself if its 'polite society' and its 'common people' part their ways and if the cultural abyss dividing them cannot be bridged.

According to Norwid (who was himself a talented painter) the best way of uniting the educated stratum with the common people was through national fine arts. The idea of national fine arts, applied to crafts and industries, and uniting folk art with sophisticated European artistry, was for him the best conception of creating a spiritual union between the 'society' and the 'people'. The common people (as had been pointed out already by Vico) 'thinks in images'; therefore, it is especially susceptible to the influence of fine arts. The task of national artists is of equal importance to the task of national political leaders: the first are 'organizing imagination', whereas the latter are organizing the political forces of their country. Art is the 'church of work', the combination of manual work with intellectual and moral efforts; therefore, it should be the most efficient means of creating a spiritual bridge between the representatives of mental work and physically working people, and, thereby, of uniting them into one national community.

Thus, the artistic intelligentsia was seen by Norwid as being able to fulfil the most important nation-building task. Sometimes Norwid allotted this task to the Polish intelligentsia in general, defining it as the only social stratum which could bridge the cultural gap between the gentry and the common people.

One of the leit-motifs in Norwid's thinking was his sharp, bitter criticism of existing Polish society, both in the homeland and in the emigration. It is necessary to point out that he distinguished between 'society' and the 'nation': 'society' meant for him the sphere of daily work, while the 'nation' remained the field of heroic 'deeds'. He repeated many times that the Poles were 'the meanest nation as society' and 'the superb society as nation', that 'the Polish society is as mean as the Polish nation is superb' (cf. A. 79, VIII. 77 and 112). The Poles were supreme as a nation because their heroism in crucial moments, in uprisings and on the battlefields, was superb; they were the meanest as a society because they were deficient in the

virtues of will and character indispensable in normal, every-day
life. This distinction enabled Norwid to reconcile his utterly
pessimistic appraisal of his compatriots with an ardent belief in
the greatness of the Polish national cause. Thus, in 1861, he was
full of admiration for the great patriotic manifestations in
Warsaw but, at the same time, did not close his eyes to the
Polish national faults. On the contrary; it was precisely by then,
on the eve of the January uprising of 1863, that his awareness of
the sharp, grotesque contrast between 'Poland as a society' and
'Poland as a nation' had become most acute and found the most
powerful expression. Let us quote:

> This is the Polish society!—this is the nation which is undeniably great as
> far *as patriotism* is concerned but which *as a society* represents nothing.
> Everything which concerns patriotic and historical feelings is so great and
> so noble in this nation that I am ready to raise my hat before an urchin of
> Warsaw;—but everything which one can expect not from the *national* but from
> the *social* feelings is merely budding here and so insignificant, almost mean,
> that I fear even to think about it.
> We are *no society* at all.
> We are a great *national banner*.
> Perhaps some good people will hang me sometimes for these truths, but
> even if I have today a halter on my neck I would say, chokingly, that Poland is
> the last society and the first nation on earth. (A. 79, IX. 63–4.)

Let us make this bitter diagnosis more concrete. What kind of
reproaches did Norwid level against the Polish society of his
day?

The most general reproach was: the lack of respect for man.
The Poles, argued Norwid, do not respect their own great men
enough, that is to say, they do not respect themselves. They are
not able to appreciate greatness in men with whom they do not
agree; they have forgotten the parliamentary tradition of
'differing from each other in a decent way' (A. 79, III. 589–90).
They offended Prince Adam Czartoryski many times, at the
same time allowing his great adversary, Lelewel, to die in utter
poverty.

A particularly drastic example of the Polish disrespect for
man was, in Norwid's eyes, the slight towards the representatives of mental work. He bluntly stated that 'nowhere on earth
is the Intelligentsia more dependent and more humiliated than
in Poland' (A. 79, IX. 125). He meant the lack of respect for
intellectual work characteristic of the gentry culture, the

inability to recognize that mental work is work, and not enjoyment, that it should be paid and that paying for it is not charity, but a duty. He wrote sarcastically about *energy* (a 'sacramental word' in Mickiewicz's vocabulary!) and military virtues, describing Poland as a society whose energy—represented, at present, by 87 generals and 2,530 other officers—is always getting ahead of intelligence (ibid., p. 150), in which deeds are always premature and books always too late. As a result of this, he concluded, each generation of Poles has to pass through an inevitable slaughter.

Another characteristic feature of the anti-intellectualism of Polish gentry culture was seen by Norwid in the excessive attachment to a peaceful, lazy life among one's own family and one's own neighbours, in an infantile love for amusements and good food combined with an almost complete inability for serious conversations. Society, he argued, is reduced in Poland to the neighbourhood, to a network of personal relations. That is why everything in Poland is 'personalized' (A. 79, IX. 343, 380, 518), i.e. dependent not on the anonymous rule of law but on personal relations, such as protection, family ties, liking or disliking, and so forth. Norwid saw this as something typically Slavonic and insisted that he himself, as an admirer of Roman law, had nothing in common with these 'idyllic, Slavonic traditions' (ibid., p. 382).

The author of *Promethidion* was, of course, fully aware that nineteenth-century Poles made great efforts to overcome the traditional, 'Slavonic' laziness. He stressed, however, that they understood their national responsibility in a one-sided way, extolling heroism on the battlefield and neglecting the 'heroism of thought'.[23] As a result, their cult of heroism, finding expression in romantic ideologies, became yet another source of anti-intellectualism. The 'heroic deed' became an excuse for the 'vacuum of thought'. In such a way the increased feeling of responsibility for the nation was transformed into an irresponsible eagerness for action, endangering the very existence of the Polish nation.

Norwid formulated this conclusion under the impression of the disastrous consequences of the defeat of the uprising of 1863–4. This impression was so strong that he revised even his favourite conception of the contrast between 'Poland as a society' and 'Poland as a nation': he began to think that Polish

patriotism was also very far from being 'superb'. He now saw
Polish patriotism as 'unenlightened', irresponsible, glorifying
soldierly valour but neglecting moral courage, and destroying
the European character of Polish culture by promoting national
exclusiveness. In a splended essay entitled 'The Annihilation of
the Nation' he warned against transforming patriotism into an
'unjustified religion': the best way of destroying any secular
idea, he argued, is to develop a religious attitude towards it.

During his lifetime Norwid was underestimated, lived in
poverty, and deeply felt—sometimes even exaggerated—his
isolation and loneliness. He was 'discovered' at the turn of the
century by a neo-romantic writer, Zenon Miriam Przesmycki,
who recognized in him one of the greatest Polish poets and
published the first collected edition of his works. From that time
on his reputation as a poet was never seriously questioned,
although his place in Polish literature was a matter for dispute.
Many writers and scholars saw him as the last great
representative of Polish Romanticism, while others presented
him as a great precursor of new trends in twentieth-century
European poetry. It seems fair to say that there were elements
of truth in both views: he was a great innovator being, at the
same time, a product of his epoch. Nevertheless, the term 'last
romantic' does not seem to be appropriate: it obscures Norwid's
conscious effort to overcome his romantic inheritance.[24]

Norwid's place in Polish intellectual history is an even more
controversial problem. His reputation as a thinker, as a
moralist and an educator of the nation, seems to be firmly
established; his maxims are sometimes quoted with such
reverence as would fit verses from Holy Writ. Their meaning,
however, and the general meaning of his thought as well, are
often understood in many different ways. His idea of the
fatherland as 'a collective duty, *un devoir collective*', provided
inspiration for the young patriotic poets who took part in the
Warsaw uprising and (to quote from Słowacki) 'went forth to
their death, like stones thrown by God upon a great rampart'.
Soon afterwards many intellectuals, including many former
soldiers of the uprising, found the most important part of his
legacy in his criticism of romantic heroism. Still later he was
quoted in support of a new version of the positivistic programme of organic labour; needless to say, he could have been
quoted as well in support of the view that organic labour as such

was not enough. He was presented both as an orthodox Catholic, always obedient to the Church, and as a thinker whose Catholicism was in fact very different from the standard, clerical version of the Catholic faith, much more sophisticated in its traditionalism than the usual forms of Catholic mentality.[25] His conception of the relationship between the national and the universal was understood by many people as providing arguments for an enlightened, modern nationalism; others, putting emphasis on Norwid's criticism of national 'exclusiveness', interpreted it as a rejection of all forms of nationalism.

I shall not try to answer the question who was right in these controversies and to what degree. My own point of view is implied in the above presentation of Norwid's ideas, but I do not think that other points of view lack legitimacy. Therefore, I shall limit myself to the most general conclusion: Norwid's importance in Polish intellectual history consisted, among other things, in the fact that he was overcoming the heritage of romantic nationalism without embracing the tenets of Positivism and without paving the way for the post-positivistic integral nationalism.

PART FOUR

Changing Perspectives

I. The Legacy of Political Romanticism and the Emergence of Integral Nationalism

As I have already noted, the events of the Springtime of the Peoples marked the culmination of Polish romantic nationalism on the one hand, and the painful breakdown of its idealistic belief in a universal brotherhood of nations, on the other. Nevertheless, the romantic heritage was so deeply embedded in the Polish political tradition that it managed to survive the crisis. In January 1863 the Russian part of Poland became the scene of the largest of the Polish national insurrections (15 months of fighting, about 1,200 skirmishes and 200,000 active insurgents). Its inevitable defeat was followed by a number of disastrous consequences for Polish national life. The tsarist government adopted a policy of systematic destruction of the autonomous institutions of the Congress Kingdom accompanied by brutal repressions of Polish cultural life. The school system became thoroughly russified. Polish children had to be taught in Russian (their native tongue was strictly forbidden in school buildings, even if used only in private conversations). At the same time the international situation was becoming extremely unfavourable for the Poles. There is no exaggeration in Peter Brock's statement that 'the Franco-Prussian war and the Eastern crisis in the seventies finally removed the Polish question from the agenda of European diplomacy' (B. 18, p. 329).

In these circumstances the crisis of the romantic type of nationalism was soon reached. The belief in the victory of the just cause, which was to be achieved with the brotherly help of other nations and would pave the way for establishing the rule of moral principles in international relations, disappeared from the mainstream of Polish political thought. The very term 'political Romanticism' began to be used in a pejorative manner, as a synonym for idealistic daydreaming and irresponsible actions, leading, as a rule, to national disaster.

Roman Dmowski, one of the founders of the anti-romantic, integral nationalism which emerged in Poland at the end of the nineteenth century, gave the following recapitulation of the legacy of 'political Romanticism' in Poland:

> In no other country, it seems, was the political heritage of the first half of the 19th century so marked as in Poland. It involved a belief in justice ruling the relations between nations, in the success of impartial European opinion in claiming one's due rights, and a conviction that historical events can be defined as 'crimes' or 'wrong-doings'. Added to this was a trust in the final victory of the right cause, a refusal to reckon with the actual distribution of power and a failure to understand that the turn of each cause depends first of all on material forces.
>
> This attitude of building political prospects on purely illusory grounds, together with the tendency of embarking on political activity with no specific aim in view and with no prior estimation of the means at disposal, has been called 'political Romanticism'. (A. 17, p. 212.)

Hence, it was natural that in specifying the tasks of his own party, called National Democracy, Dmowski shifted to the foreground the necessity of 'eradicating the vestiges of political Romanticism' and replacing it with the ideas that 'pursuing its own interests is the primary duty of the nation' and that 'the only principle of international relations is that of strength or weakness, never that of being morally right or wrong' (ibid., pp. 235–6).

Needless to say, there were in Poland many other attempts to overcome the legacy of romantic nationalism, either by discrediting it and getting rid of it or by trying to reinterpret it in accordance with the new conditions. Presenting and analysing all of them would amount in practice to writing a history of the problem of the nation and nationalism in Polish thought from the middle of the nineteenth century until the present day, which, of course, does not fall within the scope of this book. However, in order to see Polish romantic nationalism in a historical perspective, it seems proper to give here a brief (and necessarily schematic) account of the most significant and characteristic attitudes towards it which have appeared in, and left their impact on, Polish intellectual history.

The most extreme reaction to the double defeat of Polish national aspirations—the defeat on the battlefield and the liquidation of the relative autonomy of the Congress Kingdom, which followed—was expressed in a brochure entitled *Poland*

and Russia in 1872 (A. 45).[1] It was written by Kazimierz Krzywicki, a former member of the State Council of the Congress Kingdom. Nations, he argued, are not unchangeable; history creates them and dissolves them as well. If a nation loses its independent existence, it becomes reduced, in fact, to a nation-less human society whose fate depends on its assimilation to the dominant nation in the state into which it has been incorporated. The aim of all forms of socialization is the moral education of individual men. The most powerful force of socialization is patriotism, i.e. the love of one's fatherland, but *national* patriotism is not the only form of patriotism; in certain situations the 'fatherland of the heart', i.e. the fatherland of the national tradition, can and should be replaced by the 'fatherland of work'. With the liquidation of the remnants of her political autonomy, Poland has finally ceased to exist as a nation. The people who are called Poles should, therefore, cease to maintain their national identity. It is in their own interests as human beings to accept the accomplished fact, to become loyal patriots of the Russian Empire, to work for its benefit, and in particular, to help the Russian government in combating the destructive forces of nihilism and socialism, demanding in return full civil rights for themselves. The children of today's Poles will, sooner or later, acquire a new sense of national identity. Russia, embodying the idea of Slavonic Unity, will be for them not only the 'fatherland of work' but the *national* community, 'the fatherland of heart' as well.

Another, much less extreme variant of the conciliation (*ugoda*) between Poles and the Russian government was set forth by Włodzimierz Spasowicz, a Pole who became a famous Russian lawyer and who proclaimed the idea of the Polish-Russian cultural rapprochement without abandoning a Polish national identity. Krzywicki's views were defined by him as a 'policy of national suicide'. However, he agreed with Krzywicki that the Poles should become advocates of Slavonic unity and sincere patriots of the Russian Empire. Like Krzywicki, he believed that the Poles represented in fact a socially conservative element, and that their role in the Russian state should consist in strengthening the moderate conservative forces, supporting liberal reforms, but firmly resisting nihilistic revolutionism. In 1882 he found in St. Petersburg the periodical *The Country* (*Kraj*) which was devoted almost entirely to promoting the idea of a Polono-Russian political 'conciliation'.

Different arguments were used by so-called Warsaw Positivists who emerged as a group at the beginning of the 1870s and for some 15 years represented the dominant trend in the intellectual life of Russian Poland (see B. 145). Disciples of Comte, Buckle, Mill, Spencer, and Darwin, opponents of all forms of 'metaphysical nonsense', they were able to appreciate the greatness of romantic poetry while rejecting out of hand the legacy of philosophical and political Romanticism, making it an easy object of ridicule and presenting it as one of the main causes of Poland's economic and intellectual backwardness. Their acknowledged leader, the publicist and writer Alexander Świętochowski, did not hesitate to proclaim that all ties between his group and the older, 'romantic' generation had been severed. The new programme for the nation was outlined by him in a series of articles entitled 'Work at the Foundations' (1873). In fact it was not as new as he himself imagined: all the ideas which were developed in it could be found in earlier programmes of 'organic works', elaborated in the Romantic Epoch. The main difference came to the fore later, in Świętochowski's article 'Political Directions' (1882), which explicitly stated that the value of national life depended not on independence or political autonomy, but mainly, if not solely, on its participation in universal civilization. Thus, in contrast to the thinkers of the 1840s, the Warsaw Positivists conceived of 'organic work' not as a means to political ends but only as a means of furthering economic and cultural modernization. As a nineteenth-century liberal, a follower of Spencer and J. S. Mill, Świętochowski was convinced that politics as such was not very important and that the political sphere of life might be easily and neatly separated from the socio-economic sphere, which could and should develop with the least possible interference on the part of the state. On the other hand, following, often unconsciously, the dominant tradition of Polish thought, he saw nations as a particular kind of social organism and not as nation-states. Therefore, it was easy for him to identify the solution of the Polish problem with the problem of Polish survival and success in economic and civilizational competition. From this point of view, the lack of political independence was not necessarily a disadvantage: Świętochowski felt that incorporation into an alien state could be a blessing because it could free the given nation from the burden of foreign policy and from military ambitions, thus enabling it to concentrate on 'work at the foundations', i.e. on the tasks of economic and cultural/civilizational progress. Such was, in his view, the case of Poland. Incorporation in the Russian Empire opened the vast Russian and Asian markets to Polish industrial products and, thus, greatly contributed to the rapid development of Polish industry which took place after the emancipation of the peasants in 1864. It may seem strange now, but in Świętochowski's eyes this was more important than the russification of the Polish schools, the severe censorship, and even the restrictions put on the usage of the Polish language. He seems to have believed, like many other liberals, in the miraculous power of economic development and to have thought, too optimistically perhaps, that successful economic and social modernization was quite sufficient for resisting the denationalizing policies of an alien government.

Another type of criticism of the legacy of the Romantic Epoch was developed by the conservative politicians from Galicia whose views were articulated by the so-called Cracow School of historiography. Unlike the Polish lands under Russian and Prussian rule, Galicia enjoyed a political autonomy which, however limited, established a Polish administration and representative institutions in this province. In such conditions the Galician landowners, who saw themselves and were recognized by the Habsburg monarchy as a 'historical stratum', i.e. as legitimate leaders of society, had no need to withdraw from political activities. Like the Warsaw Positivists they proclaimed reconciliation with the existing state, condemned all kinds of irredentism, and committed themselves to 'organic labour'; in contradistinction to Positivists, however, they understood 'organic work' in a more political way, putting emphasis on the struggle for further administrative and constitutional changes. They wanted to establish relations between Galicia and Austria which would revive the principles of the ancient union between Lithuania and Poland.

The attitude of the Galician conservatives to the Warsaw Positivists was rather ambiguous. They appreciated their fight against political and philosophical idealism; as far as scholarship was concerned, the representatives of the Cracow school of historiography were very close to the positivistic scientism.

However, as unashamed conservatives and devout Catholics, they profoundly disagreed with the Positivists' anti-clericalism, with their alleged or real materialism, and, last but not least, with the bourgeois-democratic tendency of their thought. Little wonder, therefore, that their criticism of the romantic legacy was sometimes very different from that of the Positivists. Świętochowski, for instance, saw Romanticism as a typical product of the culture of the gentry, expressing the attitudes and values of a parasitic leisure class and, even, providing a sophisticated defence of the interests of that class by ascribing to it a peculiar spiritual mission. The Galician conservatives, on the other hand, accused the romantic generation of seeing the Polish nobility as an embodiment of all evil and of striving for its complete liquidation. Józef Szujski, a leading representative of the Cracow school, pointed to the existence of some similarities between Romanticism and the mentality of the Polish gentry, but interpreted this in a different way than the Positivists. He deplored the weakness of executive power and the absence of a strong hierarchical principle in the last 300 years of Polish history and, from this point of view, condemned both the 'gentry democracy' of the ancient Polish Commonwealth and the romantic democratism of gentry-revolutionaries, seeing the latter as an extension and consequence of the former (A. 95). The Positivists, and particularly Świętochowski were repelled by the religious metaphysics or religious mysticism of romantic thinkers. The Galician conservatives, on the other hand, directed their criticism against the heretical and anti-clerical tendencies of romantic thought. In spite of all these differences, however, both sides fully agreed in the condemnation of the romantic conspiracies and insurrections, by acknowledging the necessity of 'conciliation' with the partitioning powers, and in setting forth programmes of political realism, i.e. of 'organic work' within the existing political structures.

It should be noted that the commitment to 'organic labour' was not always bound up with a negative attitude towards romantic nationalism. Eliza Orzeszkowa, the famous novelist who was closely connected with the positivist movement and thought of herself as a disciple of Spencer, published a book entitled *Patriotism and Cosmopolitanism* (1880) which, in spite of its scientific appearance, had much in common with romantic theories of the nation (A. 81). She declared that nations are necessary 'individualizations of mankind', that one can serve the common cause of human progress only through the medium of one's own nation, that all nations should love and respect each other, and that the final solution of all national questions (a solution already predicted, as she put it, by the ancient prophets of Israel[2]) will consist in introducing and observing ethical principles in international relations. At the same time she paid tribute to the positivistic glorification of productive work, and even to the ideas of social Darwinism, by declaring that the productivity of work and the capacity for winning the struggle for survival depend on the strength of emotional motives, the best of which is patriotism. She also appealed to the romantic cult of sacrifice and to the populist idea of paying off the debt which the educated classes owe to the many generations of heavily exploited common people. In order to discharge this debt, she argued, it would be necessary to assume the existence of a collective national individuality embracing both the living generation and the generations of the past; otherwise the living generation should not feel burdened with responsibility for the deeds of their forefathers.

In Galicia an important attempt to reconcile these new trends with the romantic legacy was made by the pioneer of industrialization in the province, Stanisław Szczepanowski. This utterly practical and sober man who in 1888 shocked Polish public opinion by publishing the book *Galician Misery* (in which he showed that the food consumption of the average man from Galicia was one half of that of the average European, and his productivity one fourth) was capable of combining his sober-mindedness with deep sentiment for the insurrection of 1863 and with a profound admiration for the Polish romantic philosophers and poets whose works were in his eyes the 'Polish national revelation'. He managed to combine an extremely bitter criticism of his compatriots with an exalted vision of Polish virtues, arguing that the Polish misery was a corroboration of the general rule: 'corruptio optimi pessima' (the corruption of the best results in the worst). He dreamed of reconciling romantic idealism with positivistic realism, and not without reason saw the forerunners of this ideal in Trentowski, Cieszkowski, and Libelt (see A. 94).

In Poznania, formerly the main centre of the philosophical movement of the 1840s, the second half of the century was extremely unfavourable for the development of Polish culture. The heavy pressure of germanization, exercised both in schools (from which the Polish language had been banned) and in the economic sphere (the deliberate efforts to bring to ruin Polish artisans, peasants, and landowners in order to replace them by German colonists), reduced the tasks of the Polish leaders of the province to the most narrowly conceived 'organic work', almost to the simple struggle for survival. Nevertheless, the break with the traditions of the Romantic Epoch was felt there much less sharply than in the Congress Kingdom. One of the reasons for this was certainly the fact that the leaders of the Poznań intellectual movement of the forties, Cieszkowski and Libelt, were not only 'political romantics' but also great pioneers of 'organic work'.

The first attacks against the ideology of 'triple loyalism' and narrowly conceived 'organic work' came, naturally, from the milieu of the political radicals in the emigration. The generation which had witnessed the tragic consequences of the defeat of the January Uprising was, as a rule, immune to their arguments—later, however, the situation began to change. At the beginning of the 1880s a marxist socialist party 'Proletariat' was organized in the Congress Kingdom. It programmatically rejected raising the issue of Polish national independence, but, at the same time, powerfully contributed to undermining the Positivists' belief that the Poles had, allegedly, no other choice except reconciliation with the existing Russian state. Another group of Polish socialists, headed by Boleslaw Limanowski (1835–1935), tried to combine socialism with an active, romantically-tinged patriotism striving for the recovery of national independence (see B. 30 and B. 92). The trend of thought represented by them paved the way for the foundation of the Polish Socialist Party (1893) which was to become a powerful mass organization, having in its ranks both convinced Marxists, like Kazimierz Kelles-Krauz, and conscious inheritors of the Polish insurrectionary tradition, like Józef Piłsudski. Equally important was the growing political radicalization of non-socialist democrats, who saw new hope for Polish nationalism in the awakening national consciousness of the enfranchised peasants. In 1887 Jan Popławski (1854–1908), in the columns of the Warsaw weekly *The Voice* (*Głos*), severely condemned the atmosphere of apathy and the 'lowering of ideals', setting against it—although not without important reservations—the example of the heroic Romantic Epoch. The editorial board of *The Voice* was in close touch with the Polish League, an organization that had been founded in Switzerland by Zygmunt Miłkowski (T. Jeż), formerly a prominent member of the Polish Democratic Society, and by a number of veterans of the January Insurrection.

These new trends in Polish political thought are described by Peter Brock as 'the second phase of romantic nationalism'—a phase which, at least in its early years, 'was either populist or socialist and sometimes both' (B. 18, p. 335). Was this really so? From the point of view of the present book this question is too important to be left unanswered.

In Limanowski's case, the quoted generalization seems to be entirely justified and acceptable. He was a disciple of Comte, the author of the first book in Polish on Comte's sociology, but, at the same time, he was steeped in the tradition of the Polish social and political thought of the Romantic Epoch, which was to become the main object of his historical studies. He was not inspired by romantic Messianism, and never spoke about 'national missions', but it cannot be denied that his patriotic socialism was strongly influenced by Stanislaw Worcell (about whom he wrote an excellent monograph) and by other early Polish socialists. The affinity between his version of nationalism and the romantic legacy can be summarized in three points. First, he believed in the possibility of the rule of ethics in political relations and in the universal brotherhood of nations. Secondly, he conceived of nations as communities integrated from within, by means of commonly shared spiritual values, and not by mere economic interests or external political institutions. Thirdly, in defining nationality he disregarded linguistic and ethnic criteria, paying attention, above all, to common historical tradition (and loyalty to the values inherent in it). In other words, he continued to support the notion of a multiethnic and multilingual nation and, like the democrats and socialists of the Romantic Epoch, believed in the possibility of restoring the multiethnic Polish Commonwealth. It should be added that he made a sharp distinction between 'patriotism; and 'nationalism', supporting the first and combating the latter. Patriotism, in his conception, was the expression of love and loyalty to one's own nation without any prejudice against other nations; an expression of the attachment to the higher values which cement a given nation and mould its historical individuality. Nationalism, on the other hand, was seen by him as the ideology and policy of the immoral modern state in its relations with other states; as the ideology of pursuing one's interests at the cost of others, of 'my country, right or wrong', of worshipping power for its own sake, and as the policy of aggression, domination, and limitless expansion. It followed therefrom that in a stateless nation, like Poland, nationalism had no real function to perform; if it did, none the less, exist, it could be explained only as an inappropriate imitation of foreign models, as a betrayal of patriotism, and as a testimony to the degeneration of political culture.[3]

Like Limanowski, Popławski decided to fight against the dominant apathy and opportunistic reconciliation with the political status quo. In doing so, he invoked the example of the unbending, heroic spirit of the romantic generation. He even made a gesture of sending a wreath to Mickiewicz's tomb in Cracow with the romantic motto, 'measure your strength by your purpose'. Nevertheless, unlike Limanowski, he was in fact very far from the romantic variety of nationalism. He confessed that *emotionally* he was close to romantic patriots, but was careful to add that *intellectually* he represented a completely different school of thinking, born out of different historical experiences and nourished on different ideas. He accused the Positivists of neglecting the emotions of the masses but at the same time he condemned 'emotionalism in politics', seeing it (like the Positivists) as a characteristic feature of all the currents of political thought of the Romantic Epoch.

The main differences between Popławski's views on national questions and the romantic legacy can be summarized in the following points:

(1) The first point concerned the attitude to the peasantry. Popławski, influenced to a certain degree by Yuzov (I. Kablits) and other representatives of the right wing of Russian populism, was convinced that a truly national culture should be based upon the indigenous culture of the peasantry. In this respect his ideas, whether he was aware of it or not, were similar to the views of many populist (or pre-populist) Polish thinkers of the Romantic Epoch. In spite of that, however, there was also an important difference. The romantic populists wanted to win the

peasants to the Polish national cause by promising them land and freedom. Hence, the tragic fact that the peasants of the Congress Kingdom were enfranchised in 1864 by the tsarist government drove many of them to utter despair about the possibility of the national awakening of the Polish popular masses. In contrast to this, Popławski saw the enfranchised Polish peasants not as a mass of people who had to be won for the national cause and raised to the level of national self-consciousness, but, simply, as people who *were* Poles, who *had* a distinctively Polish national consciousness and culture (although different from the consciousness and culture of the gentry) and whose interests were not only socio-economic but national as well. The Polish peasants, like other Poles, want to live under the Polish administration, to have their children educated in Polish schools, to create institutions which would be able to further their interests and help them in the economic struggle with different foreigners (Germans, Jews), and so forth. Therefore, already in their present state they constitute a firm social basis for a renewal of Polish nationalism. In contrast to the old nationalism of the gentry, this new plebeian nationalism should not soar to the sphere of lofty ideals and indulge in messianic illusions. It should be realistic and down-to-earth; it should strive ultimately for national independence, organizing the social forces of the nation on a much larger scale and for more ambitious goals than was envisaged by the positivistic theorists of 'organic labour', but, at the same time, it should reject the romantic faith in a political miracle, i.e. in a successful national insurrection.

(2) Closely bound up with this was Popławski's conviction that the new nationalism should be concerned, above all, with national *interests* and not with the national honour or national glory. The political, economic, and cultural interests of one's own nation, he thought, should be more important for a responsible patriot than moral imponderabilia or ideological Absolutes. It followed that the programme of the nationalists should be very flexible; non-committed to the tenets of a universalistic social creed. If the national interests of a given nation happen to coincide with the interests of a radical social movement, the place of a true nationalist will be on the left. In other circumstances, however, the defence of national interests could place him on the right wing of the political spectrum.

(3) Finally, as Peter Brock has rightly pointed out, 'the nation in Popławski's view, was the product of ethnic differentiation rather than of the state and of historical development' (B. 18, p. 339). It was a logical consequence of his view that the new nationalism should base itself upon the ethnic nationality of the Polish peasantry rather than upon the political tradition of the ancient Polish Commonwealth of the gentry. Popławski, however, did not draw from this the conclusion that the non-Polish nationalities of the former Commonwealth should be granted the right of national self-determination. On the contrary, he repeated many times that purely ethnic and linguistic criteria were not enough for defining a nation, because national individuality was also a product of a common political history. He put forward this thesis whenever he defended the interests of the Polish minorities in the ethnically mixed territories of the eastern borderlands, especially in the eastern part of Galicia where the position of the Poles was seriously threatened by the growing strength of the Ukrainian national movement. Nevertheless, the emphasis on ethnic and linguistic differentiation was much more characteristic of his nationalism than the appeal to historic rights. Like the populist Bolesław Wysłouch, he wanted to reverse the tide of history by awakening the sense of Polishness among the Polish-speaking population of Upper Silesia, Mazuria, and other territories which had not belonged to the old Commonwealth for centuries. He did not condemn the Jagellonian tradition of eastward expansion, but thought that in the present situation the Poles should return rather to the tradition of their medieval Piast monarchy, i.e. to concentrate above all on the German danger (see A. 85, II. 15). He accused Polish politicans of stubbornly cherishing dreams of Vilno and Kiev while, at the same time, neglecting Poznań, almost forgetting about Gdańsk (Danzig) and completely forgetting about Królewiec (Königsberg). His claim to the Piast heritage of the Poles was based not only on linguistic and ethnic grounds but on geo-political factors as well. He thought that without Poznania, Silesia, and access to the Baltic Sea, a future Poland would be too weak to exist as a truly independent state. He prophetically predicted that Polish access to the sea would never be safe if Eastern Prussia remained part of Germany. Therefore, he categorically demanded the incorporation of this

territory into a future Poland, in spite of the fact that only a part of its population spoke a Polish dialect.

As to the eastern borders of the future Poland, Popławski rejected both the 'ethnographical principle' (i.e. purely linguistic and ethnic criteria) and the romantic dream of the restoration of the ancient, multiethnic and multilingual Commonwealth. He wanted to incorporate into the future Polish state only those parts of the Ukrainian, Belorussian, and Lithuanian territories in which the Poles were, in his estimation, strong enough to dominate the non-Polish population and to succeed in its gradual polonization. Thus, his emphasis on 'common history' as an important factor in the nation-building process had nothing in common with the notion of a historically constituted multiethnic, multilingual, and multicultural nation. His ideal was a homogeneous national state. Lelewel's view of the Polish nation as a community composed of many different ethnic and linguistic groups was in his eyes a characteristic feature of the mentality of the gentry, that is to say, a relict of feudalism, incompatible with modern nationalism and with the realities of the modern world.

In 1893 the Polish League changed its name into the National League. Soon afterwards the new nationalist movement, started by the Polish League and by Popławski's *Voice*, finally crystallized and consolidated itself under the name National Democracy. Except for Popławski, the main role was played in it by Zygmunt Balicki and Roman Dmowski. In 1895 these three men began to publish in Lvov the *All-Polish Review* (*Przegląd Wszechpolski*)—a mouthpiece of the movement, propagating the ideas of the new nationalism in all three parts of partitioned Poland. Politically, the movement made a large step towards the right. In spite of the populist overtones in its initial ideology and in spite of its energetic educational activity among the peasants, it was socially too conservative to transform itself into a peasant party. Before the end of the century its ideology, thanks to the contributions of Balicki and Dmowski, became a Polish variant of a full-fledged integral nationalism.

Balicki, the philosopher and sociologist of the movement, proclaimed the necessity of unashamed 'national egoism' as a precondition for a healthy state of national life. Very significantly, perhaps in conscious opposition to Limanowski, he made a sharp distinction between 'nationalism' understood as the policy of national egoism, and the romantic tradition of 'patriotism'. The latter was in his eyes a sentimental ideology of the weak; an ideology exalting a nation but in fact betraying its real interests for the sake of chimerical humanitarian ideals, idealizing heroic defeats and martyrdom instead of teaching the nation how to win in the struggle for survival; believing stupidly in an inevitable victory of justice, and thus giving people a pretext for tolerating passivity and carelessness in their every-day life. The replacement of 'patriotism' by a consistent 'nationalism' was for him a *conditio sine qua non* of the Polish national revival.

Roman Dmowski, whose opinion about 'political Romanticism' I have already quoted above, was equally out-spoken about the fundamental difference between his own nationalism and the humanitarian tradition of romantic Polish patriotism. In his book *The Thoughts of a Modern Pole* (A. 14) he accused his countrymen of clinging to the ideas of their romantic poets, that is to the comforting illusion that all nations were brothers and that conflicts between them could be solved on the basis of an abstract 'justice'. This illusion, he argued, was one of the products of the abnormal historical evolution of Poland. The Polish nobles had ceased to think in terms of struggle because no other class in ancient Poland was strong enough to fight against their absolute domination in society. In such hothouse conditions the 'noble nation' had lost its warlike virtues and become a 'feminine nation'. From this point of view, strongly influenced, as we can see, by social Darwinism, the best traditions of the old Polish Commonwealth, such as religious toleration, attachment to civil liberties and political freedom, even the equality of the Lithuanian and Ruthenian gentry, appeared to Dmowski as expressions of political immaturity and the laziness of a comfortable élite lacking the experience of every-day struggle. Even worse, in his eyes, was the romantic idealization of ancient Poland. He saw it as an idealization of weakness, as an effort to comfort the Poles with the thought that moral superiority was more important than victory in the struggle and lording over others. Especially repellent to him were the messianic ideas of the soteriological meaning of the 'crucifixion' of Poland and of the Poles' sacred mission of fighting for the salvation of all other nations. Each nation, he maintained, should think only about its own interests; no nation can claim to be innocent. Moral criteria, as such, should be applied only in the sphere of private life but not in the sphere of international relations. The partitions of Poland were not a 'crime' but a natural result of Poland's weakness. The Poles should not appeal to a non-existent conscience of mankind but should learn, instead, from their enemies how to win in a brutal struggle. They should rid themselves of moral scruples and pursue their political and economic interests in the same way as the German Hakatists were pursuing German interests in the Prussian part of Poland.[4] Poland's struggle should not be only defensive but aggressive as well. It should be directed not only against the partitioning powers but also against the national minorities, especially against the Ukrainians in Galicia and the Jews. The Ukrainians, Dmowski argued, should be glad to face this challenge. If they were capable of becoming a separate nation they would become hardened and strengthened in the struggle, and if they were not—they would become polonized. In either case, the conflict would cease to exist for the benefit of both sides. On the Jewish question Dmowski underwent an evolution from a relatively moderate economic anti-semitism to a violent racial anti-semitism, based upon the assumption that Jewish blood is poisonous for the Polish national spirit. The same evolution was characteristic of his entire party; Popławski, the main ideologist of the early stage of the 'new nationalism', would have been dismayed by the anti-Jewish excesses committed by the 'National Democrats' in the interbellum period.

The main assumption of Balicki's and Dmowski's theories was the idea of the nation as an organic whole to which the individual belongs, or should belong, entirely and to which he owes an unlimited, undivided loyalty. Socially unattached intellectuals, alienated from their own nation, were defined by Balicki as 'social psychopaths'. For Dmowski any attempt to approach national problems not from the point of view of the concrete interests of one's own nation, but from the standpoint of an abstract justice, was tantamount to eschewing respon-sibility, and a cowardly betrayal of the most sacred duty. It should be noted, however, that in the ideology of the 'National Democrats' the demand for absolute loyalty to one's own nation and the categorical rejection of supra-national standpoints were not bound up with national megalomania. On the contrary, Dmowski was extremely critical of his compatriots, accusing them, among other things, of being infected by romantic illusions as to their moral superiority, while in fact being simply weaker and less disciplined than their neighbours. Sometimes he even seemed to doubt if the Poles could make good nationalists. In his view of Polish history he remained as far as possible from romantic idealizations of ancient Poland. Instead, he was very close to the critical and pessimistic appraisal of the Polish past of the conservative Cracow historians. This should not surprise us: according to integral nationalists, the loyalty to one's own nation should be absolute and one should not excuse oneself for one's nationalism by referring to a peculiar value represented allegedly by one's own particular nation. The Polish romantics tried to justify their ardent patriotism by ascribing to Poland a great, universal mission. For Dmowski every nation existed for its own sake, and not for the sake of universal progress;[5] his nationalism, therefore, did not need to be supported by an idealized image of the nation.

An important part of Dmowski's criticism of the legacy of Polish Romanticism was, of course, his criticism of romantic heroism, as expressed in the national insurrections of the Romantic Epoch. In assessing this legacy he was much more severe than Popławski, who criticized not national insurrections as such but only the attempts to continue the insurrectionary tradition in changed historical conditions, both domestic and international. Dmowski had the civil courage to state that the whole tradition of nineteenth-century national uprisings, so dear to the hearts of his compatriots, was a tradition of humiliating defeats whose celebration would have been incompatible with his political doctrine. In an eloquent passage he said:

Many people in three generations were deeply moved by listening to the words of a patriotic song:

Rise, Poland, crush your chains,
Today is the hour of triumph or death.

As for me, these words offend my moral sense and my deepest feelings. The man who really means this, is a criminal. The very idea that Poland might die, is a crime.

Everybody can risk his private property and sacrifice his own life. Sometimes it can be a moral duty. But no individual, no organization, and no generation can expose to danger the very existence of Poland. Because Poland does not belong to an individual, to a party or even to a single generation of Poles. She belongs to the entire chain of generations, to those of the past, those of the present and those of the future as well. The man who exposes to a risk the existence of his nation resembles a gambler who plays with someone else's money. (A. 15, p. 56.)

In such a manner the new, integral nationalism of the 'National Democracy' cut itself off from the older, romantic nationalism of heroic insurgents, metaphysical philosophers, and prophetic poets. True, many historians, especially historians of literature, managed to combine adherence to Dmowski's party with a deep reverence for the romantic legacy. Many of them deliberately tried to obscure the fact that the new nationalism was in reality a betrayal of the humanitarian values of the Romantic Epoch. The facts, however, remained so and could not be changed.

As I have already pointed out in connection with Boleslaw Limanowski, the tradition of romantic nationalism was defended and continued by the patriotic Left, especially by the ideologists of the Polish Socialist Party (PPS). Dmowski's greatest political rival—the leader of the Revolutionary Faction of the PPS and the future head of the restored Polish state, Józef Piłsudski—was deeply steeped in the romantic tradition. In the cultural sphere the post-positivistic period (1895–1914) witnessed a genuine revival of romantic tendencies in literature and philosophy; because of this it is often called the 'neo-romantic epoch'. Writers, publicists, and philosophers of this epoch—one need name only Stanislaw Przybyszewski, Artur Górski, and the world-famous philosopher Wincenty Lutosławski (cf. A. 52, A. 53)—tried, among other things, to resuscitate and develop the romantic theory of the nation. They looked for metaphysical foundations of nationalities (in contrast to states and tribes which, according to them, were devoid of noumenal existence) and ascribed to each nation a peculiar universal mission. Like the messianic poets they combined the theory of the nation as 'a group of spirits united in a common mission' with the belief in progressive reincarnation, thus treating nations not as ends in themselves but as means in individual perfection; finally they indulged in idealizing the ancient Polish Commonwealth, presenting it as a prefiguration of the future world-system. Like the romantic generation they dreamed of the rule of moral principles in politics and saw this idea as a peculiarly Polish contribution to political thought. Like Słowacki, whose influence on their thinking was especially important, they were fascinated by the *liberum veto*: it harmonized, they thought, with their élitist individualism which defended the individual against the masses and claimed that the mechanical majority was always blind and deaf to the higher truths.[6]

There is no place in this book for a fuller characterization of neo-romantic trends in the broadly conceived Polish nationalism. The main aim of this chapter is to show the emergence of integral nationalism in Poland, the contrast between this type of nationalism and the older, romantic variety, and, finally, to emphasize the fact that the romantic tradition in Polish nationalism managed to survive and to defend itself against the attacks of Dmowski's followers. The general conclusion which one can draw from a comparison between the romantic and the integral nationalism is obvious: the latter betrayed the humanitarian values of the former. This difference was very deeply felt and it was the main reason for the fact that the humanitarian nationalists in Poland preferred to call themselves 'patriots', thus cutting themselves off from the National Democrats who had been the first to introduce the term 'nationalism' into the vocabulary of Polish politics.

It would be a great oversimplification to overlook the fact that their criticism of the Polish romantic tradition—or, rather, of the attempts to continue it in the new conditions—the new nationalists were sometimes correct, or, at least, partially correct. It seems justified even to say that the weaknesses of romantic-inspired nationalist thinking were, possibly, one of the main sources of the growing strength of integral nationalism in Poland. Intellectually, the so-called Polish 'neo-romanticism' of the years 1895–1914 was indeed a rather irritating example of escaping from real, contemporary problems into an idealized past and opiating self-contentment based on a comfortable and gratifying sense of an alleged moral superiority. Politically, the tradition of romantic nationalism supported the illusion that the spirit of the Polono-Lithuanian union was still alive and that the eastern nationalities of the former Commonwealth still wanted to live in a common, Polish-dominated state. Dmowski was right that this was ana-chronistic thinking—although one should add, to see the other side of the coin, that his own party greatly contributed to the growing hostility of the Ukrainian and Lithuanian population towards the Poles. After Poland had regained her independence the tradition of romantic hero-worship passed into the camp of Piłsudski's followers and served the growing cult of the leader. Thus the phraseology of romantic heroism and activism became associated with the *Führerprinzip* and, naturally, began to evoke suspicion and antipathy among the leftist intelligentsia; an antipathy which was sometimes mechanically transferred to include the whole romantic tradition. Finally—last but not least—the tradition of political Romanticism had its large share of responsibility for the tragedy of the Warsaw uprising of 1944; an uprising whose price in human lives was terrible and whose outcome left 'nothing but honour' (cf. B. 195).

The 'new nationalism' of Popławski, Balicki, and Dmowski can be credited with making Polish nationalism more realistic, more modern, and even more modest in its aims (if only by abandoning the crusading spirit of romantic idealism). By the same token it was more understandable for the average man; it had a down-to-earth, plebeian quality, sharply contrasting with romantic nationalism which was, after all, even in its most populist variants, an ideology of the intellectual élite of the nation. Despite Popławski's initial intentions, all these changes brought about a considerable 'lowering of ideals'. One could argue, however, that this was a necessary price to be paid for making nationalism the ideology of a modern mass movement. The noble-minded nationalism of speculative philosophers and messianic poets could hardly become the ideological foundation of a powerful political party.

Nevertheless, we are aware—or should be aware—of the final results of this evolution. Like all other forms of integral nationalism everywhere in the world, Polish integral nationalism had become discredited both morally and politically. In the restored Poland, a country where the masses were poor, frustrated, and where one third of the entire population was non-Polish, the growing influence of integral nationalists (although they were never in power) proved to be politically disastrous. Instead of solving existing problems they created new ones, increasingly difficult to solve. One of the sad results of this policy was the fact that even the word 'nation' came to be associated not with brotherhood and freedom, as it had been before, but with discrimination against national minorities and with anti-semitism.

In view of such experiences—and, also, in view of the universal experience of our century—some of the old ideas of Polish Romanticism deserve, I think, to be treated as relevant to our contemporary problems. The idea of a nation as a spiritual community grounded in a common devotion to some higher, universal values should not be ignored by the world facing the processes of social atomization caused by a permanent crisis of values. The peculiar combination of ardent national feelings and a heroic defence of national identity with an equally ardent desire to submit nations to universally recognized ethical rules and to solve international conflicts peacefully, by means of supra-national institutions, is, obviously, not irrelevant to the world torn by dangerous, egoistic rivalries and, at the same time, having at its disposal most powerful means of destruction. The romantic idea that the national personality realized itself most fully in contributing to the universal regeneration of mankind was, perhaps, too idealistic as a political precept for a subjected and partitioned country but, perhaps, it also contained a great truth; after all, mere egoism leads only to a disintegration of personality, because true personality (both individual and collective) is impossible without a commitment to supraindividual, universal values. Even Polish romantic Messianism, seen from this perspective, represents above all a splendid example of the longing for a deeper meaning in history and of heroic 'hoping against hope'—qualities that seem to be much needed in the world suffering from 'de-utopianization', although by no means free from 'ideologies' (in Karl Mannheim's sense of these terms).

However, let us return to nineteenth-century viewpoints. It is evident, as I have tried to show throughout this book, that Polish romantic nationalism—its hopes and its disillusionments—was a function of the international status of the Polish question. One can say with a small degree of oversimplification, that the self-image of the Poles was dependent on the Western image of Poland, and that the latter was a more or less faithful reflection of the importance of the Polish question in European politics. Romantic nationalism flowered in Poland at the time when European public opinion glorified the Poles as heroes of universal freedom. Its crisis began when events had shown that beautiful words were merely words, and that neither the governments nor the peoples of the West would organize a crusade for Poland's sake.

There are several reasons why I have decided to add to this book a separate study on Marx's and Engels's views on the Polish question. First, they are interesting in themselves, shedding much light on one of the least known aspects of Marx's and Engels's theories. Secondly, the works of Marx and Engels contain, I think, the best arguments defending the whole tradition of Polish 'political Romanticism' against its later critics. Finally, an analysis of their position on the Polish question and of their positive attitude towards Polish romantic nationalism is a good starting point for a short presentation of some Polish thinkers of the Left who were inspired by Marxism in their theorizing on the national question, and who came to conclusions completely different from the well-known standpoint of Rosa Luxemburg. It has a symbolic significance that one of them, Stanisław Brzozowski—a thinker undeservedly unknown in the West, but very widely read and influential in Poland—saw no contradiction in drawing inspiration at the same time from Marx and from the Polish romantic heritage.

II.   Marx, Engels, and the Polish Question

1. A Review of Some Essentials

'The working men have no country.' These famous words from the *Manifesto of the Communist Party* have often been quoted to support the view that the authors of the Manifesto, as ideologists of the 'country-less' proletariat, adopted a thoroughly cosmopolitan, supra-national standpoint—the standpoint of total indifference towards the national problem of having, allegedly, no relevance to the real situation and class interests of the industrial working class of Europe. In fact, however, this is a class misreading whose stubborn vitality and constant re-emergence in the vast literature on the subject are strange and regrettable indeed. It should not be so in light of S. F. Bloom's detailed study of the 'national implications in the work of Karl Marx' (B. 12).

According to Bloom, the *Manifesto* 'discussed the common taunt that the socialists proposed to abolish nationality as unworthy of serious consideration'. The usual misreading of the quoted statement from the *Manifesto* consists in taking it 'to affirm precisely what Marx and Engels were at pains to deny': that nationalities had no real existence, that they should not exist, that the emotion of patriotism was foreign to the proletariat. The point of the *Manifesto* 'was simply that the question of nationalism was bound up with the question of a stake in one's country (B. 12, pp. 22–4). The working class, according to Marx and Engels, was deprived of its fatherland but had to regain it by 'rising to be the national class', 'constituting itself *the* nation' (A. 58, VI. 501–3).[7]

Was it really so? It may seem doubtful to those students of Marxism who have become too much accustomed to thinking that historical materialism consists of reducing everything to class struggles and in seeing the class structure as the only true reality in social life. Such sceptics, however, should follow

Bloom's advice and carefully read Marx's letter to Engels of 20 June 1866—a letter in which French members of the First International, who considered all nations to be merely 'antiquated prejudices', were accused by Marx of 'Proudhonized Stirnerism; and of an unconscious French national egotism (see A. 25). The term 'Stirnerism', as applied to the national question, could refer only to Max Stirner's view that *all* allegedly supra-individual structures, like nation or class, humanity or state, are merely divinized 'phantoms'. Rejecting 'Stirnerism' amounted therefore to aserting that nations *did* have a real, tangible existence of their own. Moreover, if the negation of nations was no less than 'Stirnerism', this clearly implied that such a negation was bound up, logically at least, with a nihilist negation of social classes and generic humanity as well.

However, one can acknowledge the reality of nations while, at the same time, treating national patriotism as a rival and hostile ideology, and as an obstacle to raising one's class consciousness to the level of self-awareness. Indeed, this would be the most simple, but also the most simplistic, solution of the inevitable conflict between loyalty to the nation and loyalty to the class, or between any other forms of vertical and horizontal group consolidation. Such a simplicity, however, was alien to the authors of the *Manifesto*. Their own solution of this problem is to be found in their theory of 'national class'. The importance of this theory has recently been emphasized by George Lichtheim. According to him, the famous phrase: 'The working men have no country', was merely a splendid slogan, having 'absolutely no significance, save as a protest against the alienation of the industrial proletariat from society'. In contrast with this, he asserted, 'Marx's concept of the national class is altogether original and extremely relevant to the theory and practice of modern communism. Rather surprisingly, it has been ignored' (B. 100, p. 86).[8]

The theory of national class is a theory of a possible convergence between the interests of a class and the interests of a given nation as a whole. Briefly defined the national class is that class in a nation whose interests at a given moment coincide with the interests of society as a whole and which, therefore, is best qualified to lead the nation along the line of progress, raising it to a higher economic and social level. It follows therefrom that leadership by a national class is perfectly legitimate, and that patriotism—in so far as it expresses the standpoint of a truly national, i.e. truly progressive class—does not contradict the principle of the primacy of class interests over narrowly defined national loyalties. Moreover, it was envisaged that a situation might arise in which it would be necessary to subordinate narrowly conceived proletarian interests to broader national tasks. Such was in fact the case of Germany. As a backward country Germany was not yet ripe for a proletarian revolution; her proletariat, although more progressive than her bourgeoisie and becoming more and more independent of bourgeois ideological tutelage, was not yet strong and mature enough to become a 'national class'. It could and had to prepare itself to assume the role of national leader in the future, but for the time being it had to subordinate itself to the progressive bourgeoisie which was still Germany's 'national class'. This did not mean that the German proletarians should not have embarked on developing their own class-consciousness, awareness of the essential conflicts within bourgeois society, and ideas of a socialist future (in that case, it would have been an anachronism to write for them a *Communist Manifesto*). What it meant in practice was that the tasks needed for a bourgeois-democratic transformation of Germany had to be completed before the path of socialist transformations could be followed. One of the most important of these tasks was the unification of Germany—a task which was by definition patriotic *par excellence*. Without national unification—without 'one nation, with one government, one code of laws, one national class-interest, one frontier, and one customs-tariff' (A. 58, VI. 489)— the organizing of German workers on the national scale and their preparation for their future national leadership would have been impossible. Therefore there was no contradiction between the *Manifesto of the Communist Party*, on the one hand, and editing a 'bourgeois-democratic' newspaper, *Neue Rheinische Zeitung*, on the other. If, during the Springtime of Peoples, Marx and Engels were 'blowing the patriotic bugle as hard as possible' (B. 100, p. 74), it was by no means inconsistent, let alone a betrayal of the proletarian cause.

German workers were seen, thus, as vitally interested in the progressive solution of Germany's national problem. Hence they had to have their own foreign policy. This policy was to be, of course, the policy of furthering Germany's alliance with the progressive, advanced European countries in order to oppose the Holy Alliance of the three absolute monarchs—the main bulwark of European reaction and the main obstacle to the progressive, democratic solution of the German national question.

It was quite natural that the Polish question, seen from this perspective, loomed large as a 'great European question', highly relevant to the cause of all-European progress and especially to the cause of democratic transformations in Germany. It would be no exaggeration to say that Marx and Engels saw it as the most important national question in Europe. It is really surprising that this important fact has been largely ignored or neglected in the vast literature on Marxism— even in publications specially focused on the national problem in Marxist thought.[9]

The reason behind the peculiar importance of the Polish question for the all-European, and particularly German, revolutionary strategy was seen by Marx and Engels in the obvious circumstance that Polish patriots had virtually no other choice than to struggle against the Holy Alliance, striving at the same time, in order to make this struggle successful, for a democratic transformation of their own country. They faced the alternative: 'Poland must either be revolutionary or perish' (A. 65, XVIII. 526), and proved able to make the right choice. Due to this Poland became a revolutionary nation, a counterpart of France in the East of Europe, 'a revolutionary part of Russia, Austria, and Prussia' (A. 58, VI. 373). In such a manner the Polish national-liberation movement became a natural ally of Western revolution, whether socialist (as in England or France) or bourgeois-democratic (as in Germany). Its peculiar significance for the German democrats stemmed from the fact that it was directed first of all against tsarist Russia—a state which actively supported feudal reaction in Germany and without which, it was believed, the absolute regimes in Austria and Prussia would not have been able to resist the pressure of democratic forces.

In 1848 Engels summed up this argument in the following words:

A French historian has said: *Il y a des peuples nécessaires*—there are *necessary* nations. The Polish nation is undoubtedly one of the necessary nations of the nineteenth century.

But for no one is Poland's national existence more necessary than for us, Germans . . .

From the moment the first robbery of Polish territory was committed Germany became dependent on Russia. Russia ordered Prussia and Austria to remain absolute monarchies, and Prussia and Austria had to obey. . . .

So long, therefore, as we help to subjugate Poland, so long as we keep part of Poland fettered to Germany, we shall remain fettered to Russia and to the Russian policy, and shall be unable to eradicate patriarchal feudal absolutism in Germany. The creation of a democratic Poland is a primary condition for the creation of a democratic Germany. (A. 58, VI. 350–1.)

2. Marx, Engels, and the Historical Evolution of the Polish Question

Let us turn now to a brief chronological presentation of Marx's and Engels's views on the Polish question.[10]

The first period of Marx's and Engels's interest in Polish affairs was the years 1846–9. Like the whole European Left, from democratic nationalists like Mazzini or Michelet to English Chartists, they were deeply stirred up by the Manifesto of the Polish Revolutionary Government of 22 February 1846. They saw in it a programme for a revolutionary transformation of the whole of Eastern Europe — a programme for an agrarian revolution which would give land to the peasants and abolish all remnants of feudalism in the political and juridical spheres. There is no evidence which would allow us to conclude that 'agrarian revolution' meant for them a total expropriation of the gentry; manorial farms, transformed into the modern, bourgeois-type land property, were to be allowed to coexist with peasant farms, although the latter, of course, would predominate. It is interesting to note that this programme, supported in the *Manifesto of the Communist Party*, was in fact in tune with the demands of the *moderate* wing of the Polish democratic movement. Marx and Engels apparently did not know that it was severely criticized by more radical groups in the Polish revolutionary movement, primarily by the revolutionary socialists who demanded the nationalization of all land and the replacement of bourgeois property with socialist property. As we know, Edward Dembowski, the virtual leader of the Cracow uprising, was also a revolutionary socialist. In later years the two friends became aware of this: in 1880, they called the Cracow events of 1846 'the first political revolution which had set forth socialist demands'.[11]

At the end of 1847 Marx and Engels took part in the international meeting organized by Fraternal Democrats to mark the anniversary of the Polish uprising of 1830. The speeches which they delivered there contained the first public announcement of the need to create an international organization of the workers. At this time they already had a considerable knowledge of Polish history derived from Joachim Lelewel's *Histoire de Pologne* and Ludwik Mierosławski's *Débat entre la révolution et la contre-révolution en Pologne*. Lelewel had become their personal friend. He spent New Year's Eve 1847–8 with them and drank to the success of a 'united, powerful, democratic, and indivisible Germany'.

Even more important were the speeches made by Marx and Engels in Brussels, in February 1848, on the occasion of the second anniversary of the Cracow uprising. Engels, contrasting the Cracow revolution to the 'conservative revolution' of 1830, spoke of the former in the following words:

At Cracow, it was clearly seen that there were no longer men who had much to lose; there were no aristocrats; every step that was taken bore the stamp of that democratic, I might almost say proletarian boldness which has only its misery to lose and a whole country, a whole world, to gain. (A. 58, VI. 551.)

The same ideas were formulated by Marx, for whom the restoration of Poland 'has become the point of honour for all the democrats of Europe' (ibid., p. 549).

This polonophile standpoint found full expression in *Neue Rheinische Zeitung*. Its most important contribution to the Polish cause was a series of Engels's articles entitled 'The Frankfurt Assembly Debates the Polish Question'. It was, perhaps, the most important *polonicum* in Marx's and Engels's early writings. We find in it so many significant passages that it is impossible to quote all of them. Instead, let us make a brief enumeration: the words about Poles being a 'necessary nation', quoted above; a severe condemnation of the anti-Polish attitudes of the Germans and Jews from Poznania and Pomerania; an equally severe condemnation of the Frankfurt Assembly for its betrayal of the Poles; the theory of agrarian revolution as the only way of overthrowing 'patriarchial feudal barbarism' in Eastern Europe, and the acknowledgement that it was the Poles who had been the first to embrace this idea; an assertion that 'the Poles have every prospect of finding themselves very soon in the van of all Slav nationalities' (ibid., VII. p. 373); the demand for the restoration of the Polish state with special emphasis on the claim that the restored Poland 'must have at least the dimensions of 1772', that 'she must comprise not only the territories but also the estuaries of her big rivers and at least a large seaboard on the Baltic' (ibid., p. 352); and, finally, the call for a German-Polish revolutionary alliance and for a revolutionary war against tsarist Russia.

Along with Engels's articles, in August 1848 *Neue Rhenische Zeitung* published the text of the 'Protest of the German Democratic Society in Cologne Against the Incorporation of Poznań in the German Confederation'. This protest, submitted to the National Assembly in Frankfurt, was made at a general meeting of the Cologne Democratic Society presided over by Marx.

No wonder that Polish politicians, both democrats and liberals, even liberal-conservatives, were very fond of Marx's and Engels's newspaper. In September 1848 a wealthy Polish landowner, Władysław Kościelski (in later years an outspoken conservative), gave Marx 2,000 thalers, as a Polish subsidy for *Neue Rheinische Zeitung*.[12] Very probably Kościelski was only an intermediary between Marx and a group of Polish politicians in Berlin who wanted to support the most polonophile German newspaper. If this hypothesis is true, the decisive voice in this delicate question belonged, undoubtedly, to August Cieszkowski.

In 1849 Marx and Engels pinned their hopes on the Hungarian insurrection—an insurrection in which thousands of Poles took part and whose commanders-in-chief were Polish *émigrés* (Generals Józef Bem and Henryk Dembiński). Later in this year a revolutionary insurrection broke out in Baden and the Palatinate; this time Engels himself took part in it, serving under the Polish commander-in-chief, Ludwik Mierosławski (Engels's direct superior was another Polish officer— F. Sznajde). Since there was at that time no revolutionary movement in Poland, all these events, naturally enough, over-shadowed Polish affairs for a while. Nevertheless, Marx and Engels always remembered the services rendered to European revolutions by Polish patriots and often returned in their articles to the Polish question. Engels often contrasted the Poles to the other Slavonic nations, claiming that the former, together with the Hungarians, Italians, and Germans, belonged to the great revolutionary nations of Europe, while the latter—the smaller Slavonic nations, infected by Russian Panslavism— were merely ethnic nationalities, 'relics' of history, having neither a historical past nor a future and doomed to be instruments of reaction. He included in the same category the Ruthenians of Galicia, accusing them of an 'obdurate narrow-mindedness' (A. 65, VI. 507–8). Poland will be restored because 'the words *Pole* and *revolutionary* have become identical' (A. 64, p. 81); Czechs, Croats, and other 'reactionary nations' will 'disappear from the earth' in the great revolutionary war of the future, so 'that nothing is left of them but their names' (ibid., p. 67).

Everybody will agree today that this was a rather extreme position, and that Engels was simply wrong in his prophetic capacity. It is difficult also to deny that there were in his articles some overtones of a genuine and uninhibited German nationalism, bordering on apologia for force and 'iron ruthlessness' in history. We must remember, however, that Engels's lack of scruples in condemning whole nations for inevitable destruction was rooted not so much in his German patriotism but, rather, in his revolutionary zeal, ruthlessly subordinating everything to the cause of overwhelming the reactionary Holy Alliance, and, no less, in his Hegelian belief in historical necessity which had never had any scruples in paving the way of universal progress.

After the defeat of the Springtime of the Peoples, Engels cooled his zeal and started to make a critical reappraisal of past events. His attitude to the Poles underwent a sharp, although brief, volte-face. In his letter to Marx of 23 May 1851, the Poles were described as a 'nation foutue', brave but lazy, and unable to be a real civilizing force. The evidence of this was seen in the inability of the ancient Polish Commonwealth to polonize its national minorities, and the conclusion was that the Russians, who had shown an excellent russifying capacity, were more likely to spread civilization in the East. The Poles could be used as tools by the Western revolutionaries but only until Russia herself embarked on the path of agrarian revolution. Another conclusion was that the Germans should never abandon their territories east of Memel (Klaipeda) and Cracow (including Poznania)—surrendering even an inch of these territories to the Poles would amount to the betrayal of civilization.

It should also be added that similar thoughts were expressed by Engels in print, in a series of articles, 'Revolution and Counter-revolution in Germany'.[13] It is worth while also to note that in the first half of 1853 Engels became aware of the fact that the eastern lands of the former Polish state were inhabited predominantly by Ukrainian and White Russian peasants for whom the restoration of Poland would mean the restoration of the political power of the Polish gentry.[14] This newly acquired knowledge made him even more sceptical about the real effectiveness of Polish revolutionary activities.

Most likely Engels's scepticism as to the Poles was shared at that time, partially at least, by Marx. Nevertheless, when the Crimean War turned their attention once more to the Russian menace to Europe, both friends quickly recovered their faith in Poland. Marx resumed his studies of Polish history and, as a result, became convinced that Poland had always been an 'outside thermometer' of Western revolutionary movements in the sense that every movement in the West had its counterpart in Poland and that the inner dynamism of Western revolutionary movements since 1789 could be measured quite correctly by their attitude to the Polish question.[15] In 1858 Marx and Engels published in the *American Encyclopaedia* an article on General Bem, stressing that he was unsurpassed in guerrilla warfare and deserved credit for his policy of reconciling the Magyars with the non-Magyar nations of Hungary. In a word, they became pro-Polish once again, ready to welcome a new revolutionary or insurgent movement among Poles.

They did not have to wait long. In January 1863 a new Polish uprising broke out. It was preceded by an agreement with the Russian revolutionaries; its outbreak was synchronized with the proclamation of a Manifesto in which the revolutionary Polish government declared that the peasants' land was their own property and that all feudal duties of peasants were abolished.

Was it not the expected agrarian revolution in the East—the revolution which Marx and Engels had predicted would come, seeing it as a prerequisite of a proletarian revolution in the

West? Apparently it was! No wonder that after a few weeks of hesitation they began to believe that an 'era of revolution' was again 'fairly opened' in Europe.[16]

Contemporary Polish historians are right in indicating that the radicalism of the Polish insurgents was restrained in practice by their desire not to alienate the patriotic gentry. In spite of this, however, there is no doubt that the January insurrection, although defeated, gained a victory as regards the agrarian question: tsarist government could not afford to alienate the Polish peasants by depriving them of the land they had been given, and, therefore, it had to enfranchise them on better terms than in Russia. There is no doubt also that the insurrection was permeated and accompanied by a truly internationalist spirit. Every nation in Europe gave it a smaller or greater number of volunteers, the greatest number being provided by the Russians. Francesco Nullo, the adjutant officer and closest friend of Garibaldi, and Andrej Poetbnia, an eminent Russian revolutionary, friend of Alexander Herzen, suffered heroic deaths in it. Marx in his talk with Colonel Łapiński wholeheartedly approved the idea of organizing a German legion which would fight under its own flag on the Polish side (B. 14, pp. 371–88).[17] Despite Proudhon, who did everything to present the Polish insurrection as a reactionary, Catholic, and aristocratic movement, the working class and the socialists of Europe spontaneously supported the heroic Poles and energetically defended the Polish cause against the bourgeois press (which, incidentally, repeated the arguments of Proudhon and of the chauvinistic Russian press). English and French workers wanted their governments to declare war on Russia; a petition to Napoleon III, demanding of him an effective military succour for the Poles, was signed by 6,467 workers (see. B. 75, p. 73). The German *Arbeiterbildungsverein* in London published a proclamation (written by Marx) which announced that the 'restoration of Poland'—an honourable slogan betrayed by bourgeois liberals—had become a blazing watchword of the German working class.[18] A meeting of French and English workers, organized in London in July 1863 to support the Polish struggle, was the place where the idea of organizing an international association of workers—the future International—was born. Marx and Engels remembered this fact and gave it symbolic significance.[19]

A touching testimony of Marx's emotional attitude to the Polish uprising is a photograph which shows him with his daughter Jenny who is wearing on her neck the Catholic cross of a Polish insurgent of 1863.[20] Documentation of his intellectual reactions to this event can be found in five manuscripts on Poland, Prussia, and Russia, written by him in the early spring of 1863, in connection with the anti-Polish Prussian-Russian convention of 8 February 1863. They were destined for a pamphlet entitled 'Germany and Poland—Military and Political Considerations', which Marx and Engels wanted to write together. The fate of Engels's part of his pamphlet (on military considerations) is unknown; Marx's manuscripts, curiously enough, remained unpublished for a hundred years. They were published only quite recently in Holland (by the Amsterdam Institute of Social History) and, later (in German and in Polish), in Poland (see A. 61 and A. 63).[21]

The main argument of the manuscript runs as follows: the restoration of Poland is the only way of annihilating Russia's domination over Eastern and Central Europe, and, by the same token, of destroying her ambitious plans to rule over the world. Therefore a restored Polish state is necessary for the Germans. On the other hand, the restoration of Poland would mean inevitable downfall for Prussia. Without Polish lands Prussia, a former lackey of Poland, would never have been able to achieve her present status in Europe and Germany. She had robbed Polish lands and established her position in Germany with the help of Russia, at the cost of permitting Russia to play a decisive role in German politics. 'The decline of Poland was the cradle of Prussia; the rise of Russia was the law of development of Prussian power. That is why Prussia was always a "jackal of Russia".' At present the relationship between Russia and Prussia is a dialectical one: Russian support is necessary for upholding Prussian domination in Germany; Prussia, in her turn, is necessary for Russia as the only safeguard of Russian rule in Poland, and as the strongest outpost of Russian influence in Germany and in Europe. Prussian interests therefore are directly opposed to the interests of German democrats, representing the legitimate general interests of Germany. The restoration of Poland is an absolute necessity for Germany because there is no other way of liberating her from the reactionary tutelage of Russia. If the restoration of Poland is incompatible with Prussian *raison d'état*, all the worse for Prussia: it means that Prussian interests are incompatible with the well-understood general interests of Germany, and, consequently, that the Prussian state should be destroyed.[22]

The general conclusion was simple and lucid: 'For Germany all questions of foreign policy can be reduced to one task: the restoration of Poland' (A. 63, p. 77).

In his presentation of Polish history Marx was guided by Polish authors—Lelewel, Mierosławski, Sawaszkiewicz, and others. He fully shared Lelewel's view that the decline and fall of the Polish state was preceded and accompanied by an inner process of national regeneration. Very often he literally repeated the opinions of Polish historians; he apparently felt that Polish views on Polish history were more reliable than Russian and Prussian ones. In his exposition of the making, defending, and overthrowing of the Constitution of 3 May 1791 he closely followed the historical account of the main architects of this Constitution (Hugo Kołłątaj and others), published in German under the title *Vom Entstehung und Untergang der polnischen Konstitution von 1791.* Unlike his practice in his other historical writings, he did not try to avoid moral judgements, sometimes very strong and emotional. Thus, for instance, the so-called 'guaranty' of the Polish political system, imposed upon Poland by her absolutist neighbours in order to prevent any attempts at modernizing and strengthening the Polish state, was in his eyes the most wicked treaty in the history of international relations.

Among the newly published manuscripts of Marx there is also a manuscript in English—first drafts of the polemic with Peter Fox, a member of the General Council of the International who had proposed a resolution concerning Poland. Marx could not agree with Fox's reasonings about the allegedly pro-Polish policy of France. French workers, he argued, are indeed pro-Polish, but none of the different French governments did anything for Poland. In fact, the recent history of France and Poland is a history of the Poles saving France many times and of France betraying them each time.

The defeat of the Polish uprising was, in Marx's estimation, one of the two most important events in European history since 1815.[23] The other was the Russian conquest of the Caucasus. Thus, the most important political process after the Napoleonic wars and the Congress of Vienna was for Marx the growing strength of tsarist Russia. Such a diagnosis could only strengthen his commitment to the Polish cause, his desire to make it the most important point of the foreign policy of the international proletariat. Consistently, he drafted a resolution concerning Poland and submitted it to the General Council of the newly created International. The proposal consisted of two points: (1) a statement that the defeat of the Polish uprising was a serious blow to the cause of progress and civilization, (2) a declaration that Poland has an absolute right to fight for her independence and to demand from the advanced nations of Europe help in this fight (see A. 83, p. 286). On 25 November 1864, the resolution was passed.

In the next year the General Council started to prepare for the first Congress of the International. Marx and Engels were fully aware that the Polish cause would have many opponents: many proletarian organizations, especially in France, were deeply impressed by Proudhon, who, as we know, presented the Polish national-liberation movement as a reactionary movement of the nobility, completely alien to the Polish workers. The Polish question was to be the ninth point on the agenda of the Congress. Marx, who was not able to participate in the Congress, wrote special instructions for the delegates of the temporary General Council (see A. 25, pp. 93–4), explaining to them the importance of Poland for the all-European revolutionary strategy. Engels, for his part, engaged in polemics with the Proudhonists in an important theoretical article entitled, 'What Have the Working Classes to do with Poland?', published a few months before the convention of the Congress. In the opening phrases he reminded his readers that the restoration of Poland had always been the main aim of proletarian foreign policy:

Wherever the working classes have taken part of their own political movements, there, for the very beginning, their foreign policy was expressed in the few words—Restoration of Poland. This was the case with the Chartist movement so long as it existed; this was the case with the French working men long before 1848, as well as during this memorable year, when on the 15th of May, they marched on to the National Assembly to the cry of 'Vive la Pologne!—Poland forever!' This was the case of Germany, when, in 1848 and 1849, the organs of the working class demanded war with Russia for the restoration of Poland. It is the case even now; with one exception [Proudhon]—of which more anon—the working men of Europe unanimously proclaim the restoration of Poland as a part and parcel of their political programme, as the most comprehensive expression of their foreign policy. (A. 64, p. 95.)

In spite of Marx's and Engels's efforts, the ninth point of the proposed resolution was rejected by the Congress. It should be added, however, that it was strongly supported by a considerable minority, especially by English and German workers, and that the Congress was nearly dissolved because of disagreements about the Polish question.

Soon afterwards, in January 1867, a great international meeting was held in the Cambridge Hall in London to celebrate the fourth anniversary of the last Polish uprising. It was organized by the International, with Marx delivering the key address. He called Poland 'the immortal knight of Europe', warning at the same time that, worn out by the accumulated betrayals of Europe, she might become 'a whip in the hand of the Muscovite' (A. 64, pp. 105–6). It is very naïve to believe, he claimed, that times have changed and 'Poland has ceased to be a necessary nation'. In fact, 'there is but one alternative for Europe. Either Asiatic despotism under Muscovite direction, will burst around its head like an avalanche, or else it must re-establish Poland, thus putting twenty million heroes between itself and Asia and gaining a breathing spell for the accomplishment of its social regeneration' (ibid., p. 108).

The impression made by this speech was immense. The meeting passed four resolutions in favour of Poland, one of them making it clear that Poland should be restored within the boundaries of 1772. It seemed that Proudhonism had been finally defeated.

After 1864, proletarian meetings organized by the International were almost the only place where words such as those quoted above could be heard. This explains the curious fact that the International had its sympathizers not only among the Polish radical Left but also among the Polish liberals, many of them being quite conservative otherwise (see B. 13, p. 73). To the latter group belonged, among others, the historian F. Duchiński who, in contrast to Lelewel, flatly denied that the Russians had any right to the common Slavonic heritage: in fact, he maintained, they were the descendants of an Asiatic race of Turanians, having nothing in common with the Slavs.

On the other hand it should be stressed that some of the

leaders of the Polish insurrectionary Left began to pin their hopes on the European proletariat quite independently from Marx's and Engels's pro-Polish stand. One of them, General Jósef Hauke-Bosak, the commander of the insurrectionary forces in the Sandomierz and Cracow voivodships, became active on the left wing of the international League of Peace and Freedom. He demanded the socialization of land and of the means of production (by giving the latter to workers' associations); in his brochure *La Grève* (1869) he set forth the idea of a general strike for the introduction of an eight hours' working day. In the Franco-Prussian War he fought under Garibaldi and gave his life in defence of the French Republic.

Another figure of importance, General Jarosław Dąbrowski, a member of a revolutionary circle of Polish officers in St. Petersburg, was the initiator and co-organizer of the revolutionary movement within the Russian army in the Congress Kingdom. Arrested before the insurrection, he succeeded, nevertheless, in steering the movement from prison. He has the credit of being one of the first Polish politicians to recognize the Ukrainians as a separate nation and acknowledge their right to self-determination. In 1871, like hundreds of his compatriots, he decided to fight as a simple soldier of the Paris Commune; soon he was made commander-in-chief of one of three armies of the Commune and, later, the commander-in-chief of all the military forces of the revolutionary city. He was killed on a barricade. The motives of his actions were explained later by his brother Teofil in the following words: 'We joined the Paris revolution because we saw in it a social revolution which, if successful, could overthrow the existing order in Europe. Could Poland lose anything in it? Nothing. Could she win something? Yes, everything' (A. 12, p. 163).

The third important representative of the 1863 generation was General Walery Wróblewski, one of the leaders of the Polish insurrectionary forces in Belorussia. He fought in the Paris commune as the commander-in-chief of the army defending the whole left bank of the Seine. He organized the last point of resistance against the troops of Versailles and defended it to the end. After the defeat he became a member of the General Council of the International and a close friend of Marx and Engels whose houses were for him (in his own words) 'les seules et véritables maisons fraternelles' (B. 14, p. 47). He never became a Marxist, but was sometimes very useful for Marx and Engels in their fight against Bakuninists and Proudhonists. The two founders of 'scientific communism' did everything they could to help him in poverty and illness; they seemed to like his cavalier spirit, his constant readiness 'to mount on a horse', and his jovial sense of humour. His presence in the General Council supported the pro-Polish tendencies within the International. He was active also among the Polish socialists in exile, siding with Boleslaw Limanowski who strove for a synthesis of socialism with democratic, humanitarian nationalism.

The prominent part played by the Poles in the Paris Commune brought discredit to their cause in bourgeois public opinion. We can clearly see in retrospect that the Franco-Prussian War, the Paris Commune, and the unification of Germany which followed, were a real turning point after which, from the point of view of European governments, the Polish question ceased to be an international question.

It was not so, however, in the International. Marx and Engels never forgot that, as they put it, the Polish exiles gave the commune her 'best generals and most heroic soldiers',[24] that for the Courts-Martial in Versailles 'it was sufficient to be a Pole in order to be shot'.[25] At the same time Engels repeated once more his classicial diagnosis of 1848, and went even further, saying: 'Even more than France, Poland, due to its historical development, is faced with the choice either of becoming revolutionary or of perishing.' This point, he added, with French Proudhonists in mind, 'invalidates all the silly talk of the essentially aristocratic character of the Polish movement' (A. 64, p. 114). Supporting his view with a list of historical examples of the Polish irrevocable commitment to democracy he concluded: 'In 1870 the great mass of the Polish émigrés in France enlisted in the service of the Commune. Was that a deed of aristocrats? Does that not prove that these Poles stand fully in the forefront of the modern movement?' (ibid.)

Very significantly, the question of Polish national independence became the platform on which Marx's and Engels's views sharply clashed with the views of the first Polish Marxists who at the end of the 1870s started to publish in Geneva their own journal named *Równość* (*Equality*). The editors of *Equality* understood proletarian internationalism as the opposite of patriotism. Moreover: they were convinced that

Polish patriotism had become the instrument of reactionaries trying to prevent the emergence of class-consciousness among the Polish workers. In 1880 they organized an international meeting in Geneva, to celebrate the 50th anniversary of the Polish uprising of 1830, and proclaimed on this occasion that the old slogan 'Long live Poland!' had lost its revolutionary content. The new slogans for Polish revolutionaries were to be: 'Away with patriotism and reaction! Long live the International and Social Revolution!' In contrast to this, Marx and Engels greeted the meeting with a long letter attesting the revolutionary content of the cry 'Long live Poland!' and proclaiming the Polish cause to be still worthy of wholehearted support by European revolutionaries, including the Russians.[26]

In his letter to Kautsky of 7 February 1882, Engels made the following comment on the Geneva meeting: 'It appears that the *Równość* has been impressed by the radically sounding phrases of the Geneva Russians' (i.e. by the Russian anarchists and populists, dismissing *political* questions as allegedly irrelevant to *social* revolution (cf. B. 176, pp. 80–106). In the same letter he presented a deep theoretical explanation of his and Marx's position. It runs as follows:

> Every Polish peasant or worker who wakes up from the general gloom and participates in the common interest, encounters first the fact of national subjugation. This fact is in his way everywhere as the first barrier. To remove it is the basic condition of every healthy and free development. Polish socialists who do not place the liberation of their country at the head of their programme, appear to me as would German socialists who do not demand first and foremost repeal of the anti-socialist law, freedom of the press, association, and assembly. In order to be able to fight one needs first a soil to stand on, air, light and space. Otherwise all is idle chatter. (A. 64, p. 117.)[27]

The same line on the Polish question was pursued by Engels after Marx's death. In 1890, in a long article entitled the 'Foreign Policy of Russian Tsarism', he repeated all the arguments for his and Marx's conception of the peculiar importance of Poland for the revolutionary transformation of Russia, adding to it an interesting parallel between Russian policy in eighteenth-century Germany and Russian policy in eighteenth-century Poland.[28] In 1882, in the preface to the Polish edition of the *Manifesto of the Communist Party*, he pointed out that in Germany, Italy, and Hungary the national problem had already been solved while the Polish question remained unsolved—despite the fact that the Poles had contributed more to the cause of revolution than Germany, Italy, and Hungary together. The rapid development of Polish industry, much quicker than in Russia, was in his view a new proof of the vitality of the Polish nation and a new guarantee of the imminent restoration of the Polish state. From the point of view of the International the restoration of Poland was desirable and necessary, because without the national independence of each country an honest, sincere collaboration between the nations of Europe was simply inconceivable.

Thus, it was quite natural that the old Engels had friendly relations with the leaders of the Polish Socialist Party (PPS), although the latter were accused of nationalism. Not only Plekhanov but he too could not agree with 'la belle m-elle Luxemburg' who defended the view that at the international congress in Zurich the Poles should be represented according to their formal citizenship, i.e. as parts of the Russian, Prussian, and Austrian delegations. Engels must have shared Plekhanov's opinion that the adoption of such a principle would amount to a new partition of Poland. If there are any doubts about it, let us recall his view on the relations between the Irish sections and the British Federal Council:

What would be said if this Council called upon Polish sections to acknowledge the supremacy of a Russian Federal Council in Petersburg, or upon Prussian, Polish, North Schleswig, and Alsatian sections to submit to a Federal Council in Berlin? Yet what was asked to do with regard to Irish sections was substantially the same thing. If members of a conquering nation called upon the nation they had conquered and continued to hold down to forget their specific nationality and position, to 'sink national differences' and so forth, that was not Internationalism, it was nothing else but preaching to them submission to the yoke, and attempting to justify and to perpetuate the dominion of the conqueror under the cloak of Internationalism. (A. 60, p, 303.)

3. Peculiar Features of Marx's and Engels's Theory of the Nation

Let us now turn to theoretical problems. Is it justified to say that Marx and Engels created a theory of the nation and of national independence, a theory of their own, stemming from, or at least meaningfully related to, their historical materialism?

I think that we can give a positive answer to this question. If

Marx and Engels supported the Polish struggle for independence, but, at the same time, refused to acknowledge the right
to self-determination of the Habsburg Slavs, it was *not only*
because of their understanding of the practical interests of the
German workers, or Germany as a whole, but *also* as a logical
consequence of their theoretical understanding of some general
laws governing the historical process.

One of the basic premises of Marx's and Engels's view of the
nation is the theory of 'national class' to which I have referred at
the beginning of this chapter. This premiss, however, does not
explain why the two authors of the *Manifesto of the Communist
Party* divided nations into two groups, the 'historical nations',
having the right to self-determination, and the 'history-less
peoples', devoid of this right (cf. B. 49, p. 22). Nevertheless this
very fact, curious as it may seem today, is of crucial significance
for the proper understanding of Marx's and Engels's theory of
nations.

Let us begin with a few quotations, shedding light on some
other premises of this theory. All of them are from Engels's
article 'Democratic Pan-Slavism' (1849). The first of them
deals with the growth of civilizations:

. . . will Bakunin reproach the American people for waging a war, which to be
sure deals a severe blow to his theories based on 'Justice and Humanity', but
which none the less was waged solely in the interests of civilization? Or is it
perhaps a misfortune that the splendid land of California has been wrested
from the lazy Mexicans who did not know what to do with it?

Is it a misfortune that through rapid exploitation of the gold mines there the
energetic Yankees have increased the medium of circulation, have concentrated in a few years a heavy population and an extensive trade on the most
suitable part of the Pacific coast, have built great cities, have opened up
steamship lines, are laying railroads from New York to San Francisco, which
will actually open the Pacific Ocean to civilization for the first time, and for the
third time in history will give a new orientation to world trade? Because of this
the 'independence' of a few Spanish Californians and Texans may be injured,
but what do they count compared to such world historical events?

Now on the issue of 'history-less' peoples:

Peoples which have never had a history of their own, which from the moment
they reached the first, crudest stages of civilization already came under foreign
domination or which were only forced into the first stages of civilization
through a foreign yoke, have no vitality, they will never be able to attain any
sort of independence.

On historical necessity:

. . . at a time when everywhere in Europe great monarchies were an 'historical necessity', what a 'crime', what an 'accursed policy', that the Germans and Magyars bound these tiny, crippled, powerless little nations together in a great Empire, and thereby enabled them to take part in an historical development which, if left to themselves, would have remained entirely foreign to them! To be sure such a thing is not carried through without forcibly crushing many a delicate little national flower. But without force and without an iron ruthlessness nothing is accomplished in history.

Finally, on centralization:

Now, however, as a result of the formidable advances in industry, trade and communications, political centralization has become an even greater need than it was then in the 15th and 16th centuries. What still has to be centralized is becoming centralized. (A. 64, pp. 71–2, 76.)

What is implicit—or even explicit—in the above quotations can be called, I think 'the historic right of superior civilization'. In a conflict between superior and inferior civilization, superior and inferior culture, the superior one is bound to win and rule, and nobody should have any moral scruples about it; it must win at all costs because its victory is in the interest of historical progress, in the interest of universal human Civilization. In history, being 'right' means only 'being on the side of progress', 'being a vehicle of civilization'. Referring to allegedly 'absolute' moral standards is nothing more than sheer sentimentalism and unhistoricism.

Was it historical materialism and not yet another variant of vulgar Hegelianism? Certainly: the terminology had sometimes a Hegelian tinge ('historical necessity', 'historical nations', and so forth), yet it was Hegelianism thoroughly reinterpreted in accordance with the distinctively Marxist view of history. It was distinctively Marxist to claim that the main criterion of progress is the development of productive forces and that every-thing else should be subordinated to it. Seeing historical progress, including the future transition from capitalism to socialism, as an objective process, not to be measured by abstract, moral criteria, was a distinctive feature of Marxist 'scientific' socialism, as opposed to 'Utopian' socialism. Finally, it was very Marxist to conceive of progress as an incessant increase of centralization; it was not *distinctively* Marxist, because there were many other thinkers (to mention only Saint-Simon) who fully shared this view but, nevertheless, it was a characteristic feature of Marxism.

All of these ideas were very relevant to the national problem. It followed therefrom that in order to make a sound judgement concerning national conflicts one must refer not to moral absolutes but to historical laws and, first of all, must answer the question: whose victory is in the interest of general human progress? The same question should be asked in a case of direct conquest, because an absolute moral condemnation of any conquest is a sentimental stupidity (see B. 12, p. 49). Pre-socialist progress has always been cruel, it has always been achieved at somebody's cost. 'History', wrote Engels in a letter to a Russian populist, 'is about the most cruel of all goddesses, and she leads her triumphal car over heaps of corpses not only in war, but also in "peaceful" economic development' (A. 59, p. 510). The same view was developed by Marx in his famous article on English rule in India. Progress, he wrote, would 'cease to resemble that hideous pagan idol, who would not drink the nectar but from the skulls of the slain', only 'when a great social revolution shall have mastered the results of the bourgeois epoch, the market of the world, and the modern powers of production, and subjected them to the common control of the most advanced peoples' (quoted from B. 12, p. 54).

How can those nations which are advanced, 'progressive', representing the interests of Civilization, be distinguished from the others? The simplest answer to this question is purely economic: an advanced nation represents a higher stage or, at least, a higher level of economic development; in any conflict between an advanced and a backward nation, historical right—the 'right of a superior civilization'—is as a rule (i.e. when no additional circumstances are involved) on the side of the former.

For Marx and Engels this was true, but not enough to make a final judgement. They knew that Czech lands were economically quite well developed, and yet they were strongly opposed to the national aspirations of the Czechs. They supported the Polish national movement, although they were aware of the economic backwardness of Poland. They sympathized with the Irish struggle against English rule in spite of the obvious fact that Ireland was economically much less developed than England. It was so, because they were thinking not only in purely economic terms, but in politico-economic, political and cultural terms as well. The mechanistic 'economic determinism', represented by some of their disciples, was deeply alien to their thought.

In politico-economic terms the chief tendency of progressive capitalist development was conceived of by Marx and Engels as the abolition of 'independent, or but loosely connected provinces' and the establishment of large, highly centralized nation-states (see A. 58, VI. 489). It was consistent with their view of the increasing importance of centralization in economic life: large-scale polities create better conditions for large-scale economies and, therefore, the assimilation of smaller nationalities is a progressive process (see B. 12, p. 36). It was never assumed, of course, that a forcible assimilation was desirable, but it was assumed that sometimes it could be necessary. A gradual process of assimilation to a superior civilization as was the case with the polonization of the Ruthenian and Lithuanian nobility,[29] or with the germanization of the upper layers of the Czechs, was considered to be quite natural and progressive. Moreover: it was strongly emphasized that such an assimilation was irreversible, because the results of the historical civilizing process could not and should not be reversed. From this point of view the Panslavism of the Habsburg Slavs, i.e. the movement for the national 'awakening' of the small Slavonic nations, was considered to be 'reactionary', running foul of the chief tendency of progress. Another obvious consequence was the support of the idea for the restoration of Poland within the historical boundaries of 1772, in spite of the fact that the eastern territories of ancient Poland were not ethnically Polish—if Poland was to be restored, it had to be restored as a big state, because only big states are in accordance with the progressive development of history.

An extremely interesting comment to those views is Engels's article 'What have the working classes to do with Poland?' It was written after the Polish uprising of 1863–4, in order to refute the standard argument of the Proudhonists who argued that the 'principle of nationalities' is a 'Bonapartist invention', used and abused for reactionary aims and having nothing in common

with the class interests of the workers. In answering this argument Engels made an important distinction between
'nationality' and 'nation'. A 'nationality' is an ethnic group
whose natural boundaries are those of language; a 'nation' is a
product of history, a politically organized territorial subdivision
of mankind;[30] its boundaries depend on its inner vitality and its
ability to be a vehicle of civilization. Every European nation has
been composed of many ethnic nationalities, and a great
majority of nations are still inhabited by people of different
nationalities. To support separatist movements of the ethnic
nationalities means to contribute to the disintegration of the
multiethnic political nations; hence, the 'principle of
nationalities' has nothing in common with 'the old democratic
and working-class tenet as to the right of the great European
nations to separate and independent existence'. 'The "principle
of nationalities",' wrote Engels,

. . . raises two sorts of questions; first of all, questions of boundary between
great historic peoples; and secondly, questions as to the right to independent
national existence of those numerous small relics of peoples which, after
having figured for a longer or shorter period on the stage of history, were
finally absorbed as integral portions into one or the other of those more
powerful nations whose greater vitality enabled them to overcome greater
obstacles. The European importance, the vitality of people is as nothing in the
eyes of the principle of nationalities, before it, the Roumans of Wallachia, who
never had a history, nor the energy required to have one, are of equal
importance to the Italians who have a history of 2000 years, and an
unimpaired national vitality; the Welsh and Manxmen, if they desired it,
would have an equal right to independent political existence, absurd though it
would be, with the English. The whole thing is an absurdity, got up in a
popular dress in order to be used as a convenient phrase, or to be laid aside if
the occasion requires it (A. 64, pp. 99–100).

As we can see from this quotation, Marx's and Engels's
approach to national conflicts could not be reduced to the
simple question of 'levels of economic development'. It involved
also other criteria, such as political and cultural development,
'the European importance', or, even, a somewhat vague notion
of the 'vitality of people'. The emphasis on 'having a history'
may seem surprising, since we are inclined to think of every
ethnic group as having a history of its own. And we are right, of
course, especially from the point of view of economic and social
history. Nevertheless, Engels's intention is quite clear. He
wanted to stress that a nation should have a *political* history,

showing proofs of its capacity to shape its own historical fate. We may conclude, therefore, that a nation (in contrast to a mere 'nationality') should be an active agent of historical development, a conscious 'subject' (in the philosophical sense), and not merely a 'raw material' of history. It is understandable that a nation conceived in such a manner should display 'vitality' and 'energy', an acute feeling of dignity, a capacity for civilizational and cultural expansion, and even warlike qualities (cf. B. 120, p. 254).

The application of this argument to the Polish question was rather obvious. Poland was not a 'nationality' but one of the *political* nations of Europe. Like many other nations in the present and the past she was a multiethnic nation; the 'principle of nationalities', supporting the claims of non-historic, ethnic nationalities, was very dangerous from the point of view of Polish interests. Engels did not hesitate to assert that this principle was in fact 'a Russian invention concocted to destroy Poland': it was more than one hundred years old, because the Russians had used it as a pretext for the partitions of Poland.[31] 'Therefore, if people say that to demand the restoration of Poland is to appeal to the principle of nationalities, they merely prove that they do not know what they are talking about, for the restoration of Poland means the re-establishment of a state composed of at least four different nationalities' (A. 64, pp. 100–1).

The theoretical source of this view was an absolutization of the 'French model' of nation-forming processes: Engels thought that in the restored Polish state the Ukrainians, Belorussians and Lithuanians would become parts of the Polish nation in the same way as the Alsatians, Bretons, Basques and Provençals had become parts of the one and indivisible nation of France. History has shown, however, that the 'French model' could not be successfully followed in East-Central Europe: neither in the case of the former Polish Commonwealth, nor in the case of the lands of St. Stephen's Crown (cf. B. 24).

4. Marx, Engels, and Romantic Polish Nationalism

It is evident that Marx's and Engels's theory of the nation, presented above, was incompatible with modern nationalism, defining nations by linguistic and ethnic criteria. It was no less incompatible with the democratic viewpoint that the right of self-determination should be extended to every nation. On the other hand, interestingly enough, it was in harmony with some characteristic tendencies of the romantic Polish nationalism of the time of the great national uprisings. It was not accidental that Joachim Lelewel, the first Polish friend of Marx, was a typical romantic nationalist and a democratic internationalist at the same time. The same is true about Wróblewski, the best Polish friend of Marx and Engels and, perhaps, the greatest epigone of romantic nationalism, wholeheartedly believing in the brotherhood of nations and in the natural alliance between Polish patriotism and European revolutionism.

True, there were many differences, very often, from a theoretical point of view, most important ones. Polish romantic thinkers were as a rule, as far as possible from programmatic scientism and economic determinism; Marx and Engels, in their turn, were as far as possible from the ethicism (sometimes religiously tinged) of Polish romantic thought. Yet, in spite of this, let us try to point out some points of convergence between Marx's and Engels's approach to national problems and the views of their Polish contemporaries.

First, the historical, political, and territorial concept of the nation, as opposed to the ethnic, linguistic concept. For Lelewel the Polish nation consisted of the Poles of Great Poland, the Poles of Little Poland, Mazovians, Lithuanians, Ruthenians, and so forth (cf. B. 17, p. 13). Himself of Polish-German background, he considered even Polish Germans to be simply German-speaking Poles. This view was fully shared by Engels, in whose eyes the German Burghers living for centuries in Poland 'became Poles, German-speaking Poles' and 'never regarded themselves as politically belonging to Germany any more than did the Germans in North America' (A 58, VI. 339). For Lelewel the ancient Polish Commonwealth was one great multiethnic nation. He wanted to preserve the ancient Polish notion of being 'gente Ruthenus (vel Lithuanus), natione Polonus'. It is easy to notice that what he meant by 'gens' corresponded to Engels's 'nationality', and what he meant by 'natio' was equivalent to Engels's 'nation'.

The ideologists of the Polish Democratic Society, following the example of the French Jacobin nationalists, emphasized that the restored Poland should be a centralized state, with no room for regional autonomy. In this respect they disagreed with Lelewel, who highly appreciated the federal structure, regional self-government, and inner diversity of the ancient Polish Commonwealth. The main reason for this was the apprehension of anarchy and counter-revolution. Unlike the French Jacobins, who wanted the French language to be obligatory for all citizens of the republic (cf. B. 51, pp. 64–5 and B. 79, p. 91), they did not demand a forcible linguistic polonization of Lithuanians or Ruthenians; nevertheless, they strongly felt that separatist tendencies based upon linguistic or religious grounds had to be reactionary and could not be tolerated in an 'orderly republic'. We may add that this position was in fact very similar to that of Marx and Engels. Another important similarity was the fact that they conceived of 'nation' in the same way as Marx and Engels, i.e. as a historical, political, and territorial concept, and disregarded the significance of linguistic and ethnic differences.

Very close to the hearts of the Polish patriots of the Romantic Epoch was Marx's and Engels's view that not all nations were equally important for Europe, that the importance of a given nation depended on its services to the universal cause of progress. This was precisely the intellectual and moral ground of the Poles' ardent belief in revolutionary internationalism, of their commitment to the cause of an all-European revolution, of their firm conviction that the restoration of Poland would be a necessary outcome of the imminent overthrow of the reactionary 'Old World'. I have tried to show that Marx and Engels fully shared this view.

The similarity of views on the Polish question was even deeper. For Marx and Engels Poland was an Eastern-European counterpart to France. They thought that Poland had to perform the same revolutionary task for the East as France had performed for the West and, therefore, that the revolutionary movements in the West had their natural ally in the Polish national movement. They saw Poland as the main bulwark of civilization among the Slavs and the main carrier of revolutionary ideas east of the Elbe; very often they spoke of Polish 'sacrifices' to the cause of revolution in the West, especially of the services rendered by the Poles to different revolutions in France, and, as a rule, they were inclined to exaggerate their importance. Such an attitude to Poland not only pleased the Polish patriots but confirmed their cherished belief in the peculiar 'mission' of their nation.

5. A Few Remarks on Post-Marxian Marxism

As I have already noted, after the defeat of the Polish uprising of
1863–4 and, finally, after the Franco-Prussian War, the Paris
Commune, and the unification of Germany, the Polish question
ceased to be an important European question. In contrast to
this, the political liberalization of the Habsburg Empire, bound
up with the social advance and growing political importance of
the masses, made the national movements among the Austro-
Hungarian Slavs stronger, more mature, and more important.
The Ukrainian national movement in Galicia also grew up; its
energetic fight against Polish rule in the province made it
evident that the old formula 'gente Ruthenus, natione Polonus'
had become an anachronism. In these changed circumstances
Marx's and Engels's views on the national problem in Eastern
Europe became anachronistic as well. The Austrian Marxists
were the first to realize this and to draw the necessary conclusions. Their leading theorist, Karl Kautsky, made the
following statement in his letter to Victor Adler of 12 November
1896:

I think that the old standpoint of Marx concerning the Eastern question and
the Polish question, as well as his attitude towards the Czechs, have become
unsupportable. To close one's eyes to the facts and to cling stubbornly to the
antiquated standpoint of Marx would be utterly un-Marxist. (A. 1, p. 221.)

Another factor which served as a catalyst in the process of
revaluation of the Marxian viewpoint on the Polish question
and on the national question in general was the challenging
theory and practice of Rosa Luxemburg. She applied to Poland
Marx's theory of the necessary process of economic integration
in such a way as to enable her to argue that the Polish economy
had become so much integrated with the Russian that the idea
of Polish national independence was merely a petty-bourgeois
nationalist illusion, used by reactionaries in order to hinder the
development of class consciousness among the Polish workers.
The restoration of Poland, she thought, was not only impossible
but also undesirable; she reluctantly agreed to embrace the
cause of limited autonomy for the former Congress Kingdom,
but even this was a forced concession on her part (cf. B. 124, II.
847). She willingly supported the liberation of Balkan Slavs
from the Turkish yoke because she saw Turkey as a stagnant,
reactionary state; in contrast to this, she believed so strongly in

the socialist future of Russia that even to hint at the idea of an independent Poland was for her a vicious ideological diversion. Thus, her position regarding Poland versus Russia was diametrically opposite to that of Marx, although justified, as in Marx's case, by referring to an all-European revolutionary strategy. She could never agree with Lenin who insisted that all the nations of the tsarist Empire should have, formally, the right of self-determination. Her extremism and quite unreasonable lack of flexibility on this point cannot be explained by theoretical or tactical reasons; as her recent biographer has correctly noted, emotional motives were, possibly, the most important. Her hatred of the 'social-patriots' from the Polish Socialist Party was so strong because she herself 'transferred all the energy and satisfaction of patriotic consciousness to the working class' (B. 124, II. 861–2). Her peculiar greatness and tragedy stemmed from a strenuous effort to conceive of internationalism not as collaboration between nations but as a complete liberation from national loyalties.

The Austrian Marxists were much more moderate. They still believed that large states were necessary for economic progress but, on the other hand, they realized that a denial of national self-determination—i.e. a rejection of 'the principle of nationalities' so much ridiculed by Engels—would contradict the principles of political democracy to which they were more and more committed. Thus, they acknowledged the right of self-determination trying, at the same time, to interpret it in such a way as to avoid the fragmentation of the existing states. A sophisticated solution to this problem (acceptable even to Rosa Luxemburg) was provided by a learned jurist, Karl Renner, who interpreted national self-determination not as a right of territorial self-determination but as an extra-territorial personal right to preserve and develop one's cultural identity. This solution was adopted by Otto Bauer who sincerely, even ardently, supported cultural nationalism, but, at the same time, tried to de-politicize national movements by limiting their aims to strictly cultural issues (such as national schools, newspapers, literature, and so on).

The new dominant attitude towards the Polish question found expression in the resolution passed by the London Congress of the International in 1896. It rejected both the proposal of the Polish Socialist Party and the counter-proposal set forth by the Polish Social Democrats headed by Rosa Luxemburg. The first proposal proclaimed that the restoration of Poland should be treated as a matter of peculiar importance for the working class in Europe; the other proposal declared such a goal to be reactionary and utopian. Having rejected both of them, the Congress proclaimed instead that, in principle, each nationality has a right of self-determination and that the working class should fight against all forms of oppression, including national oppression. Thus Marx's and Engels's distinction between 'nations' and 'nationalities', as well as their emphasis on the *peculiar* importance of the Polish question, found no endorsement in the Second International.

An interesting Marxist contribution to the theoretical explanation and practical solution of national problems was made by a Polish sociologist, a member of the Polish Socialist Party, Kazimierz Kelles-Krauz (1872–1905). His works on the national question, written in Polish in the years 1900–4 (see A. 34, II) are ignored by Western specialists who, as a rule, concentrate on Rosa Luxemburg and do not try to become acquainted with the arguments of her socialist opponents in Poland. Such an attitude finds support in the widespread belief that the PPS was not a Marxist party and had no interesting theoreticians in its ranks. This is, however, only partially true: Kelles-Krauz, an influential figure in the PPS, was undoubtedly a gifted thinker and an ardent Marxist.

Polemizing with Rosa Luxemburg, Kelles-Krauz concentrated, of course, on the Polish question. He dismissed her argument that Russian markets were necessary for the development of Polish industry and that for that reason Poland should remain united with Russia. Incorporation, he argued, is not necessary for economic co-operation and trade; it cannot even guarantee that the tsarist government will not reintroduce a tariff-wall between the Congress Kingdom and Russia, if it happens to serve the interests of Russian industrialists. In general, reducing important political questions to economic considerations is a kind of 'economism', characteristic of the 'apoliticism' of the anarchists and populists, but deeply alien to Marxism. The most important Marxist argument for the independence of Poland is the fact (pointed out by Engels) that the Polish working class is more developed, more mature, and, proportionately, much more numerous than the working class in Russia. Russian rule over Poland hinders the democratic transformation not only in Poland but also in Russia because, as Marx and Engels repeatedly stressed, 'a people which oppresses another cannot emancipate itself'.

Kelles-Krauz was fully aware that some aspects of Marx's and Engels's views had become unsupportable. He welcomed the national awakening of 'non-historical' peoples and did not deny them the right of political self-determination. Like Kautsky (and unlike Marx and Engels) he emphasized the growing nation-creating role of native languages and explained this by referring to the processes of vertical and horizontal social mobility, characteristic of capitalist development and greatly increasing the role of all means of communication. He agreed, therefore, to define nationalities by linguistic criteria and to abandon Marx's and Engels's distinction between 'nationalities' and 'nations'. He agreed even (which was something rare at that time) to treat the Jews as a separate, although non-territorial, nationality. The most difficult for him was the problem of the Lithuanian, Latvian, Belorussian, and Ukrainian populations of the ancient Polish Commonwealth. In accordance with the old standpoint of Marx and Engels, Kelles-Krauz treated these nations as not mature enough for independent statehood and, taking into account the visible growth of their national consciousness, proposed that they enter into a federation with a restored, socialist Poland. Such a federation, he argued, would be much better for their further national development than remaining within the boundaries of the autocratic and essentially 'Asiatic' Russian state. It seemed to him that Latvia (where he was born), Lithuania, and Belorussia would become autonomous parts of the restored Poland, while the Ukraine would choose a more loose form of federation. The final solution of these problems, as well as the solution to the Polish question, was made dependent on the organizational and educating activity of the Polish socialists: the future boundaries of Poland, he thought, would be delimited by the territorial range of activities of the Polish Socialist Party.[32]

Kelles-Krauz's contribution to the general theory of nationalism consisted in an interesting analysis of the dialectical relations between the nation-building processes and political democratization. Political democracy, he argued, is a necessary condition for the normal, civilized forms of class struggle; on the other hand, genuine political democracy, i.e. a political system in which different minorities are ready to accept the decisions of the majority, is possible only in a society whose members consider themselves as belonging to the same nation. Therefore, an independent national state is necessary both for the bourgeoisie and for the working class. The latter needs it even more because the proletarian class interest demands *full* political democratization, and cannot be satisfied with half-measures. The Polish bourgeoisie would gladly accept a limited national autonomy, but the Polish workers, being a 'national class', would never cease to struggle for full national independence.

Another interesting Polish thinker whose name should be mentioned in this context was Stanislaw Brzozowski (1878–1911). He underwent a fascinating intellectual evolution in which Marxism was only a phase, although a very important one. He was most close to Marxism in the years 1906–8, but even then interpreted it in a spirit very different from the naturalistic determinism of the intellectual leaders of the Second International, such as Plekhanov or Kautsky. It is justified to say that, like György Lukács, he had discovered some of the basic philosophical intuitions of young Marx before the main works of the young Marx, such as his *Economic and Philosophic Manuscripts of 1844*, were published. He saw Marxism as a philosophy of action; in order to avoid connotations of idealistic activism he preferred to call it a 'philosophy of work'. In his Marxist phase he thought that purposeful work in order to survive and develop, above all physical productive work, was the most important form of human activity, the ultimate source of our knowledge of the external world and the basis of human domination over the elemental forces of nature. He endowed work with a creative capacity and thought of it in sociological and historical terms. Philosophically, this meant that the so-called 'classical definition of truth' is a nonsense because the external world, as we know it, is not something 'given'; it is something *created* by ourselves in the historical and social process of collective work. It followed from this that the working people have always been the vanguard of mankind in its eternal struggle with resistant 'nature', and that the notion of the so-called 'objective laws of nature' (or 'laws of history') represented a false, reified image of the world, resulting from the alienation of intellectuals, which, in turn, was the result of the divorce between the non-working producers of ideas, for whom the world, such as they knew it, was something 'given', and the working people, who, in fact, had created this world. If the workers themselves had an illusion of the 'objectivity' of natural and social processes, it was only because of their social enslavement which for a long time had been necessary for the development of productive forces. The modern industrial proletariat was seen in this perspective as an oppressed class which, for the first time in history, had a chance to liberate itself without causing thereby a regression in human mastery over nature.

Brzozowski's importance for the Marxist theory of nationalism and for the Marxist approach to the Polish question lies in the fact that, like Kelles-Krauz, he saw the Polish proletariat as the most developed, most mature, most modern class of Polish society, i.e. as the 'national class' in the Marxian sense of this term. In opposition both to Rosa Luxemburg and to traditional patriotism he considered the class consciousness of the Polish workers not as something alien, irrelevant, or hostile to Polish patriotism but as the highest, most modern form of Polish national consciousness. The events of the revolution in 1905–7, he thought, proved that the Polish working class was the only force fighting national independence and, at the same time, making the most important contributions to the economic and spiritual modernization of Poland. At the beginning of the twentieth century, when the Marxian idea of 'national class' was almost entirely forgotten, this was an original standpoint, worthy of mention as an attempt at combining Marxism with a progressive, proletarian nationalism.

From the point of view of this book it is relevant to point out that Brzozowski's nationalism was strongly influenced by the Polish romantic heritage, and that his philosophical activism drew inspiration not only from Marx's 'Theses on Feuerbach' but also from Mickiewicz's cult of heroism, Cieszkowski's 'philosophy of action', and from many other Polish thinkers of the Romantic Epoch.[33]

To sum up. Marx and Engels put forward four conceptions concerning nationalism. First, the conception of the 'law of superior civilization', leading to the conclusion that the more advanced nations—more advanced not only in the economic sense, but also from the point of view of cultural development or revolutionary activity—are the legitimate leaders of humanity, representing the interests of an all-human civilization; this conception, as we know, was defended by Engels in his articles on the Habsburg Slavs. Secondly, the conception of the 'national class' and of the national tasks of the workers. Thirdly, the distinction between historical 'nations' and linguistic/ethnic 'nationalities'. Finally, the viewpoint that national interests should be subordinated to the universal cause of revolution. This viewpoint might be interpreted in two different ways, having in common only the denial of the universal applicability of the right of national self-determination. Marx and Engels themselves combined this viewpoint with their theory of the 'national class', and inferred from it that the working class should actively support those national movements whose victory would bring about a desirable change in international relations. On the other hand, their theory implied that if the proletariat is not ripe enough to become a 'national class', its class interests should be subordinated to national interests. Rosa Luxemburg (the other interpretation) also thought that some national movements might serve the cause of progress, but she insisted (in glaring contrast to Marx's and Engels's standpoint) that the proletariat as such could not have separate national tasks, and that true internationalism consisted in the total eradication of patriotism. Other conceptions, such as those developed by the Austrian Marxists, could be, perhaps, more or less compatible with Marxism, but there was nothing *distinctively* Marxist in them. (I deliberately refrain from analysis of Lenin's conception because that is a topic for another, separate work.)

A few words should be added concerning Marx's and Engels's attitude towards the Polish question. It is evident that they were wrong when they insisted that Poland and Hungary were the only nations east of the Elbe which deserved independence and had a chance to win it. Quite often they somewhat exaggerated the European importance of Poland. Nevertheless, it seems useful to recall their views. A majority of Western historians, referring to the socio-economic theory of modernization, conceive of nineteenth-century Poland as a backward East-European country, i.e. a country of essentially the same type as Russia; it is therefore appropriate to recall that Marx and Engels—the two thinkers who had discovered the importance of the economic factor in history—were very far from such a one-sided view, that they took into account historical heritage, political culture, and always treated Poland as part and parcel of Europe, and as an eastern outpost of the West. Some specialists know that the Polish question was an important European problem, but the average educated man (sometimes even in Poland!) is ignorant of this. Eulogies in honour of heroic Poles by such writers as Lamennais, Michelet, Mazzini, or Victor Hugo can be dismissed as shallow romantic rhetoric; the opinions and analyses of Marx and Engels—the most influential nineteenth-century thinkers—have to be taken more seriously. It is not necessary to agree with them, but it is useful to know them, if only as an antidote to the prevalent indifference towards the history of those European nations which, as a result of political divisions, do not belong to the contemporary 'West' and, because of this, are treated by many people, often unconsciously, as not belonging to Europe as well.

Notes

INTRODUCTION

[1] Let me quote just two examples:

F. Ponteil (B. 136). One might legitimately expect that a major part of this book would be devoted to Poland. In fact the Polish question is discussed only on pp. 238–42 and 276–9, each time with errors. The Great Emigration, Polish Democratic Society, the activities of Prince Czartoryski's camp among the Slavs, and so forth, are not even mentioned. Even Lelewel, writing in French and well known in contemporary Europe, does not exist for the author of this book.

Anthony D. Smith (B. 149). The author uncritically accepts Trevor-Roper's formulation according to which Polish nationalism—in contrast to Hungarian, Italian, and German nationalisms—belongs to the category of 'secondary' nationalisms, that is to the same category as Ukrainian, Slovak, Romanian, and even Belorussian nationalism (p. 29)! I hope that my present book will make clear the absurdity of such an irresponsible classification.

[2] However, it seems worth while to point out that in the English language the word 'nationalism' has also been used sometimes in its narrower meaning. In the English translations of Mazzini's works we often find the opposition between the 'spirit of nationalism' and the 'spirit of nationality'. The first, according to Mazzini, was the real cause of the disappointing outcome of the Springtime of the Peoples: 'it was the narrow spirit of nationalism substituted for the spirit of nationality' (A. 67, p. 5).

PART ONE

[1] It is interesting to note that similar arguments were put forward by supporters of slavery in the Southern States of the U.S.A. (see B. 129, II. 99–103).

[2] According to the estimations of such contemporary Polish historians as B. Leśnodorski, J. Tazbir, and T. Łepkowski. It should be added, however, that in ethnically Polish territories of the former Commonwealth the percentage of the gentry (according to the same authors) was much higher.

[3] Of course, the attitude towards Jews in ancient Poland was far from being homogeneously friendly. As a rule, the Jews were protected by the king and the gentry, whereas the Catholic Church, the burghers, and the peasants (especially Ukrainian peasants, because of the services rendered by Jews to Polish landlords) remained more or less hostile to them.

[4] It remained within the borders of the Commonwealth only until 1621. In 1621 and in 1629 the greater part of Livonia was ceded to Sweden and only its south-eastern province (Latgale) remained under Polish–Lithuanian rule.

[5] The most terrible was the so-called massacre of Humań (1768) where about 30,000 people (landlords, their employees, petty gentry, and Jews) lost their lives.

[6] The translation of this saying as 'For the lack of order Poland stands' does not render its true meaning.

[7] Leszczyński's authorship of this book has recently been questioned by

E. Rostworowski. It is certain, however, that it was inspired by Leszczyński and expressed his views.

[8] The best analysis of the changing situation of the Polish gentry in the years 1764–1863 is J. Jedlicki's book (B. 61). For a brief analysis of how the lower strata of the Polish gentry became transformed into the Polish intelligentsia, see A. Gella (B. 41).

[9] P. Sugar (B. 155, p. 46). On p. 49 the author asserts that Polish nationalism 'remained aristocratic until the end of the second World War'. Happily, Peter Brock's study of Polish nationalism, published in the same volume, corrects this picture.

[10] A more sophisticated, although also one-sided analysis of this aspect of the reception of the ideas of Enlightenment in the 'old republics' was given by Franco Venturi. 'It is of immense interest', he wrote, 'to see the transplanting, the partial and difficult transformation of old ideas of freedom into eighteenth-century constitutional concepts and humanistic spirits blossoming again on old stock. These are processes which were ideal rather than relevant to immediate politics, even if they were to achieve a considerable degree of effectiveness in Poland, the United Provinces and Geneva' (B. 171, p. 31).

[11] According to Kołłątaj one should have at least 135 hectares (7.5 *włóki*) of arable land in order to enjoy political rights. Poorer landowners were considered by him to be too ignorant and too dependent on others to represent an independent judgement.

[12] For the genesis of this conception see F. Bronowski (B. 22). It is an ironical fact that the Polish word for 'commune' (*gmina*) is not of Slavonic origin but derives from the German *Gemeinde*.

[13] See A. 49, pp. 218–20, 221–6, 246–50. It should be added that Lelewel's views on the ancient Russian freedom, expressed in his lengthy review of Karamzin's *History of the Russian State* (published in the Russian periodical *Severnyi Arkhiv*, 1823), exerted some influence on the Decembrists' philosophy of Russian history. See B. 173, pp. 314–18.

[14] See the recent books by S. Kalembka (B. 64) and A. Barszczewska-Krupa (B. 9). For a good selection of the Society's documents, see A. 2. The best work in English is P. Brock's article reprinted in B. 17.

[15] A good summary of Hoffman's views on Polish history is contained in his article 'On the Equality of the Gentry in the Old Poland' (1841), reprinted in A. 106, pp. 977–88.

[16] See J. Czyński, 'What is Democracy?' (1844), in A. 106, pp. 845–7.

[17] On physiocratism in Poland see B. 116 and B. 43.

[18] This point of view is shared, among others, by S. Kieniewicz.

[19] The arguments for the opposite view are presented in Kieniewicz, B. 70, pp. 45–9. From my point of view the term 'feudalism' should not be applied to the social realities of the Duchy of Warsaw and the Congress Kingdom. Labour services of the Polish peasants of that time are comparable to the *otrabotki* of the Russian peasants at the end of the nineteenth century.

[20] Like Jan Czyński, he came from a converted Jewish family.

[21] Cf. the following characterization of the Polish *émigré* democrats by General Ludwik Mierosławski (who was himself one of them): 'They all were gentry, defeated gentry doing penance, redeemed by wounds of the soul and body—but gentry' (quoted in B. 123, p. 14, note 7).

[22] Cf. A. 2, pp. 91–2 and 120–1. The opposition between the eighteenth-century idea of the 'rights of men' and the nineteenth-century idea of the 'duties of man' was popularized later in Mazzini's book, *The Duties of Man* (the first chapter of which appeared in 1844).

[23] This point of view found expression in the quoted book by Kieniewicz (B. 70).

[24] Marx's letter to Engels of 25 March 1868. Quoted from A. 62. p. 140.

[25] Boris Nikolaievsky put forward the thesis that Herzen and Bakunin might have been influenced by Lelewel's theories concerning the primitive Slavonic commune and, therefore, that he may be regarded as 'the ancestor not only of Polish, but also of

Russian narodnichestvo' (B. 125); see also Benoit Hepner (B. 54). Lelewel himself was a democratic republican, and not a populist. As far as direct influence is concerned, Mickiewicz's influence on Herzen (see above p. 274) seems to be more important than Lelewel's. What is true, however, is that the primitive Slavonic commune was 'discovered' first in Poland and only afterwards in Russia, and that Lelewel's contribution to this discovery was of paramount importance. (Cf. B. 182).

[26] On the history of Slavophile ideas in Poland see Z. Klarnerówna, *Słowianofilstwo w literaturze polskiej lat 1800–1848*, Warsaw 1926. Chodakowski's essay is reprinted in A. 5.

[27] For a detailed presentation of Gurowski's fascinating intellectual evolution (which led him ultimately to belief in the 'Manifest Destiny' of America and to committing himself to the cause of abolitionism) see B. 175 and B. 38.

[28] It should be stressed, however, that—in accordance with the centralist leanings of the TDP—he was against giving autonomy to the provinces of the state.

[29] The most comprehensive monograph of Ściegienny (with an edition of archival sources) is the recent book by the Soviet historian W. Djakow (B. 34). For a monograph on Królikowski, see B. 167.

[30] See E. J. Hobsbawm (B. 57), V. Lanternari (B. 94), and Y. Talmon (B. 160).

[31] Cf. B. 63, pp. 93–4. Królikowski's articles, published in *Le Populaire* in summer 1842, were 'the beginning of a new doctrinal thrust that played an important role during the middle years of the Icarian movement and culminated in the publication of *Le Vraie Christianisme* early in 1846' (ibid., p. 94).

[32] Ściegienny was influenced also by Lamennais's *Paroles d'un croyant*, which had been, in turn, partially at least, a product of Mickiewicz's influence.

[33] Reprinted in A. 96 and A. 106.

[34] From Meinecke's point of view any idea of limiting national sovereignty by submitting nations to any kind of supra-national institutions is a manifestation of 'cosmopolitanism'.

[35] See, for instance, the criticism of this principle by A. Cobban (B. 28) Even more violent criticism of it is to be found in E. Kedourie (B. 67). 'The national principle', he writes (p. 79), 'far from providing continuity in European diplomacy, means a radical subversion of the European state system, an endless attempt to upset the balance of power on which the system must rest.'

[36] The systematization of 'The Kohn Dichotomy' was made by L. L. Snyder (B. 150, pp. 118–20). Reprinted by A. Kemiläinen (B. 69, pp. 234–7).

[37] Such a tendency was especially characteristic of General Ludwik Mierosławski, who defined Polish nationality as 'le propre, libre et normal développement de la civilisation slave'. See A. 74, p. ix.

[38] An interesting example of criticism of Semenenko's article from the point of view of a 'political' conception of nation was provided by Jan Czyński. He criticized Semenenko not for ignoring the linguistic criteria but for ignoring the fact that the Polish nation was composed not only of peasants and nobles but also of burghers and Jews.

[39] See his article 'Narodowość (Centralizacja)' in *Postęp*, Paris 1834, pp. 82–8 and 97–102. Reprinted in A. 106, pp. 800–8. According to Krępowiecki, 'provincialism' represented the spirit of counter-revolutionary schism and rebellion.

[40] One of the first Poles who became conscious of this was Count Leon Rzewuski who already in 1848 expressed his readiness to acknowledge the right of the Ruthenians in Galicia to separate from the Poles and to develop as an independent nation.

[41] See the last chapter of this book.

[42] Carlton J. H. Hayes (B. 51) worked out an interesting typology of nationalism. The weakest point of this typology is a strange disregard for progressive romantic nationalism as a separate type of nationalist thinking. Mazzini has been classified by Hayes as a 'liberal nationalist', i.e. as a thinker belonging to the same category as Bentham! It is difficult to imagine a more mistaken judgement.

[43] Along with the German conservative romantics a particularly good example of this type of nationalism was presented by the Russian Slavophiles. See. B. 180.

[44] See his article 'The Old and New Patriotism' in *Demokrata Polski*, v (1842), 225–43.

[45] On Mazzini's influence among the Poles see Kieniewicz, B. 71.

[46] The author of the quoted article, entitled 'About Means and Ends of Our Revolution' (Dziennik Powszechny, 6 January 1831), was O. Szaniecki.

[47] See the chapter on Golovin and Sazonov in W. Śliwowska's book (B. 158).

[48] The title of Stroynowski's book is: *Nauka prawa przyrodzonego, politycznego, ekonomiki politycznej i prawa narodów* (3rd edn., Wilno 1791).

[49] Such as Kajetan Skrzetuski, Wincenty Skrzetuski, Antoni Popławski, and others. At the beginning of this tradition one should place the exiled king Stanisław Leszczyński and his 'Memorial de l'affermissement de la paix general'.

[50] See B. 91, p. 31. J. Skowronek (B. 146, p. 51) points out that young Czartoryski propagated not only the idea of national self-determination but also the idea of federalism. He wanted to create, under the sceptre of Alexander I, a federation of Slavonic peoples (without the Balkan people) in which the whole of Poland was to be included.

[51] Therefore, from Meinecke's point of view Polish romantic nationalists could be accused of 'cosmopolitanism'. This is an excellent illustration of the important difference between their type of nationalism and the nationalism of a 'Nationalstaat', let alone the so-called 'integral nationalism'.

PART TWO

[1] The full story of Wroński's relations with Arson is to be found in B. 169.

[2] D'Arcy gave a very high appraisal of Wroński's philosophy of creation and its relevance to contemporary philosophical thought.

[3] Cieszkowski's 'Diary' is preserved in the library of the University of Poznań. I have read it from a typescript prepared for printing by T. Kozanecki.

[4] Early Polish Hegelianism is discussed in detail in B. 7.

[5] See the correspondence between Cieszkowski and K. L. Michelet printed in B. 90.

[6] See especially the books by A. Cornu (B. 29), H. Stucke (B. 154), N. Lobkowicz (B. 102), and S. Avineri, *The Social and Political Thought of Karl Marx*, Cambridge 1968, pp. 124–30. The first comprehensive monograph on Cieszkowski's thought in English is the recent book by A. Liebich (B. 101; see also his Introduction to A. 10). In Kolakowski's recently published history of Marxism a whole chapter is devoted to Cieszkowski's ideas (B. 80, Vol I).

See also the following statement in *Marxism, Communism and Western Society. A Comparative Encyclopedia* (ed. by C. D. Kerning, Vol. VI, 1973, p. 296): '. . . Marx, influenced perhaps by von Cieszkowski's *Prolegomena zur Historiosophie*, in which the author urged that the philosophical understanding of history should promote *Praxis*, sought a philosophy that would, at the same time, be both an understanding of history and a socialist transformation of human society' (article 'Philosophy', written by H.B. Acton and K. G. Ballestrem).

[7] Thus, in Cieszkowski's intention, the term 'Historiosophie' (coined by him) was by no means a synonym for 'philosophy of history'. By creating 'historiosophy'—the absolute knowledge of history—Cieszkowski wanted to complete the 'age of Thought' and, by the same token, to transcend it.

[8] For a detailed analysis of the reception of Cieszkowski's ideas in Germany see J. Garewicz's article in B. 135.

[9] For an English translation of the relevant fragment of this letter see B. 180, p. 356.

[10] Herzen stressed also that the author of *Prolegomena* was a Slav.

[11] Cieszkowski's role in Herzen's intellectual evolution is strongly emphasized in G.

Shpet (B. 142). See also R. Labry (B. 93) and M. Malia (B. 111). For a comprehensive analysis see A. Walicki, 'Cieszkowski and Herzen', in B. 135.

[12] The manuscript of it was, reputedly, destroyed in Krasiński because of fear that it might be confiscated by the Russian police and that his friend might be compromised as representing very unorthodox religious views.

[13] It was given to Jacob Sengler, the editor of a clerical journal *Kirchenblätter.*

[14] See *Journal of Speculative Philosophy*, Vol. IV, 1870, pp. 62–83 (Introduction to the Logic of Trentowski), Vol. XVI, 1882, No. 3, pp. 244–9 and No. 4, pp. 413–22 (The Sources and Faculties of Cognition), Vol. XVII, 1883, No. 2, pp. 163–9 (continued) and No. 4, pp. 356–66 (continued). The translation was done by I. Podbielski, professor in Havana College, Cuba.

[15] German 'das Ich' or 'Ichheit', Polish 'jaźń' (the word introduced to Polish by Trentowski; one of his few neologisms which became widely accepted). I follow here Podbielski's translation (see above, note 14).

[16] Part of it is published in A. 101.

[17] Norbert Wiener (B. 189) acknowledged the fact that the priority in using the term 'cybernetics' belongs to 'a Polish philosopher'.

[18] See Trentowski's review of Engels's brochure *Schelling und die Offenbarung* (reprinted in A. 103).

[19] Belief in the Russian origin of the word 'intelligentsia' is expressed even in the *Concise Oxford Dictionary*. See also A. J. Toynbee (B. 166, p. 153) and M. Malia (B. 112, p. 441). Toynbee's comment is especially misleading.

[20] Cf. Hegel's *Encyclopedia of Philosophical Sciences*, §573.

[21] For a more comprehensive analysis of Libelt's aesthetics see my article on Libelt in B. 183.

[22] It is worth mentioning that a translation of Kamieński's treatise on the 'People's War' appeared in France under the Nazi occupation to serve the needs of the French resistance movement. This rare edition was published in 1943 under the title *Insurrection est un art* (translated by J. Tepicht).

[23] See H. Temkinowa's article in B. 135.

[24] Published in the journal *Warsaw Library*, 1846.

[25] I have stressed the word 'romantic' because Kamieński, whose revolutionism was not of a romantic variety, was not against the novel; on the contrary, he himself wrote a realistic novel, describing the daily life of the Polish gentry.

[26] Cf. Marx's letter to Engels of 25 March 1868. Quoted from A. 62, pp. 139–40.

[27] The title of Ziemięcka's article (reprinted in A. 106) was 'Thoughts on Philosophy'. It was an indirect answer to Cieszkowski's article 'On the Ionian Philosophy'.

[28] Tadeusz Rejtan was the member of the Polish Diet who heroically protested against the second partition of Poland.

[29] In fact the 1840s were a 'philosophical epoch' not only in Poland but also in Russia, although Rzewuski was apparently not aware of this. It is true, however, that the main Russian thinkers of the epoch (Belinsky, Herzen), in contrast to the Polish philosophers, did not try to compete with the Germans in creating all-round philosophical systems.

[30] This was the consequence of the fact that the upper classes of Russian society had become Westernized, and the traditions of the ancient 'holy Russia' was preserved mainly among the peasantry. In Russia, as the Slavophile Y. F. Samarin put it, 'the only haven of Toryism is the peasant's hut' (A. 89, pp. 401–2). Rzewuski could not make a similar statement because the traditions of ancient Poland in his beloved Ukraine were represented exclusively by the Polish (or polonized) nobility.

PART THREE

[1] See G. Maver, 'Mazzini and Mickiewicz,' in B. 1.

[2] See the histories of Polish literature by M. Kridl (B. 86) and C. Milosz (B. 119), two monographs by M. M. Gardner (B. 39 and B. 40), and the monograph on Mickiewicz by W. Weintraub (B. 187). Unfortunately, there is no monograph in English on Juliusz Słowacki.

[3] It is probable that this redeemer was to be Mickiewicz himself. Cf. the following comment: 'Mickiewicz's mother, descended from a converted Frankist family, was of 'alien' blood; and his own name, Adam, omitting the unvoiced 'A', has the numerical value of 44. Such Kabbalistic notions were gleaned from the writings of the French mystic, Louis-Claude de Saint-Martin.' (*Encyclopedia Judaica*, Vol. XI, Jerusalem 1871, p. 1501.)

[4] For a later edition in French see A. 72.

[5] The most important of the many influences reflected in Towiański's teaching was that of Swedenborg.

[6] Millenarian influences reached Towiański through German pietism as expressed by J. A. Bengel in his *Erklärte Offenbarung St. Joannis*, 1740. See B. 133, pp. 187–90.

[7] In fact, Mickiewicz was the first popularizer of Emerson's ideas in France; this was recognized by Margaret Fuller who met him in Paris and was very impressed by him. It is worth adding that Mickiewicz translated two of Emerson's essays ('History' and 'Over-Soul') into Polish.

[8] According to D. Halévy (and to Michelet and Quinet as well) the greatest among them was Mickiewicz: 'Mickiewicz is the greatest, Mickiewicz is great. Messianic exaltation will soon dim his mind, but the dimming of one's mind does not exclude greatness. The more I think about this episode, the more am I convinced that in order to understand Michelet, to appreciate this moment of his life as it can and should be appreciated, it is necessary to get acquainted with this unusual greatness, the greatness of Mickiewicz' (B. 46, pp. 97–8).

[9] Two books have recently been published in Polish on the 'Trinity from Collège de France': by W. Weintraub (B. 188) and by M. Wodzyńska (B. 191). See also the older work by Mickiewicz's son: W. Mickiewicz, *La Trilogie de Collège de France*, Paris 1924.

[10] See also Fabre's article in B. 1, p. 159.

[11] I should stress, however, that in some historical situations 'reactionary' ideologies ('reactionary' in the sense of their *Weltanschauung* content) perform a progressive function. The case of Mickiewicz is a good illustration of this.

[12] The best, still unsurpassed, studies on Słowacki's messianic philosophy are the books by J. G. Pawlikowski (B. 130) and J. Kleiner (B. 72). The most comprehensive recent study is A. Kowalczykowa's contribution to B. 183.

[13] Czesław Miłosz has rightly noted that 'in its main lines, Słowacki's vision of a cosmic evolution is strangely similar to the thesis proposed some hundred years later by a French Jesuit anthropologist, Teilhard de Chardin' (B. 119, p. 241).

[14] Thus, if 'democracy' means the rule of the masses—'the rule of the inferior', as Edgar Jung put it—Słowacki's republicanism was the opposite of democracy. On the other hand, however, we should remember that in Słowacki's eyes the common people were not necessarily 'inferior': in some moments of history they could represent spiritual superiority.

[15] The poetical polemic between Słowacki and Krasiński is analysed in the excellent study by M. Janion (B. 60).

[16] For a comprehensive analysis of Mickiewicz's criticism of Trentowski and vice versa see B. 178, pp. 89–172.

[17] Lessing's pamphlet *Die Erziehung des Menschengeschlechts* was a secularization of the chiliastic philosophy of history, as preserved in German pietism. Cieszkowski called Lessing 'One of the rare true sages of mankind' (A. 8, I. 25). The similarities between

Lessing's and Cieszkowski's views have been discussed in an interesting article by B. Hepner (B. 55).

[18] To enumerate some of them: the programme of the sanctification of work and earthly life; the conception of the calling of man consisting in constant self-creating and in transforming the world into a 'New Jerusalem'; the idea of the immanent presence of God in the world and of the gradual disappearing of the difference between the 'secular' and the 'sacred'; the peculiar combination of religiosity with the cult of science and progress; the vision of the future 'planetary' mankind united by a common synethetic (or syncretic) culture and living in eternal peace; the idea of universal evolution leading to the emergence of a supra-human being, and so forth.

[19] Reprinted in A. 109 (pp. 361–5) and (in Polish) in A. 106.

[20] For a more comprehensive analysis see B. 177.

[21] In Norwid's eyes Cieszkowski was the greatest philosopher in the contemporary world.

[22] It is worth while to mention that the Russian Slavophile K. Aksakov used the same words ('the inner truth') in his description of the basic principle of the Russian commune.

[23] In his poem 'Fulminant', written during the Polish uprising of 1863, Norwid set against military heroism the heroism of Archimedes, Socrates, and Plato. See A. 79, III.

[24] One of the best studies on Norwid is entitled 'Norwid's Romanticism' (B. 153). In spite of this title, however, the author shows Norwid as a writer consciously overcoming Romanticism, both artistically and intellectually.

[25] It seems proper to note in this connection that Norwid himself emphasized that Christianity is older than the catechism, and that one should be obedient not only to the Church, whom we called 'our Mother', but also to our Father in Heaven (A. 79, IX. 196).

PART FOUR

[1] For a detailed analysis of this brochure see W. Karpiński, in B. 42.

[2] Orzeszkowa, like other Positivists, was a staunch opponent of all forms of anti-semitism. She wrote a series of novels on Jewish themes in which she treated the Polish and Lithuanian Jews with great understanding and sympathy.

[3] For a detailed analysis see J. Kurczewska's article in B. 42.

[4] The word 'Hakatist' was coined after the initials of the founders of the *Deutscher Ostmark Verein*: Hansemann, Kennemann, and Tiedeman. The chief aim of this organization was colonization and thorough germanization of the 'eastern marches'. In Polish political vocabulary the word 'Hakatism' became synonymous with militant chauvinism.

[5] Popławski expressed the same thought in the following words: 'We want to live and to develop our national individuality, this conscious will is for us the highest law, the foundation of our patriotism. To justify this patriotism, to legitimize it by referring to "universal" ideas, would amount to degrading its dignity' (A. 85, I. 68).

[6] For a detailed analysis of the 'neo-romantic' trends in Polish nationalism see H. Floryńska, in B. 42.

[7] The same point has recently been made by a Polish philosopher, J. Kuczyński (B. 89).

[8] It should be noted that Lichtheim has ignored Bloom, in whose book the problem of the national class is discussed in a separate chapter.

[9] S. F. Bloom has devoted a separate chapter of his book to the national problems of England, France, Germany, Russia, and the U.S.A.; strangely enough, he has not paid much attention to the problems of Italy and Ireland; even more surprising is the fact that he did not devote a special chapter to the Polish question in Marx's and Engels's thought.

[10] For a more detailed presentation see the books by J. W. Borejsza (B. 14) and C. Bobińska (B. 13). Cf. also the recently published book by I. Cummins (B. 31. It appeared when this study had already been written and prepared for printing).

[11] Cf. the letter to the Geneva meeting in honour of the 50th anniversary of the Polish uprising of 1830, signed on 27 November 1880 by K. Marx, F. Engels, P. Lafargue, and F. Lessner (A. 57).

[12] See Kościelski's letter to Marx of 18 September 1848, in B. 13 (pp. 70–1) and B. 14 (p. 203).

[13] Published in the *New York Daily Tribune*, 1851–2.

[14] See Engels's letter to Weydemeyer of 12 April 1853.

[15] See Marx's letter to Engels of 2 December 1856.

[16] See Marx's letter to Engels of 13 February 1863. The quoted words were written by Marx in English.

[17] Cf. Marx's letter to Engels of 12 September 1863.

[18] The text of this proclamation is available (in Russian) in the 13th volume of the Russian edition of Marx's and Engels's works, and in A. 57, I. 390–2.

[19] Cf. their letter to the Geneva meeting, 1880 (see above, note 11).

[20] Reproduced in A. 57, II.

[21] The Polish edition, prepared by a group of Soviet, Polish, and East German historians, is better, but, unfortunately, much less available in the West.

[22] Cf. Marx's letter to Engels of 24 March 1863.

[23] See Marx's letter to Engels of 7 June 1864.

[24] K. Marx, 'On the Polish Question', speech delivered in honour of the Polish uprising in 1863, London 1875. Quoted from A. 57, II. 105. The original of this speech (in German) was destroyed in the last war in Warsaw together with other documents from Polish *émigré* archives in Rapperswil Castle.

[25] Cf. the letter to Geneva meeting, 1880 (see above, note 11).

[26] See above, note 11.

[27] It is noteworthy that Engels was concerned with the national feelings of the Polish *workers*, refuting thereby the widespread misinterpretation of the famous slogan: 'The working men have no country.'

[28] Tsarism wanted to profit from the anarchic state of affairs in both countries and, therefore, in both cases imposed on them a 'guarantee' of the existing political order in which every German prince and every member of the Polish Parliament could exercise the right of veto; in such a manner, Germany was to become, after Poland, 'the next object to be partitioned' (A. 64, p. 35).

[29] Cf. Engels's words: '. . . due to the higher civilization of the Poles the White Russian and Ukrainian nobility has become strongly polonized' (A. 64, p. 30).

[30] Engels wrote only about European nations, and it seems that he saw modern nations as products of the historical development of Europe. In any case, such a view would harmonize with the characteristically 'Eurocentric' facet of Marxism (cf. B. 120, p. 238).

[31] It should be added that this was only an argument 'from hindsight', used by nineteenth-century Russia. Catherine II in her justification of the partitions of Poland never used arguments which could undermine the principle of dynastic legitimism. The fact that eighteenth-century Russians made use of the anti-Polish rebellions of Ukrainian peasants (which they themselves, later, cruelly suppressed) is another issue.

[32] In the first years of the Polish People's Republic Kelles-Krauz was condemned as a Polish nationalist, or even 'imperialist', disguised as a socialist, and, as such, providing quasi-Marxist', arguments for the future Kiev expedition of Piłsudski (cf. B. 139). Today he is treated as an outstanding Marxist thinker; his articles on the national problems are, usually, highly esteemed, with the exception of his view on the desirable Eastern boundaries of Poland (see M. Waldenberg, in B. 42).

[33] For a detailed analysis of Brzozowski's intellectual development see B. 181.

List of Works Cited

Not including titles just mentioned in the book. For a bibliography of the Polish philosophy of the epoch see A. Kadler and I. Raczyńska, *Bibliografia filozofii polskiej 1831–1864*, Warsaw 1960.

A. *Primary Sources*

1. Adler, V., *Briefwechsel mit August Bebel und Karl Kautsky*, Wien 1954.
2. Baczko, B., ed., *Towarzystwo Demokratyczne Polskie, Dokumenty i pisma*, Warsaw 1954.
3. Belinsky, V. G., *Polnoe sobranie sochinenii*, Vol. XII, Moscow 1956.
4. Brodziński, K., *Wybór pism*, ed. A. Witkowska, Wroclaw 1966.
5. Chodakowski, Z. D., *O slowiańszczyźnie przed chrześcijaństwem*, ed. J. Maślanka, Warsaw 1967.
6. Chojecki, E., *Wizerunki polityczne*, Vol. III, Leipzig 1865.
7. Cieszkowski, A., *Gott und Palingenesie*, Berlin 1842.
8. Cieszkowski, A., *Ojcze Nasz*, Poznań 1922.
9. Cieszkowski, A., *Prolegomena zur Historiosophie*, Berlin 1838.
10. Cieszkowski, A., *Selected Writings*, ed. A. Liebich, Cambridge, Mass. 1979.
11. Czartoryski, A. J., *Essai sur la diplomatie. Manuscript d'un Philhellène publié par M. Toulouzan*, Paris–Marseille 1830.
12. Dąbrowski, J., *Listy*, Warsaw 1960.
13. Dembowski, E., *Pisma*, eds. A. Śladkowska and M. Żmigrodzka, Warsaw 1955.
14. Dmowski, R., *Myśli nowoczesnego Polaka*, Lwów 1903.
15. Dmowski, R., *Polityka polska i odbudowanie państwa*, Warsaw 1925.
16. Dmowski, R., *The Problem of Central and Eastern Europe*, London July 1917.
17. Dmowski, R., *Rosja, Niemcy i kwestia polska*, Lwów 1908.
18. Engels, F., *Ludwig Feuerbach and the End of Classical Philosophy*, Moscow 1949.
19. *Filosofskie i obshchestvenno-politicheskie proizvedeniya petrashevtsev*, Moscow 1953.
20. Gołuchowski, J., *Die Philosophie in ihrem Verhältnisse zum Leben ganzer Völker und einzelner Menschen*, Erlangen 1882.
21. Gołuchowski, J., *Filosofia otnosyashchaysia k zhizni narodov i kazhdogo cheloveka*, Perevedeno akademikon i professorom D. Vellanskim, St. Petersburg 1834.
22. Gołuchowski, J., *Rozbiór kwestii włościańskiej w Polsce i w Rosji w 1850 r*, Poznań 1851.

23. Gurowski, A., *La Civilisation et la Russie*, St. Petersburg 1940.
24. Gurowski, A., *La Vérité sur la Russie et la révolte des provinces polonaises*, Paris 1834.
25. Haupt G., Lowy M., Weill C., eds., *Les Marxistes et la question nationale 1848–1914*, Paris 1974.
26. Haxthausen, A. F. von, *Studies on the Interior of Russia*, ed. S. F. Starr, Chicago 1972.
27. Heltman, W., Janowski, J. N. *Demokracja polska na emigracji*, Warsaw 1965.
28. Herzen (Gertsen), A.I., *Sobranie sochinenii*, Moscow 1954–65.
29. Holowiński, I., 'O stosunku bezpośredniej filozofii do religii i cywilizacji naszej', Tygodnik Petersburski 1846.
30. Hugo, V., *Oeuvres complètes*, Paris 1969-72.
31. Kamieński, H., *Filozofia ekonomii materialnej ludzkiego spoleczeństwa z dodaniem mniejszych pism filozoficznych*, ed. B. Baczko, Warsaw 1959.
32. Kamieński, H., *O prawdach żywotnych narodu polskiego*, Brussels 1844.
33. Kamieński, H., *Pamiętniki i wizerunki*, Wroclaw 1951.
34. Kelles-Krauz, K., *Prisma wybrane*, Warsaw 1962.
35. Kireevsky, I. V., *Polnoe sobranie sochinenii*, Moscow 1911.
36. Kollataj, H., *Listy Anonima. Prawo polityczne narodu polskiego*, eds. B. Leśnodorski and H. Wereszycka, Warsaw 1954.
37. Kołłątaj, H. et. al., *O ustanowieniu i upadku Konstytucji polskiej 3 maja 1971 roku*, Paris 1868 (First edn., Metz 1793).
38. Kościuszko, T., *Pisma*, ed. H. Mościcki, Warsaw 1947.
39. Kozłowski, F., *Początki filozofii chrześcijańskiej wlacznie a krytyką filozofii B.F. Trentowskiego*, Poznań 1845.
40. Krasiński, Z. *Listy Lwów* 1887.
41. Krasiński, Z., *Listy do A. Cieszkowskiego*, Cracow–Warsaw 1912.
42. Krasiński, Z., *Listy do Delfiny Potockiej*, Warsaw 1975.
43. Krasiński, Z., *Pisma*, Cracow–Warsaw 1912.
44. Królikowski, L., *Wybór pism*, Warsaw 1972.
45. Krzywicki, K., *Polska i Rosja w 1872 roku*, Dresden 1872.
46. Lelewel, J., *Listy emigracyjne*, Cracow 1848–56.
47. Lelewel, J., *Polska, rzeczy i dzieje jej*, Vol. XX, Poznań 1864.
48. Lelewel, J., 'Stracone obywatelstwo stanu kmiecego w Polsce', in: idem, *Polska wieków średnich*, Vol. IV, Poznań 1851.
49. Lelewel, J., *Wybór pism politycznych*, Warsaw 1954.
50. Libelt, K., *Filozofia i krytyka*, Poznań 1845–50.
51. Libelt, K., *Samowładztwo rozumu i objawy filozofii slowiańskiej*, Warsaw 1967.
52. Lutosławski, W., *The Knowledge of Reality*, Cambridge 1930.
53. Lutosławski, W., *The World of Souls*, with a Preface by W. James, London 1924.
54. Łukaszewicz, W., Lewandowski, W. (eds.), *Postępowa publicystyka emigracyjna, Wybór źródeł*, Wroclaw 1961.
55. Maistre, J. de, *Les soirées de Saint-Pétersbourg ou entretiens sur le gouvernement temporel de la Providence*, Paris 1821.
56. Maistre, J. de, *Works*, selected, translated and introduced by J. Lively, New York–London 1965.

57. *Marks i Engels o Polsce*, with an Introduction by C. Bobińska, Warsaw 1960.
58. Marx, K., Engels, F., *Collected Works*, New York, since 1976.
59. Marx, K., Engels, F., *Correspondence 1846–1895*, London 1936.
60. Marx, K., Engels, F., *Ireland and the Irish Question*, New York 1972.
61. Marx, K., *Manuscripte über die polnische Frage (1863–1864)*, herausgegeben und eingeleitet von Werner Conze und Dieter Hertz-Eichenrode, S' Gravenhage 1961.
62. Marx, K., *Pre-Capitalist Economic Formations*, ed. E. J. Hobsbawm, London 1964.
63. Marx, K., *Przyczynki do historii polskiej (Rękopisy z lat 1863–1864)*, Warsaw 1971.
64. Marx, K., Engels, F., *The Russian Menace to Europe*, Glencoe, Ill. 1952.
65. Marx, K., Engels, F., *Werke*, Berlin 1960–8.
66. Mazzini, G., *The Duties of Man and Other Essays*, London–Toronto–New York 1915.
67. Mazzini, G., *Essays. Selected From the Writings, Literary, Political, and Religious*, London 1887.
68. Michelet, J., *Légendes démocratiques du Nord*, ed. M. Cadot, Paris 1968.
69. Michelet, K. L., *Entwicklungsgeschichte der neuesten deutschen Philosophie*, Berlin 1843.
70. Mickiewicz, A., *Dzieła*, Warsaw 1955.
71. Mickiewicz, A., *Dzieła wszystkie*, Vol. XVI, Warsaw 1932.
72. Mickiewicz, A., *Les Slaves*, Paris 1914.
73. Mickiewicz, A., *Poems*, translated by various hands and edited by G. R. Noyes, New York 1944.
74. Mierosławski, *De la nationalité polonaise dans l'équilibre européen*, Paris 1856.
75. Mierosławski, 'Demokracja jako warunek bytu Polski', *Demokrata Polski*, Vol. V, part 2, 1842.
76. Mierosławski, L., *Uwagi nad dzielem O prawdach zywotnych narodu polskiego* (an offprint from *Demokrata Polski*), Brussels 1844.
77. Mochnacki, M., *Dzieła*, Poznań 1863.
78. Mochnacki, M., *Pisma wybrane*, Warsaw 1957.
79. Norwid, C. K., *Dzieła wszystkie*, ed. J. W. Gomulicki, Warsaw 1971–6.
80. *Nouveau Christianisme. Lettres d'Eugène Rodriques sur la religion et la politique. L'éducation du genre humain par Lessing*, Paris 1832.
81. Orzeszkowa, E., *Patriotyzm i kosmopolityzm*, Wilno 1880.
82. Paszkowski, J., 'O Janie Śniadeckim', *Pielgrzym*, Vol. II, 1842.
83. *Pierwsza Międzynarodówka a sprawa polska*, ed. by J. Borejsza, H. Katz, I. Koberdowa, and M. Watle, Warsaw 1964.
84. Podolecki, J. K., *Wybór pism*, Warsaw 1955.
85. Popławski, J. S., *Pisma polityczne*, Cracow–Warsaw 1910.
86. Rzewuski, H., *Mieszaniny obyczajowe Jarosza Bejly*, Wilno 1841–3.
87. Rzewuski, H., *Pisma*, St. Petersburg 1851.
88. Saint-Simon et d'Enfantin, *Ouevres*, Vol. XLII, Paris 1877.
89. Samarin, Y. F., *Sochineniya*, Moscow 1877.
90. Słowacki, J., *Dziela*, ed. J. Krzyzanowski, Wroclaw 1949.
91. Słowacki, J., *Dziela wszystkie*, Wroclaw 1953–63.
92. Staszic, S., *Pisma filozoficzne i spoleczne*, Warsaw 1954.

93. Szaniawski, J. K., *O naturze i przeznaczeniu urzędowań w spoleczności*, Warsaw 1808.
94. Szczepanowski, S., *Myśli o odrodzeniu narodowym*, Cracow 1903.
95. Szujski, J., *Dawna Rzeczpospolita i jej pogrobowce*, 1871, in: idem, *Dzieła*, Series III, Vol. II, Cracow 1894.
96. Temkinowa, H. (ed.), *Lud Polski. Wybór dokumentów*, Warsaw 1957.
97. Trentowski, B. F., *Chowanna*, edited and introduced by A. Walicki, Wroclaw 1970.
98. Trentowski, B. F., *Grundlage der universellen Philosophie*, Karlsruhe 1837.
99. Trentowski, B. F., *Listy*, ed. S. Pigoń, Cracow 1937.
100. Trentowski, B. F., *Myślini, czyli całokształt loiki narodowej*, Poznań 1844.
101. Trentowski, B. F., *Pisma o filozofii religii* (fragments of unpublished manuscripts), ed. T. Kozanecki, Warsaw 1965.
102. Trentowski, B. F., *Przedburza polityczna*, Freiburg 1848.
103. Trentowski, B. F., *Stosunek filozofii do cybernetyki oraz wybór pism politycznych*, edited and introduced by A. Walicki, Warsaw 1974.
104. Trentowski, B. F., *Vorstudien zur Wissenschaft der Natur*, Leipzig 1840.
105. Trentowski, B. F., *Wizerunki duszy narodowej*, Paris 1847.
106. Walicki, A. (selected and introduced by), *Filozofia i myśl spoleczna w latach 1831–1864*. Vol. V of the series *700 lat myśli polskiej*, Warsaw 1977.
107. Woronicz, J., *Rzecz o monarchii i dynastii w Polsce*, Paris 1839.
108. *Wspóludzial Adama Mickiewicza w sprawie Andrzeja Towiańskiego*, Paris 1877.
109. Začek, V. (ed.), *Slovanský sjezd v Praze 1848*, Praha 1958.

B. *Secondary Sources*

1. *Adam Mickiewicz, 1855–1955. Międzynarodowa Sesja Naukowa PAN*, Wroclaw–Warsaw 1958.
2. Adamus, J., *Monarchizm i republikanizm w syntezie dziejów Polski*, Łódź 1961.
3. Arcy, Ph. d', *Hoene-Wroński. Une philosophie de la création*, Paris 1970.
4. Backvis, C., 'Individu et la societé dans la Pologne de la Renaissance', in: *Individu et société à la Renaissance*, Bruxelles–Paris 1967.
5. Backvis, C., 'Les Thèmes majeures de la pensée politique polonaise au XVI-e siècle', *Annuaire de l'Institut de Philologie et d'Histoire Orientales et Slaves*, Vol. XIV, 1957.
6. Backvis, C., 'Wymóg jednomyślności a wola ogólu', *Czasopismo prawno-historyczne*, Vol. XXVIII, 1975, No. 2.
7. Bar, A., 'Zwolennicy i przeciwnicy filozofii Hegla w polskim czasopiśmiennictwie (1830-1850)', *Archiwum do badania historii filozofii w Polsce*, Vol. V, Cracow 1933.
8. Baron, S. W., *Modern Nationalism and Religion*, Freeport, N.Y. 1947.
9. Barszczewska-Krupa, A., *Reforma czy rewolucja?*, Łódź 1979.
10. Bendix, R., *Max Weber: An Intellectual Portrait*, Garden City, N.Y. 1960.
11. Berdyaev, N., *The Russian Idea*, London 1947.

12. Bloom, S. F., *The World of Nations. A Study of the National Implications in the Work of Karl Marx*, New York 1941.
13. Bobińska, C., *Marksa spotkania z Polską*, Cracow 1971.
14. Borejsza, J. W., *W kręgu wielkich wygnańców 1848–1895*, Warsaw 1963.
15. Braun, J., *Aperçu de la philosophie de Wroński*, Rome (without date).
16. Brazill, W. J., *The Young Hegelians*, New Haven and London 1970.
17. Brock, P., *Nationalism and Populism in Partitioned Poland*, London 1973.
18. Brock, P., 'The Polish Nationalism', in B. 155.
19. Brock, P., *Polish Revolutionary Populism*, Toronto and Buffalo 1977.
20. Brock, P., 'Z. D. Chodakowski and the Discovery of Folklife: A Chapter in the History of Polish Nationalism', *The Polish Review*, Vol. XXI, 1976, No. 1–2.
21. Bromke, A., *Poland's Politics: Idealism versus Realism*, Cambridge, Mass. 1967.
22. Bronowski, F., *Idea gminowładztwa w polskiej historiografii*, Łódź 1969.
23. Butler, E. M., *The Saint-Simonian Religion in Germany*, Cambridge 1926.
24. Chlebowczyk, J., *On Small and Young Nations in Europe. Nation-forming Processes in Ethnic Borderlands in East-Central Europe*. Wrocław 1980.
25. Chmielowski, P., 'Filozof w więzach reakcji', *Ateneum*, 1889, II.
26. Chołoniewski, A., *The Spirit of Polish History*, New York 1918.
27. Ciołkosz, Lidia and Adam, *Zarys dziejów socjalizmu polskiego*, Vol. I, London 1966, Vol. II, 1972.
28. Cobban, A., *National Self-Determination*, London 1948.
29. Cornu, A., *Karl Marx et Friedrich Engels. Leur vie et leur oeuvre*. Vols. I-III, Paris 1955–62.
30. Cottam, K. J., *Bolesław Limanowski*, Boulder, Colo. 1978.
31. Cummins, I., *Marx, Engels, and National Movements*, London 1980.
32. Cygler, B., *Działalność polityczno-spoleczna J. Lelewela na emigracji*, Gdańsk 1969.
33. Desroche, H., 'Messianismes et utopies. Note sur l'origine du socialisme occidentale', *Archives de sociologie des religions*, 1959, No. 8.
34. Djakow, W., *Piotr Ściegienny i jego spuścizna*, Warsaw 1972.
35. Duker, A.G., 'The Mystery of the Jews in Mickiewicz's Towianist Lectures on Slav Literatures', *The Polish Review*, Vol. II, 1962, No. 3.
36. Fabre, J., *Lumières et romantisme. Énergie et nostalgie de Rousseau à Mickiewicz*, Paris 1963.
37. Feldman, J., *Bismarck a Polska*, Warsaw 1947.
38. Fischer, L. F., *Lincoln's Gadfly, Adam Gurowski*, Norman, Oklahoma 1964.
39. Gardner, M. M., *Adam Mickiewicz, the National Poet of Poland*, New York 1911.
40. Gardner, M. M., *The Anonymous Poet of Poland, Zygmunt Krasiński*. Cambridge 1911.
41. Gella, A., 'The Life and Death of the Old Polish Intelligentsia', *Slavic Review*, Vol. XXX, No. 1, Mar. 1971.
42. Goćkowski, J., Walicki, A. (eds.), *Idee i koncepcje narodu w myśli polskiej czasów porozbiorowych*, Warsaw 1977.
43. Grabski, S., *Zarys rozwoju idei spoleczno gospodarczych w Polsce*, Cracow 1903.

44. Grynwasser, H., *Demokracja szlachecka*, Warsaw 1948 (1st edn. 1918).
45. Guinet, L., *Zacharias Werner et l'ésotérisme maçonnique*, Paris–La Haye 1962.
46. Halévy, D., *Jules Michelet*, Paris 1928.
47. Handelsman, M., *Adam Czartoryski*, 3 vols., Warsaw 1948–50.
48. Haskins, C. H. and Lord, R. H., *Some Problems of Peace Conference*, Cambridge, Mass. 1920.
49. Haupt, G., 'Les Marxistes face à la question nationale: L'Histoire du problème', in A. 25.
50. Hayes, C. J .H., *Nationalism: A Religion*, New York 1960.
51. Hayes, C. J. H., *The Historical Evolution of Modern Nationalism*, New York 1931.
52. Hayner, P. C., *Reason and Existence: Schelling's Philosophy of History*, Leiden 1967.
53. Heller, C. S., *On the Edge of Destruction. Jews of Poland Between the Two World Wars*, New York 1977.
54. Hepner, B., *Bakounin et le panslavisme révolutionnaire*, Paris 1950.
55. Hepner, B., 'History and the Future: the Vision of August Cieszkowski', *Review of Politics*, Vol. XV, 1953.
56. Hinz, H., 'The Philosophy of the Polish Enlightenment and Its Opponents', *Slavic Review*, Vol. XXX, 1971, No. 2.
57. Hobsbawm, E. J., *Primitive Rebels. Studies in Archaic Forms of Social Movement in the 19th and 20th Century*, Manchester 1963.
58. Hubert, S., *Poglądy na prawo naródow w Polsce czasów Oświecenia*, Wroclaw 1960.
59. Isambert, F. A., *Politique, religion et science de l'homme chez Philippe Buchez*, Paris 1967.
60. Janion, M., 'Dialektyka historii w polemice między Slowackim a Krasińskim', in: idem, *Romantyzm. Studia o ideach i stylu*, Warsaw 1969.
61. Jedlicki, J., *Klejnot i bariery spoleczne*, Warsaw 1968.
62. Johnson, Ch., *Revolution and the Social System*, Stanford, Calif. 1964.
63. Johnston, H., *Utopian Communism in France*, Ithaca and London 1974.
64. Kalembka, S., *Towarzystwo Demokratyczne Polskie w latach 1832–1846*, Toruń 1966.
65. Kallenbach, J., *Zygmunt Krasiński*, Lwów 1904.
66. Kamenka, E. (ed.), *Nationalism. The Nature and Evolution of an Idea*, Canberra 1973.
67. Kedourie, E., *Nationalism*, London 1960.
68. Kelles-Krauz, K., 'La Loi de la rétrospection révolutionnaire vis à vis de la theorie de l'imitation', *Annales de l'Institut International de sociologie*, 1896 (in Polish see A. 34, Vol. I).
69. Kemiläinen, A., *Nationalism. Problems Concerning the Word, the Concept and Classification*, Iyväskyla 1964.
70. Kieniewicz, S., *The Emancipation of the Polish Peasantry*, Chicago and London 1969.
71. Kieniewicz, S., 'La Pensée de Mazzini et le mouvement national Slave', *Atti de convegno sul tema: Mazzini et l'Europe*, Rome 1974.
72. Kleiner, J., *Juliusz Słowacki. Dzieje twórczości*, Vol. IV, Warsaw 1927.
73. Kleiner, J., *Mickiewicz*, Lublin 1948.

74. Kleiner, J., *Zygmunt Krasiński. Dzieje myśli,* Lwów 1912.
75. Koberdowa, I., *Pierwsza Międzynarodówka i lewica Wielkiej Emigracji,* Warsaw 1964.
76. Kohn, H., *The Idea of Nationalism. A Study of Its Origin and Background,* 6th edn., New York 1957.
77. Kohn, H., 'Nationalism', in: *International Encyclopedia of the Social Sciences,* ed. D. L. Sills, Vol. XI, 1968.
78. Kohn, H., *Panslavism. Its History and Ideology,* Notre Dame, Indiana 1953.
79. Kohn, H., *Prelude to Nation-States: the French and German Experience, 1789_1815,* Princeton, N.J. 1967.
80. Kolakowski, L., *Main Currents of Marxism. Its Rise, Growth and Dissolution,* London 1978.
81. Kostenicz, K., *Legion włoski i Trybuna Ludów,* Warsaw 1969.
82. Kozanecki, T., 'Maurycy Michnacki i obóz Czartoryskiego', *Przegląd Historyczyny,* Vol. XLVII, 1956, No. 4.
83. Kozłowski, W.M., *Les idées françaises dans la philosophie nationale et la poésie patriotique de la Pologne,* Grenoble 1923.
84. Krasiński, A., 'Dzień Ducha Świętego', *Biblioteka Warszawska,* 1903, Vol. II.
85. Kridl, M., *Mickiewicz i Lamennais,* Warsaw 1909.
86. Kridl, M., *A Survey of Polish Literature and Culture,* 2nd edn., New York 1967.
87. Kridl, M., 'Two Champions of a New Christianity: Lamennais and Mickiewicz', *Comparative Literature,* Vol. IV, 1952, No. 3.
88. Kroński, T., *Rozważania wokól Hegla,* Warsaw 1960.
89. Kuczyński, J., *Indywidualność a ojczyzna: filozoficzna problematyka kwestii narodowej,* Warsaw 1972.
90. Kühne, W., *Graf August Cieszkowski, ein Schuler Hegels und des deutschen Geistes,* Leipzig 1938.
91. Kukiel, M., *Czartoryski and the European Unity,* Princeton, N.J. 1955.
92. Kurczewska, J., *Naród w socjologii i ideologii polskiej,* Warsaw 1979.
93. Labry, R., *A. I. Herzen: Essai sur la formation et le développement de ses idées,* Paris 1928.
94. Lanternari, V., *The Religions of the Oppressed,* London 1963.
95. Laqueur, W., *Guerilla: A Historical Study,* London 1977.
96. Laqueur, W., 'Karl Heinzen. The Origins of Modern Terrorism', *Encounter,* Aug. 1977.
97. Lerski, J. J., *A Polish Chapter in Jacksonian America. The United States and the Polish Exiles of 1831,* Madison 1958.
98. Leslie, R. F., *Polish Politics and the Revolution of November 1830,* Westport, Conn. 1969.
99. Leslie, R. F., *Reform and Insurrection in Russian Poland 1856–1865,* Westport, Conn. 1963.
100. Lichtcheim, G., *Marxism. An Historical and Critical Study,* New York 1962.
101. Liebich, A., *Between Ideology and Utopia. The Politics and Philosophy of August Cieszkowski,* Dordrecht 1978.
102. Lobkowicz, N., *Theory and Practice: History of a Concept From Aristotle to Marx,* Notre Dame–London 1967.
103. Lovejoy, A. O., *The Great Chain of Being,* New York 1960.

104. Löwith, K., *From Hegel to Nietzsche*, Garden City, N.Y. 1967.
105. Löwith, K., *Meaning in History*, Chicago and London 1970.
106. Luciani, G., *Le Livre de la Genèse du Peuple Ukrainien*, Paris 1956.
107. Łagowski, B., *Filozofia polityczna M. Mochnackiego*, Cracow 1981.
108. Maciejewski, J., 'Geneza i charakter ideologii republikantów *1767–1775*', *Archiwum Historii Filozofii i Myśli Społecznej*, Vol. XVII, Wroclaw 1971.
109. Maciszewski, J., 'Kultura polityczna Polski złotego wieku', in: Gierowski, J. A. (ed.), *Dzieje kultury politycznej w Polsce*, Warsaw 1977.
110. Makowiecka, Z. *Mickiewicz w Collège de France*, Warsaw 1968.
111. Malia, M., *Alexander Herzen and the Birth of Russian Socialism*, Cambridge, Mass. 1961.
112. Malia, M., 'What is Intelligentsia?', *Daedalus*, Summer 1960.
113. Mannheim, K., *Essays in Sociology and Social Psychology*, London 1953.
114. Mannheim, K., *Ideology and Utopia*, London 1954.
115. Manteufflowa, M., *J. K. Szaniawski. Ideologia i działalność*, Warsaw 1936.
116. Marchlewski, J., *Fizjokratyzm w dawnej Polsce (Pisma wybrane*, I), Warsaw 1952.
117. Marcuse, H., *Eros and Civilization*, New York 1962.
118. Meinecke, F., *Cosmopolitanism and the National State*, Princeton, N.J. 1970.
119. Milosz, C., *The History of Polish Literature*, New York–London 1969.
120. Molnár, M., *Marx, Engels et la politique internationale*, Paris 1975.
121. Morawski, S., *Studia z historii myśli estetycznej XVIII i XIX wieku*, Warsaw 1961.
122. Morley, Ch., 'The European Significance of the November Uprising', *Journal of Central European Affairs*, Vol. XI, Jan. 1951–Jan. 1952, pp. 407–16.
123. Namier, L., *1848: The Revolution of the Intellectuals*, Garden City, N.Y. 1964 (1st edn. 1946).
124. Nettl, J. P., *Rosa Luxemburg*, London 1966.
125. Nikolaievsky, B., 'Za vashu i nashu vol'nost'!', *Novyi Zhurnal*, New York 1944, No. 7.
126. Ogonowski, Z., *Socynianizm a Oświecenie*, Warsaw 1966.
127. Ogonowski, Z., 'W obronie liberum veto', *Człowiek i Światopogląd*, IV, 1975.
128. Palmer, R. R., *The Age of the Democratic Revolution*, Princeton, N.J. 1959.
129. Parrington, V. L., *Main Currents in American Thought*, New York 1939.
130. Pawlikowski, J. G., *Mistyka Słowackiego*, Lwów 1909.
131. Pelenski, J., 'The Incorporation of the Ukrainian Lands of Old Rus' into Crown Poland', *American Contributions to the Seventh International Congress of Slavists*, Vol. III: History, The Hague–Paris 1973.
132. Piechocki, J., *Narwidowa koncepcja Sztuki-pracy*, Poznań 1929.
133. Pigoń, S., *Z epoki Mickiewicza*, Lwów 1922.
134. Pigoń, S., *Zręby Nowej Polski w publicystyce Wielkiej Emigracji*, Warsaw 1938.
135. *Polskie spory o Hegla* (a collective work), Warsaw 1966.
136. Pónteil, F., *L'Eveil des nationalités et le mouvement libéral (1815–1848)*, Paris 1860.
137. *Prehlád dejín slovenskej filosofie* (a collective work), Bratislava 1965.
138. Robertson, P., *Revolution of 1848. A Social History*, Princeton, N.J. 1952.

139. Schaff, A., *Narodziny i rozwój filozofii marksistowskiej*, Warsaw 1950.
140. Serejski, M. H., *Europa a rozbiory Polski*, Wroclaw 1970.
141. Serejski, M. H., *K. B. Hoffman*, Lódź 1953.
K. B. Hoffman, Lódź 1953.
142. Shpet, G., *Filosofskoe mirovozzrenie Gerstena*, Petrograd 1921.
143. Sikora, A., *Gromady Ludu Polskiego*, Warsaw 1974.
144. Sikora, A., *Posłannicy Słowa. Hoene-Wroński, Mickiewicz, Towiański*, Warsaw 1967.
145. Skarga B. (ed.), *Polska myśl filozoficzna i społeczna*, Vol. II, Warsaw 1976.
146. Skowronek, J., *Antynapoleońskie koncepcje Czartoryskiego*, Warsaw 1969.
147. Skowronek, J., *Polityka bałkańska Hotelu Lambert (1833–1856)*, Warsaw 1976.
148. Skwarczyński, P., 'The Constitution of Poland Before the Partitions', in: *The Cambridge History of Poland*, Vol. II, New York 1971.
149. Smith, A. D., *Theories of Nationalism*, London 1970.
150. Snyder, L. L., *The Meaning of Nationalism*, New Brunswick, N.J. 1954.
151. Stearns, P. N., *The Revolutions of 1848*, London 1974.
152. Stefanowska, Z., *Historia i profecja*, Warsaw 1962.
153. Stefanowska, Z., 'Norwidowski romantyzm', *Pamiętnik literacki*, Vol. LIX, 1968, No. 4.
154. Stucke, H., *Philosophie der Tat. Studien zur Verwirklichung der Philosophie bei den Junghegelianer und der wahrensozialisten*, Stuttgart 1963.
155. Sugar, P. F., Lederer, Ivo, J. (eds.), *Nationalism in Eastern Europe*, Seattle and London 1969.
156. Symmons–Symonolewicz, K., *Nationalist Movements: A Comparative View*, Meadville, Pa. 1970.
157. Śladkowska, A., *Poglądy społeczno-filozoficzne E. Dembowskiego*, Warsaw 1955.
158. Śliwowska, W., *W kręgu poprzedników Hercena*, Wroclaw 1971.
159. Talmon, J. L., *Political Messianism. The Romantic Phase*, New York 1960.
160. Talmon, Yonina, 'Millenarism', in: *International Encyclopedia of Social Sciences*, Vol. X (see B. 77).
161. Tazbir, J., *A State Without Stakes*, Kościuszko Foundation, New York [1973].
162. Tazbir, J., *Kultura szlachecka w Polsce*, Warsaw 1978.
163. Temkinowa, H., *Gromady Ludu Polskiego*, Warsaw 1962.
164. Thrupp, S. (ed.), *Millennial Dreams in Action*, The Hague 1962.
165. Tillich, P., *A History of Christian Thought*, New York 1972.
166. Toynbee, A. J., *Change and Habit*, London 1966.
167. Turowski, J., *Utopia społeczna Ludwika Królikowskiego*, Warsaw 1958.
168. Ujejski, J., *Dzieje polskiego mesjanizmu do powstania listopadowego włącznie*, Lwów 1937.
169. Ujejski, J., *O cenę Absolutu. Rzecz o Hoene-Wrońskim*, Warsaw 1925.
170. Vancourt, R., *La Pensée religieuse de Hegel*, Paris 1965.
171. Venturi, F., *Italy and the Enlightenment. Studies in Cosmopolitan Century*, New York 1972.
172. Viatte, A., *Les Sources occultes du romantisme*, Paris 1928.
173. Volk, S. S., *Istoricheskie vzglady dekabristov*, Mosco–Leningrad 1958.
174. Wach, J., *Sociology of Religion*, London 1947.

175. Walicki, A., 'Adam Gurowski: Polish Nationalism, Russian Panslavism, and American Manifest Destiny', *The Russian Review*, Jan. 1979.
176. Walicki, A., *The Controversy over Capitalism. Studies in the Social Philosophy of the Russian Populists*. Oxford 1969.
177. Walicki, A., 'Cyprian Norwid: trzy wątki myśli', *Archiwum Historii Filozofii i Myśli Społecznej*, Vol XXIV, Wroclaw 1978.
178. Walicki, A., *Filozofia a mesjanizm. Studia z dziejów filozofii i myśli społecznej romantyzmu polskiego*, Warsaw 1970.
179. Walicki, A., 'The Paris Lectures of Mickiewicz and Russian Slavophilism', *The Slavonic and East European Review*, Vol. XLVI, No. 106, Jan. 1968.
180. Walicki, A., *The Slavophile Controversy. History of a Conservative Utopia in Nineteenth-Century Russian Thought*, transl. by H. Andrews-Rusiecka, Oxford 1975.
181. Walicki, A., *Stanislaw Brzozowski. Dzieje myśli*, Warsaw 1977.
182. Walicki, A., 'Les tendances principales dans le slavophilisme polonais et le slavophilisme russe', *Revue des études slaves*, LII/3, 1979.
183. Walicki, A. (ed.), *Polska myśl filozoficzna i społeczna*, Vol. I [1831–63]. Warsaw 1973.
184. Wandycz, P., *The Lands of Partitioned Poland. 1795–1918*, Seattle and London 1974.
185. Weintraub, W., 'Adam Mickiewicz, the Mystic-Politician', *Harvard Slavic Studies*, Vol. I, 1953.
186. Weintraub, W., *Literature and Prophecy*, The Hague 1959.
187. Weintraub, W., *The Poetry of Adam Mickiewicz*, The Hague 1954.
188. Weintraub, W., *Profecja i profesura. Mickiewicz, Michelet, Quinet*, Warsaw 1975.
189. Wiener, N., *The Human Use of Human Beings: Cybernetics and Society*, Boston 1954.
190. Williams, G. H., *The Radical Reformation*, Philadelphia–London 1962.
191. Wodzyńska, M., *Adam Mickiewicz i romantyczna filozofia historii w Collège de France*, Warsaw 1976.
192. Worsley, P., *The Trumpet Shall Sound*, London 1957.
193. Wszołek, J., *Prawica Wielkiej Emigracji wobec narodowego ruchu wloskiego*, Wroclaw 1970.
194. Wyczański, A., *Polska Rzeczpospolita szlachecka, 1454–1764*, Warsaw 1965.
195. Zawodny, J. K., *Nothing But Honour*, London 1978.
196. Zdziechowski, M., *Wizja Krasińskiego*, Cracow 1912.
197. Žaček, V., *Čechové a Poláci roku 1848*, Prague 1948.
198. Żaliński, H., *Kształt polityczny Polski w ideologii TDP (1832–1846)*, Wroclaw 1976.

Index

411